NEW CENTURY BIBLE COMMENTARY

General Editors

RONALD E. CLEMENTS	MATTHEW BLACK
(Old Testament)	(New Testament)

DEUTERONOMY

THE NEW CENTURY BIBLE COMMENTARIES

Not yet available in paperback
Other titles are in preparation

NEW CENTURY BIBLE COMMENTARY

Based on the Revised Standard Version

DEUTERONOMY

A. D. H. MAYES

AN ORDINATION GIFT FROM:
VIOLA SOULE'

WM. B. EERDMANS PUBL. CO., GRAND RAPIDS

MARSHALL, MORGAN & SCOTT PUBL. LTD., LONDON

Copyright © Marshall, Morgan & Scott (Publications) Ltd. 1979
First published 1979 by Marshall, Morgan & Scott, England
Softback edition published 1981

Printed in the United States of America
for
Wm. B. Eerdmans Publishing Company
255 Jefferson Ave. S.E., Grand Rapids, Mich. 49503
and
Marshall, Morgan & Scott
1 Bath Street, London ECIV 9LB
ISBN 0 551 00895 4

Library of Congress Cataloging in Publication Data
Mayes, A. D. H. (Andrew David Hastings)
Deuteronomy

(New century Bible commentary)
Includes index.
1. Bible.   O.T. Deuteronomy — Commentaries.
I. Bible.   O.T.   Deuteronomy. English. 1981.
II. Title.   III. Series.
BS1275.3.M39   1981   222'.1507   81-1804
ISBN 0-8028-1882-X (pbk.)   AACR2

CONTENTS

ABBREVIATIONS

AfO	*Archiv für Orientforschung*
ANET	*Ancient Near Eastern Texts Relating to the Old Testament* (edited by J. B. Pritchard), Princeton, 1950.
AOAT	*Alter Orient und altes Testament*
ASTI	*Annual of the Swedish Theological Institute*
ATANT	*Abhandlungen zur Theologie des Alten und Neuen Testaments*
AUSS	*Andrews University Seminary Studies*
AV	*Authorised Version*
BA	*Biblical Archaeologist*
BASOR	*Bulletin of the American Schools of Oriental Research*
BBB	*Bonner Biblische Beiträge*
BDB	*Hebrew and English Lexicon of the Old Testament* (edited by F. Brown, S. R. Driver and C. A. Briggs), Oxford, 1907.
BHS	*Biblia Hebraica Stuttgartensia* (edited by K. Elliger and W. Rudolph).
Bib	*Biblica*
BWANT	*Beiträge zur Wissenschaft vom Alten und Neuen Testament*
BZ	*Biblische Zeitschrift*
BZAW	*Beihefte zur Zeitschrift für die alttestamentliche Wissenschaft*
CBQ	*Catholic Biblical Quarterly*
EvTh	*Evangelische Theologie*
EVV	English Versions
FRLANT	*Forschungen zur Religion und Literatur des Alten und Neuen Testaments*
GK	*Gesenius' Hebrew Grammar* (edited by E. Kautzsch; 2nd English edition by A. E. Cowley), Oxford, 1910.
HTR	*Harvard Theological Review*
HUCA	*Hebrew Union College Annual*
IB	*The Interpreter's Bible*
IDB	*The Interpreter's Dictionary of the Bible*
IEJ	*Israel Exploration Journal*
Interp	*Interpretation*
ITQ	*Irish Theological Quarterly*
JAOS	*Journal of the American Oriental Society*
JB	*Jerusalem Bible*
JBL	*Journal of Biblical Literature*

7

JCS	*Journal of Cuneiform Studies*
JJS	*Journal of Jewish Studies*
JNES	*Journal of Near Eastern Studies*
JPOS	*Journal of the Palestine Oriental Society*
JQR	*Jewish Quarterly Review*
JSS	*Journal of Semitic Studies*
JTS	*Journal of Theological Studies*
KuD	*Kerygma und Dogma*
LXX	The Septuagint
MT	The Masoretic Text
MVAG	*Mitteilungen der vorderasiatischen Gesellschaft*
NEB	*New English Bible*
OTL	*Old Testament Library*
OTS	*Oudtestamentische Studiën*
PEQ	*Palestine Exploration Quarterly*
RB	*Revue Biblique*
RSV	*Revised Standard Version*
RV	*Revised Version*
Sam	Samaritan
SBL	Society for Biblical Literature
SBT	*Studies in Biblical Theology*
Schol	*Scholastik*
Syr	Syriac
Targ	Targum
TB	*Tyndale Bulletin*
ThLz	*Theologische Literaturzeitung*
VT	*Vetus Testamentum*
VTS	Supplements to *Vetus Testamentum*
Vulg	Vulgate
WMANT	*Wissenschaftliche Monographien zum Alten und Neuen Testament*
ZA	*Zeitschrift für Assyriologie*
ZAW	*Zeitschrift für die alttestamentliche Wissenschaft*
ZDPV	*Zeitschrift des deutschen Palästina-Vereins*
ZKTh	*Zeitschrift für katholische Theologie*
ZThK	*Zeitschrift für Theologie und Kirche*

BIBLIOGRAPHY
(quoted in text by short title)

LITERARY INTRODUCTION

O. Eissfeldt, *The Old Testament: an Introduction*, Oxford, 1965.
G. Fohrer, *Introduction to the Old Testament*, London, 1970.
O. Kaiser, *Introduction to the Old Testament*, Oxford, 1975.
A. Weiser, *Introduction to the Old Testament*, London, 1961.

HISTORY

J. Bright, *A History of Israel*², London, 1972.
J. Hayes and J. M. Miller (ed.,) *Israelite and Judaean History*, London, 1977.
S. Herrmann, *A History of Israel in Old Testament Times*, London, 1975.
M. Noth, *The History of Israel*², London, 1960.

COMMENTARIES *(cited by author's name only)*

A. Bertholet, *Deuteronomium (Kurzer Hand-Commentar zum Alten Testament*, hrsg von K. Marti), Tübingen, 1899.
P. Buis, *Le Deutéronome (Verbum Salutis* 4), Paris, 1969.
P. Buis and J. Leclercq, *Le Deutéronome (Sources bibliques)*, Paris, 1963.
H. Cazelles, *Le Deutéronome (La Sainte Bible)*, Paris, 1966.
P. C. Craigie, *The Book of Deuteronomy (The New International Commentary on the Old Testament)*, London, 1976.
S. R. Driver, *Deuteronomy*³ *(International Critical Commentary)*, Edinburgh, 1902.
A. Knobel, *Die Bücher Numeri, Deuteronomium und Josua (Kurzgefasste exegetisches Handbuch zum Alten Testament)*, Leipzig, 1861.
E. König, *Das Deuteronomium (Kommentar zum Alten Testament* III), Leipzig, 1917.
K. Marti, *Das fünfte Buch Mose oder Deuteronomium (Die Heilige Schrift des Alten Testaments*³, hrsg von E. Kautsch, I), Tübingen, 1909.
A. Phillips, *Deuteronomy (Cambridge Bible Commentary on the New English Bible)*, Cambridge, 1973.
G. von Rad, *Deuteronomy (OTL)*, London, 1966.
J. Rennes, *Le Deutéronome*, Geneva, 1967.
G. A. Smith, *Deuteronomy (Cambridge Bible for Schools and Colleges)*, Cambridge, 1918.

C. Steuernagel, *Das Deuteronomium*² (*Handkommentar zum Alten Testament*), Göttingen, 1923.

J. A. Thompson, *Deuteronomy* (*Tyndale Old Testament Commentaries*), London, 1974.

J. Wijngaards, *Deuteronomium* (*De Boeken van het Oude Testament* II/III), Roermond, 1971.

G. E. Wright, 'Deuteronomy', *IB*, Nashville, 1953.

SPECIAL STUDIES

Y. Aharoni, *The Land of the Bible*, London, 1966.

N. Airoldi, '*lbd mmkrjw 'l–h'bwt* (Dtn 18.8b) ', *BZ* 18, 1974, 96–101.

W. F. Albright, 'The "Natural Force" of Moses in the Light of Ugaritic', *BASOR* 94, 1944, 32–5.

—— 'Some Remarks on the Song of Moses in Deuteronomy XXXII', *VT* 9, 1959, 339–46.

—— *Yahweh and the Gods of Canaan*, London, 1968.

A. Alt, 'Zu *hit'ammer*', *VT* 2, 1952, 153–9.

—— 'Das Verbot des Diebstahls im Dekalog', in *Kleine Schriften zur Geschichte des Volkes Israel* I, München, 1953, 333–40.

—— 'Die Heimat des Deuteronomiums', in *Kleine Schriften zur Geschichte des Volkes Israel* II, München, 1953, 250–75.

—— 'The God of the Fathers', in *Essays on Old Testament History and Religion*, Oxford, 1966, 1–77.

—— 'The Origins of Israelite Law', *ibid.*, 81–132.

O. Bächli, *Israel und die Völker* (*ATANT* 41), 1962.

—— 'Zur Aufnahme von Fremden in die altisraelitische Kultgemeinde', in *Wort-Gebot-Glaube* (Walter Eichrodt zum 80. Geburtstag, hrsg von H. J. Stoebe) (*ATANT* 59), 1970, 21–6.

K. Baltzer, *The Covenant Formulary*, Oxford, 1971.

J. R. Bartlett, 'The Land of Seir and the Brotherhood of Edom', *JTS* 20, 1969, 1–20.

—— 'The Use of the Word *rō'š* as a title in the Old Testament', *VT* 19, 1969, 1–10.

—— 'The Moabites and Edomites', in *Peoples of Old Testament Times* (edited by D. J. Wiseman), Oxford, 1973, 229–58.

M. A. Beek, 'Das Problem des aramäischen Stammvaters (Deut. XXVI 5)', *OTS* 8, 1950, 193–212.

—— 'Der Dornbusch als Wohnsitz Gottes (Deut. XXXIII 16)', *OTS* 14, 1965, 155–61.

W. Beyerlin, *Origins and History of the Oldest Sinaitic Traditions*, Oxford, 1965.

J. Blenkinsopp, 'Are there traces of the Gibeonite Covenant in Deuteronomy?', *CBQ* 28, 1966, 207–19.

F. S. Bodenheimer, 'The Manna of Sinai', *BA* 10, 1947, 2–6.

H. J. Boecker, *Die Beurteilung der Anfänge des Königtums in den deuterono-mistischen Abschnitten des 1. Samuelbuches* (*WMANT* 31), 1969.

J. R. Boston, 'The Wisdom Influence upon the Song of Moses', *JBL* 87, 1968, 198–202.

G. Braulik, 'Die Ausdrücke für "Gesetz" im Buch Deuteronomium', *Bib* 51, 1970, 39–66.

C. Brekelmans, 'Die sogenannten deuteronomischen Elemente in Gen.–Num.', *VTS* 15, 1966, 90–6.

H. A. Brongers, 'Bemerkungen zum Gebrauch des adverbialen *we*ʿ*attāh* im alten Testament', *VT* 15, 1965, 289–99.

H. Brunner, ' "Was aus dem Munde Gottes geht" ', *VT* 8, 1958, 428–9.

P. Buis, 'Deutéronome XXVII 15–26: malédictions ou exigences de l'alliance', *VT* 17, 1967, 478–9.

M. du Buit,' Quelques contacts bibliques dans les archives royales de Mari', *RB* 66, 1959, 576–81.

S. Bülow, 'Der Berg des Fluches', *ZDPV* 73, 1957, 100–7.

A. Caquot, 'Remarques sur la "loi royale" du Deutéronome (17, 14–20)', *Semitica* 9, 1959, 21–33.

C. M. Carmichael, 'Deuteronomic Laws, Wisdom and Historical Traditions', *JSS* 12, 1967, 198–206.

—— 'A New View of the Origin of the Deuteronomic Credo', *VT* 19, 1969, 273–89.

—— *The Laws of Deuteronomy*, Ithaca and London, 1974.

U. Cassuto, 'The Song of Moses (Deuteronomy Chapter xxxii 1–43)', in *Biblical and Oriental Studies* I, Jerusalem, 1973, 41–6.

—— 'Deuteronomy Chapter XXXIII and the New Year in Ancient Israel', *ibid.*, 47–70.

H. Cazelles, 'Sur un rituel du Deutéronome (Deut. XXVI 14)', *RB* 55, 1948, 54–71.

—— 'La dîme israélite et les textes de Ras Shamra', *VT* 1, 1951, 131–4.

—— 'Tophel (Deut. I 1,)', *VT* 9, 1959, 412–15.

—— 'Institutions et terminologie en Deutéronome i 6–17', *VTS* 15, 1966, 97–112.

B. S. Childs, 'Deuteronomic Formulae of the Exodus Tradition', *VTS* 16, 1967, 30–39.

W. M. Clark, 'Law', in *Old Testament Form Criticism* (edited by J. H. Hayes), San Antonio, 1974, 99–139.

R. E. Clements, 'Deuteronomy and the Jerusalem Cult Tradition', *VT* 15, 1965, 300–312.

—— *God and Temple*, Oxford, 1965.

—— *God's Chosen People*, London 1968.

—— *Prophecy and Tradition*, Oxford, 1975.

A. Cody, *A History of Old Testament Priesthood* (*Analecta Biblica* 35), Rome, 1969.

F. M. Cross, 'Ugaritic *db'at* and Hebrew Cognates', *VT* 2, 1952, 162–4.

F. M. Cross and D. N. Freedman, 'A Note on Deuteronomy 33:26', *BASOR* 108, 1947, 6–7.

—— —— 'The Blessing of Moses', *JBL* 67, 1948, 191–210.

—— —— 'Josiah's Revolt against Assyria', *JNES* 12, 1953, 56–8.

—— —— 'The Song of Miriam', *JNES* 14, 1955, 237–50.

M. Dahood, *Proverbs and Northwest Semitic Philology*, Rome, 1963.

—— *Psalms (Anchor Bible)*, I 1965, II 1968, III 1970.

—— 'Hebrew-Ugaritic Lexicography', *Bib* 54, 1973, 356.

—— 'Northwest Semitic Notes on Dt 32.20', *Bib* 54, 1973, 405–406.

D. Daube, 'A Note on a Jewish Dietary Law', *JTS* 37, 1936, 289–91.

—— *Studies in Biblical Law*, Cambridge, 1947.

—— 'Rechtsgedanken in den Erzählungen des Pentateuchs', in *Von Ugarit nach Qumran (BZAW 77)*, 1961, 32–41.

G. H. Davies, 'Phylacteries', *IDB* vol. 3, 808–809.

M. Delcor, 'Les attaches littéraires, l'origine et la signification de l'expression biblique "Prendre à témoin le ciel et la terre" ', *VT* 16, 1966, 8–25.

P. Diepold, *Israels Land (BWANT V, 15)*, 1972.

W. Dietrich, 'Josia und das Gesetzbuch (2 Reg. XXII)', *VT* 27, 1977, 13–35.

G. R. Driver, 'Three Notes', *VT* 2, 1952, 356–7.

—— 'Birds in the Old Testament', *PEQ* 87, 1955, 5–20, 129–40.

—— *Canaanite Myths and Legends*, Edinburgh, 1956.

—— 'Two Problems in the Old Testament examined in the light of Assyriology', *Syria* 33, 1956, 70–78.

—— 'Hebrew Homonyms', *VTS* 16, 1967, 50–64.

S. R. Driver, *Notes on the Hebrew Text and the Topography of the Books of Samuel²*, Oxford, 1960.

F. Dumermuth, 'Zur deuteronomischen Kulttheologie und ihre Voraussetzungen', *ZAW* 29, 1958, 59–98.

W. Eichrodt, *Theology of the Old Testament*, London, vol. I 1961, vol. II 1967.

O. Eissfeldt, *Erstlinge und Zehnten im Alten Testament (BWANT 22)*, 1917.

—— 'El and Yahweh', *JSS* 1, 1956, 25–37.

—— *Das Lied Moses Deut. 32:1–43 und das Lehrgedicht Asaphs Psalm 78 samt einer Analyse der Umgebung des Mose-Liedes*, Berichte über die Verhandlungen der Sächsischen Akademie der Wissenschaften zu Leipzig. Philologisch-historische Klasse, Band 104, Heft 5, 1958.

—— 'Der Gott Tabor und seine Verbreitung', in *Kleine Schriften* II, 1963, 29–54.

—— 'Gilgal or Shechem?', in *Proclamation and Presence* (edited by J. I. Durham and J. R. Porter), London, 1970, 90–101.

H. J. Elhorst, 'Eine verkannte Zauberhandlung (Dtn 21, 1–9)', *ZAW* 39, 1921, 58–67.

J. A. Emerton, 'Priests and Levites in Deuteronomy', *VT* 12, 1962, 129–38.

—— 'A Consideration of some Alleged Meanings of *yd'* in Hebrew', *JSS* 15, 1970, 145–80.

F. C. Fensham, 'The Possibility of the Presence of Casuistic Legal Material at the Making of the Covenant at Sinai', *PEQ* 93, 1961, 143–6.

—— 'Widow, Orphan and the Poor in Ancient Near Eastern Legal and Wisdom Literature', *JNES* 21, 1962, 129–39.

M. Fishbane, 'The treaty background of Amos 1:11 and related matters', *JBL* 89, 1970, 313–18.

L. R. Fisher (ed.), *Ras Shamra Parallels* I (*Analecta Orientalia* 49), 1972; II (*Analecta Orientalia* 50), 1975.

J. A. Fitzmyer, *The Aramaic Inscriptions of Sefîre* (*Biblica et Orientalia* 19), 1967.

G. Fohrer, 'Das sogenannte apodiktisch formulierte Recht und der Dekalog', *KuD* 11, 1965, 49–74.

—— 'Twofold Aspects of Hebrew Words', in *Words and Meanings* (edited by P. R. Ackroyd and B. Lindars), Cambridge, 1968, 95–103.

M. V. Fox, 'Jeremiah 2 : 2 and the "Desert Ideal" ', *CBQ* 35, 1973, 441–50.

R. Frankena, 'The Vassal-Treaties of Esarhaddon and the Dating of Deuteronomy', *OTS* 14, 1965, 122–54.

J. Friedrich, *Staatsverträge des Hatti-Reiches in hethitischer Sprache* I (*MVAG* 34.i) 1926; II (*MVAG* 31.j), 1930.

K. Galling, 'Der Beichtspiegel', *ZAW* 47, 1929, 125–130 (= *Zur neueren Psalmenforschung*, hrsg von P. H. A. Neumann, Darmstadt, 1976, 168–75).

—— 'Das Gemeindegesetz in Deuteronomium 23', in *Festschrift für A. Bertholet*, Tübingen, 1950, 176–91.

—— 'Das Königsgesetz im Deuteronomium', *ThLZ* 76, 1951, 133–8.

—— 'Die Ausrufung des Namens als Rechtsakt in Israel', *ThLZ* 81, 1956, 65–70.

T. H. Gaster, *Myth, Legend and Custom in the Old Testament*, London, 1969.

B. Gemser, '*Beʿēber hajjardēn*: in Jordan's borderland', *VT* 2, 1952, 349–55.

—— 'The Importance of the Motive Clause in Old Testament Law', *VTS* 1, 1953, 50–66.

E. Gerstenberger, *Wesen und Herkunft des 'apodiktischen Rechts'* (*WMANT* 20), 1965.

H. Gese, 'Der Dekalog als Ganzheit betrachtet', *ZThK* 64, 1967, 121–38.

S. Gevirtz, 'West Semitic Curses and the Problem of the Origins of Hebrew Law', *VT* 11, 1961, 137–58.

H. W. Gilmer, *The If-You Form in Israelite Law* (*SBL Dissertation Series* 15), 1975.

I. Goldziher, 'Zu *Šaʿatnêz*', *ŽAW* 20, 1900, 36–7.

C. H. Gordon, 'A New Akkadian Parallel to Deuteronomy 25, 11–12', *JPOS* 15, 1935, 29–34.

—— 'An Akkadian Parallel to Deuteronomy 21 : 1ff.', *Revue d'Assyriologie et d'Archéologie orientale* 33, 1936, 1–6.

—— 'Mesopotamia', *IDB* vol. 3, 359.

—— *Ugaritic Textbook* (*Analecta Orientalia* 38), Rome, 1965.

M. Görg 'Eine neue Deutung für *kapporet*', *ŽAW* 89, 1977, 115–18.

J. Gray, *The Legacy of Canaan* (*VTS* 5), 1957.

—— *I & II Kings*² (*OTL*), 1970.

M. Greenberg, 'The biblical conception of Asylum', *JBL* 78, 1959, 125–32.

P. Grelot, 'La racine *hwn* en Dt I, 41', *VT* 12, 1962, 198–201.

J. Halbe, 'Passa-Massot im deuteronomischen Festkalender', *ŽAW* 87, 1975, 147–68.

—— 'Erwägungen zu Ursprung und Wesen des Massotfestes', *ŽAW* 87, 1975, 324–46.

J. Harvey, 'Le "Rib-pattern", réquisitoire prophétique sur la rupture de l'alliance', *Bib* 43, 1962, 172–96.

S. Herrmann, 'Die konstructive Restauration: Das Deuteronomium als Mitte biblischer Theologie', in *Probleme biblischer Theologie* (Gerhard von Rad zum 70. Geburtstag, hrsg von H. W. Wolff), München, 1971, 155–70.

W. Herrmann, 'Das Aufgebot aller Kräfte', *ŽAW* 70, 1958, 215–20.

D. R. Hillers, 'A Note on some Treaty Terminology in the Old Testament', *BASOR* 176, 1964, 46–7.

—— *Treaty Curses and the Old Testament Prophets* (*Biblica et Orientalia* 16), Rome, 1964.

—— *Covenant: the History of a Biblical Idea*, Baltimore, 1969.

T. R. Hobbs, 'Jeremiah 3, 1–5 and Deuteronomy 24, 1–4', *ŽAW* 86, 1974, 23–9.

J. Hoftijzer, *Die Verheissungen an die drei Erzväter*, Leiden, 1956.

—— 'Das sogenannte Feueropfer', *VTS* 16, 1967, 114–34.

W. L. Holladay, *The Root SUBH in the Old Testament*, Leiden 1958.

H. Hollenstein, 'Literarkritische Erwägungen zum Bericht über die Reformmassnahmen Josias in 2 Kön. XXIII 4ff.', *VT* 27, 1977, 321–36.

G. Hölscher, 'Komposition und Ursprung des Deuteronomiums', *ŽAW* 40, 1922, 161–255.

F. Horst, 'Das Privilegrecht Jahwes', in *Gottes Recht* (*Theologische Bücherei* 12), München, 1961, 17–154.

H. B. Huffmon, 'The Covenant Lawsuit in the Prophets', *JBL* 78, 1959, 285–95.
—— 'The Treaty Background of Hebrew *Yāda'*, *BASOR* 181, 1966, 31–7.
—— and S. B. Parker, 'A further note on the Treaty Background of Hebrew *Yāda'*, *BASOR* 184, 1966, 36–8.
E. V. Hulse, 'The Nature of Biblical "Leprosy" and the use of alternative medical terms in modern translations of the Bible', *PEQ* 107, 1975, 87–105.
P. Humbert, 'Le substantif *to'ēbā* et le verbe *t'b* dans l'Ancien Testament', *ZAW* 72, 1960, 217–37.
J. P. Hyatt, 'Were there an Ancient Historical Credo in Israel and an Independent Sinai Tradition?', in *Translating and Understanding the Old Testament* (edited by H. T. Frank and W. L. Reed), Nashville, 1970, 152–70.
—— *Exodus* (New Century Bible), London, 1971.
A. Jepsen, '*Amah* und *Schiphchah*', *VT* 8, 1958, 293–7.
—— '*Ṣedeq* und *ṣ*ᵉ*dāqāh* im Alten Testament', in *Gottes Wort und Gottes Land* (hrsg von H. Graf Reventlow), *Göttingen*, 1965, 78–89.
A. R. Johnson, *The Vitality of the Individual in the Thought of Ancient Israel²*, Cardiff, 1964.
—— *Sacral Kingship in Ancient Israel²*, Cardiff, 1967.
G. H. Jones, ' "Holy War" or "Yahweh War"?', *VT* 25, 1975, 642–58.
E. Junge, *Der Wiederaufbau des Heerwesens des Reiches Juda unter Josia* (*BWANT* IV, 23), 1937.
R. Kilian, *Literarkritische und formgeschichtliche Untersuchung des Heiligkeitsgesetzes* (*BBB* 19), 1963.
H. Klein, 'Verbot des Menschendiebstahls im Dekalog?', *VT* 26, 1976, 161–9.
M. G. Kline, *The Treaty of the Great King. The Covenant Structure of Deuteronomy*, Grand Rapids, 1963.
R. Knierim, 'Exodus 18 und die Neuordnung der mosaischen Gerichtsbarkeit', *ZAW* 32, 1961, 146–71.
L. Köhler, 'Hebraïsche Vokabeln I', *ZAW* 13, 1936, 287–93.
V. Korošec, *Hethitische Staatsverträge* (*Leipziger Rechtswissenschaftliche Studien* 60), Leipzig, 1931.
H. Kosmala, 'The So-Called Ritual Decalogue', *ASTI* 1, 1962, 31–61.
H. J. Kraus, *Die prophetische Verkündigung des Rechts in Israel* (*Theologische Studien* 51), Zürich, 1957.
—— *Worship in Israel*, Oxford, 1966.
E. Kutsch, 'Erwägungen zur Geschichte der Passafeier und des Massotfestes', *ZThK* 55, 1958, 1–35.
—— *Verheissung und Gesetz* (*BZAW* 131), 1972.
C. J. Labuschagne, 'The Song of Moses: its Framework and Structure',

in *De Fructu Oris Sui* (Essays in honour of Adrianus van Selms, edited by I. H. Eybers, F. C. Fensham, C. J. Labuschagne, W. C. van Wyk, A. H. van Zyl), Leiden, 1971, 85–98.

—— 'The Tribes in the Blessing of Moses', *OTS* 19, 1974, 97–112.

M. R. Lehmann, 'A new interpretation of the term *šdmwt*', *VT* 3, 1953, 361–71.

J. Leipoldt, S. Morenz, *Heilige Schriften. Betrachtungen zur Religionsgeschichte der antiken Mittelmeerwelt*, Leipzig, 1953.

N. P. Lemche, 'The Hebrew Slave. Comments on the Slave Law Ex. xxi 2–11', *VT* 25, 1975, 124–44.

J. D. Levenson, 'Who inserted the book of the Torah?', *HTR* 68, 1975, 203-233.

B. A. Levine, *In the Presence of the Lord*, Leiden, 1974.

J. L'Hour, 'L'alliance de Sichem', *RB* 69, 1962, 5–36, 161–84, 350–68.

—— 'Une législation criminelle dans le Deutéronome', *Bib* 44, 1963, 1–28.

—— 'Les interdits to 'eba dans le Deutéronome', *RB* 71, 1964, 481–503.

B. Lindars, 'Torah in Deuteronomy', in *Words and Meanings* (Essays presented to David Winton Thomas, edited by P. R. Ackroyd and B. Lindars), Cambridge, 1968, 117–36.

J. Lindblom, *Erwägungen zur Herkunft der Josianischen Tempelurkunde (Scripta Minora Regiae Societatis Humaniorum Litterarum Lundensis, 1970–71:3)*, Lund, 1971.

G. Lisowsky, 'Dtn 25,4', in *Das ferne und nahe Wort* (L. Rost Festschrift, hrsg von F. Maass), *(BZAW* 105), 1967, 144–52.

M. Liverani, 'The Amorites', in *Peoples of Old Testament Times* (edited by D. J. Wiseman), Oxford, 1973, 100–133.

S. Loersch, *Das Deuteronomium und seine Deutungen: ein forschungsgeschichtlicher Überblick (Stuttgarter Bibelstudien 22)*, 1967.

N. Lohfink, 'Wie stellt sich das Problem Individuum-Gemeinschaft in Deuteronomium 1,6–3,29?', *Schol* 35, 1960, 403–407.

—— Darstellungskunst und Theologie in Dtn 1, 6–3, 29', *Bib* 41, 1960, 105–134.

—— 'Der Bundesschluss im Land Moab. Redaktionsgeschichtliches zu Dt. 28,69–32,47', *BZ* 6, 1962, 32–56.

—— 'Die deuteronomische Darstellung des Übergangs der Führung Israels von Moses auf Josue', *Schol* 37, 1962, 32–44.

—— *Das Hauptgebot. Eine Untersuchung literarischer Einleitungsfragen zu Dtn 5–11 (Analecta Biblica 20)*, Rome, 1963.

—— 'Die Bundesurkunde des Königs Josias', *Bib* 44, 1963, 261–88, 461–98.

—— 'Die Wandlung des Bundesbegriffs im Buch Deuteronomium', in *Gott in Welt* (Festgabe für Karl Rahner, hrsg von H. Vorgrimler) I, Freiburg, 1964, 423–44.

—— 'Zur Dekalogfassung von Dt 5', *BZ* 9, 1965, 17–32.
—— *Höre Israel. Auslegung von Texten aus dem Buch Deuteronomium*, Dusseldorf, 1965.
—— 'Review of E. W. Nicholson, *Deuteronomy and Tradition*', *Bib* 49, 1968, 106–110.
—— *The Christian Meaning of the Old Testament*, London, 1968.
—— 'Dt 26, 17–19 und die "Bundesformel" ', *ZKTh* 91, 1969, 517–53.
—— 'Beobachtungen zur Geschichte des Ausdrucks '*m YHWH*', in *Probleme biblischer Theologie* (Gerhard von Rad zum 70. Geburtstag, hrsg von H. W. Wolff), München, 1971, 275–305.

O. Loretz, 'Neues Verständnis einiger Schriftstellen mit Hilfe des Ugaritischen', *BZ* 2, 1958, 287–91.

V. Maag, 'Erwägungen zur deuteronomischen Kultzentralisation', *VT* 6, 1956, 10–18.

A. A. Macintosh, 'A Consideration of Hebrew *g'r*', *VT* 19, 1969, 471–79.

J. Maier, *Das altisraelitische Ladeheiligtum* (*BZAW* 93), 1965.

J. Malfroy, 'Sagesse et loi dans le Deutéronome', *VT* 15, 1965, 49–65.

B. Marzulis, 'Gen. XLIX 10/Deut. XXXIII 2–3', *VT* 19, 1969, 202–210.

A. D. H. Mayes, 'The Nature of Sin and its Origin in the Old Testament', *ITQ* 40, 1973, 250–63.
—— *Israel in the Period of the Judges* (*SBT* II/29), London, 1974.

S. D. McBride, 'The Yoke of the Kingdom. An exposition of Dt. 6:4–5', *Interp* 27, 1973, 273–306.

D. J. McCarthy, *Treaty and Covenant* (*Analecta Biblica* 21), Rome, 1963.
—— 'Notes on the Love of God in Deuteronomy and the Father-Son Relationship between Yahweh and Israel', *CBQ* 27, 1965, 144–7.
—— 'Covenant in the Old Testament: the present state of enquiry', *CBQ* 27, 1965, 217–40.
—— 'Berit in Old Testament History and Theology', *Bib* 53, 1972, 110–21.
—— *Old Testament Covenant. A Survey of Current Opinions*, Oxford, 1972.

F. R. McCurley, 'The Home of Deuteronomy Revisited: a methodological analysis of the northern theory', in *A Light unto my Path* (Old Testament Studies in Honor of Jacob M. Myers, edited by H. N. Bream, R. D. Heim, C. A. Moore) (*Gettysburg Theological Studies* IV), Philadelphia, 1974, 295–317.

J. W. McKay, 'The Date of Passover and its Significance', *ZAW* 84, 1972, 435–47.
—— 'Man's Love for God in Deuteronomy and the Father/Teacher-Son/Pupil Relationship', *VT* 22, 1972, 426–35.
—— *Religion in Judah under the Assyrians* (*SBT* II/26), 1973.

H. McKeating, 'The Development of the Law on Homicide in Ancient Israel', *VT* 25, 1975, 46–68.

I. Mendelsohn, 'On the preferential status of the eldest son', *BASOR* 156, 1959, 38–40.

—— 'Slavery in the Old Testament', *IDB* vol. 4, 383–91.

G. E. Mendenhall, 'Covenant Forms in Israelite Tradition', *BA* 17, 1954, 49–76.

—— *The Tenth Generation*, Baltimore, 1973.

R. P. Merendino, *Das deuteronomische Gesetz: ein literarkritische, gattungs- und überlieferungsgeschichtliche Untersuchung zu Dt 12–26 (BBB 31)*, 1969.

T. N. D. Mettinger, *Solomonic State Officials (Coniectanea Biblica Old Testament Series 5)*, Lund, 1971.

J. Milgrom, 'The alleged "demythologization and secularization" in Deuteronomy', *IEJ* 23, 1973, 156–61.

P. D. Miller, *The Divine Warrior in Early Israel*, Harvard, 1973.

G. Minette de Tillesse, 'Sections "tu" et sections "vous" dans le Deutéronome', *VT* 12, 1962, 29–87.

S. Mittmann, *Deuteronomium 1:1–6:3 literarkritisch und traditions- geschichtlich untersucht (BZAW 139)*, 1975.

J. C. de Moor, 'Rāpi'ūma—Rephaim', *ZAW* 88, 1976, 323–45.

W. L. Moran, 'Some Remarks on the Song of Moses', *Bib* 43, 1962, 317–27.

—— 'The End of the Unholy War and the Anti-Exodus', *Bib* 44, 1963, 333–42.

—— 'The Ancient Near Eastern Background of the Love of God in Deuteronomy', *CBQ* 25, 1963, 77–87.

—— 'A Note on the Treaty Terminology of the Sefîre Stelas', *JNES* 22, 1963, 173–6.

—— 'The Literary Connections between Lv 11,13–19 and Dt 14,12–18', *CBQ* 28, 1966, 271–7.

R. Mosis, *Untersuchungen zur Theologie des chronistischen Geschichtswerkes*, Freiburg, 1973.

H. Motzki, 'Ein Beitrag zum Problem des Stierkultes in der Religions- geschichte Israels', *VT* 25, 1975, 470–85.

J. M. Myers, 'The Requisite for Response. On the theology of Deuter- onomy', *Interp* 15, 1961, 14–31.

G. Nebeling, *Die Schichten des deuteronomischen Gesetzeskorpus: ein traditions- und redaktionsgeschichtliche Analyse von Dtn 12–26 (Dissertation)*, Mün- ster, 1970.

M. Newman, *The People of the Covenant*, London, 1965.

E. W. Nicholson, 'The Centralization of the Cult in Deuteronomy', *VT* 13, 1963, 380–89.

—— *Deuteronomy and Tradition*, Oxford, 1967.

—— 'The Interpretation of Exodus XXIV 9–11', *VT* 24, 1974, 77–97.

E. Nielsen, *Shechem*, Copenhagen, 1955.

—— 'Some Reflections on the History of the Ark', *VTS* 7, 1960, 61–74.
—— *The Ten Commandments in New Perspective (SBT* II/7), 1968.
M. Noth, *Das System der zwölf Stämme Israels (BWANT* IV, 1), 1930.
—— *Überlieferungsgeschichtliche Studien*[2], Tübingen, 1957.
—— *Die Ursprünge des alten Israel im Lichte neuer Quellen (Arbeitsgemeinschaft für Forschung des Landes Nordrhein-Westfalen,* Heft 94), 1961.
—— 'The Laws in the Pentateuch', in *The Laws in the Pentateuch and Other Essays,* Edinburgh, 1965, 1–107.
—— 'For all who rely on works of the law are under a curse', *ibid.*, 118–31.
—— *A History of Pentateuchal Traditions,* New Jersey, 1972.
T. Oestreicher, *Das deuteronomische Grundgesetz,* Gütersloh, 1923.
L. Perlitt, *Bundestheologie im Alten Testament (WMANT* 36), 1969.
—— 'Moses als Prophet', *EvTh* 31, 1971, 588–608.
H. Petschow, 'Zur Systematik und Gesetzestechnik im Codex Hammurabi', *ZA* 57, 1965, 146–72.
A. Phillips, *Ancient Israel's Criminial Law,* Oxford, 1970.
—— '*NEBALAH*—a term for serious disorderly and unruly conduct', *VT* 25, 1975, 237–42.
—— 'Another Look at Murder', *JJS* 28, 1977, 105–126.
J. G. Plöger, *Literarkritische, formgeschichtliche und stilkritische Untersuchungen zum Deuteronomium (BBB* 26), 1967.
J. R. Porter, *Moses and Monarchy,* Oxford, 1963.
J. B. Pritchard (ed.), *Ancient Near Eastern Texts Relating to the Old Testament,* Princeton, 1950.
C. Rabin, 'Three Hebrew Terms from the Realm of Social Psychology', *VTS* 16, 1967, 219–30.
G. von Rad, *Das Gottesvolk im Deuteronomium (BWANT* III, 11), 1929.
—— *Der heilige Krieg im Alten Israel (ATANT* 20), 1951.
—— *Studies in Deuteronomy (SBT* 9), 1953.
—— *Old Testament Theology,* Edinburgh, vol. 1 1962, vol. 2 1965.
—— 'The Form-Critical Problem of the Hexateuch', in *The Problem of the Hexateuch and Other Essays,* Edinburgh, 1966, 1–78.
—— 'The Promised Land and Yahweh's Land in the Hexateuch', *ibid.*, 79–93.
—— 'There Remains still a Rest for the People of God', *ibid.*, 94–102.
—— 'The Tent and the Ark', *ibid.*, 103–124.
—— 'The Deuteronomic Theology of History in I & II Kings', *ibid.*, 205–221.
J. Reade, 'The Accession of Sinsharishkun', *JCS* 23, 1970, 1–9.
R. Rendtorff, 'The Background of the Title *'l 'lywn* in Gen. xiv', in *Fourth World Congress of Jewish Studies* I, Jerusalem, 1967, 167–70.
K. H. Rengstorf, *Die Re-Investitur des verlorenen Sohnes in der Gleichniser-*

zählung Jesu Luk. 15,11–32 (Arbeitsgemeinschaft für Forschung des Landes Nordrhein-Westfalen, Heft 137), 1967.

H. Graf Reventlow, *Gebot und Predigt im Dekalog*, Gütersloh, 1962.

—— 'Kultisches Recht im Alten Testament', *ZThK* 60, 1963, 267–304.

—— 'Gebotskern und Entfaltungsstufen in Deuteronomium 12', in *Gottes Wort und Gottes Land* (Festschrift für H. W. Hertzberg zum 70. Geburtstag, hrsg von H. Graf Reventlow), Göttingen, 1965, 174–85.

D. A. Robertson, *Linguistic Evidence in Dating Early Hebrew Poetry (SBL Dissertation Series* 3), 1972.

W. H. Ph. Römer, 'Randbemerkungen zur Travestie von Deut. 22, 5', in *Travels in the World of the Old Testament* (Studies presented to M. A. Beek, edited by M. S. H. G. Heerma van Voss, Ph. H. J. Houwink ten Cate, N. A. van Uchelen), Assen, 1974, 217–22.

M. Rose, 'Bemerkungen zum historischen Fundament des Josia-Bildes in II Reg 22f.', *ZAW* 89, 1977, 50–63.

L. Rost, 'Das kleine geschichtliche Credo', in *Das kleine Credo und andere Studien zum Alten Testament*, Heidelberg, 1965, 11–25.

N. Sarna, 'Zedekiah's Emancipation of Slaves and the Sabbatical Year', *AOAT* 22, 1973, 143–9.

W. H. Schmidt, 'Überlieferungsgeschichtliche Erwägungen zur Komposition des Dekalogs', *VTS* 22, 1972, 201–220.

R. F. Schnell, 'Perizzite', *IDB* vol. 3, 735.

W. Schottroff, *Das altisraelitische Fluchspruch (WMANT* 30), 1969.

H. Schulz, *Das Todesrecht im Alten Testament (BZAW* 114), 1969.

F. Schwally, *Der heilige Krieg im alten Israel*, Leipzig, 1901.

S. Schwertner, 'Erwägungen zu Moses Tod und Grab in Dtn 34,5.6', *ZAW* 84, 1972, 25–46.

H. Seebass, 'Die Stämmeliste von Dtn XXXIII', *VT* 27, 1977, 158–69.

I. L. Seeligmann, 'A Psalm from Pre-Regal Times', *VT* 14, 1964, 75–92.

G. Seitz, *Redaktionsgeschichtliche Studien zum Deuteronomium (BWANT* V, 13), 1971.

J. van Seters, 'The Conquest of Sihon's Kingdom: a literary examination', *JBL* 91, 1972, 182–97.

—— *Abraham in History and Tradition*, Yale, 1975.

P. W. Skehan, 'The Structure of the Song of Moses in Deuteronomy (Deut. 32:1–43)', *CBQ* 12, 1951, 153–63.

—— 'A Fragment of the 'Song of Moses' (Deut. 32) from Qumran,' *BASOR* 136, 1954, 12–15.

R. J. Sklba, 'The Redeemer of Israel,' *CBQ* 34, 1972, 1–18.

R. Smend, *Die Bundesformel (Theologische Studien* 68), 1963.

N. H. Snaith. *The Distinctive Ideas of the Old Testament*, New York, 1964.

—— 'The Meaning of *šeʿîrîm*', *VT* 25, 1975, 115–18.

J. A. Soggin, 'Kultätiologische Sagen und Katechese im Hexateuch', *VT* 10, 1960, 341–7.

J. J. Stamm and M. E. Andrew, *The Ten Commandments in Recent Research* (*SBT* II/2), 1967.

F. J. Stendebach, 'Das Schweinopfer im alten Orient', *BZ* 18, 1974, 263–71.

F. Stolz, *Jahwes und Israels Kriege* (*ATANT* 60), 1972.

A. Strobel, *Der spätbronzezeitliche Seevölkersturm* (*BZAW* 145), 1976.

W. A. Sumner, 'Israel's Encounters with Edom, Moab, Ammon, Sihon and Og according to the Deuteronomist', *VT* 18, 1968, 216–28.

D. Winton Thomas, '*KELEBH* "dog": its origin and some usages of it in the Old Testament', *VT* 10, 1960, 410–27.

—— 'Some Observations on the Hebrew word *raʿanān*', *VTS* 16, 1967, 387–97.

M. Tsevat, 'Alalakhiana', *HUCA* 29, 1958, 109–134.

P. H. Vaughan, *The Meaning of 'BĀMĀ' in the Old Testament*, Cambridge, 1974.

R. de Vaux, 'Une hachette essénienne?', *VT* 9, 1959, 399–407.

—— *Ancient Israel: its Life and Institutions*, London, 1961.

—— *Studies in Old Testament Sacrifice*, Cardiff, 1964.

—— 'Les Hurrites de l'histoire et les Horites de la Bible', *RB* 74, 1967, 481–503.

—— 'Le lieu que Yahvé a choisi pour y établir son nom', in *Das ferne und nahe Wort* (L. Rost Festschrift, hrsg von F. Maass) (*BZAW* 105), 1967, 219–28.

—— 'Ark of the Covenant and Tent of Reunion', in *The Bible and the Ancient Near East*, London, 1972, 136–51.

—— 'The Sacrifice of Pigs in Palestine and in the Ancient East', *ibid.*, 252–69.

S. J. de Vries, 'Review of E. Nielsen, *Die zehn Gebote*', *VT* 16, 1966, 530–34.

L. Wächter, Die Übertragung der Beritvorstellung auf Jahwe', *ThLZ* 99, 1974, 801–816.

V. Wagner, *Rechtssätze in gebundener Sprache und Rechtssatzreihen im israelitischen Recht* (*BZAW* 127), 1972.

E. von Waldow, *Der traditionsgeschichtliche Hintergrund der prophetischen Gerichtsreden* (*BZAW* 85), 1963.

G. Wallis, 'Der Vollbürgereid in Deuteronomium 27,15–26', *HUCA* 45, 1974, 47–63.

S. D. Waterhouse, 'A land flowing with milk and honey', *Andrews University Seminary Studies* I, 1963, 152–66.

E. F. Weidner, *Politische Dokumente aus Kleinasien. Die Staatsverträge in akkadischer Sprache aus dem Archiv von Boghazköi* (*Boghazköi-Studien* 8), Leipzig, 1923.

—— 'Der Staatsverträge Assurnirari VI von Assyrien mit Mati'ilu von Bit-Agusi', *AfO* 8, 1932–3, pp. 17–27.

M. Weinfeld, 'Traces of Assyrian Treaty Formulae in Deuteronomy', *Bib* 41, 1960, 417–27.

—— 'The Origin of Humanism in Deuteronomy', *JBL* 80, 1961, 241–7.

—— 'Deuteronomy—the present state of enquiry', *JBL* 86, 1967, 249–62.

—— 'The Covenant of Grant in the Old Testament and in the Ancient Near East', *JAOS* 90, 1970, 184–203.

—— *Deuteronomy and the Deuteronomic School*, Oxford, 1972.

—— 'On "demythologization and secularization" in Deuteronomy', *IEJ* 23, 1973, 230–33.

—— '*B*ᵉ*rît*—covenant vs. obligation', *Bib* 56, 1975, 120–28.

J. Weingreen, *From Bible to Mishna*, Manchester, 1976.

D. H. Weiss, 'A Note on '*šr l' 'ršh*', *JBL* 81, 1962, 67–9.

G. J. Wenham, 'Deuteronomy and the central sanctuary', *TB* 22, 1971, 103–118.

—— '*B*ᵉ*tūlāh*—a girl of marriageable age', *VT* 22, 1972, 326–48.

P. Wernberg-Møller, 'Pleonastic *Waw* in Classical Hebrew', *JSS* 3 1958, 321–6.

C. Westermann, *Die Verheissungen an die Väter* (*FRLANT* 116), 1976.

J. Wijngaards, '*ḥwṣy* and *h'lh*—a twofold approach to the Exodus', *VT* 15, 1965, 91–102.

H. Wildberger, *Jahwes Eigentumsvolk* (*ATANT* 37), 1960.

—— 'Die Neuinterpretation des Erwählungsglauben Israels in der Krise der Exilszeit', in *Wort-Gebot-Glaube* (Walter Eichrodt zum 80. Geburtstag, hrsg von H. J. Stoebe) (*ATANT* 59), Zürich, 1970, 307–324.

F. V. Winnett, 'Mining', *IDB* vol. 3, 384–5.

D. J. Wiseman, 'The Vassal-Treaties of Esarhaddon', *Iraq* 20, 1958.

H. W. Wolff, 'Das Kerygma des deuteronomistischen Geschichtswerks', in *Gesammelte Studien zum Alten Testament* (*Theologische Bücherei* 22), München, 1964, 308–324.

—— *Anthropology of the Old Testament*, London, 1974.

G. E. Wright, *The Old Testament against its Environment* (*SBT* 2), 1950.

—— 'The Levites in Deuteronomy', *VT* 4, 1954, 325–30.

—— 'The Lawsuit of God: a form-critical study of Deuteronomy 32', in *Israel's Prophetic Heritage* (edited by B. W. Anderson and W. Harrelson), London, 1962, 26–67.

E. Würthwein, Die Josianische Reform und das Deuteronomium', *ZThK* 73, 1976, 395–423.

Z. Zevit, 'The ʿegla Ritual of Deuteronomy 21:1–9', *JBL* 95, 1976, 377–90.

W. Zimmerli, 'Ich bin Jahwe', in *Gottes Offenbarung* (*Theologische Bücherei* 19), München, 1963, 11–40.

—— 'Das zweite Gebot', *ibid.*, 234–48.

—— *The Law and the Prophets*, Oxford, 1965.

F. Zimmermann, 'Some Studies in Biblical Etymology', *JQR* 29, 1938–39, 241–6.

H.-J. Zobel, *Stammesspruch und Geschichte* (*BZAW* 95), 1965.

INTRODUCTION
to
Deuteronomy

A. TITLE AND PLACE IN THE CANON

The Hebrew title of the book, as usual derived from the first or the first significant words, is 'these are the words'. It is a title which is in fact peculiarly appropriate to the book, for we find here (see below) heavy and extensive influence from the form and terminology of extra-biblical treaty texts, where 'words' is frequently found as the term used to describe their contents. The English title *Deuteronomy* derives from a Latinized form of the LXX title: *Deuteronomion*. The latter is based on an ungrammatical LXX rendering of Dt. 17:18. The Hebrew text there can only mean 'a repetition (or copy) of this law'. The LXX, however, translated it as 'this second (or repeated) law', understood with reference to the whole book of Deuteronomy. As 'this second law' the LXX title is suitable in the sense that Deuteronomy understands itself, even if only late in its history, as belonging in the context of a second covenant, which Moses made with Israel in Moab on the borders of the land, a covenant distinct from the covenant made at Sinai/Horeb (see 29:1). However, the title is not suitable in that it takes no account of the fact that Deuteronomy incorporates much of what is already found in the preceding books (for example, about fifty per cent of the Book of the Covenant in Exod. 20:23–23:33 is paralleled in Deuteronomy). This perhaps makes the alternative understanding of the LXX title, 'this repeated law', more appropriate. However, neither understanding represents an accurate rendering of the Hebrew of 17:18. That verse makes no reference, either explicit or implicit, to older compilations of law outside the book of Deuteronomy.

As the fifth book of the Old Testament, Deuteronomy belongs to the Pentateuch, the earliest section of the Bible to achieve canonical status. Since it is only the Pentateuch which enjoys this status with the Samaritans, it is likely that it was accepted as canonical before the Samaritan schism. So already by the fourth century BC Deuteronomy in the context of the Pentateuch was canonical. However, the book has a 'canonical history' which goes far behind this point, and indeed it is in the context of the history of Deuteronomy that the history of the early stages of the canon should be traced. Before it became part of the Pentateuch, Deuteronomy was connected with the following books and marked the opening of the so-called deuteronomistic history (see below); and before that stage it was an independent book perhaps having some connection with the reform of Israel's cultic life carried out by Josiah in 621 BC (see below). For the beginning of the formation of the canon the essential periods in this history were the time of the original book of Deuteronomy and the stage of its being edited in the context of the deuteronomistic history of which it came to form a part.

The original Deuteronomy was a lawbook (see below), analogous to the lawcodes found outside Israel. As such it differed significantly in some respects from other collections of law which were probably already not unknown in Israel. The latter would have taken the form of shorter collections, of cultic material attached to sanctuaries, of legal material used in the administration of justice, and so on. But now, apparently for the first time, there came into existence a more extensive collection of law, authoritative for the conduct of the national life, and ascribed for its authorship to Moses. A written document had become binding, a source of guidance on which one should meditate and which one should teach to each successive generation (cf. 6:4–9).

The standing which Deuteronomy thus acquired was strengthened when, as part of the deuteronomistic history, it was heavily influenced by a deuteronomistic editor. For at this stage Deuteronomy came to incorporate elements of the extra-biblical treaty tradition and to reflect in its structure the form of these extra-biblical treaties. The growth of the canonical principle can hardly be separated from this treaty influence, for even if a written document was not in every case essential for the validity of a treaty, the general importance ascribed to the written texts and the care taken for their preservation (on this see especially McCarthy, *Treaty*, 38ff.) constitute an element which was carried over from that specific treaty context (or from the general legal context which includes the treaties) into this stage of the formation of Deuteronomy (cf. 31:9–13, 24–29; also comment on 4:2). At this stage Deuteronomy understands itself as 'Scripture', the will of Yahweh authoritatively set down in writing (cf. 17:18; 28:58, 61; 29:20f.). Thus the canonical status which the Pentateuch was accepted to possess by the fourth century is by no means the beginning of the process of formation of the canon, but rather a stage in the history of the canon in which Deuteronomy plays a central role.

B. STRUCTURE

The following discussion of the structure of Deuteronomy has the purpose of describing the process by which the book has reached its present form. It is difficult to say to what extent the view here put forward fairly reflects current study of and opinion about the book, for it is impossible to discern anything like a dominant approach to Deuteronomy in current scholarship; widespread agreement exists on some broad and basic issues, but otherwise the range of divergence of opinion is considerable.

The first two sections of what follows give an impression of some recent work: firstly, the study of the formal structure of the whole, and, secondly, the study of the literary growth which culminated in that form. The discussion which follows in the next two sections brings together and supplements the detailed results of the commentary, in separating out and describing the nature and purpose of two deuteronomistic stages in the growth of Deuteronomy to its present form, and, behind those stages, the content and character of the original Deuteronomy. That such stages are to be discerned in Deuteronomy's origin and development would be widely admitted; the content, nature and purpose of each of these stages is one area where considerably more study is necessary. The editing of the original Deuteronomy may well have been a process rather than an event or events, and, consequently, the separation of distinct layers of editing may be carried through only with diffidence. The two layers which are here separated, on the basis of the historical concerns of the one and the covenant law concerns of the other, should be seen as two parts of this process within the deuteronomistic movement.

The problem of the extent and nature of the original Deuteronomy is no more easily soluble: but it must be within the context of the book itself, rather than by appeal to rather uncertain proposed historical backgrounds, that the discussion must proceed. Our conclusion is that this original book was a lawcode, incorporating some already existing collections of law, with a parenetic introduction. As a result of the first stage of deuteronomistic editing it became associated with the event of covenant-making on Sinai and the imparting to Israel of the decalogue. As a result of the second stage of deuteronomistic editing, Deuteronomy itself took on the characteristics of covenant (or treaty) law under the influence of ideas, forms and expressions derived from the extra-biblical treaty tradition.

(a) *The Form of Deuteronomy*
Older studies of Deuteronomy (for which see especially the comprehensive account in Loersch, *Das Deuteronomium* or, more briefly, Eissfeldt, *Old Testament*, 171ff.), when they were not concerned with the chronological dating of the book, the time of its origin and its relation to Josiah's reform, concentrated especially on the analytical criticism of the book. While the latter has by no means been abandoned and the highly detailed analysis of Deuteronomy, as found in the commentaries of Bertholet, Marti, Steuernagel and others in the past, finds its modern advocates in the work of, for example, Merendino (*Das deuteronomische Gesetz*) and Mittmann (*Deuteronomium 1:1–6:3*), the study of Deuteronomy and the application of literary analysis to it has proceeded in recent years within a context which began its development only in 1938. That year marked the first appearance of von Rad's study 'The Form-Critical Problem of the Hexateuch' (now in *Problem*, 1–78), which was primarily concerned with the structure of the Hexateuch, but which also included a suggestive study of the form of Deuteronomy as an organic whole.

Von Rad observed that in structure the book has four sections: (a) a historical and parenetic introduction in chs. 1–11; (b) the presentation of the law in 12:1–26:15; (c) the sealing of the covenant in 26:16–19; (d) the blessings and curses in chs. 27ff. In this structure von Rad was able to recognize the form of a cultic ceremony of covenant making or covenant renewal, a form which appears also in the Sinai pericope in Exod. 19–24. The proximity of Deuteronomy to this ceremony, despite the book's presumed late date of origin, was clear to von Rad by the constant use of the word 'today', through which the divine revelation and covenant making on Sinai became present realities for those to whom Deuteronomy is addressed. Other passages, such as Pss. 50, 81, confirm the existence of this cultic ceremony, 'a great cultic drama, the distinctive features of which are undoubtedly the divine self-revelation and the subsequent communication of God's purpose in the form of apodeictic commandments'. Deuteronomy does not explicitly name any sanctuary as the place where such a covenant ceremony was celebrated, but when Dt. 11:29ff.; 27, are seen along with Jos. 8:30ff.; 24, it is clear that there is only one place which can come in for consideration here: the sanctuary at Shechem. It was here that the covenant tradition, reaching back to Sinai, was preserved from early times in the context of a covenant festival.

It was not proposed by von Rad that Deuteronomy as it stands may be taken simply to reflect this cultic festival. The problem of understanding the precise process of growth of the book was not minimized; but what did emerge was that the end result of this process of growth was an organic unit which as a whole and also in many of the particular units of which it was composed was constructed on the pattern of a covenant-making ceremony.

Von Rad's results represented the beginning of a new era of research into Deuteronomy, an era which has, moreover, in large part tended to confirm rather than invalidate his views in at least some of their essential aspects. This has been mainly as a consequence of the development of one particular area of research, that of the forms of ancient Near Eastern treaties and the influence of these forms and their vocabulary on the Old Testament covenant forms. The extra-biblical treaties exhibit a variety of forms, but this variety may in fact be reduced to two broad categories which are themselves not totally independent (see particularly McCarthy, *Treaty; idem, Old Testament Covenant*, 24ff.; and, for earlier studies, with somewhat different emphasis, Mendenhall, *BA* 17, 1954, 49ff.; Beyerlin, *Origins*, 52ff. The literature on the subject is vast and cannot possibly be either listed or reviewed at this point. Selections of treaty texts will be found in McCarthy, *Treaty*, 181ff.; *ANET*, 201ff. For the Hittite treaties the main collections are those of Friedrich, *Staatsverträge*, and Weidner, *Politische Dokumente*. The primary study of their forms is that of Korošec, *Hethitische Staatsverträge*. For the Mesopotamian treaties see especially Weidner, *AfO* 8, 24ff.; and Wiseman, *Iraq* 20, 1958): these two groups are, firstly, treaties deriving from the Hittite empire of 1400–1200 BC, and secondly, treaties from Mesopotamia deriving from a somewhat later time in the first millennium BC.

For the former group a fairly constant pattern may be discerned consisting of the following elements: (a) a titulature, in which the great king who offers the treaty identifies himself, giving his titles and appellations; (b) a historical prologue in which the great king outlines in direct personal form of address the relationships which have existed until then between the two parties: particular emphasis is laid on all that the suzerain has done on behalf of the vassal; (c) the stipulations of the treaty are now presented. This section may be divided into two parts: first, a statement of the basic and fundamental demand which constitutes a general obligation defining the total relationship between the two parties; and, secondly, the detailed and particular demands concerning a wide variety of subjects though all concerned precisely with the treaty relationship being established. (d) Sometimes a 'document clause' dealing with the preservation and regular public reading of the treaty text now follows, but generally the section immediately following the stipulations consists of the list of witnesses; this list includes the gods of both parties, together with natural phenomena, mountains, rivers, sea, heaven and earth, wind and clouds. (e) The final section is a (usually quite stereotyped) curse and blessing in case of violation or observance of the terms of treaty.

This is the 'standard' form of Hittite treaty, but it is far from being rigid. Its flexibility is apparent in the occasional omission of certain elements (including the historical prologue; see the discussion of the matter in McCarthy, *CBQ* 27, 1965, 227, n.23; *idem*, *Old Testament Covenant*, 26f., n. 29) and the variation in emphasis within others (so, for example, the curse and blessing formula does not always have a balanced stereotyped form, but may vary to give chief emphasis to the curse, as in the treaty translated in *ANET*, 205f.); yet it is the general pattern of these treaties and one which serves to distinguish them as a group within the general treaty tradition which later reappears with the ninth-century treaties from Mesopotamia.

The Mesopotamian treaty texts come from the Assyrian empire. From a formal point of view they are more difficult to deal with than the Hittite treaties. The reason is that with the exception of the Esarhaddon treaty, of which a full version may be obtained from all its various copies, they are in a fragmentary condition. Nevertheless, as a group they are clearly distinguished in form from the Hittite treaties by two factors in particular: firstly, by the general absence of a historical prologue; and, secondly, by the long and colourful curses without any corresponding blessings. Otherwise, however, as McCarthy, *Treaty*, 80ff., has shown, the later and the earlier groups of treaties do stand within the one treaty tradition. They have common elements—stipulations (often expressed in the apodictic 'thou shalt [not]' form), curses, lists of gods as witnesses, etc.—which firmly connect the varying manifestations of the treaty tradition in different cultural contexts. The common aim of imposing under oath the will of a superior on an inferior is effected through the medium of a form which, though varying slightly within each of the groups and to a larger extent between the groups, preserved the essential features of a known and used tradition of treaty-making which can be traced over several centuries in the ancient Near East.

That there is a connection between Deuteronomy and this extra-biblical treaty tradition is certain. The relationship is clear not only in formal structure (particularly in the succession of historical review, laws/stipulations and blessing-curse), but also in many details. Reference is made to these points of contact in the commentary below (cf. for example, 6:5 on the command to 'love' Yahweh; 9:24 on the verb 'know'; 13:4 on the treaty use of 'walk after', 'fear', 'obey the voice of', 'serve', 'cleave'; 23:6 on 'peace' and 'prosperity'; and the introduction to ch. 28 with the commentary on 28:23, 29, for the treaty background of the curses). This contact is with the treaty tradition as a whole rather than with any particular part of it. The argument that it is the Mesopotamian manifestation of the treaty tradition which is particularly reflected underestimates the importance which Deuteronomy assigns to the role of history, which with its persuasive, didactic, and warning function parallels closely what is to be found in the Hittite treaty texts. On the other hand, the Hittite treaties do not offer a fully satisfactory background for the extensive curses which Deuteronomy contains in ch. 28; these find a much better parallel in the Mesopotamian context.

It is in fact doubtful if the attempt to isolate one particular phase of the treaty tradition as offering the closest parallel to Deuteronomy serves any very useful purpose. This is for two reasons. In the first place, the attempt tends to underestimate the significance of the treaty *tradition* to which all the treaties belong, as opposed to the individual treaties or groups of treaties. But, secondly, and perhaps more important, the attempt seems frequently to proceed by bypassing a fundamental problem in this whole discussion. This problem concerns the considerable lack of clarity which exists on the precise nature of the relationship between Deuteronomy and the treaties. Deuteronomy is not a treaty document, nor is it presented as a treaty document. It is presented as a speech of

Moses shortly before his death; it is in effect his testament. That in itself constitutes a link with the tradition, for, as Baltzer, *Covenant Formulary*, 63ff., (cf. also von Rad), has noted, the occasion of a change in leadership was also the occasion of making or renewing treaty relationships. Yet Deuteronomy is still not the text of a treaty or covenant. That it goes back to a treaty document (see below on Josiah's reform) is a possibility; for the moment, however, our concern is with Deuteronomy as it now stands.

In its present form Deuteronomy is not a treaty document; it is not presented as such, and some elements of the treaty form it does not include (for example, the titulature), and indeed there are elements of the book which cannot be included in a treaty form. This is true especially of the last three chapters of the book, which include the Song of Moses, the Blessing of Moses and the account of his death. So in its present form the book of Deuteronomy can- not be held to follow exactly the form of treaty, which in turn means that it cannot simply be taken as a 'literary imitation' of the treaties (as argued by Weinfeld, *JBL* 86, 1967, 252f.; *idem*, *Deuteronomy*, 57). This permits a most important negative con- clusion: there is clear evidence in Deuteronomy that treaty forms and vocabulary have influenced the form, vocabulary and the ideas of the book, but it is not possible to transfer directly and immediately from the literary context of the extra-biblical treaties to the literary context of Deuteronomy. This in turn means that arguments for the unity of Deuteronomy which are based on its supposed treaty form (Weinfeld, *Deuteronomy*, seems implicitly to accept the unity of Deuteronomy because of its treaty background; explicit arguments for unity on this basis—and indeed also for Deuteronomy's origin in Mosaic times—appear in Kline, *Treaty*, and in a vaguer way also in Craigie) are inadmissable, and it is even doubtful to what extent the literary criticism of Deuteronomy as frequently practised in the past is vitiated by arguments and observations deriving from the ancient Near Eastern treaties. In so far as the literary contexts of Deuteronomy and of the extra- biblical treaties are, as already indicated, independent, the literary criticism of Deuteronomy must in the first instance proceed quite independently of the treaties.

(b) The literary development of Deuteronomy
That Deuteronomy presents a complex problem relating to its origin and growth is indicated by a number of factors. In the first

place there is extensive duplication of material. This is the case
not only with particular laws, as with the demand for centralization of sacrificial worship which appears three times in ch. 12
(vv. 5f., 11f., 13f.), but especially in the introductory chapters
where chs. 1–4 and 5–11 both present historical material and
parenesis leading up to the law. Secondly, there is a remarkable
mixture of historical and parenetic material within each of these
introductory sections. It is true that several of the treaty texts
already referred to, particularly the Hittite treaties, also present
such a mixture, but in Deuteronomy large sections of the historical
material, though presently joined with the parenetic, stand quite
apart from the latter as history recounted not perhaps simply for
its own sake, but certainly not with the object of inducing a feeling
of gratitude in Israel for favours shown her by Yahweh in the
past. So, for example, there is a clear distinction between the
historical section in chs. 1–3 and the historical references which
appear in ch. 8. Even if Seitz, *Studien*, 29, is correct in his view
that 1:9–15, 16f., 18, has in mind the deuteronomic law (which,
however, seems doubtful; vv. 9–18 deal simply with the administrative and judicial organization of Israel, and lead up to the
conclusion of the section in v. 18), there is no way in which chs. 1–3
may be understood as an attempt to inculcate a spirit of obedience,
which is part at least of the intention of the historical prologue of
the treaties; on the other hand, this is precisely the intention of the
reference in ch. 8 to Israel's experiences in the wilderness. Thirdly,
the presentation of Deuteronomy as speech of Moses to Israel
occasionally, as in ch. 27, breaks down to become narrative about
Moses and Israel. Fourthly, there is remarkable interchange of
second person singular and plural forms of address (preserved in
the AV and RV translations, but not in the RSV which translates
'you' and 'your' for both singular and plural).

The last-mentioned phenomenon in particular has been widely
used as a means towards adopting a source critical approach to the
problems which Deuteronomy otherwise presents. Among the
older commentators, Steuernagel in particular used it as a criterion
for determining stages of growth, an approach which has been revived and strengthened more recently by Minette de Tillesse, *VT* 12,
1962, 29ff. However, it can by no means be used on its own as the
key to the solution to all Deuteronomy's difficulties. Not only has
such a change in form of address been observed in extra-biblical
documents (references in Baltzer, *Covenant Formulary*, 33n. 71; cf.

also the Sefîre inscription I B, lines 21–45, for this variation within the stipulations of a treaty: text in Fitzmyer, *Aramaic Inscriptions* 16ff.), but even within the book of Deuteronomy itself there are many passages where the application of this criterion for the purpose of source division succeeds only in doing unacceptable violence to the text. A test case is 4:1–40 (unfortunately not treated by Minette de Tillesse), the unity of which must be upheld despite its frequent change of use of singular and plural forms of address (see the introduction to ch. 4 and especially comment on v. 19). Lohfink, *Hauptgebot*, 30f., 239ff., 244ff., 252ff., sees the question in a stylistic context (in this being followed by e.g. Lindblom, *Erwägungen*, 15f.: cf. also Buis, 30f.). Every change of number is a new form of address, a new assault on the listener. The singular is the standard form by which the cult community is addressed, while it is in the preaching of the law that the desire for effect and emphasis demanded a change to the plural, so that the community is no longer addressed as a unit but as a collection of individuals. The individual is no longer lost in the unit but stands as an individual. This is the case, for Lohfink, in the parenetic sections, while in the narrative passages different rules apply. Here when the listeners are referred to as having participated in the events of the story being related then the plural is used; but when narrative is joined to parenesis the usage becomes confused.

Lohfink's study represents the most sustained attempt to explain the phenomenon on stylistic grounds. Whether or not his precise description of the purpose and effect of the change is correct (and there are many passages where it is difficult to apply; cf., for example, the singular address in 7:11 and the plural in 8:1), it must be true that for some passages at least in Deuteronomy, and particularly for 4:1–40 and other texts deriving from the same hand, the change is a stylistic feature of the work of a single author, and cannot be used for source division purposes. On the other hand, however, it is clear that there are several occasions where the change of address coincides with other differences between passages, where assignment of sections to different authors is based on grounds other than change of address. In this connection the other pointers to the hands of different authors in Deuteronomy, referred to above, become relevant.

The use of different forms of address presents a problem which has by no means been satisfactorily solved. In the present context the results of our study seem to confirm the widespread view that

the original introduction to the laws of chs. 12–26 was formulated
in singular form of address. This, however, is a conclusion reached
not only on grounds of change of address but primarily for reasons
unconnected with that phenomenon (see further below). It also
appears to be the case that the author responsible for the incorporation of Deuteronomy within the larger context of the deuteronomistic historical work (see below) used the plural form of address
—again, a view widely held and particularly promoted by Minette
de Tillesse. Otherwise, however, the consistent use of singular or
plural does not characterize the work of any one author; both
forms are used by the same author in the same literary unit. As
already mentioned, this is to be seen in 4:1–40 together with
several other passages in later chapters apparently deriving from
the same hand.

Literary-critical approaches to the problem of Deuteronomy in
the past have been dominated by two views which are adopted
independently or in some form of combination. These two views
may be classified as the documentary and the supplementary.
The former view found its representative in Steuernagel (following
Wellhausen in particular, though differing in important respects,
especially on the question of what constituted the 'original
Deuteronomy') and several of his followers, who attempted
a literary-critical division of Deuteronomy into documents.
Steuernagel saw the present book as the result of the combination
of three editions of the original work. Three layers could be
distinguished in chs. 1–11, two using plural form of address and
the third singular. In the law, however, this division could be
carried through only in ch. 12; traces of different editions otherwise almost disappear. His view represents the extreme to which
this particular approach to Deuteronomy could go, and it resulted
not only in a minute division of sources (which, however, in itself
should not be taken as a criticism of the approach), but more
significantly in the understanding of individual editions which
were very thin in content and which seemed highly improbable
when the true nature of the full, expansive and repetitive nature
of the style of the literature was appreciated.

Those who adopted the supplementary approach thought in
terms of an original Deuteronomy which was gradually supplemented through the addition of more or less extensive sections.
This approach is widely adopted to some degree, at least for the
legal sections of the book. It has been worked out in detail by

Horst (*Gottes Recht*, 17ff.) who saw a decalogue containing a 'law of privileges of Yahweh' as basic to chs. 12–18, which has undergone supplementation which eventually introduced the idea of centralization. Hölscher (*ZAW* 40, 1922, 161ff.) extended the approach to the whole book, seeing the singular nucleus of chs. 6–11 as the introduction to the original collection of law. More recent advocates of the approach, as Noth, *Studien*, 16f., and Weiser, *Introduction*, 129f., do not show the same inclination towards a detailed analysis but propose, rather, a process of growth, this being either a literary process (Noth) or one carried out 'within the framework of the oral, partly sermon-like recital at the festival cult of the covenant' (Weiser).

Finally, a combination of the documentary and supplementary approaches finds advocates in Eissfeldt and Fohrer. The former is a close follower of Wellhausen in that the original Deuteronomy is understood to have been the lawbook (this, however, having developed through a series of supplements and amplifications). This lawbook, which included blessing and curse from the first, now has an introduction in chs. 1–11 in which two parallel strands have been combined, through being set one after the other (1:1–4:40 and 4:44–11:32; cf. Eissfeldt, *Old Testament*, 18f., 225ff.) Fohrer, on the other hand (cf. Fohrer, *Introduction*, 169ff.), points out that the original Deuteronomy, as a lawbook like the Hammurabi Code, would from the beginning have had an introduction and conclusion: the original one is now to be found in 4:44–9:6; 10:12–11:32, while the secondary addition to it is in 1:1–4:43; 9:7–10:11. Within this secondary addition it is not possible to take chs. 1–3 as the work of an editor who incorporated Deuteronomy into the deuteronomistic historical work (as Noth; see further below); rather, the chapters function to connect Deuteronomy with the Pentateuchal tradition.

This brief sketch outlines the main approaches to the literary-critical problems of Deuteronomy, and may give some indication of the diversity of views adopted. Even as a sketch, however, it cannot be considered in any way adequate without some reference being made to two more recent significant contributions to the question, those of Lohfink, *Hauptgebot*, and Seitz, *Studien*.

The work of Lohfink is a strict stylistic study, in which it is the vocabulary used, the phrases and combinations of terms, that determine the authorship of passages. It is confined to chs. 5–11, and in summary form its most significant results may be catalogued as

follows: (a) chs. 5 and 6 belong together as a unit; (b) chs. 9–11
are in some ways distinct from what precedes; (c) language typical
of the decalogue is missing from chs. 10–11; (d) within chs. 5–8
the basis is formed by a Gilgal covenant text (see introduction
below to chapter 7) which is basic to ch. 7 on the one hand, and
the decalogue material of chs. 5–6 on the other; (e) a secondary
layer of ch. 7 together with ch. 8 arose from the working together
of these two basic texts; (f) the same editor compiled 9:1–7, which
was intended as a key to the interpretation of chs. 9–11, and so
must be regarded as responsible for the final form of the complete
section chs. 5–11; (g) 10:12–11:17, in that it contains no decalogue
language, is earlier than chs. 5–6, and is indeed the earliest part
of chs. 5–11; (h) 9:9–10:11, on the other hand, in that it tells of
covenant breaking, presupposes the story of covenant making in
chs. 5–6, and so cannot be the original prelude to 10:12–11:17.
The overall conclusion is, therefore, that 10:12–11:17 is the oldest
section; it was used by the author of chs. 5–6 who then composed
9:9–10:11; the editor who combined with this the Gilgal covenant
material of ch. 7 also composed the later parts of ch. 7, ch. 8, and
9:1–7 as the key to what follows.

Lohfink's approach, which can only adequately be discussed in
the treatment of the various texts to which he refers (see the
commentary), has been severely criticized by Mittmann,
Deuteronomium 1:1–6:3, 3ff., as arbitrary and subjective, and as a
method by which any text can be taken as a unit. This is somewhat
extreme in view of the highly controlled analysis to which Lohfink
subjects the text; but, aside from the detailed points of criticism
which are made in the commentary, there is at least one general
respect in which the method may lead to false results: this lies in
the fact that it pays inadequate attention to the conservative
nature of literary forms in the ancient Near East, for this tends to
minimize the particularity of the styles of individual writers, so
that stylistic analysis may easily lead to the erroneous separation
of passages as deriving from different authors when in fact they
come from the same hand. However, in at least one major respect
the commentary below follows Lohfink: this is in the view that the
decalogue does not belong to the basic layer of chs. 5–11, though
in the determination of that layer there is considerable diversity.

The proposals of Seitz are at once more traditional and at the
same time a considerable advance on what has already been done.
Proceeding from a view of Deuteronomy as a whole, he notes that

the book contains a series of superscriptions which may be divided into two groups. They are to be found in 1:1; 4:44; 28:69 (EVV 29:1); 33:1 on the one hand, and 4:45; 6:1; 12:1 on the other. The latter group is distinguished from the former in being fuller and in not being connected to its contexts by a linking word introducing direct speech (e.g. 'and he said'). These superscriptions belong to their contexts and may be held to mark stages of redaction or stages in the history of the growth of the book. The first mentioned group, in so far as it covers a larger extent of material than the second, belongs to the later of the two stages of redaction which the superscriptions mark. It is not suggested that absolutely everything now to be found in Deuteronomy must be seen as having found its present place in association with one or other of these superscription systems. On the one hand, there are later additions, such as the Song of Moses in Dt. 32; and, on the other hand, there was a most important stage of development which preceded the first superscription system. This was the stage of collection of the deuteronomic laws. This was marked especially by the connection of already existing law collections with the centralization laws (see further below); but this collection has no preserved introduction. The latter was provided with the earlier of the two superscription systems (4:45; 6:1; 12:1) which brought in complexes of material, such as the decalogue, the narrative of the events at Horeb, and the war speeches, now to be found in chs. 5–11, which had no original connection with Deuteronomy. This stage of redaction also saw the addition of further laws to the law corpus, and resulted broadly speaking in the present chs. 5–26, 28. The second redactional stage is marked by the later superscription system (1:1; 4:44; 28:69 (EVV 29:1); 33:1) which has its closest parallels in the deuteronomistic historical work (Seitz, *op. cit.*, 31, refers in this context to Jos. 12:1, 7; 13:2; 14:1 and Jg. 3:1) It comes from the time of incorporation of Deuteronomy into the deuteronomistic historical work, and brought with it chs. 1–4; 27; 28:58ff.; 29ff., along with certain other expansions and additions to the material incorporated.

Once again the commentary below follows Seitz in seeing the decalogue, and material dependent on it, as no original part of Deuteronomy, and agrees with many aspects of his detailed exegesis of the text. However, in two major respects there is considerable divergence from his views. Firstly, it seems that too much weight is placed by Seitz on the two groups of superscriptions as (a) coming from two identifiable stages, and (b) as bringing with them major sections of the present Deuteronomy. It is not clear that all the superscriptions said to belong to each of these stages of redaction do in fact belong together, and it seems preferable to see at least one of them (33:1) as simply the heading to the Blessing of Moses incorporated as an independent addition. Secondly, it is by no means certain that a characteristically deuteronomic collection of law (characterized by the theme of centralization) can be shown to have existed apart from introductory material now contained in chs. 5–11. A basic layer of these chapters may in fact be assigned to the stage of collection of the deuteronomic law.

(c) Deuteronomistic editing of Deuteronomy
Our study of the text of the first three chapters of Deuteronomy confirms the view proposed especially by Noth, *Studien*, 14ff., that there is here not an introduction to the deuteronomic law, but rather the beginning of a much more extensive historical work. The chapters have no essential contact with the law beyond bringing the reader up to the historical point in time at which the law was proclaimed. Their focus is rather on the history of the people Israel, a history which indeed stands under and is judged by the law proclaimed at its beginning. However, while the history thus stands in some connection to the law, the important point in the present context is that the history is seen in the first instance as a whole; Dt. 1–3, though clearly sharing with the rest of the larger history this connection to the law, is yet in the first place a part of that history, and only as such a part does it gain this connection with the law.

The history to which these sections of Deuteronomy belong continues until the end of the second book of Kings. The details of the redactional history of that work are not certain, particularly with regard to the possibility of there having existed an edition which came into existence before the fall of Jerusalem in 587 BC, an edition which was then later supplemented during the exile in order to incorporate material dealing with later events. For the moment this is not a fundamental issue (on this see further below); it remains clear that the passages mentioned in Deuteronomy belong to this history, rather than to the law, and so, following the title 'deuteronomistic historical work' commonly given to that work, they may be called deuteronomistic passages in Deuteronomy.

Dt. 1–3, therefore, do not on their own account belong with the law; they do not lead up to it or introduce it. Rather they lead up to and introduce the history of Israel which as a whole stands under the law. This can be seen in the stylistic connections between these chapters and the early parts of Joshua in particular (see introductions to 1:6–3:11 and 3:12–29), but especially also in the clear continuity in subject and concern between these chapters and 31:1–8, 14f., 22f., where the commissioning of Joshua by both Moses and Yahweh is related as fulfilment of the command of 3:27f.; for those parts of ch. 31 are clearly intended to lead on into the future history of Israel narrated in the succeeding books.

The book of Deuteronomy thus contains at least a framework which derives from a deuteronomistic hand, a framework which appears in chs. 1–3 and parts of ch. 31, but also in 34:1*, 2–6, where there is found the fulfilment of the divine command to Moses, also given in 3:27f., to ascend Pisgah in order to view the land. Yet between these two ends of the book it appears that the hand of the same author is again to be seen. Once again it may be determined mainly from the historical concern which is the primary element. The most important passages in this connection are 5:1–6:3 containing the decalogue, and parts of 9:1–10:11 dealing with Israel's breaking the covenant and its renewal. The latter story depends on the former since it is in 5:1–6:3 that the original covenant making is described, and several detailed points of contact show that the writer responsible for 5:1–6:3 (apart from several later additions; see the introduction to the section) is also responsible for 9:9–12, 15–19, 21, 25; 10:1–5.

For a number of reasons the pericope within which the decalogue is contained, and hence also the story of the covenant breaking in chs. 9f., must be understood as later additions, and probably deuteronomistic additions, to the present context. First of all, there is here again historical narrative. The decalogue is certainly to be understood in itself as a collection of divine demands, but in the context of the pericope within which it stands it is subservient to the category of history. The giving of the decalogue to the people is seen as an event in Israel's past history. Secondly, it is impossible to see how the decalogue, understood as a collection of divine demands, could possibly be original in its present position. It may indeed be understood as the fundamental demand, the divine law, on which the remainder of the detailed law in chs. 12–26 is dependent: the latter is intended to draw out

the detailed implications of the decalogue demands. However, it is
clear that this cannot be taken as an original intention of the laws
of chs. 12–26, but rather must be a secondary idea of the purpose
of these laws arising from the secondary placing of the decalogue
in its present position. Had it been an original intention the connections between the two would have been clearer and indeed
closer; for the decalogue is presently separated from the laws of
chs. 12–26 by an abundance of other material. Thirdly, as will be
taken up in detail in the introduction to 5:1–6:3, the decalogue at
present has a form which suits the deuteronomistic rather than the
deuteronomic background particularly well.

Further possible contributions to Deuteronomy from this
deuteronomistic author are difficult to isolate. One passage may
be pointed to with some confidence: 12:8–12, 16. This is one of
the three versions in that chapter of the law concerning the
limitation of sacrificial worship to one central sanctuary. Consider-
ing the importance which the deuteronomistic historian in the
books of Kings has attached to this demand as the single criterion
by which judgment is meted out to Israel's kings (cf. 1 Kg. 15:14;
22:43; 2 Kg. 12:3, etc.), it is only to be expected that he should
have been responsible for part of this elaboration of that law (see
further on 17:14–20).

It should be emphasized, however, that this deuteronomistic
contribution to the growth of Deuteronomy represents but one
strand in the deuteronomistic editing of the book. For there is no
doubt but that the work of the deuteronomistic circle represents a
process or movement which was not completed in the context of a
single editing event incorporating Deuteronomy into the deuteronomistic history. The latter represents an early if not the earliest
stage in that deuteronomistic movement, identifiable mainly from
its historical interest. To be distinguished from it, however, there
is clearly a later deuteronomistic contribution. To investigate
whether the distinction being drawn here would coincide with
stages in the redaction of the deuteronomistic history generally
would go beyond the limits possible in this context, but whatever
about the other books which now form part of the deuteronomistic
history, it must be proposed that in the case of Deuteronomy there
is clear evidence of more than one deuteronomistic edition. In the
context of our understanding the work of the deuteronomistic
circle as a process or movement, it must of course follow that the
assignment of passages to particular editorial layers is often very

uncertain. Nevertheless, there seems to be at least one further deuteronomistic layer in Deuteronomy, apart from that already described, which may be isolated fairly easily. This is the layer which takes its starting point in 4:1–40. It presupposes the existence of the other layer, and is, therefore, the later of the two.

As already mentioned in connection with the earlier discussion of the significance of the phenomenon of change in form of address, 4:1–40 is a single literary unit. With its introductory 'and now', it clearly presupposes the existence of chs. 1–3 and was brought in to follow them (see comment on 4:1). The theme, however, is quite separate from that of the first three chapters, and even though in the context of possible treaty influence on the form of the book, 4:1–40 would in any case be understood to begin a new section, this is nevertheless clearly a secondary connection between chs. 1–3 and 4:1–40, based on a view of chs. 1–3 as a historical prologue to be followed by a general demand for obedience. It was not as a historical prologue, however, that chs. 1–3 first came into existence, but rather as the introduction to the deuteronomistic history.

The dominant theme of the chapter is obedience to the law in general and to the prohibition of images in particular. The style of the chapter is marked by an unexplained diversity in use of second person singular and second person plural forms of address, and by the use of certain characteristic terms and phrases: statutes and ordinances, teach, do, possession, inheritance, with all your heart and with all your mind, signs and wonders, a mighty hand and an outstretched arm, it may go well with you, prolong your days. The appearance of this subject and style through many other passages in Deuteronomy indicates that the author of 4:1–40 did not confine his contribution to that chapter, but, as would be expected, made further extensive additions to the work which lay before him. The history of Israel does not feature in his writing; rather it is Israel standing before the divine demand, with a promise of blessing for obedience. In connection with the latter point a certain characteristic of this author's thought requires particular notice. This is the view that curse and blessing do not stand before Israel only as alternate possibilities dependent on her disobedience and obedience to the law; curse and blessing also appear as occurring in historical succession as characteristic of succeeding phases of Israel's history (cf. McCarthy, *Treaty*, 137, 147). The former understanding of curse and blessing is to be found in 6:10ff.;

8:19f.; 11:13ff.; 28:1–44; and the latter in 4:25ff.; 28:45ff.; and
30:1. In the latter the curse is understood to be the consequence
of Israel's disobedience while the blessing will follow on her
repentance and turning again to God after the disobedience which
brought the curse.

It is by no means clear, however, that the difference in understanding of curse and blessing is an indication of difference in
authorship. The view of curse and blessing as alternate possibilities
is the usual one, and frequently associated with law collections
both within and outside the Old Testament. It is this view which
we would, then, expect to see most strongly represented in any
collection of law with blessing and curse attached to them, and
so it is the view found most frequently in Deuteronomy. Deuteronomy is presented at all levels as a body of law demanding obedience, and it is to that obligation that blessing and curse attach
themselves. However, the work of the deuteronomistic circle, at
any rate in its later stages (see further below), was set against the
background of Israel in exile. The destruction of the people and
the land, the ruination of the cities and the deportation of their
populations, had already taken place, and therein lay the operation of the curse for Israel's disobedience to the law. The curse had
already come, and to a people who saw themselves as the victims
of that curse the deuteronomistic editor also wished to address a
word of encouragement. This he did by presenting curse and
blessing as successive features of Israel's life. Through doing this
he could say that, although Israel had been disobedient and
although she now suffers the consequences of that in the coming
into effect of the curse attached to the law, yet even now if Israel
repents and turns back to God the blessing of God will come on
them. The deuteronomistic editor sees his task as a double one:
on the one hand he must present the law as that which still must
be obeyed, as the conditions on which Israel's true prosperity
still depends, and as bringing with it, therefore, both curse and
blessing. On the other hand, however, to his dispirited contemporaries he also addresses a word of hope by saying in effect that
the disasters they have experienced represent the operation of the
curse of the law; the curse is now over. But that law also carries
with it a blessing, and it is that which Israel if she returns to
Yahweh may now expect.

The work of this second deuteronomistic editor is most extensive
in ch. 4, where vv. 1–40 are to be ascribed to him. His editorial work

continued, however, in later sections of the parenesis. Apart from some isolated additions to the earlier deuteronomistic pericope which introduced the decalogue in 5:1–6:3, it is to be found mainly in 6:10–18; 7:4f., 7–16, 25f.; 8:1–6, 11*b*, 15f., 18*b*–20; 10:12–11:32. Here the aim was more fully to integrate the decalogue than had already been done. It had originally been introduced within the context of a narrative of an event of Israel's history. The later deuteronomist, however, has emphasized its actual demand for the exclusive worship of Yahweh, so continuing the theme already established in 4:1–40, and so has modified the original general exhortation of these chapters into a specific demand. Within the law corpus itself some material may also be ascribed to this later deuteronomist. This is particularly the case in ch. 12 where he has not only given his own version of the sanctuary law in vv. 1–7, but through the addition of v. 32 he has effected a strong connection of the law on centralization of worship with the law on the purity of worship. This latter theme continues through the next two chapters and has been filled out by the later deuteronomist through the addition of specific illustrative material in 14:1, 4–21. Other additions to the law corpus do occur, but their assignment to this deuteronomistic editor is by no means certain. He may be at work in 15:4–6 emphasizing the connection between obedience to the law and prosperity, in 17:2f., where there is a link with the decalogue, and also in the supplements to the law corpus in 25:17–19; 26:1–15. Later, however, linguistic and thematic connections with 4:1–40 show the late deuteronomistic authorship of the covenant passages in 26:16–27:26, though here, however, still later additions have also been made. Ch. 28 may also be claimed to belong to the work of the deuteronomistic circle, even though it is difficult to be more precise on its origin (see the introduction to that chapter), but the work of the author of 4:1–40 is probably contained more clearly in chs. 29f. The language and thought of the sermons in these chapters, along with the general background which they presuppose, point to the later deuteronomist. This is the case also with the provisions for the regular public reading and the preservation of the law in 31:9–13, 24–29. The work of this editor is then brought finally to a close in 32:45–47.

Aside from the two deuteronomistic contributions to the book, some other later additions must also be isolated. Many of these are occasional supplements to the text, filling out and explaining particular points, and are of quite unknown origin. In some cases, however, it is possible to assume that the background of the additions is the literary stage at which Deuteronomy was to some extent detached from the deuteronomistic history in order to become part of the Pentateuch (on this see especially Noth, *Studien* 18off.). The 'Pentateuch' before the inclusion of the book of Deuteronomy comprised the JE sourses set within the framework of the Priestly writing. The latter concluded with the death of Moses, which meant that it could not stand simply as the immediate prelude to the deuteronomistic historical work beginning with Deuteronomy styled as speech of Moses. The uneven break between the JEP account and the deuteronomistic history was smoothed over by the transfer of the Priestly account of the death of Moses to the end of Deuteronomy, where it is now to be found in 34:1*, 7–9.

This connection of the two blocks of material also directly caused the repetition in 32:48–52 of the Priestly story of the announcement of Moses' death in Num. 27:12–14. Other additions, deriving from the same occasion, though not from the Priestly writing, are in 4:41–43; 34:10–12. Otherwise, the occasion of the post-deuteronomistic additions to Deuteronomy cannot be determined. Apart from some isolated verses, the chief of these additions are, firstly, the Song of Moses in 31:30–32:44, with its introduction in 31:16–22; and, secondly, the Blessing of Moses in ch. 33.

(d) The original Deuteronomy

By 'original Deuteronomy' is here meant the form of the book as it existed prior to the first deuteronomistic editing which incorporated it into the deuteronomistic historical work. It is, of course, not to be denied that additions were made to the book between the time of its origin and its incorporation into that historical work. However, these are to be seen as unconnected, isolated additions which do not constitute a systematic editing and reworking of the content. Likewise, it is also clear that before the time of origin of the original Deuteronomy there existed shorter or longer collections of law. On the other hand, however, behind the stage at which the deuteronomistic editing of the work began it is in fact possible to discern only one stage which marked the time when earlier collections of law were brought together into the context of an overall presentation which is recognizably deuteronomic, i.e. which constitutes a form of the book of Deuteronomy of such a character that subsequent work on it in the context of the deuteronomistic circle would take the form of editing an already existing book.

The original book of Deuteronomy, therefore, seems to have included the following: 4:45; 6:4–9, 20–24; 7:1–3, 6, 17–24; 8:7–11*a*, 12–14, 17–18*a*; 9:1–7*a*, 13–14, 26–29; 10:10–11; 12:13–15, 17–19 (20–28), 29–31; 13:1–18*; 14:2f., 21*; and nearly all 14:22–25:16, with the omission of some isolated deuteronomistic and later additions. Certainly, clear characteristics of the original may be deduced from these passages. In the first place it had a heading which referred generally to statutes and ordinances which Moses gave Israel after leaving Egypt. The book was styled as a speech of Moses and though the precise location of its being imparted to Israel was not given it was clearly at some stage of Israel's life between Egypt and the occupation of the land. No reference was made in the book to the Sinai revelation or the giving of law then or to a covenant concluded then. This book was simply a collection of law given by Moses to Israel.

Yet at the same time the general parenesis, in which Israel is exhorted to obedience, makes it clear that this law comes to Israel also under the authority of Yahweh (6:24); these laws given by Moses are statutes of Yahweh by which Israel shall live and prosper. Therefore, this teaching must be with Israel continually and she must be careful in the transmission of it to future generations. For the rest, the parenesis is concerned with Israel's relationship to the land. Given the fictional standpoint of the book the presentation is, of course, that of Israel outside the land on its way to take possession of the land. But the actual emphasis lies more generally on Israel and the meaning of the land for her. Israel is a people holy to Yahweh, whom Yahweh has chosen for his own possession. Therefore, the non-Israelite inhabitants of the land are to be destroyed. Only in this way can Israel's relationship to Yahweh remain uncontaminated (ch. 7). The land is a 'good land' (8:10), which Yahweh is giving Israel in fulfilment of his promise to the patriarchs (6:23; 9:5; 10:11). This Israel should be careful to remember, and not to ascribe to her own power her possession of the land. It is Yahweh who gives the enemy into her hand (7:22ff.: 8:17). Nor should Israel misinterpret her status as the people of Yahweh and her receiving from Yahweh the gift of the land as the consequence of her own righteousness. Israel has

already shown in her history that she can make no such claim
(9:7a), and in fact it is for the wickedness of the nations that
Yahweh is driving them out before Israel.

The purpose of this exhortation is not just generally to encourage obedience to the law; more specifically, it is to encourage the
view that Israel is Yahweh's own possession, to whom he has given
the land. This place of Israel is to be preserved through its
obedience to the law given through Moses. The law which then
follows is itself, at least in its early stages, presented within a
parenetic or preaching context, which points back to the
deuteronomic exhortation in chs. 6–11 (on the originality of the
connection of the basis of chs. 6–11 with the deuteronomic law see
also introduction to 5:1–11:32). In the latter part of the collection
of law, however, the parenetic elements tend to disappear, and
the impersonal style of the casuistic form of law comes to predominate (see especially from 21:10 to the end). The impression
which the collection of law thus gives (and this is true whatever
stage of redaction is taken as the standpoint) is of an unfinished
mixture of material of varied origins which has not had a uniform
history or a systematic and polished presentation. This is undoubtedly true of the material to some extent, and it represents a
problem in the understanding of the law corpus which has defied
complete explanation.

A novel attempt to deal with the problem, focusing particularly
on the question of the (apparently quite haphazard) order of the
laws has been made by Carmichael, *Laws* (cf. also *idem, JSS* 12,
1967, 198ff.). According to Carmichael one must think in terms of
a deuteronomic author whose technique for drafting laws involves
the expression of material presented at the beginning of his code
with material taken from earlier laws in the Book of the Covenant
(Exod. 20–23) and earlier narrative traditions. His method is
discursive, allusive and expansive, and consequently the arrangement of laws which results is not necessarily a logically consistent
one in the context simply of the content and immediate concern
of those laws. So 16:18–19:21 takes up and further expands the
laws of 12:1ff. using earlier legal and narrative material. There is
no doubt that Carmichael is right in his view that a variety of
factors governs the order of the laws quite apart from any rational
association from the modern legal point of view. This has been
demonstrated for the Code of Hammurabi by Petschow (*ZA* 57,
1965, 146ff.) in particular, who points to associations of thought

and wording, connections which are governed by chronological order of circumstances regulated by the laws etc., in order to explain the order of Hammurabi's laws. So also Daube, *Studies*, 74ff., points to similarly 'illogical' arrangements in both Roman and Hebrew Law, where new provisions are sometimes joined to an existing code as an appendix, instead of being worked in at that point of the existing code required by the subject matter of the new provisions. So in principle Carmichael's approach has much in its favour. There are two points, however, which suggest caution. In the first place, some of the associations which Carmichael establishes with earlier legal and narrative texts are purely fanciful; sometimes they do not succeed in showing what Carmichael thinks they do show; and sometimes when they are possible they are in fact much more probably wrong. For example, if the place of 21:1–9 is to be accounted for (a) by the coincidence of subject with 19:1ff. (homicide), and (b) by the method of bringing in laws suggested by historical material which is related to the homicide laws of ch. 19 (cf. Carmichael, *Laws*, 136), then 21:1–9 should come before 19:15–21. Again, the law on the prophet in 18:16ff. is said to have its background in 4:1–40, so explaining why this law is followed in 19:1ff. by the law on the cities of refuge, for the latter has its background in 4:41–43. However, the background of the prophet law in 18:16ff. would much more probably (on Carmichael's method) lie in ch. 5, for it is only there that the question of the (prophetic) mediator between God and the people arises, and not in ch. 4. Secondly, Carmichael's approach pays little or no attention whatever to the different forms of law in Deuteronomy and to the phenomenon, already pointed to, that the parenetic material is heavily represented at the beginning but is hardly present at all in the latter parts of the collection.

It wou'd seem best to apply Carmichael's approach more selectively, rather than as a general principle to show the gradual growth of the whole law corpus; that is, it may succeed in explaining the presence of certain individual laws (as, for example, the landmark law in 19:14) or perhaps even groups of laws in their present contexts. However, the differences in style and form in the laws suggest that already existing laws and already existing arrangements of laws within collections have been incorporated by the author of the original Deuteronomy. It is along these lines that Merendino, *Gesetz*, finds several legal sources: cultic laws, 'abomination' laws, laws concluding with the purging formula, marriage laws, humanitarian laws, apodictic laws. Such laws there undoubtedly are at present in Deuteronomy, but this mixed classification according to both content and form conceals a situation in which it is very likely that many laws within any of these groups are in fact secondary compilations (by the deuteronomic author), in form based on older laws but containing no ancient content. So, for example, those laws which terminate in the purging formula (13:5; 17:7, 12; 19:19; 21:21; 22:21, 22, 24; 24:7) would on the face of it apparently belong together, and be or derive from a series of laws using such a formula (see particularly L'Hour, *Bib* 44, 1963, 1ff.); however, a study of the content of the relevant laws is enough to show that they cannot all be set on the same level: it is unlikely that laws on apostasy, on marriage and family relations and social laws, to all of which the formula is now attached, originally belonged together in a single series. The formula itself makes no reference to Yahwism (or to Israel, if 'from Israel' in 17:12; 22:22 is seen as secondary in relation to 'from you' which otherwise occurs), and may well have originated outside that context. If so, then the laws on apostasy using that formula would be secondary formations. That this should be so, and that the deuteronomic author should himself be responsible for many such secondary formations, is entirely credible. From the point of view of his understanding of the holiness of Israel (7:6) and of their exclusive relationship to Yahweh such a formula would suit his outlook well; in its form using direct second person singular address, it would also have been suitable, for the deuteronomic author shows a clear preference for this direct address form, even to the extent of using it in the context of casuistic laws which are otherwise impersonal (on deuteronomic partiality for the 'if you . . .' style, see particularly Gilmer, *If-You Form*, 45ff., where it is also pointed out, however, that the form is not a deuteronomic innovation, being found in all legal corpora as well as in treaty texts and in both biblical and extra-biblical wisdom literature. See also below, the introductions to 12:29–13:18 and to 16:18–17:7.)

Much the same is true of those laws which conclude by describing the crime as an abomination to Yahweh (17:1; 18:12; 22:5; 23:18; 25:16). The condemnation of an act as an 'abomination' is by no means confined to Deuteronomy. It has many examples in Proverbs and also in extra-biblical wisdom (see comment, with references, on 7:25). In its occurrences in Deuteronomy probably only two (18:12; 25:16) can be classed as pre-deuteronomic usages of the term in connection with the laws. Otherwise it is due to the deuteronomic legislator adopting the expression secondarily for laws where he thought it particularly appropriate. There is, therefore, very little likelihood of these laws having formed an original series or collection which has been split up by the deuteronomic legislator (as proposed by, for example, L'Hour, *RB* 71, 1964, 481ff.; cf. also Merendino, *op. cit.*, 326f. See comment on 18:12.)

The deuteronomic legislator must be regarded as the originator or formulator of much of the material now in the law corpus. The theme of centralization of worship to a single sanctuary may indeed have a history (see below), but the law on the subject in ch. 12 is one of the most distinctive characteristics of this deuteronomic author. It is quite true (cf. von Rad) that the law is not presupposed throughout the deuteronomic law, but this does not mean that it may be easily removed as just a layer of this law (as proposed by Maag, *VT* 6, 1956, 10ff.). It stands at the beginning of the deuteronomic law corpus and informs many of the laws which follow; it is a deuteronomic law in the light of which all further laws in that law corpus are to be seen. It is formulated by the deuteronomic legislator with the intention that it should be programmatic for the whole.

However, there are many laws, particularly in the later parts of the whole corpus, which do not refer to centralization, which are irrelevant to the subject, and which either are not expressed in the parenetic form which characterizes the centralization law, or which are simply a deuteronomic reformulation of an older law. Such laws are especially the casuistic laws in 19:4ff., 11f., 15–21; 21:1–9, 15–17, 18–21; 22:13–21, 22, 23–29; 24:1–4, 5, 7; 25:5–10, and also the rather differently formulated laws on war in 20; 21:10–14; 23:10–15. Deuteronomic influence on these laws is slight, being found, for example, in the occasional introduction of direct form of address in the otherwise impersonal casuistic laws (cf. 19:19; 22:24, 26). There is nothing to show that it was the deuteronomic legislator who brought together either the independent casuistic laws or the casuistic laws as a whole with the war laws, and the absence of such indication makes it more likely that the casuistic laws with the war laws existed already before the deuteronomic legislator as a collection (see on this especially Seitz,

Studien, 110ff., 223ff.). That this is so, at least for the casuistic laws as an existing collection, is supported by the fact that the two subjects with which these casuistic laws are concerned—death and marriage—are also associated outside Deuteronomy, not only in the decalogue but also in Jer. 7:9. The embedding of the war laws in the casuistic laws, most probably before the creation of the deuteronomic law collection, would have come about simply through the interpretation of one of those casuistic laws (21:1–9) as possibly referring to the death of someone killed in battle (see introduction to 19:1–21:9). It is this complete collection of casuistic and war laws which the deuteronomic legislator adopted and connected with his centralization laws, and it is its already complete form which explains the minimal deuteronomic influence which can be traced in it. This event would also have provided the occasion of the adoption or creation of further laws by the deuteronomic legislator, suggested to him by the subject and the forms contained in the larger collection of casuistic and war laws. It seems, therefore, that the explanation for most of the characteristics of the deuteronomic law corpus, with respect to its content and to the order of laws which it treats, is to be sought not simply in the creative work of the deuteronomic legislator, but mainly in the process of redaction, which will have included the formation of pre-deuteronomic collections of law, which culminated in the formation of the deuteronomic law corpus.

In concluding this section some further general remarks are necessary on the original Deuteronomy and the effect on it of the successive stages of editing to which it has been subject. First of all, the original Deuteronomy was a law book and only in so far as similar collections of law outside the Old Testament are formally related to treaty documents was the original Deuteronomy also related to the treaty form. There are some similarities in structure between lawcodes and treaties, but there are also essential differences, both in form and in setting presupposed. The lawcodes contain a system of laws imposed by a ruler on his subjects, the treaty on the other hand is designed to ensure the loyalty of the treaty partner. In form they may overlap in containing historical prologue followed by laws and blessings and curses, but they are clearly distinguishable in their content and purpose. The laws of a lawcode govern the whole life of a community and the relationships of its members, but the stipulations of the treaty are designed to ensure the faithfulness of one partner to the other. It is to the lawcodes that the original Deuteronomy bears the closest resemblance. Its laws too are designed for the direction of the whole life of the community and are directed towards the regulating of the mutual relationships of the members of that community rather than towards the loyalty of the community to Yahweh. There are no distinctively treaty characteristics in the original Deuteronomy. It is with the deuteronomistic editing of Deuteronomy, particularly in its second stage, that the treaty elements are introduced. The first stage of deuteronomistic editing set the book in the context of the deuteronomistic history and introduced the Sinai/ Horeb material; in the second stage, however, not only was the long curse and blessing element brought in and elaborated, which in itself would not have changed the character of the original law book, but the strong covenant or treaty elements in 26:16–27:26 were also introduced. This is a crucial contribution to Deuteronomy, for the latter now becomes a covenant or treaty between Yahweh and Israel. The older character of Deuteronomy as a lawcode does not, however, completely disappear, and so, for example, Weinfeld, *Deuteronomy*, 148ff., finds that the lawcode and treaty forms have converged in Deuteronomy. It is a convergence, however, which arises out of the secondary introduction of treaty elements into the original book.

One at least of the impulses towards doing this must be related to the problem, which arose after the first deuteronomistic editing, of the relationship between the deuteronomic law and the revelation and covenant making on Sinai. This was not a problem with which the original Deuteronomy, which made no reference to Sinai, had to deal. However, once the decalogue had been added in the first stage of deuteronomistic editing, the question of the relationship between this decalogue and the event on Sinai on the one hand, and the deuteronomic law given by Moses to Israel in the wilderness on the other hand, had to be faced. The decalogue was by this time understood as covenant law, and the event on Sinai, whatever its original significance in the tradition, was seen as a covenant ceremony in which the relationship between Yahweh and Israel was based on a set of expressed stipulations which set out to regulate Israel's life. Since, however, the deuteronomic law also had this purpose of regulating Israel's existence, and since it was already a feature of the original Deuteronomy (cf. 6:24) that this law stood under the authority of Yahweh, it was inevitable that the concept of treaty or covenant should be carried over to the deuteronomic law. For this reason it is set by the later deuteronomistic editor within the context of a covenant in Moab and described as 'the words of the covenant which the Lord commanded Moses to make with the people of Israel in the land of Moab, besides the covenant which he had made with them at Horeb' (29:1; see comment). The question of the precise relationship between the two covenants and the two laws is resolved through presenting the one covenant as standing on a level with the other, and the deuteronomic law as the law which Moses had in fact received from Yahweh at Sinai at the time of the first covenant.

C. THEOLOGY

(a) Israel in Deuteronomy

Deuteronomy lends itself to being described as the expression of an intensely nationalistic faith. It centres on Israel, the community of 'brothers', living in the land in covenant with its God, and whose existence in the land is uncorrupted by contact with non-Israelite peoples. This element of exclusiveness cannot be ignored, yet it must be seen in its whole context and must be defined more closely for what it actually is. The Israel of Deuteronomy is not the state of Israel in any of the forms by which that state is known. The community to which the law is addressed is not defined by its citizenship within a state headed by the king and expressed through the existence of the various institutions and forms of which a monarchic state is composed. The king is barely mentioned in the book, and when the law does concern itself with him (17:14–20), he is treated as one of the brothers comprising the people who, like his people, is subject to the divine law. Rather, the Israel of the book of Deuteronomy is the people of God, held together by the common worship of its God.

This is not to say that Deuteronomy has a genuine openness, showing a willingness to accept as 'brothers' all who acknowledge Yahweh as their God. For one thing, certain people are explicitly excluded from membership in the 'community of the Lord' (23:1ff.). Secondly, the limits of the people are demarcated more precisely by reference to those who acknowledge a common tradition of sojourn in Egypt and occupation of the land. The worship of Yahweh involves the adoption as one's own of a history in which Yahweh made himself known, a history which took concrete form not only in an escape from Egypt but also in the violent occupation of a land through the forced dispossession of its former inhabitants. Thirdly, Deuteronomy (4:19) sees non-Israelite peoples as having their own forms and objects of worship which have been assigned to them. The worship of Yahweh is the expression of the faith of the chosen people. Finally, Deuteronomy expresses no sense of Israel with a mission to the world. Of the three elements in the blessing of Abraham in Gen. 12:1-3, only the first two, land and posterity, are taken up into Deuteronomy (the former being dominant, the latter only occasionally appearing, as, for example, 1:10f.), while the third, that Abraham will exemplify to the world the significance of what it is to be blessed by God, does not appear.

Deuteronomy, then, has a definite community of the people of Yahweh in mind. Noth, *Laws*, 28ff., identified this community as the old, pre-monarchic Israelite amphictyony which the monarchy never replaced and which expressed itself as a sacral community united in the worship of its God at its amphictyonic sanctuary. The existence of such an amphictyony in pre-monarchic Israel presents certain problems, and its survival into the monarchic period cannot be shown through the clear existence of an amphictyonic institution in later time. If an amphictyony existed in Israel, it is perhaps this which provided the picture of an ideal Israel which survived especially in the prophetic tradition. But whether or not such an amphictyony existed, it is of no actually existing Israel that Deuteronomy speaks; for Israel in the period of Deuteronomy's origin (see below) was a monarchic state. It is *to* this Israel that Deuteronomy is addressed, but it speaks to this Israel of an Israel that should exist, a people of God. It is an ideal which it represents. This is not necessarily, however, an ideal for the future, as Alt, *Kleine Schriften* II, 250ff., proposed, when he saw in Deuteronomy the reform programme of a renewal movement in northern Israel after 722 BC, a restoration programme designed for the time when Assyrian overlordship might be ended; rather, it is an ideal for the present, a picture of Israel as it should be, held up to the Israel that is. The ideal does not exclude the actual, but rather seems to presuppose it, for it is clear that there is and could be no Israel for which Deuteronomy could act as a sufficient constitution. There are no laws here for civil damages, protection of property and so on which would be required in a lawcode for an actual Israel. This is a collection of often quite unenforceable laws which is designed to educate, to inculcate religious convictions and attitudes, to show how such attitudes express themselves in the life of the people of God, within the framework of an actually existing Israel, whatever constitutional form that Israel might take. It is unlikely, therefore, that Deuteronomy, at least in its original 'lawbook' form, is intended to replace the Book of the Covenant in Exodus, as proposed by Weiser, *Introduction*, 131, and Eissfeldt, *Old Testament*, 221. Only about fifty per cent of the Book of the Covenant is taken up in Deuteronomy, and none of the laws on pecuniary matters which make the Book of the Covenant suitable as state law, is represented in Deuteronomy. It is within the framework of an existing Israel, functioning on the basis of laws such as those contained in the Book of the Covenant, that Deuteronomy takes its place. Within that framework Deuteronomy sees Israel as a holy people (7:6; 14:2), and it attempts to show what this means in the context of the daily problems of its social, political and religious life (cf. Clements, *God's Chosen People*, 37ff.).

In order to authorize and legitimize its teaching, Deuteronomy gives it the authority of antiquity and the sanctity of the word of Moses. However, this presentation as speech of Moses brought with it the fictional setting of pre-settlement times, the law appearing as the teaching of Moses to Israel on the eve of the occupation of the land. This setting added significantly to the effect and purpose of the laws, quite apart from the authority of Mosaic authorship which it introduced. For the laws addressed Israel from outside the land, from a historical and geographical point at which the history of Israel in the land had not yet begun. As von Rad, *Studies*, 70ff., has suggested, the effect of this was to bring Israel back to its pre-settlement days, to the age of its establishment as the elect people of God, to the time before its corruption through involvement in and with the people of the land. That history, which was a history of sin and rebellion against God, is in effect cancelled out, so that Israel now has the chance of a new beginning with Yahweh through obedience to the laws designed for its life in the land.

(b) God

The general theme of Deuteronomy can be comprehensively stated in a single sentence: it is a call to the service of one God by an elect people centered around one sanctuary, through obedience to the law in the land which God has given. First of all, it is a call. Only in the broadest sense can the content of Deuteronomy be termed law; rather, it is teaching and exhortation. The aim is to persuade rather than to command, to encourage rather than to force. This aim is achieved through the use of first person of the speaker, through direct form of address, through the building up in series of verbs aimed at inculcating the right attitude to the law: hear, learn, keep, observe, do, etc. (cf. 5:1, 27, 32f.; 6:3; 7:12, etc., and the table in Lohfink, *Hauptgebot*, 200ff.), and through the many references to history as showing God's favour towards Israel as the basis for Israel's obedient response to God (see comment on 8:2–6). Throughout, Deuteronomy calls Israel to acknowledge this claim which God has on her.

Deuteronomy is not generally interested in promulgating a theoretical monotheism. Occasionally in ch. 4 (cf. vv. 35, 37) the absolute uniqueness of Yahweh is affirmed, but even there (cf. 4:19f.) as well as elsewhere in Deuteronomy it is the uniqueness of Yahweh for Israel which is to the fore. In this Deuteronomy stands in line with the decalogue, for there too it is Israel's worship of Yahweh rather than monotheism which is the issue. Anything which may compromise the sole lordship of Yahweh for Israel must be ruthlessly extirpated from her midst. This is the case with the nations in the land which Israel is to occupy: they are to be utterly destroyed (7:1ff.); it is the case also with all those within Israel who may entice the people to apostasy: that source of evil is to be purged from her midst (ch. 13). It is only Yahweh who has a claim on Israel, for it is only he who has acted in her history.

Deuteronomy emphasizes both the immanence and the transcendence of Israel's God. The transcendence (cf. Clements, *God and Temple*, 88ff.) is emphasized positively in ch. 4 (see v. 36) in the declaration that from heaven Yahweh let Israel hear his voice and see his fire, though Yahweh himself did not descend to Israel, and negatively in ch. 10 (vv. 1–5) in the portrayal of the ark simply as a container for the tablets of the law rather than as the throne of Yahweh. It comes out too in the fact that for Deuteronomy Yahweh is not to be coerced or persuaded through sacrificial offerings. Sacrifices have their place in private worship as an expression of gratitude to God in the fulfilment of vows (12:6, 11, 17, 26; 23:21ff.); but they belong chiefly in the context of the humanitarian behaviour which the Israelite must adopt towards the poor, for they are to be shared with the poor, the Levite, the stranger, the orphan and the widow. What Weinfeld (*JBL* 86, 1967, 258ff.; *idem*, *Deuteronomy*, 210ff.; cf. also Milgrom, *IEJ* 23, 1973, 158ff., and Weinfeld, *IEJ* 23, 1973, 230) has called secularization in Deuteronomy probably also belongs here. That is, there is a tendency in Deuteronomy towards the liberation of religious institutions and practices from primitive magical elements, taboo regulations and so on; the tendency is manifested in the fact that profane slaughter is permitted, in the humanitarian use of sacrifices and tithes, in the disappearance of the apotropaic character from the regulations relating to Passover (16:1ff.) and of the magical elements in, for example, regulations relating to exemption from military service (20:5ff.), and also in the humane character of the motivations attached to laws on Sabbath observance (5:12ff.), slavery (15:12ff.) and the poor (e.g. 24:14ff.). This may be called secularization provided that term is understood, as Weinfeld emphasizes, not to imply opposition to religion. For the religious spirit with which the laws are imbued is unmistakable and indeed that law is as a whole understood to be a sign of divine grace (4:7f.). This may be termed also a spiritualizing tendency, a move towards freeing the divine from the control of man, towards separating God from man so that the actions of man in sacrifice as also in prayer and confession, come to express that right attitude to God which Deuteronomy requires, rather than a means by which the divine may be made to conform to the wishes of the worshipper.

Yet Yahweh is also immanent; he is no spectator watching Israel from a distance, but is active in her history punishing and rewarding. The epithets by which he is described: jealous (4:24; 5:9; 6:15); great and terrible (7:21); faithful (7:9); merciful (4:31), point to an involvement with Israel which may be described only in terms of his active presence in her life and history. At times this presence is in fact stated explicitly (23:14), and it must be presupposed when actions at the sanctuary are said to take place 'before the Lord your God' (16:11, 16; 26:10, 13; cf. Wenham, *TB* 22, 1971, 112f.). In this connection the 'name theology' of Deuteronomy is significant. This aspect of Deuteronomy's theology has often been stressed as an illustration of the transcendence of God in Deuteronomy: God himself is not present in the sanctuary, only his name is there (cf. e.g. Kaiser, *Introduction* 132f.; McCurley, in *Light*, 308). In fact, however, this introduces a false distinction between Yahweh and his name. The name and the reality signified thereby are not distinguishable; when Yahweh is said to have caused his name to dwell at a sanctuary the intention is to indicate the real and effective presence of Yahweh himself at that sanctuary (see comment on 12:5, and Myers, *Interp* 15, 1961, 28). For Israel indeed there is no other nation 'that has a god so near to it as the Lord our God is to us, whenever we call upon him' (4:7).

(c) Election and Covenant
The immanence of God is presupposed also in a fundamental feature of deuteronomic theology: that Israel is an elect people. What is really distinctive in Deuteronomy is that the whole life of the people is regulated from the point of view of its relationship with Yahweh, and the basic element here is that Israel was chosen by Yahweh. As von Rad, *Gottesvolk*, 27f., and Clements, *VT* 15, 1965, 305ff., have shown, the application of election terminology to the people as a whole is an original deuteronomic contribution to Israelite faith (cf. 4:37; 7:6; 10:15; 14:2). Here for the first time the notion of the people as chosen appears. Yet the verb *bāḥar*, 'choose', even in the sense of divine election, does have a pre-deuteronomic history. In this history, however, it is used not of the people but of the king. It is the king of the Davidic line who was chosen by Yahweh to reign in Zion. Both the historical books of Samuel (cf. 1 Sam. 16:8ff.; 2 Sam. 6:21; 16:18) and the Psalms (Pss. 78:70; 89:19) presuppose the existence of a royal ideology connected with the Davidic dynasty which held that the king was the chosen of Yahweh. This act of Yahweh, in choosing his king, issued in a relationship between himself and the Davidic king which is described both as a covenant relationship (Ps. 89:28, 33f.) and as a father–son relationship (2 Sam. 7:14; Ps. 2:7, etc.). It was a relationship founded on an act of grace on the part of Yahweh, yet it did not exclude the element of obligation imposed on the recipient of divine grace (cf. 2 Sam. 7:14; Pss. 89:30ff.; 132:12). The kings of the Davidic line were subject to the divine law and stood under the threat of punishment for disobedience.

It is from this context that the idea of divine election in Deuteronomy ultimately derives. The deuteronomic law has a certain interest in the king (cf. Dt. 17:14ff.); but even though there too the king is the one chosen by Yahweh (this part of 17:15 may, however, be secondary; see comment on 17:15) the intention of the law is not to exalt him above his brothers, but rather

negatively to express the idea that it is only the one chosen by
Yahweh, and not any other, whom the Israelites may set over
themselves as king. The true sense of divine election, as involving
the setting apart of a person for special relationship with God, is in
Deuteronomy 'democratized' in order to apply to the people as a
whole, a people who are considered to be brothers. In the light of
the background of the election theme it must indeed be considered
probable that the deuteronomic view of the divine election of the
people is intended as an implicit rejection of the idea of divine
election centered on one individual or dynasty. Explicitly, however, Deuteronomy says nothing of this. The deuteronomic
parenesis in 7:6; 9:5 refers to Israel's election and the fact that she
can lay no claim to righteousness; rather, in giving Israel land
Yahweh is acting to fulfil his promise to the patriarchs. The
deuteronomistic edition in 7:7f. expands this by presenting the
background of the people's election as a twofold one: first,
Yahweh's unmerited love for his people, and, secondly, the oath
which Yahweh swore to the fathers. Yahweh's choice of Israel as
'a people for his own possession', expressed through his bringing
them out of Egypt and giving them land, is a sign of his love and
the fulfilment of his promise to the fathers.

The theme of election is not confined in Deuteronomy to the
people. It is in the parenetic introduction to the law that this theme
appears; in the law itself, however, the divine election focuses on
the one sanctuary at which the people may worship Yahweh
(12:5, 11, 14, 18, 21, 26; 14:23–25; 15:20; 16:2, 6, 11, 15; 17:8, 10;
18:6; 26:2). That sacrificial worship in Israel should be confined
to a single sanctuary is expressive of the unity and uniqueness of
God (see comment on 6:4). A multiplicity of sanctuaries would
lead to the existence of different conceptions of God and so open
the way to the assimilation of the worship of Yahweh with the
worship of other gods. To this extent, then, the desire to purify the
worship of Israel is a motive in the centralization law. This law is a
fundamental feature of Deuteronomy. It cannot be treated (as by
von Rad) as belonging to a relatively late layer which may easily
be removed. It is expressed through the use of a stereotyped
formula 'the place which the Lord your God shall choose', which
may be extended by 'from all your tribes' or 'in all your tribes'
(12:5, 14), and also by the statement of purpose 'to set his name
there' (12:5, 21) or 'to cause his name to dwell there' (12:11;
16:2, 6, 11). These different formulations appear in different

layers of the law (12:14 is part of the deuteronomic lawcode, while 12:5, 11 belong to the stages of deuteronomistic editing), and one should probably understand that there has been a growth in the law which has its origins in pre-deuteronomic times. The fact that there is a stereotyped formula, to which various additions are made in Deuteronomy, suggests that this is a pre-deuteronomic formula which is here adopted (cf. Jos. 9:27). It may be, however, that in pre-deuteronomic time the formula had a distributive sense: any place which Yahweh shall choose, while the deuteronomic contribution has been to use it of a single sanctuary (see comment on 12:5, 14). This is suggested by the altar law of Exod. 20:24 where there is clearly no concern to establish a single sanctuary. In pre-deuteronomic time the formula would have referred to those places which had proved themselves as legitimate sanctuaries through some revelation of Yahweh, while Deuteronomy refers the formula to one place only.

Nevertheless, there is clear indication that before the time of Deuteronomy the theme of Yahweh's election of a sanctuary had attached itself to one sanctuary in particular: the sanctuary of Zion. No claim to exclusiveness appears until the time of Hezekiah who attempted to carry through a policy of centralization (2 Kg. 18:4, 22), but already before that Jerusalem was considered pre-eminent among Israel's sanctuaries. Jerusalem is 'the city of God', 'his holy mountain', 'the city of the great king' (Ps. 48:1f.), it is the city which 'he chose' and which 'he loves' (Ps. 78:68), it is the city which Yahweh has 'desired for his habitation' (Ps. 132:13). The ultimate background of these ideas is undoubtedly to be seen in the originally non-Israelite mythological motif of the divine mountain, which at Ugarit appears in the belief in Mount Zaphon as the abode of Baal (for a fuller account see, for example, Driver, *Canaanite Myths*, 96ff.; Johnson, *Sacral Kingship*, 31ff.). This belief is associated with the god Elyon ('Most High') in Isa. 14:13f., and Elyon was the god worshipped in pre-Israelite Jerusalem (cf. Gen. 14:18ff.). Through pre-Israelite beliefs attaching to Jerusalem the divine mountain theme gained entry into Israelite faith and was strengthened through the actions of David and Solomon in making Jerusalem the political capital of the kingdom and also the religious centre, the site of the temple and the home of the ark of God (2 Sam. 6; 1 Kg. 8). Not only, however, did the actions of those Davidic kings strengthen the doctrine of the mountain as the divine abode, but they also resulted in a strong connection between the theme of the election of Zion and that of the election of David, a connection which finds expression in Ps. 2:6; 78:68ff.; 132:11f. One cannot separate these election traditions, as Wildberger, in *Wort*, 312f., who sees the election of Israel in the context of Israel's salvation history and that of Jerusalem in the cultic context of temple celebrations. Both election traditions belong closely together and as a single complex have their background in beliefs attaching to the Jerusalem temple.

The specific impulse which led from the view of Jerusalem as pre-eminent to that of Jerusalem as exclusive, a view which is found first in the time of Hezekiah, is difficult to determine. There may have been a strong political motive in the sense that Hezekiah may have attempted centralization with the object of renewing the political unity of the people which had been broken since the death of Solomon (cf. Nicholson, *VT* 13, 1963, 38off.). In any event, however, it is the cultic pre-eminence with which Jerusalem had long been associated which made this claim to exclusiveness at all possible. Here lie the roots of the deuteronomic law on the single sanctuary, and, in the associated tradition of the election of David, the roots of the deuteronomic view of the chosen people.

Belief in the election of Israel by Yahweh to be his own people lies behind the nationalistic exclusiveness which informs Deuteronomy. Israel is separated from the nations as the object of Yahweh's special concern, and so her life is lived in isolation from the nations. The land she is to occupy will, through the action of Yahweh, be completely vacated by its former inhabitants so that Israel may live uncontaminated by the presence of the nations (ch. 7). Israel's separation from the nations as the people of Yahweh is presupposed throughout Deuteronomy. This is obviously the case with those laws, as in ch. 14 (see especially 14:21), which prescribe what is clean and what is not clean for Israel; but in fact the whole of the law is directed to the same situation, to the regulation of the life of a people which has been set apart by God. Israel, however, was a people in the world, and the other nations of this world could not be simply ignored; yet such references to these other nations as do exist are hostile. Deuteronomy is thoroughly and aggressively opposed to everything which is not of the people of Yahweh. This opposition finds particular expression in the martial character of the book. There are laws relating to warfare and the camp in chs. 20, 23; and these, together with the military concerns of the parenetic introduction with Israel's attitude to the nations (chs. 7, 9), help to give the impression that Israel for Deuteronomy is precisely the people of Yahweh in camp, preparing for war against the enemies of both Yahweh and Israel. This, indeed, is the fictional setting of this speech of Moses to Israel just before her entry into the land.

In von Rad's view (cf. *Studies*, 45ff.; *idem*, *Theology* 1, 73ff.) the background of this martial spirit is Israel's ancient holy war tradition from the time of the pre-monarchic sacral amphictyony. The authors of Deuteronomy are reviving the ancient holy war as a means towards bringing about revival and renewal of the nation in their own time. Junge, *Wiederaufbau*, 24ff., has indeed proposed that after Sennacherib's invasion of Judah in 701 BC the financial resources for rebuilding the army when opportunity later arose were non-existent. This was particularly the case in the time of Josiah, and, in order to meet the situation, the old holy war ideology, involving the conscription of all those capable of bearing arms, was revived. More recent study suggests, however, that holy war ideology or theology is a deuteronomic creation, and that this has been responsible for the schematization of older traditions dealing with Israel in the pre-monarchic period (see comment on 20:1); and if this is correct the extent to which any background to the deuteronomic spirit of holy war may be found in older martial tradition is doubtful. The essential aspect of the holy war in Deuteronomy is the people Israel united in the camp under Yahweh in opposition to the foreign nations. This finds an adequate explanation against the background of the exclusiveness and intolerance of the deuteronomic doctrine of Israel the elect people of Yahweh.

In a more positive way this deuteronomic doctrine also issues in the view that Israel and Yahweh stand in a covenant relationship, though it is not in fact until the stage of deuteronomistic editing of Deuteronomy that covenant thought is made explicit in the book. This is not necessarily to say, however, that the belief that a covenant relationship existed between God and Israel is a deuteronomistic creation which could have been formulated only after the appearance of the deuteronomic form of the election tradition. Covenant and election belong together, but the latter existed in Israelite faith long before it was expressed through the use of the verb *bāḥar*, 'choose', in the deuteronomic literature. The tradition that Yahweh had brought Israel out of Egypt implied, though it did not use the vocabulary of, the deuteronomic doctrine of election, and this tradition is of ancient origin. It is expressed or hinted at in a variety of ways, as through the use of the verb 'know' in Am. 3:2 (cf. also Am. 3:1; 9:7), so that in so far as this doctrine is basic to covenant faith in Israel, the belief in such a covenant relationship may have a pre-deuteronomistic origin.

The word *bᵉrît*, 'covenant' (on the word see comment on 4:13), is used in theological contexts outside Deuteronomy in relation to Abraham (Gen. 15:18), Sinai (Exod. 19:5), David (2 Sam. 23:5) and also in Hosea (6:7; 8:1). The non-theological uses of the word (cf. e.g. 1 Kg. 5:26, EVV 12) are not here of concern, but in relation to its theological use it is widely argued that it reflects the theology of the deuteronomic school. It is proposed (cf., for example, Kutsch, *Verheissung*, 88ff.; Perlitt, *Bundestheologie*, 6off.; Wächter, *ThLZ* 99, 1974, 811ff.) that in the theological context the first application of the term 'covenant' was to the divine promise of land to Abraham, the intention being to strengthen that promise and the historical background of the application being, therefore, a time of uncertainty and danger when Israel's continued occupation of the land was in doubt; in this context the strengthening of the divine promise would have reassured Israelites of the reality and certainty of their possession of the land. A suitable historical context would be during the reign of Hezekiah towards the end of the eighth century BC, for Sennacherib's invasion of Judah in this period would have vividly illustrated the tenuous nature of the Judean hold on its land. The activities of the deuteronomic school in the seventh century BC, resulting in Deuteronomy and later in the deuteronomistic historical work, are not far separated from this time. So, it is proposed that it was in the context of deuteronomic theologizing that the term 'covenant' received an extended application so that it came to include the obligations laid on Israel. Perlitt, *op. cit.*, 114, proposes that originally the relationship between Yahweh and Israel was analogous to that between Chemosh and Moab (Jg. 11:23f.), and that it was prophetic opposition to this very nationalistic form of faith which led to the deuteronomic view that Yahweh and Israel are related by covenant. As far as specific covenant texts outside Deuteronomy are concerned, if these are not to be taken as deuteronomic additions to older material (for example, Hos. 6:7; 8:1), they can be understood to have been subject to a process of reinterpretation which has imposed the novel covenant category on originally non-covenant ideas and traditions. So, for example, Exod. 24:9–11 may be seen as an ancient text, not presupposing a covenant, however, but preserving a theophany tradition (see especially Nicholson, *VT* 24, 1974, 77ff.). Only as a result of later editing of the tradition, especially through Exod. 19:3ff., which took place in deuteronomic (see comment on 7:6) or, following Brekelmans, *VTS* 15, 1966, 94, 'proto-deuteronomic', circles, was the old tradition reinterpreted in covenant form.

The major advantage of attributing to deuteronomistic (or deuteronomic) theologians the introduction of covenant theology is that it explains the otherwise very remarkable reticence of the pre-deuteronomic prophets on the covenant. If covenant faith is taken to be original to such contexts as the Sinai tradition, one is compelled to assume that for some reason the belief found no favour with the prophets, at least in so far as that belief is bound up with the word 'covenant'. So, for example, Eichrodt, *Theology* 1, 51f., supposes that the prophets avoided using the term 'covenant' because it was not compatible with their understanding of the nature of the response demanded of Israel to the actions of God on her behalf. It is, of course, possible, that just as with the belief in Israel's election by Yahweh so also with the covenant, the thought might be present without the use of the word. This has been argued for particularly by McCarthy, *Bib* 53, 1972, 110f., with reference especially to Exod. 24:11. In this instance, however, Nicholson has clearly shown that one need not go outside the category of theophany for the whole passage of which the verse forms a part. The reference to eating and drinking may refer not to any covenant-making ceremony but simply to rejoicing at the sanctuary in the presence of God (see, for example Dt. 12:7; 14:26; 27:7). Yet in principle it remains true that the application of the word *berît* to the relationship between God and Israel may well have been simply the introduction of a new term into a context well prepared to receive it, rather than the introduction of a completely novel category of belief into an essentially different context. In this respect there would exist a close parallel to the traditional background to the use of the theme of election in Deuteronomy.

If this is so, then on the one hand it might be argued (see, for example, Perlitt) that the necessary background for the use of the term covenant was created by the prophetic protest against

nationalistic religion and that the introduction of the element of
moral obligation into Israel's faith, which the deuteronomistic
view of the relationship presupposes, was the result of this prophetic
preaching. On the other hand, however, it might be argued that
this moral element, involving certain demands made on Israel by
God, was long a feature of Israel's faith which the prophets were
concerned to highlight with particular force. The portrayal in
Deuteronomy of Israel's faith as a covenant faith would then be the
presentation of a traditional doctrine which has received a fresh
emphasis in the context of the application to it of the word
'covenant'.

It is clear that an important aspect of this problem concerns the
context within which Old Testament law was understood and
taught in pre-deuteronomic times, and to this we shall turn
shortly. With regard specifically to the use of the term 'covenant',
it is true that it is in the literature of the deuteronomic school that
'covenant' comes to prominence, and in that literature the word
has a variety of applications (see comment on 4:13). However, it is
not absolutely clear that in the use of the word *berît* in this context
there is a deuteronomistic original contribution. It is not possible
here to investigate all the particular examples of use of the word
berît in what are apparently pre-deuteronomic contexts, in order
to determine whether or not they are original usages. Several of
these (such as Hos. 6:7; 8:1) may indeed be the result of later
editing of the literary contexts in which they now appear. Yet one
passage does deserve attention: Exod. 24:8. The phrase which
appears here, 'the blood of the covenant', is impossible as an
expression of deuteronomic or deuteronomistic belief; for with its
clearly ritualistic presuppositions it stands in complete contrast
with the deuteronomistic emphasis on the words or the law by
which Israel's relationship with Yahweh is established.

It is true that this is only one passage which clearly stands apart
from the general deuteronomic and deuteronomistic context; yet
the possibility must be granted that this is enough to establish a
pre-deuteronomistic basis for the use of *berît* in this context. That
this term has been emphasized in the deuteronomistic context, so
that the covenant relationship is presented as the almost exclusive
category by which Israel's relationship with Yahweh may be described, is not in question; but it would seem that the deuteronomist
has not invented this category but rather has taken it as the one
of a number of already existing categories (such as the father–son

and marriage analogies; cf. Hos. 1–3; Isa. 11:1; 1:2, etc.) by
which he considered this relationship could best be expressed.

The existence in pre-deuteronomic time of a covenant tradition
is suggested also by the strong association of covenant ideas with
Shechem. Outside Deuteronomy this association is found especially
in Jos. 8:30ff.; 24, and within Deuteronomy in 11:30; 27:1ff. In
all cases the passages stand in a deuteronomistic context, and to
trace pre-deuteronomistic material in them is a quite uncertain
undertaking. However, on the other hand, it is difficult to account
for the insistence of 11:30; 27:1ff. that the covenant ceremony
should take place on Ebal and Gerizim, the two mountains by
Shechem, unless on the assumption that a strong pre-deotero-
nomistic covenant tradition was located there. Early deuteronomistic literary activity, which produced the deuteronomistic
historical work, viewed Jerusalem as the only legitimate sanctuary for Israel. Subsequent deuteronomistic editing of Deuteronomy would not have willingly detracted from this by naming,
even for pre-Solomonic time, any other sanctuary as legitimate.
It was the deuteronomistic emphasis on covenant as the category
by which the relationship between God and Israel should be
described which involved attachment to already existing covenant
thought, associated with Shechem, and so also the naming of
these two mountains by Shechem. However, the deuteronomist
has also minimized the risk that Shechem would detract from the
exclusive status ascribed to Jerusalem; he has done this through
presenting the sanctuary at Shechem not as important and significant in its own right, but rather as being the place at which Israel,
on first entering the land, must arrive (see comment on 11:30;
27:2). It is quite incidental for the deuteronomistic editor that
the covenant ceremony took place at the sanctuary of Shechem;
what is important is that it took place as soon as Israel entered
the land. Entry into the land and entry into the covenant relationship are inseparable.

It is clear, however, that while the deuteronomist may not have
been original in using covenant ideas and probably also terminology in this context, these ideas did get powerful reinforcement
through the work of the deuteronomist. It is now that covenant
becomes almost the exclusive category by which Israel's relationship with God might be described. It is difficult to go beyond this
in assessing the precise nature of original deuteronomistic contributions to covenant thought, since inferences for pre-deutero-

nomistic time can be of only a most general character. This means that with regard to the form by which this belief in a covenant relationship was concretely expressed it is not possible to be clear on the precise extent of deuteronomistic originality. As already noted in the discussion of the structure of Deuteronomy, the book makes particular use of the form and language of extra-biblical treaties. Deuteronomy is not the text of a treaty and there are problems in describing the relationship between the treaties and the book, but it is quite clear that the influence of treaty forms and language is strong. That the deuteronomist was responsible for the introduction of this form of expression is possible but by no means certain. It is with the deuteronomist that it is particularly associated; but, on the other hand, the link is with the treaty *tradition*, rather than with any particular section of that tradition which might help in fixing the adoption of the form to a particular period. It is true that especially in Dt. 28 there is a strong connection with the treaty tradition as it appears in the Mesopotamian treaties of the time of the Assyrian empire in the eighth and seventh centuries BC. This has encouraged speculation (see especially Weinfeld, *Deuteronomy*, 158ff.) linking the authorship of Deuteronomy specifically with those familiar with Mesopotamian treaty forms (see further below), which in turn could suggest that it was then that the treaty form was first used to express the covenant relationship. This could be supported by the fact (see above) that it is in specifically deuteronomistic rather than deuteronomic parts of Deuteronomy that the treaty elements appear. However, Deuteronomy's use of history constitutes a firm link with the Hittite treaty form, so that it is clearly more appropriate to think in terms of the influence of a general treaty tradition on Deuteronomy, rather than any more specific influence. Moreover, the fact that the original Deuteronomy did not show treaty elements does not necessarily imply that this form was not used in a covenant context in Israel until deuteronomistic time. It was only as a result of the need to deal with the question of the relationship between the deuteronomic law and Sinai that the deuteronomic law came to be presented as covenant law, and so then the forms used in covenant expression, treaty forms, were introduced.

The treaty expression of the covenant relationship may, therefore, be pre-deuteronomistic. Nevertheless, it is from the deuteronomistic context that it is possible to appreciate how this form and terminology were used and the possible modifications to the

form that were made. The question of deuteronomistic responsibility either for the adoption of the form in the first place or for
the modifications to the form which were made must be set aside.
Lohfink, in *Gott in Welt*, I, 428ff., has described a number of
respects in which treaty conceptions have been modified in the
adoption of the form into the Israelite context. It is with respect
to the use of the treaty form in Deuteronomy, whether or not this
reflects earlier ideas, that the modifications may be described.
Firstly, the treaty was a form designed to regulate the relations of
two human parties. Deuteronomy, however, emphasizes the
transcendence of Yahweh (a) through the description of the
theophany by which Yahweh came to his people (cf. 5:24ff.), and
(b) through the declaration that 'heaven and the heaven of
heavens, the earth with all that is in it' belong to Yahweh (10:14).
Secondly, the treaties frequently imply or express that in certain
situations the chief partner to the treaty is also under an obligation:
if the vassal fulfils the demands made on him then his suzerain will
protect him, assure him and his successors of their throne, etc.
The possibility that Yahweh might be seen in the same light is
countered in 9:4ff. (a) by the assertion that Israel is not righteous
and that it is only because of the unrighteousness of the nations
that they are being expelled from the land, and (b) by the
reference to the oath sworn to the patriarchs in fulfilment of which
Yahweh is giving Israel the land. Thus the freedom of Yahweh
in relation to the covenant between himself and Israel is maintained. Thirdly, in the treaties blessing and curse are alternate
possibilities depending on obedience or disobedience to the
demands of the treaty. There is an absolute character about them,
so that the curse for disobedience implies the end of the relationship expressed in the treaty. In Deuteronomy, however, this
possibility is largely cancelled out through the presentation of
curse and blessing not as alternate possibilities but as successive
events in history in that order, connected by repentance and
forgiveness. In 4:25ff.; 30:1ff. (see comment on 4:29) the breach
of covenant which brings the curse is followed by repentance,
divine forgiveness and the restoration of the blessing.

These are fundamental modifications which have transformed a
legal category into an instrument by which expression might be
given to a relationship in which divine election and love together
with divine transcendence and freedom are basic features. They
presuppose a long period of theological reflection on the nature of

Yahweh and his relationship with Israel, and do not represent simply the result of the use of an alien model in a religious context. The model is largely an alien one; but the context into which it was brought seems to have been a well formed one in which, expressed through different models perhaps, ideas were already in existence which suggested the treaty form as a means by which they could be expressed more effectively. So the father–son analogy would have expressed both the superiority of God and the necessity for appropriate behaviour in a relationship with him. Through the treaty form these ideas were strengthened, while at the same time the importance of Israel's response to divine initiative could be emphasized. But while the legal form strengthened the legal element in the relationship, it also preserved that relationship from becoming one of mere legalism; for the divine demand is at all times balanced by the divine love and set within the context of a relationship which depends not first on obedience to law but on the free act of divine love.

(d) Law and Land

The relationships established by covenants or treaties were regulated by the laws which formed part of those contracts. However, this cannot be taken as an adequate statement of the content and purpose of Old Testament law, and especially of the law of Deuteronomy. The original Deuteronomy was a lawcode in form (see above), and its characteristics were carried over into the treaty form which the deuteronomistic editing introduced. But neither lawcodes as known from outside the Old Testament nor the law of Deuteronomy can be taken as legal collections to be used in the daily administration of justice. Extra-biblical lawcodes often appear to have the purpose of vindicating the king before the gods through presenting the laws by which the king exercised the authority granted him by the gods (see Phillips, *JJS* 28, 1977, 105ff.), and even if this is not the case in the Old Testament it is clear that there too the law collections are not designed as judges' rules on which their judicial decisions would be based. The laws are not addressed to the judiciary, they are addressed to Israel; they are not presented as laws, but rather as teaching. They are embedded in exhortation and encouragement which has the object of persuading those addressed. As Gemser, *VTS* 1, 1953, 50ff., has pointed out, motive clauses are found attached to both casuistic and apodictic laws, and there is a discernible increase in the proportion of laws with motive clauses between the Book of the Covenant in Exodus (seventeen per cent) and Deuteronomy (sixty per cent). There are different types of such clauses—some have an ethical content (for example Dt. 24:6), others a cultic or theological content (for example, Dt. 17:1) and some refer to Israel's saving history (for example, Dt. 15:15)—but they are all united in having the purpose of persuasion in the context of teaching rather than demanding in the context of law.

The clearly humanitarian concerns of Deuteronomy conform with this conclusion. This attitude is apparent in the teaching on the generous treatment which is to be accorded to slaves (15:12–18), the stranger, the fatherless and the widow (10:18; 24:17, 19, 20, 21; 27:19), the Levite (12:18; 16:11, 14; 26:12, 13); in the command that gleanings are to be left to the poor (24:14ff.), all of which are concerns which usually could not easily be the subject of legal enforcement. Yet in many cases these laws do undoubtedly derive from general legal practice. This is the case, for example, with the marriage and family laws scattered through chs. 21ff. These laws have a casuistic form, appropriate to the background from which they came, and collections of them originated on the basis of cases tried by the elders at the city gates, or at a later stage by the royally appointed judges (see introduction to 16:18–17:7). Such casuistic laws arose out of concerns common to the administration of justice generally throughout the ancient Near East, and the connections between Old Testament and ancient Near Eastern law, particularly in casuistic laws, are correspondingly close. Variations in precise descriptions of the cases, and in the exact punishments provided, do occur; but the general form and content is common to the whole ancient Near East. The form of the laws consists of a conditional clause, introduced by *kî*, 'when', in which the main case is described; the case may then be defined in more detail through the use of subsidiary conditional clauses, introduced by *'im*, 'if'. Finally, the punishment, graded according to the severity of the offence described, is stipulated.

That Israel used or would have required such laws in the time before her settlement in the land is doubtful, though some have thought that the semi-nomadic context would have presented cases requiring decision through such laws (cf. for example, Fensham, *PEQ* 93, 1961, 143ff.; Kilian, *Heiligkeitsgesetzes*, 2f.). In content the laws reflect rather a settled society and in form they presuppose the administration of justice as this is done in a settled environment. It is most probable, therefore, that as Alt, *Essays*, 98ff., has suggested, Israel began the use of this form of law after settlement in the land, and the laws were in large measure general ancient Near Eastern laws mediated to her through the Canaanites. In an important respect, however, these casuistic laws often appear in a modified form in Deuteronomy. The modification lies in the use of the direct form of address within or in close association with a law which in its original casuistic form was impersonal throughout. So in 22:13–21, 22, the impersonal casuistic laws are supplemented with the expression: 'so you shall purge the evil from the midst of you/from Israel,' while 22:23f. not only has this expression but even within the law itself uses the direct form of address (cf. also 22:26; 24:4, 7, etc. On the 'if-you' style of law see above, p. 51). This change reflects a situation in which the casuistic laws have been divorced from their original context in the actual administration of justice and applied to a new didactic purpose. The context is no longer that of providing a code of laws for legal use, but rather that of inculcating a way of behaviour through teaching and exhortation.

At least one other form of law is to be found in Deuteronomy. This is the type classified by Alt as apodictic. Alt described such laws as being characterized by their concern with fundamental issues, by their religious background (the authority behind them being God), by their concise rhythmical form, by their appearance in series and by the fact that they combine religion, morality and law. Within Old Testament law he distinguished three groups of such apodictic laws: (a) those formed as Exod. 21:12 'Whoever strikes a man so that he dies shall be put to death'; (b) those formed as Dt. 27:16 'Cursed be he who dishonours his father or his mother'; and (c) the prohibition as Dt. 14:21 'You shall not eat anything that dies of itself'. The first two resemble casuistic law in describing a case and fixing a punishment, but are distinct in their form which is rhythmical and in which the case is described by means of a participial clause, and also in the fact that only the punishment of death is prescribed ('Cursed' being understood as carrying this implication). The third group is distinct from both casuistic and the other apodictic laws in being simply a prohibition; no case is described and no punishment is stipulated. Furthermore, it is only here that the direct form of address appears. All these groups of apodictic laws have the common characteristics mentioned above, however, and these distinguish them as a type from casuistic.

In order to elucidate their background Alt appealed to the context in which one of the groups of apodictic appears: the list of curses in Dt. 27. They are recited in public before the assembled people. It is law proclaimed in the context of Israel's public worship, and Dt. 31:9ff. may preserve an ancient custom in providing for such a public reading every seven years during the Feast of Tabernacles. Here the law would have functioned to remind Israelites of their obligations to God; the context could be described as one of covenant renewal.

Detailed accounts of the history of the study of apodictic law since Alt are provided by Nielsen, *Commandments*, 68ff. and Clark, in *Form Criticism*, 109ff. In so far as Deuteronomy in particular is affected by later studies, the following modifications to Alt's views are clearly necessary. First of all, the three groups of apodictic law proposed by Alt cannot be seen form critically as belonging to the same type. They are different forms, and these differences are to be accounted for by the different backgrounds from which they have emerged. The first group, as represented by Exod. 21:12, bears close resemblances to casuistic law, and despite the fact that it is rhythmical and appears in series, it cannot be divorced from the legal context. Whether or not Schulz, *Todesrecht*, 6ff., 40ff., is correct in his view that these laws depend on the prohibitions and presuppose a situation in which the norms represented by the prohibitions are being incorporated into the legal context, it is clear that these laws in participial form do have a legal function (see also Schottroff, *Fluchspruch*, 125ff.). Their penalty ('shall be put to death') is not a cultic formula proclaiming the inevitability of this punishment, but a legal pronouncement giving sentence for a certain crime. Its legal nature is indicated by Gen. 26:11; Exod. 15:12; Jg. 21:5, and from Lev. 20:2, 27; 24:16; Num. 15:35 it may be concluded that the method of punishment was community stoning. The time of origin of the type is not certain, but the distinct ethical concerns of the law and its uncompromisingly rigorous method of treating defaulters point to the pre-settlement period before Israel became familiar with the refinements and gradations possible in casuistic law. For the form of the curse, as in Dt. 27, a similar conclusion is indicated. Recent studies have shown (see comment on 27:15) that 'cursed' does not have originally a cultic background; rather it is a legal sentence and declares expulsion from the clan. The only difference between these two forms lies, therefore, in the punishment prescribed. The context of origin of both is the same.

The third group of apodictic laws, the direct prohibition, is the type to which the term 'apodictic' as a formal designation is now generally restricted. It is perhaps most important in the present connection since this type predominates in Deuteronomy. Here again Alt's thesis must be modified. The present context of these laws is a covenant context, but from two points of view it is clear that this cannot be taken as the context of origin of the type of law which the prohibition represents. On the one hand, such forms are to be found outside the Old Testament (references in Gevirtz, *VT* 11, 1961, 138: see also Gerstenberger, *Wesen*, 130ff., and McCarthy, *Treaty*, 35ff.). On the other, the Old Testament itself offers enough indication that the original concern of this type of law is not with the covenant relationship betweenYahweh and Israel and that its original authority is not that of God. Even in Deuteronomy, apart from the decalogue, the speaker addressing Israel is not Yahweh, but Moses. It is true that behind Moses stands the divine will; but other contexts of use offer different possibilities as an original background. Lev. 18:7ff. now appears as the word of God to Israel through Moses. The content of this series of direct prohibitions is, however, such as to make it probable that the original context of their use is the extended family and the original authority behind them that of the elders of the semi-nomadic clan. Moreover, even when the content of the prohibitions is theological, it frequently refers to God in the third person (for example, Exod. 22:27, EVV 28), so presupposing a human authority on the basis of which the prohibition is made. However, as Gerstenberger has shown, the concern of the majority of these forms is with everyday life, and with cultic matters in so far as they impinged on everyday life; their application is to human relationships and their concern is with the ordering of social groups. Jer. 35:6f. preserves a series of such apodictic prohibitions, which (though expressed in the second person plural rather than the singular as usual with these prohibitions) may be taken to represent the typical context from which they emerged. The prohibitions are here the authoritative commands of Jonadab, the 'father' of the Rechabites, a clan which preserved its original semi-nomadic way of life long after Israel's settlement of the land. The use of the direct personal form of address has its origin, therefore, not in divine speech in the covenant cult, but in instruction by the elders in the context of the clan. The authority behind the prohibitions is not the absolute will of Yahweh, but the authority of the elders (see Gerstenberger, *op. cit.* 109ff.). The context of origin of the prohibitions then bears some general similarity to the place of origin of the first two groups of what Alt styled apodictic law: in all cases the background is a pre-settlement one and the general context that of the semi-nomadic clan. However, the precise contexts are different: on the one hand, a clearly legal context of origin, but with the prohibitions this is not the case. Here there is instruction, not law; the advice of the elder, backed up by the authority of the clan, intended as the means of preserving and transmitting the ethos of the clan.

Many of the particular examples of this apodictic law did not have this place of origin. Such prohibitions as 'you shall have no other gods before me' (Dt. 5:7) can only have originated in the context of Israel's cult and the authority can only be that of Yahweh. But this can be said with assurance only of those apodictic laws which in content are like the first commandment of the decalogue. Otherwise, apodictic law shows no such original relationship to the covenant cult. But apodictic law in general (as well as casuistic law) is *now* to be found in this cultic context. No matter what the particular place of origin of such examples of this law may be, it is all now understood to be divine law, the conditions of the covenant between Yahweh and Israel. In this respect Deuteronomy has a view of Israel's law in common with other collections in the Pentateuch. Clearly a transformation in understanding of the law has taken place. Its authority is no longer that of the clan elders, or of the elders sitting in judgment at the city gates; it is the authority of Yahweh declaring this law as the condition of his relationship with Israel.

Behind this transformation there lies a process whereby on the one hand the narrow terms of the relationship between Yahweh and Israel came to be defined in more and more detail, and on the other hand the view gained currency that Yahweh was a God governing all spheres of life so that laws and teaching primarily concerned with non-cultic areas came to be seen as covenant demands. This idea would have been promoted by the fact (to which Reventlow, *ZThK* 60, 1963, 278f., draws attention) that even in the original clan context the apodictic law would have had some connection with the cult; the clan lived under the aegis of the gods, and so the teaching of the elders or the laws which they administered would have derived their authority from the sanctified order which the elders represented. However, the distinction between the clan context and the immediate authority of the elders on the one hand, and the cultic context and the immediate authority of God on the other, must be preserved in the determination of the influences which led to the particular form by which apodictic law is expressed.

The process of transformation in the understanding of apodictic (and casuistic) law is difficult to mark out in chronological stages. The problems here are similar to those already encountered with the covenant theme, for corresponding to the difficulty in determining the existence of a covenant concept in pre-deuteronomistic time in Israel there is also difficulty in determining the degree to which law in this period was understood to be divine law, issued on the authority of Yahweh. For Gerstenberger, *op. cit.*, 107f., the process of coming together of covenant and apodictic law, so that the latter came to be considered divine law, extended over the whole pre-exilic period. If this is to be followed the implication is that the norms of behaviour championed by the pre-exilic prophets cannot be understood as deriving from anything like covenant law. Rather, they reflect the customary norms of behaviour as transmitted and promulgated especially by the wisdom teachers. But this is far from certain. Even though it is difficult to trace in the prophets specifically cultic forms presupposing covenant law (such as the lawsuit form; see the introduction to 31:30–32:43), it is clear that such temple 'entrance liturgies' as are preserved in Pss. 15; 24:3ff. presuppose the transmission and promulgation of law in a cultic context, while it is most unlikely that the Book of the Covenant in Exod. 20:22–23:33, which is presented as divine law, is to be assigned to such a late time. It neither refers to nor presupposes the monarchic period in Israel, and consequently attests a very early understanding of the relationship between Yahweh and Israel as depending on the observation of certain norms of behaviour.

Whatever the history of it may be, the process of the adoption of law into the context of Yahweh and Israel is well advanced in Deuteronomy. Here the dominant and central concern is the proclamation of law, obedience to which is required by Yahweh. So much in fact is the law pushed into the foreground that it is tempting to see the book in the context of the legalism of later

Judaism, where it is through the observance of the law by individuals that the community of the people of God is constituted. This
view of Deuteronomy is to a certain extent supported by those
passages where the blessing of God is directly dependent on the
observance of law; it is the law, therefore, which is the means by
which Israel found its life (cf. for example, 4:40; 6:3; 11:13f.). In
general, however, Deuteronomy must be absolved from the charge
of legalism. The covenant which stands as the framework within
which the law is proclaimed provides a context in which Israel,
the people of Yahweh, exists before the law (see on this Noth, *Laws*,
6off.; and Zimmerli, *Law*, 47). Even in the extra-biblical treaty
texts, at least those from the Hittite empire, the historical prologue
may be interpreted in these terms; the relationship between the
sovereign and his vassal is established on the initiative of the
sovereign, and is now being defined in terms of the treaty stipulations (see Lohfink, *Christian Meaning*, 106ff.). On the other hand,
however, the regular and uniformly balanced blessing and curse
sections in these treaties designate the blessing not as the continuation of an already existing state of things (the security and
prosperity of a relationship with the sovereign), but as the goal of
obedience to the stipulations. It is through such obedience that
the vassal and his state can exist. In Deuteronomy, on the other
hand, the view that the blessing of standing in covenant with
Yahweh results from·obedience to the commandments (see, for
example, 7:12) is balanced and indeed outweighed by the view
that Israel's status as the people of Yahweh is something real and
actual before the covenant demands are made (see especially
27:9f.). And in the event of Israel's disobedience to these demands
the operation of the covenant curse does not always mean that the
covenant relationship is brought to an irrevocable end (see above
p. 70). Through introducing the possibility of repentance and forgiveness the tension between the idea that Israel's status as the
people of Yahweh precedes and is independent of the covenant,
and the idea that disobedience to the covenant demands brings
punishment and destruction is to some extent resolved.

In this connection the land plays a significant role as the very
point at which the tension is perhaps at its most taut. On the
one hand the land is the place where the law is to be obeyed (see,
for example, 6:1, 10ff.); but on the other, it also appears as the
place which Israel cannot possess unless she obeys the law (see,
for example, 4:1). These.views are not simply to be assigned to

different authors or editors in Deuteronomy; rather they result
from the adoption and modification of the covenant or treaty form
in which Deuteronomy is presently expressed. That possession of
the land results from obedience is a view which belongs clearly
within the covenant or treaty category of reward; that the law is
for Israel's life in the land is a fundamental modification which
results from Israel's conception of her place as the elect people of
God (see above), for this election is expressed not simply through
the rescue of Israel from Egypt but also through the bestowal on
Israel of the land of Palestine. It is this which fulfils God's promise
to the patriarchs. On the basis of this promise the land is Israel's
'inheritance' (see comment on 4:21), which, whether understood
to include both east and west Jordan (cf. 1:6ff.; 2:24, 31; 4:45ff.;
11:24) or seen as west Jordan alone (cf. 9:1; 11:31; 30:18), is a
single unit, the gift of Yahweh to his people. It is the gift of God
which is realized in Israel's obedience to the commandments.
Israel's possession of the land is in this respect the link between the
promise to the patriarchs and Yahweh's covenant with Israel: it
fulfils the one and is the realization of the other.

The land is in fact central to Deuteronomy's whole theology,
and in this theme too Deuteronomy has taken an element of
Israel's tradition and brought it to special prominence. The
background of this tradition is not at all certain, and even on
fundamental points there is wide divergence of opinion (for
comprehensive summaries of studies of the tradition see Plöger,
Untersuchungen, 66ff.; Westermann, *Verheissungen*, 92ff.). One of the
first major studies of the subject was carried out by Alt, who saw
the divine promises to the patriarchs of land and descendants as
originally distinct and independent elements of tradition, the
one deriving from the nomadic context and the other added to it
after settlement in the land. The one, the promise of descendants,
reflects the concern of the nomadic tribe for its preservation and
strengthening, and belongs to the pre-settlement time; the other,
the promise of land, reflects the claim to possession of land on the
part of those who have in fact settled, and is therefore a post-
settlement element of the tradition (cf. Alt, *Essays*, 65). Von Rad,
on the other hand, did not preserve this distinction, and, as Noth
also (cf. Noth, *Pentateuchal Traditions*, 54ff.: von Rad, *Problem*, 79ff.),
saw both promises as elements of pre-settlement tradition.

An adequate understanding of the element of promise in the
patriarchal traditions is possible only after an examination of the

traditions in which the promises appear within their present literary contexts, such as that carried out by Westermann. The purpose of such a study is that of determining the originality of the element of promise within the whole context. In the first place it is clear that in most cases the promise has been secondarily introduced into a narrative (cf. Gen. 22:15–18; 26:2–5; 28:13–15, etc., and Westermann, *op. cit.*, 114ff.). Secondly, the promises do not all concern land and descendants. Gen. 18 is significant in this respect, for the whole story is here given over to just one promise, that of a son. It suggests that the tradition which contains only one promise has a stronger claim to originality than that in which there is a combination of promises. Thirdly, as far as the promise of land in particular is concerned, it has a fairly constant formulation. So, when it is addressed to Abraham (as this promise mostly is), God says: I will give this land to you and to your descendants (cf. Gen. 12:7; 13:15; 15:18; 24:7; 28:13). There is a formula used here which is proper not to the context of promises but rather to the legal context of the actual transfer of ownership in the present (cf. Westermann, *op. cit.*, 135f.). Gen. 48:22, using the same verb 'give', indicates that the legal context is the one to which the formula is really appropriate.

If this is so, then those apparent promises of land to Abraham and his descendants in fact presuppose the situation of the descendants who actually possess the land as a result of settlement: they express a claim to the land which says in effect that this land belongs to us by virtue of the fact that ownership of it has been legally transferred to us. Thus, the tradition of the promise of land in no case preserves actual promises which go back to the patriarchal period.

This does not mean, however, that the historical background presupposed by the formulation of these 'promises' is one in which Israel's possession of the land is endangered by invasion and conquest, so that one would look to the latest pre-exilic or exilic periods as the time from which these promises come (cf. Hoftijzer, *Verheissungen*, 99). It is doubtful that the stories in which these promises are to be found can be dated to such late time; and, in any event, the claim to possession which the promises express presupposes not specifically a time of danger to Israel's possession, but rather generally a justification for Israel's having taken possession of the land. So, although the settlement of Israel in the land is presupposed, the time of origin for this tradition of promise is probably the early post-settlement period. It is through this tradition that Israel justified her dispossession of the former inhabitants of the land.

Deuteronomy has emphasized this promise and made it central to the whole theological presentation. It is the land which is the focus of promise, the land which is either reward for obedience or the place where the law is to be obeyed, possession of the land which expresses Israel's status as the elect people of Yahweh (see above). For Deuteronomy life itself means life in the land in covenant with Yahweh.

D. HISTORICAL BACKGROUND

(a) General background
For the general historical background of Deuteronomy we must go to the later years of the Judean kingdom. As we have noted, many of the theological ideas in the book have a history which reaches back to early years, but in general Deuteronomy is the distillation of the teaching of priests, prophets, and wise men (see below on authorship) presupposing the long existence of that teaching in Israel. Moreover, its language most closely resembles that of the seventh century BC and later in Judah, coming to expression in the work of the deuteronomistic historian (see below) and the later parts of Jeremiah. So the general time in the context of which the book must be seen is that of the last decades of the existence of the Judean kingdom. It may be, of course, that Deuteronomy has antecedents in written collections of a larger or smaller nature (see above pp. 52f., on the casuistic and war laws), but there is no evidence of the existence in Israel of a covenant document reaching back to earliest days, which eventually in the course of gradual supplementation, developed into Deuteronomy in much the form that is now presented to us. This view has been promoted especially by Lohfink (*Bib* 44, 1963, 461ff.; *idem, Höre Israel*, 18ff.). As we have seen, however, even if the existence of a pre-deuteronomic or pre-deuteronomistic covenant faith in Israel is established, it is only with the deuteronomist that covenant and treaty characteristics came to be attached to Deuteronomy. There is no indication of an association of the original Deuteronomy with covenant thought. This means that the history of origins of Deuteronomy may be described only in a limited way in terms of the coming together of smaller collections of law; these were

probably not, until the formation of Deuteronomy characterized by its parenetic introduction, understood or presented as the law of Moses. The real background of Deuteronomy itself, as the law of Moses with its parenetic introduction and centralization demand, lies in the history of the late monarchic period in Judah.

The history of this period is described in detail in the histories of Noth, Bright, Herrmann, Hayes-Miller, and others; only its outline need be sketched here in so far as this is relevant to the conditions out of which Deuteronomy emerged. The beginning of the seventh century marked the closing years of the reign of Hezekiah. It was a period of turmoil in Judah which had just experienced invasion by the Assyrian king Sennacherib in his attempt to crush a revolt on the part of the Judean monarch, a revolt which had been encouraged by a change in Assyrian leadership, the recovery of Egyptian power and the rebellion of other subject states against their Assyrian overlord. The interpretation of 2 Kg. 18f. and of the Assyrian records relating to these events is complicated and uncertain, but it seems clear at least that while Judah was decimated by Sennacherib and Hezekiah was forced to submit and send tribute, Jerusalem itself was not taken.

Hezekiah is remembered as a king who did what was right in the eyes of Yahweh, having instituted a reform in temple worship and abolished the high places. By contrast his successor Manasseh, who came to the throne in 696 BC, is remembered as an evil king who thoroughly corrupted the worship of Yahweh. In the light of the study by McKay, *Religion*, one should beware of a too one-sided interpretation of these evaluations; yet it remains probable that they are not unconnected with internal political policies in Judah in the reigns of these kings. The favourable conditions for revolt against Assyria towards the end of the eighth century may well have fostered nationalistic anti-Assyrian policies in the Judean court in the reign of Hezekiah, while the resurgence of Assyrian power under Sennacherib and Esarhaddon in the time of Manasseh may on the contrary have encouraged policies of appeasement in the face of Assyrian oppression. The spirit which manifested itself in Hezekiah's revolt would also have tended to express itself in the purification of Israel's worship, while in the case of Manasseh the spirit of the age which favoured appeasement was probably also to be seen in the syncretism of cultic practice in that period.

The general impression given by Assyrian records is that Manasseh was a consistently faithful vassal; but the account in 2 Chr. 33:11ff. of Manasseh being brought in chains to Babylon by the Assyrians (cf. Hayes-Miller, *History*, 454f.) is perhaps to be taken as going back to an attempted revolt against Assyria when its decline began with the accession of Asshurbanipal in 669 BC. The situation remained unchanged under Manasseh's son Amon, who ruled for only two years (642–640 BC) before being assassinated. The reason for his murder is not clear; it was a court intrigue of some kind, possibly arising from hopes of independence from the weakening Assyria, hopes which Amon's continued subservience to Assyria did nothing to promote. If this is so, then Amon's assassins were an anti-Assyrian group of Judean religious and political nationalists. Their own subsequent assassination by 'the people of the land' would then probably have been the work of those who considered the time not yet opportune for such rebellious moves and who feared reprisals from Assyria. In any case the outcome was the accession of Josiah in 640 BC at the age of eight.

The political situation in Assyria in the final years of Asshurbanipal until his death in 627 BC is obscure; but one known feature of his reign deserves attention since it apparently reflects a general phenomenon in the ancient Near East in this period. This was his collection of cuneiform writings in his library at Nineveh, which included copies of ancient Babylonian myths and epics. Similarly in Egypt, especially under Asshurbanipal's contemporary there, Psammetichus I, there was a similar interest in the copying of texts and the revival of ancient cultic practices. Herrmann, in *Probleme*, 169f. (including in this context Josiah's reform, understood to have been based on the deuteronomic law), refers to this time as a renaissance, not just the reviving of old norms and ideas, but the proclamation of new norms and ideas through the editing of traditions.

Under Asshurbanipal's successor Sin-shar-ishkun the pace of decline of Assyria was even more marked. In 625 BC Nabopolassar gained control of Babylon and founded the Neo-Babylonian empire. At the same time the Medes under Cyaxares invaded the Tigris region of the Assyrian empire and eventually formed an alliance with Nabopolassar. Nineveh, and the Assyrian king Sin-shar-iskun who ruled from there, fell to their combined attack in 612 BC, Cyaxares having already two years previously taken Asshur the ancient Assyrian capital. Though the Assyrians under

Asshur-uballit held out for a time in Haran, that city too was captured in 610 BC and Assyrian power was destroyed.

Throughout this period Egyptian intervention in affairs in Mesopotamia is not lacking. Already in 616 BC Psammetichus appeared at the side of the Assyrians against Babylon. Egyptian policy seems to have been prompted by a fear of the power of the alliance of the Babylonians and Medes and a desire to ensure its own presence and influence at least in Palestine and Syria. To this end a further intervention under Necho was undertaken on behalf of the Assyrians in 609 BC in a bid to shore up Assyrian remnants. Apparently in the course of an attempt to stop the Egyptian forces reaching Assyria, Josiah was killed at Megiddo.

The death of Josiah marked the end of a brief period of Judean independence. Josiah's reform (for which see the detailed account below) was in part a cultic reform of worship in the Jerusalem temple, intended to rid it of Assyrian cult objects and practices. It must probably also be seen in the context of a general reorganization of his kingdom in which former areas of the Israelite kingdom which had been absorbed into the Assyrian provincial system were brought under Judean control. While the use of the detail in 2 Kg. 23:4–20 in this context is an uncertain basis for reconstruction (see below) it has been plausibly proposed (cf. Noth, *History*, 273ff.) that Jos. 13; 15; 18; 19 go back in part to an administrative reorganization of Judah under Josiah. Judean expansion in this time is also suggested by archaeological results at the Dead Sea, Ein Gedi, and Arad (cf. Hayes-Miller, *op. cit.*, 464). With the death of Josiah the independence of Judah came to an end. Although Necho failed in his attempt to bolster up Assyria, he did retain control of Palestine, as a result of which he was able to depose Josiah's successor Jehoahaz and set his brother Eliakim (with his name changed to Jehoiakim) on the throne in his place. Judah was now under Egyptian control.

The defeat of the Egyptians in 605/4 BC persuaded Jehoiakim to change his allegiance, however, and he became a vassal of Nebuchadnezzar, who had succeeded his father Nabopolassar as king of Babylon. But an unsuccessful Babylonian attempt to invade Egypt in 601 BC prompted Jehoiakim to renounce his allegiance and turn to Egypt once more. The eventual result was Babylonian invasion in 598 BC. Shortly before Jerusalem surrendered Jehoiakim died and was succeeded by his son Jehoiachin who, with other citizens, formed the first deportation from Judah to Babylon. The second decisive conquest of Judah and Jerusalem by Babylon was delayed only a further decade. Jehoiachin's uncle Zedekiah was put on the throne of Jerusalem. Incitement to rebellion was not lacking all through his reign (cf. Jer. 27), and eventually in 589 BC, along with Tyre and Ammon, and apparently with the understanding of Egyptian backing, rebellion against Babylon materialized. The Babylonian reaction came in the following year, and by 587 BC Jerusalem was captured. Zedekiah was brought into exile with a further proportion of the population, and the state of Judah was brought to an end. It is within this context that the movement which resulted in the production of Deuteronomy and also of the deuteronomistic historical work is to be set.

(b) Deuteronomy and the reform of Josiah
It has long been held that a relationship of some sort is to be posited between Deuteronomy and the reform of Josiah in 621 BC (for bibliography on this see Nicholson, *Deuteronomy*, 1ff.), and perhaps most frequently this has meant that Deuteronomy, or a part of that book, has been identified with the book of the law which 2 Kg. 22f. describes as having been found in the Jerusalem temple. Following this acccount, in the course of repairs being carried out on the temple in the eighteenth year of the reign of Josiah the book of the law was found. The high priest Hilkiah handed the book over to Shaphan the secretary who, having read it, brought it to the king. The king's reaction on hearing Shaphan read the book to him was to rend his clothes and to send a deputation to enquire of God 'concerning the words of the book that has been found'. The deputation went to Huldah the prophetess who replied with two oracles: in the first doom was threatened for Jerusalem and its inhabitants for their apostasy, and in the second Josiah was promised that he would 'be gathered to (his) grave in peace, and (his) eyes shall not see all the evil which I will bring upon this place'. Josiah then assembled all the people to the temple where he read the book to them. He then made a covenant, in which the people joined, to obey the demands of the book. Consequently a reform was instituted, involving the purification of the Jerusalem temple, the deposition of the priests of the high places and the defiling of those high places along with Topheth in the valley of the Son of Hinnom. The sanctuary of Bethel too was destroyed together with those of

the 'cities of Samaria'. The king then commanded that a Passover be observed at Jerusalem; and, finally, he put away 'the mediums and the wizards and the teraphim and the idols and all the abominations that were seen in the land of Judah and in Jerusalem.'

Although deuteronomistic responsibility for the present form of this account (apart perhaps from some later additions) is generally recognized, it is also frequently understood that much of the account constitutes a record (so Noth, *Studien*, 92, with reference to 22:3–23:3) incorporated by the deuteronomist, so that no difficulty, or very little difficulty, is felt to stand in the way of deriving reliable historical information from the essential parts of the story. These essential parts would be the finding of the book in the temple, the consultation of Huldah and Josiah's reform measures. Huldah's oracle is stressed because it is usually understood to conflict with the actual historical end of Josiah, which was a violent death at Megiddo (2 Kings 23:29f.); this conflict tends to support the historicity of Huldah's oracle which in turn supports the place of the book in the story. As far as actual historical reconstruction is concerned, however, chief emphasis lies on the book found in the temple and Josiah's reform measures.

In the description of the general historical framework within which these two elements of the story are to be fitted different possibilities exist. Even within the Old Testament there is not unanimity on the matter. The account in Kings describes repairs being carried out on the temple in Josiah's eighteenth year, during which the book was found, and suggests that everything which followed was consequent on the book's discovery. Josiah's reform is thus understood to have been based completely on the demands made in that book. In Chronicles, however, a rather different picture emerges. There (2 Chr. 34f.) it is described how 'in the eighth year of his reign, while he was yet a boy, he began to seek the God of David his father; and in the twelfth year he began to purge Judah and Jerusalem of the high places, the Asherim, and the graven and the molten images. . . .' The book of the law found in the temple in his eighteenth year led to the consultation of Huldah and the covenant to keep the demands of the book. Subsequently a Passover was celebrated in Jerusalem. Here the book of the law finds its place within a reform already under way, and functions to confirm the validity of what Josiah had already done.

The discrepancy between these accounts is not to be resolved simply by interpreting the 'repairs' to the temple described in Kings as activities arising from reform measures undertaken before the discovery of the law book; nor can the historical basis of the accounts be reconstructed simply by adopting a composite picture which will accommodate both. The tendency has been, therefore, to move the main emphasis away from the Old Testament accounts to the general historical situation in the ancient Near East as providing the necessary framework; and so to see the event of Josiah's reform as an event in ancient Near Eastern history, which must be interpreted first of all in that context (see on this Noth, *History*, 273ff.: Bright, *History*, 312ff.; Herrmann, *History*, 263ff.; Cross and Freedman, *JNES* 12, 1953, 56ff.). The chief feature of the general history of the period is the declining power of Assyria which had long dominated Mesopotamia and Syria-Palestine. The general course of this decline has been sketched above; the particular part of the process which is relevant at this point begins with the death of Ashurbanipal in 627 BC, or his abdication some years earlier in 631 BC (on this see the discussion in Reade, *JCS* 23, 1970, 1ff.). The occasion of a change in rule was always the occasion of revolt on the part of subject states, and in this instance the weakness of Assyria and its absorption with the threat posed by enemies on its very borders provided an opportunity for revolt by Judah which could not be more favourable to success.

A precise correlation between the various stages in Josiah's reform as presented by the Chronicler and major changes in the political situation in Assyria, as attempted by Cross and Freedman, is at best an optimistic undertaking. It demands both accurate knowledge of Assyrian chronology and an acceptance of the account of the reform as described by the Chronicler. Nevertheless, in general events in Judah should be seen against that background, and a reform by Josiah is, given the nature of the situation, most probably to be construed at least partially as a revolt by a subject nation against the overlord. Even if its measures were purely religious, they would, in the light of the syncretistic cult promoted particularly by Manasseh as an Assyrian vassal, constitute an assertion of nationalistic independence from external influence. In this framework the book of the law, as a basis for reform measures, could then be understood not as the total basis for the reform but as having contributed to a particular phase of that reform (so, for example, Nicholson, *Deuteronomy*, 12f., distinguishes the first stage of the reform, as a political move on the part of Josiah which involved the removal of Assyrian and other foreign cults from Judah and Jerusalem and which took place before the discovery of the law book, from the second stage which was based on the book and aimed at purifying the cult of Yahweh).

However, before any worthwhile move can be made to describe events in Judah against the general ancient Near Eastern background, the account of Josiah's reform must be treated in detail. This really means the account of 2 Kg. 22f., for the Chronicler's version clearly uses Kings as a source here, while there is no evidence of any other independent source used by the Chronicler which might account for the discrepancies between the two versions. Mosis, *Untersuchungen*, 195f., notes that the twelfth year, which is the earliest to which the Chronicler puts part of Josiah's reform, would have been the year of Josiah's majority when he could act independently of any other ruling influences, and suggests that the chronological details of the Chronicler's account may be adequately understood from the desire to show the king acting as soon as possible to purify the cult. It is, therefore, the Kings account which is the primary witness to the events of the period.

The story of Josiah's reform in 2 Kg. 22f. has been analysed by Lohfink, *Bib* 44, 1963, 261–88, 461–98, who finds that the part of the story dealing with the finding of the book of the law (22:3–20; 23:1–3, 21–23) falls into four sections, all of which begin and end with a reference to the king (22:3–11; 22:12–20; 23:1–3; 23:21–23). Moreover, the sections begin alternately with 'the king sent' (22:3; 23:1) and 'the king commanded' (22:12; 23:21). The concerns of each section have been summarily described by Lohfink as: repentance, oracle of salvation, covenant renewal, festival; and these are taken to be the four acts which comprise a covenant renewal ceremony. Covenant renewal is central to the story, and the whole world of the story is the world of covenant making. It is perhaps not altogether justifiable to separate 23:4–20 from this description; for it too begins and ends with reference to Josiah, and, though disturbing the alternating pattern, it begins with 'the king commanded'. The one point which really distinguishes 23:4–20 from the other sections is that it makes no reference to the book of the law. However, this has its background in the origin of the section (see below) and cannot justify

distinguishing 23:4–20 from its context at the deuteronomistic
stage of the history of the account to which Lohfink's description
applies. Moreover its inclusion with the other sections does not
seriously disturb the overall pattern which Lohfink has observed,
for 23:4–20, in describing the actual reforms carried out by Josiah,
provides concrete illustration of the obligations inherent in the
covenant renewal.

The general context within which the story of Josiah's reform
now stands is that of the deuteronomist. The extent of this work
and the background against which it was produced are of some
relevance here in so far as they must determine the perspective
and the context from which the account of Josiah must be ap-
proached. Clearly the chronological framework at least of the
story of Josiah, in 2 Kg. 22:1–3; 23:28–30, belongs in the context
of a deuteronomistic edition of the books of Kings which extends
beyond Josiah. How far beyond Josiah is not certain. According
to Noth, *Studien*, 91ff., the books of Kings in their entirety are
the work of the deuteronomist working in the exilic period. More
probably, however, one should think in terms of a late pre-exilic
deuteronomistic history which was then supplemented to bring
it to its present proportions (cf. Gray, *1 & 11 Kings*, 6ff., 753f.).
References to the exile of Judah within this work, as in 2 Kg.
17:19f., give the impression of being exilic additions to an already
existing work which did not know of Judah's destruction. Gray
has made it very probable that this pre-exilic work was composed
during the reign of Jehoiakim. This is suggested by an apparent
break in the records between Jehoiakim's rebellion against Nebuchadnezzar (2 Kg. 24:1) and the siege of Jerusalem in the time
of Jehoiachin. Furthermore, the note on Jehoiakim's death (2 Kg.
24:6) does not conform with earlier such notices in that it omits
reference to his burial. The verse may be an imitation of the
deuteronomistic royal death notices, marking the beginning of
the exilic supplement to the deuteronomistic history. If this is so,
the pre-exilic deuteronomistic history would have been compiled
in 598 BC when Jehoiakim revolted against Nebuchadnezzar. So
the account of Josiah's reform was put into its present chronological context and framework some twenty-three years after his
eighteenth year.

However, the determination of the background of the material
contained in this framework is another issue. Lohfink, *Bib* 44,
1963, 469f., isolates 22:3–20; 23:1–3, 21–3 as a unit deriving from

the time of Josiah. That it is a unit is a conclusion based on its structure, and that it derives from the time of Josiah is evidently based on the observation that it does not presuppose knowledge of the violent way in which Josiah met his death.

There are two points which must be made here. First of all, it may be accepted that the story has a definite structure which (even with 23:4–20) is that of a ceremony of covenant renewal. Yet it must be emphasized that it is not a covenant renewal ceremony which is described here; rather it is a story about certain actions carried out by Josiah which is presented structurally on the pattern of a covenant ceremony. It is on the basis of the presupposed structure that the existence of a unit may be claimed here, but that this may be isolated from its context violates its character as a story of events in Josiah's lifetime which is continued outside that unit. It is not impossible that a historian, supposing a reform carried out by Josiah to have had the character of covenant renewal, to have presented the account of that reform, within the context of his own history, on the pattern of a covenant renewal ceremony. The account of the reform then need not necessarily be treated as a unit which may be divorced from its context. Secondly, that the account does not betray knowledge of the violent death of Josiah is presumably a reference to the oracle of Huldah where, in 2 Kg. 22:20, Josiah is promised that he will be gathered to his grave 'in peace'. It is probably true (see below) that this oracle is to be taken in the way presupposed in Lohfink's argument, viz. as conflicting with and so earlier than the actual death of Josiah; but this supports an early date for Huldah's oracle only and not necessarily for the whole literary context in which it is now to be found.

In the first part of the story, in 22:3–11, there are two subjects: the repairs being carried out on the temple and the finding of the book of the law. The former provides the context for the latter and gives it the appearance of historical reliability. However, this impression must be revised in the light of the clear connection between the account of the repairs to the temple in 2 Kg. 22 and a similar account in 2 Kg. 12:9–16. There is a clear literary relationship between the two accounts (compare, for example, 12:12 and 22:5), which is to be explained on the assumption either that the same hand is at work in both or that one account has been used in the formulation of the other by a different hand. The differences between the two accounts suggest that the first

alternative is unlikely, and Dietrich, *VT* 27, 1977, 18ff., has shown
that these differences do in fact indicate that ch. 22 is dependent
on ch. 12 for the account of repairs to the temple. For example,
it is more likely that 22:7 is an abbreviated version of 12:13–16
than that the latter should be an elaboration of the former. The
story of the repairs to the temple is, therefore, a secondary construction which has the purpose of providing a historically credible
context for the story of the finding of the book of the law. The latter
may be easily separated in 22:8, 10f. V. 10 with its fresh introduction is clearly not the continuation of v. 9, but rather of v. 8. V. 9
functions to link the story of the law book with that of the repairs
to the temple. This does not necessarily mean, however (as
Dietrich proposes), that there existed two already formed literary
units, one dealing with the repairs to the temple and the other
with the law book, which the deuteronomist combined. Much
more probable is the conclusion that the one responsible for the
secondary construction of the story of repairs is the deuteronomist,
and that the reason for the construction is to provide a context
not for an already existing story, but rather for a story which he
himself composed.

One may ask, nevertheless, if there is behind the story of the
finding of the book a tradition on which the deuteronomist de-
pended and which may be relied on as reflecting an actual event
in the eighteenth year of Josiah. Lohfink, *Bib* 44, 1963, 28off., has
pointed out that the account refers not to 'a book of the law', but
to 'the book of the law'. This indicates, for Lohfink, that the book
was well recognized and familiar; it was, in short, the old covenant
document of the Jerusalem temple which now, having been lost,
is found. This may explain the way in which the book is referred
to; but one must ask if it is possible to make this immediate transfer
from the literary to the historical level. In other words, the reference
to 'the book' rather than 'a book' is explicable within the literary
context of the deuteronomistic history and does not necessarily demand the historical explanation which Lohfink proposes. For the
deuteronomistic historian Israel's history ran its course under the
judgment of the law of Moses presented in Deuteronomy, and it
is specifically to Deuteronomy as 'the book of the law' that the
deuteronomist refers on several occasions in his history (cf. Jos.
1:8; 8:31, 34: 23:6; 2 Kg. 14:6); the present reference can only be
seen in that context. 'The book of the law' is the book which the
deuteronomistic history has continually presented as the funda-

mental element in Israel's history, and it is to this book within the literary presentation of the deuteronomistic history that 2 Kg. 22f. refers. This reference is to be explained primarily, therefore, within the literary context of the particular construction of the deuteronomistic history. That it may be explained adequately within that context, without reference to a historical book of the law existing since the time of Moses and found in the temple in the time of Josiah is a point to which we shall return.

The second part of the story in 22:12–20 concerns Josiah's sending of a deputation to consult Huldah the prophetess, and the reply of Huldah to this enquiry. Here again an impression of historical credibility has been deliberately created, this time through the reference to the actual individuals who formed Josiah's deputation. Such detail, however, is not in itself decisive, for it is precisely this means that is used by the Chronicler with the purpose of giving the impression of historicity. In fact, of the four individuals mentioned, three are known from Jer. 26 and other passages, and only one, Asaiah, is known only from the present passage (on this see Würthwein, *ZThK* 73, 1976, 402f.). The impression intended by the giving of this detail is, moreover, counterbalanced by the general vagueness of the story in so far as these individuals are associated with it. They are reported only to have 'talked with' Huldah (22:14), which is not the language of a royal annal or a historical chronicle. Moreover, the reference in 22:13 to the great anger of Yahweh which 'is kindled against us' presupposes rather a situation where disaster has either already come or is imminent, in fact the situation of the deuteronomistic historian, not that of Josiah in 621 BC. The historical setting which the account provides does not, therefore, of itself give convincing reason for concluding that a course of events corresponding to this account took place in Josiah's eighteenth year.

In reply to the enquiry made of her Huldah is represented as imparting two oracles: the first in 22:16–17 and the second in 22:18–20. Of these the first is widely and correctly recognized as a deuteronomistic composition (cf. Würthwein, *op. cit.*, 404ff.; Dietrich, *op. cit.*, 25ff.; and especially now Rose, *ZAW* 89, 1977, 52ff.). The language of the oracle is late: the formula 'behold I will bring evil on . . .' is found in late layers of Jeremiah (19:3, 15; 32:42), as is also the expression 'that they might provoke me to anger' (Jer. 7:18; 25:7; 32:29); there is nothing concrete and specific in the oracle; it is general and formulaic, and is concerned

to give expression to a particular understanding of history as
running its course in fulfilment of the prophetic word (see comment on Dt. 18:21, 22).

This is not the case with the second oracle in 22:18–20, which
is directed to Josiah personally. Rose, *op. cit.*, 54ff., has pointed to
some elements of this oracle which may be deuteronomistic, such
as the expressions 'a desolation and a curse' and 'the evil which
I shall bring'; but apart from these there is no formulaic language
in the oracle; rather it is concrete and specific in its references to
Josiah and particularly in the promise that he shall be gathered
to his grave in peace. This means that it cannot be from the same
hand as the first oracle. This being the case, the question of its age
in relation to the first oracle immediately arises: is it earlier than
22:16f. or later? The commonly held view is that it is in fact
earlier, and that, moreover, it must be dated to the time of Josiah
himself. This is because of the evident conflict between the content
of Huldah's promise to Josiah, that he should be gathered to his
grave in peace, and the historical end of Josiah, his violent death
at Megiddo. An oracle containing such a promise could not have
originated after Josiah's death.

Würthwein, *op. cit.*, 404f., has, however, pointed out that this
promise should not be separated from its foundation in 22:19,
Josiah's having become penitent and having humbled himself;
and the thought that is here expressed—the repentance of a king
leading to a warding off of evil—is typical of the Chronicler. In
support of this Würthwein points out that the verbal form 'humble
oneself' is found in the religious context otherwise only in 1 Kg.
21:29; Lev. 26:41; and the Chronicler. In this case the reference
to Josiah's being gathered to his grave 'in peace' would have to be
understood to refer not to the nature of Josiah's death but rather
to the fact that Josiah himself would not see the ruin and destruction which was to come on Jerusalem and its inhabitants. However
it is doubtful that this is an adequate exegesis of the passage. To
be gathered to one's grave in peace is to die naturally (cf. Rose,
op. cit., 59); it is inconceivable that an oracle containing these
words would have been secondarily introduced into the already
existing deuteronomistic account of Josiah's reign and death. This
would suggest that the oracle containing these words is older than
its deuteronomistic context.

The contrary argument that the words 'gathered to (his) grave
in peace', had they been understood to refer specifically to a

natural death for Josiah, would have been omitted by the deuteronomist in order not to conflict with the account of the actual
death of Josiah, is not compelling. An attempt has in fact been
made to diminish the tension between this part of the oracle and
the account of Josiah's death. This has been done through setting
the oracle in a context which diverts attention from the question
of Josiah's own fate to that of the fate of Jerusalem. This context
must include the reference to Josiah's humbling himself (22:19)
and to his eyes not seeing the evil which God will bring on
Jerusalem (22:20), which, in the light of 1 Kg. 21:29, may be
claimed as deuteronomistic language. Deuteronomistic authorship
of this context is supported by the fact that there is a clear affinity
between the reference to God bringing evil on 'this place' in v. 20
and the first oracle of Huldah (22:16f.) which has already been
seen to be composed of deuteronomistic formulaic language.

The second oracle of Huldah stands in tension with its wider
context in promising Josiah a peaceful death; it stands in some
tension also with its immediate context: it refers to Josiah having
'wept before me' which points to an act of penitence in the temple,
but the context (22:11) refers only to Josiah's having rent his
clothes in the palace; the oracle describes Josiah's actions as a
reaction to having heard 'how I spoke against this place and
against its inhabitants', while the context (22:8, 11) refers to 'the
book of the law.' In view of these tensions it is not possible to
consider the oracle either a subsequent insertion into an already
existing deuteronomistic account, or as coming from the hand
of the deuteronomistic historian. The oracle must, then, be older
than the deuteronomistic history. This is supported by the fact
that it is supplemented in several places by deuteronomistic
phrases. These would have come in at the time of the incorporation of the oracle into the history, and would have had the purpose
of adapting the oracle to its new context.

If this is true, the pre-deuteronomistic oracle of Huldah would
have referred to Josiah's having wept before God as a result of
hearing how God spoke against Jerusalem, and would have contained a promise that he would be gathered to his grave in peace.
There is no indication that it referred to the book of the law. All
such references belong within the deuteronomistic contribution
to this section, and thus continue the deuteronomistic account in
22:3–11. This finds some support in 22:13. This verse is introduced
by 'Go, inquire of the Lord', which is a regular formal element in

such contexts (cf. for example, Gen. 35:22; 1 Kg. 22:5, 8; 2 Kg. 3:11; 8:8, etc.) and cannot be claimed to be specifically deuteronomistic. It is followed, however, by a very full commission which in its two parts has no parallel outside this passage. The first part 'for me, and for the people, and for all Judah' is paralleled in Isa. 8:19; Jer. 21:2; the second, 'concerning the words of this book that has been found', has a parallel in 1 Kg. 14:5 (slightly emended), but with both parts together the commission is here awkward, overfull and without analogy. If it is a question, then, of one part being a later addition, it is the second which must be considered as such; it is highly unlikely that the first would have been added before an already present second part. This addition would then belong with the other references to the book of the law, that is to the deuteronomistic stage of incorporation of the oracle into the history, while the remainder of the first part of 22:13 may have belonged as the introduction to the original oracle.

The third part of the account in 23:1–3 is central to the present form of the story. On the basis of the book and Huldah's oracle Josiah gathered the people to the temple and there made a covenant, in which the people joined, to obey the commandments of the book. The section is a single unit, portraying the king not as set apart to stand in a special relationship with God, but as one of his people who functions as did Moses (Exod. 24:3–8) and Joshua (Jos. 24) in the obligating of the whole people, including himself, to the laws of the covenant. Appropriately at this point reference is made to 'the book of the covenant', by which, however, is clearly intended 'the book of the law' already mentioned; these are alternative designations and come from the same hand. That this hand is a deuteronomistic one is clear from a number of considerations: firstly, the section is the continuation of the deuteronomistic account in the preceding sections; secondly, on the supposition that what is referred to here is the book of Deuteronomy, it is with the deuteronomistic stage(s) of redaction of that book (see above on the structure) that the term 'book of the covenant' has its closest association; thirdly, the building up of terms to describe the law in Deuteronomy is typical of deuteronomistic parts of Deuteronomy, and the specific combination of terms here, 'his commandments and his testimonies and his statutes', is closely paralleled in the deuteronomistic Dt. 6:17. The possibility of a tradition in this section on which the deuteronomist depends and which he brings to expression in his own words is, therefore, the same problem as we have already met in connection with 22:3-11, viz. does the total literary context in which the section stands, that of the deuteronomistic history governed by Deuteronomy, provide an adequate explanation for this section, or must the existence of a historical tradition, understandable only in terms of an actual event in the time of Josiah, be assumed? This problem will be taken up after the last two sections of this story of Josiah's reform, 23:4-20 and 23:21-25, have been examined.

In 23:4-20 details are given of the actual reform measures of Josiah. In the treatment of this section reference must be made first to Oestreicher, *Grundgesetz*, 13ff., who distinguished 23:4-15, 19 from its context on stylistic grounds. While the context is written in a broad narrative style, the verses which detail the reform measures have a short, compact style, simply enumerating the actions of Josiah. Furthermore, while the use of the '*waw*-consecutive' characterizes the context, these verses show a remarkably high incidence of use of the '*waw*-conjunctive'. One must add to these points the observation that while in the present context it is clearly presupposed that the reform measures were based on the book found in the temple, there is in this section no reference back to such a book. In fact, the section reveals characteristics which have already appeared with 22:12-20, viz. signs from both its language and its content that there is here a basic layer which has been taken up and edited on at least one occasion.

This general conclusion indicates the necessary approach towards explaining one further notable characteristic of these verses, which is their disorder as far as content is concerned. Not only are the same subjects treated more than once (for example, v. 8 anticipates v. 13), but there is no consistency with respect to the place where the reforms were carried through and the kinds of reforms involved: reforms in Jerusalem are referred to in vv. 4, 6f., 8b, 10-12, and scattered among these references attention is directed to cities and sanctuaries outside Jerusalem; some reforms are apparently aimed at purifying the cult of Yahweh (for example, vv. 6ff., 14f.) while others are apparently concerned with the cults of foreign gods (vv. 10ff.), though no effort is made to distinguish them.

Hollenstein, *VT* 27, 1977, 326ff. (cf. also Würthwein, *op. cit.*,

412ff.), has distinguished three stages in the development of this text. In the first place there is the basic text, secondly there is the deuteronomistic redaction of this text, and thirdly there is the post-deuteronomistic redaction. The deuteronomistic material is fairly easy to distinguish. V. 4, because of its clear contacts in style of opening with 22:3, 12; 23:1, and with 2 Kg. 17:16; 21:3; 25:18 in referring to the priests, the priests of the second order and the keepers of the threshold, and also to Baal, Asherah, and all the host of heaven, is deuteronomistic. On the other hand, however, deuteronomistic passages do not generally refer to 'the temple of the Lord', but rather to 'the house of the Lord'; nor to 'vessels' in connection with the worship of foreign gods. In these two cases there may be pre-deuteronomistic material here edited. The final phrase of v. 4, 'and carried their ashes to Bethel', together with v. 5, use the 'waw-conjunctive' which is not typical of the deuteronomist. On the other hand, for two reasons this usage may be taken as not belonging to the basic layer: firstly, had this usage been found in the source used by the deuteronomist (and it does not appear in other verses which may be assigned to this source) or in a pre-deuteronomistic edition of that source, it would have been modified to conform with normal deuteronomistic usage. Secondly, while the deuteronomist might make the kings of Judah responsible for corrupt worship, it is most unlikely that his source would have done so, if this source is to be seen in any way as an official account of the reforms of Josiah. The end of v. 4, along with v. 5, may be taken, therefore, as belonging to a post-deuteronomistic redaction. Vv. 6–8a are deuteronomistic, referring to 'the house of the Lord', to the removal of the Asherah (alluding to its introduction in 2 Kg. 21:7) and its burning at the Kidron (cf. 1 Kg. 15:3), and to the cult prostitutes, the Asherah and the high places as characterizing the corrupt state of Judah (cf. 1 Kg. 14:22–24). With these verses go also vv. 9, 13, for here too the references to the 'high places' and the 'abominations' must be seen in the light of the summary description of Judah's sin given by the deuteronomist in 1 Kg. 14:22–24. On the other hand, vv. 8b, 10 use the form of the 'waw-conjunctive', which connects them with the post-deuteronomistic redaction already seen in the end of v. 4 and v. 5. In vv. 11f. an edited version of the pre-deuteronomistic layer appears. Here the detailed reforms of Josiah are enumerated. They have been edited in the addition of 'that the kings of Judah had dedicated' and 'which the kings of Judah had made, and the altars which Manasseh had made in the two courts of the house of the Lord', ascribing responsibility for corruption to the kings of Judah, and also in the final phrase of v. 12, 'and cast the dust of them into the brook Kidron' which uses the '*waw*-conjunctive'. Otherwise, however, these two verses reveal the particular concerns of the basic layer, which are with the forms of Assyrian cultic practices which Josiah expelled from the Jerusalem temple. It is the deuteronomistic historian who has not only extended this to include reforms outside Jerusalem, but also to refer in general terms to Canaanite cult practices and to the worship of the high places. The post-deuteronomistic redaction is continued in v. 14 and the final phrase of v. 15, 'also he burned the Asherah', where the '*waw*-conjunctive' is found. This stage of editing, which is not apparently presupposed here by the Chronicler's version of the reform, is concerned with exalting Josiah even beyond the idealistic picture which the deuteronomist had already painted. The deuteronomistic historian, who intends to show how Josiah removed all the cultic abuses which he has mentioned throughout his history, is responsible for most of v. 15 and vv. 16–20. There is an apparent conflict within them since v. 15 tells of the destruction of the altar of Bethel, while v. 16 presupposes its existence. However, the apparent conflict arises from the incorporation into his story by the deuteronomist of an aetiological explanation of a grave·monument at Bethel, which he used in order to give expression to his interest in prophecy and fulfilment (cf. 1 Kg. 13): the monument is that of the man of God who predicted that Josiah would defile the altar of Bethel by burning men's bones upon it. The deuteronomistic account in this section then concludes with vv. 19f.

Two significant points in particular emerge from this study. In the first place, even if the details of the analysis adopted here are subject to some modification, it is clear that the existence of 'the book of the law' is nowhere presupposed. Moreover, this is not just the arbitrary separation of a section of this account in order to exclude reference to the book of the law; vv. 4–20 constitute a clearly separate unit with its own beginning and ending. Secondly, the pre-deuteronomistic basis of the story makes no reference to the centralization of worship through the abolition of the high places. It is only with the deuteronomistic stage of redaction that this is introduced. If the pre-deuteronomistic layer reflects a reform instituted by Josiah, then that reform was aimed at ridding the

Jerusalem temple of the apparatus of Assyrian cultic practices in connection with the worship of sun and stars.

The final section of the account of Josiah's reform is contained in 23:21–25. Two subjects are treated here: firstly, the command of Josiah to keep the Passover, and, secondly, his removal of 'the mediums and the wizards and the teraphim and the idols and all the abominations' from Judah and Jerusalem. In both cases these are reforms explicitly based on the book found in the temple. That immediately connects the section with the deuteronomistic contribution in 22:3–23:3, a connection which is confirmed by two further points: firstly, as with the earlier sections, so also here the deuteronomist has at the beginning referred to the king having commanded (or sent), and at the end referred once more to the king; secondly, the deuteronomistic redaction in the previous section extended Josiah's reform to Canaanite cult practices and the corruption of the worship of Yahweh. This is the concern also of this final section, in v. 24 (for 'abominations' see 23:13) and also in vv. 21ff. in so far as the institution of the centralized Passover festival is presented as a necessary reform of the worship of Yahweh.

Würthwein, op. cit., 407ff., has, however, proposed that the reference to the institution of a centralized Passover festival is a later addition. The reason adduced is that the festival, which was a spring festival, is said to have been celebrated in Josiah's eighteenth year, the same year as that in which the book of the law was found according to 22:3; there is not sufficient time allowed for the organization of such a festival, based on the book of the law. Even though our analysis so far has yielded no indication of a book of the law as the basis of Josiah's reform, it remains true that it is difficult to see the Passover festival in the context of Josiah's reform measures. Gray, op. cit., 742, notes that the account 'exasperates us by its silence as to the specific motive for the innovation'. The other reforms were carried out in order to remove corruptions in the temple cult; but here no such reason is given or implied. Now, for the first time, it is the book of the law alone which is seen as sufficient reason for the measure. Furthermore, it is a centralized Passover to which the verses refer: it is kept in Jerusalem. This can only be understood in the context of the measure to centralize all sacrificial worship at one sanctuary, and that is only understood in the deuteronomistic sections of what has preceded dealing with the removal of the high places. But against

Würthwein, this reference to Passover is probably best treated as deuteronomistic rather than any later. Its style of introduction is deuteronomistic; it makes specific reference to Dt. 16, and other such clear references to Deuteronomy, in the phrase 'the book of the law', have already been seen to be deuteronomistic. In any case, there is no sign of a pre-deuteronomistic basic layer in the verses on Passover.

Our study of the text relating to Josiah's reform shows, therefore, a deuteronomistic account which has post-deuteronomistic additions inserted in 23:4–20, and a clear pre-deuteronomistic basis in only the oracle of Huldah, now edited in 22:12–20, and the reform measures of Josiah, now edited in 23:4–20. In neither passage does the pre-deuteronomistic basis refer to the book of the law. Apart from these passages there is a consistent deuteronomistic story of the finding of the book of the law, its authentication by Huldah, and the covenant and reform carried out on the basis of it. Despite the fact that there is no evidence of a pre-deuteronomistic basis here, one must ask if the deuteronomist is here relying on some tradition relating to a book found in the temple in the time of Josiah, and if not how then this account originated. That there is any old tradition here is unlikely for two main reasons. In the first place, the account is historically improbable: it is unlikely that such a reform would have been carried out simply on the basis of a book found in the temple in the course of repair work; it is even more unlikely that such a book would have been treated so casually by Hilkiah and Shaphan, while it would have caused Josiah to rend his clothes. This is a theological story which has its main focus not on the finding of the book of the law in the temple, but on pushing forward Josiah as a righteous king who acted in accordance with the law of Moses. Secondly, the book of the law is not presupposed by those elements of the story which may be claimed as pre-deuteronomistic and in fact there is some tension between these elements and the notion of a book of the law. The references which belong to the pre-deuteronomistic basis of the account in 23:4–20 do not presuppose the book of the law; they do not, however, exclude the possibility of a book of the law. The original oracle of Huldah, on the other hand, does not presuppose a book of the law, but also tends to exclude such a book. That to which Josiah reacted, according to this oracle, was a word of God (22:19 'how I spoke') which presupposes a prophetic word rather than a book of the law; and

certainly a book of the law presented as speech of Moses to all
Israel would be a highly unsuitable reference for this oracle.

The full original setting of Huldah's oracle is not preserved, and
so the occasion of his sending to enquire of God is unclear; one
may only suggest possible occasions. By analogy with similar
situations earlier (see especially 1 Kg. 22:5, 8) the occasion may
have been one in which Josiah was preparing for a specific undertaking, in order to determine the outcome of which he sent to
Huldah. Her reply was one of encouragement and assurance that
God had heard him (22:19) and that his venture would be successful (22:20), because he had shown himself as faithful to God
(22:19). Historically, this could belong to one of a variety of
possible situations; in the context of the actual information which
we have on Josiah this specific undertaking may have been his
attempt to restrain Necho from going to the aid of Assyria (23:29),
while the manner in which Josiah had earlier shown himself faithful to God was through his reform measures already carried out
(23:4*, 11f.).

If the story of the finding of the book of the law is not then based
on historical tradition, why has the deuteronomist introduced it?
It is important to emphasize here that the historicity of a reform
instituted by Josiah is not in doubt. The only explanation for the
pre-deuteronomistic basis of 23:4–20 is that it is an account of
measures carried through by this king. The measures would have
been recorded in royal annals, and these annals containing the
written account of Josiah's reforms were the source for the deuteronomistic historian. Josiah was then known historically as a
righteous king who had carried out reforms in the worship of the
Jerusalem temple. On the other hand, the deuteronomist had
constructed his history on the basis that it stood under the judgment of God. This was effected through his incorporation of the
existing original book of Deuteronomy at the beginning of his work
as a standard by which he intended his readers to judge the
history. The book of the law, by which title he referred to Deuteronomy, was presupposed as existing throughout Israel's history.
It was the standard by which Israel's history was to be judged; it
was therefore also the standard by which the righteousness of any
individual in that history could be determined. Josiah, known as
a righteous king, could have been such only because he fulfilled
the law, and his reforms must have been carried out in conformity
with this law. It was inevitable, then, that his reforms should have

come to be seen as based on the book of the law. As to why this book should be presented as having been 'found' in the temple, this may be the means by which it was felt that the contrast between the reign of Josiah and that of his two predecessors, Manasseh and Amon, could best be expressed. The account of the reigns of these kings could scarcely have described an event in which the book of the law became lost; but this could be implied through presenting the book of the law as 'found' in the time of Josiah. In the reigns of Manasseh and Amon Judah reached depths of corruption; the book of the law must in that time have been lost. In the time of Josiah there was a return to Yahweh; the book of the law, the guide for the life of Israel since Moses, was found once more.

A further motive was probably at work in connecting the book of the law with Josiah. If it is true that the deuteronomistic history was compiled in 598 BC (see above), then those to whom it was addressed were themselves children at the time of Josiah's reform. Through the presentation of this reform as a covenant into which all the people 'both great and small' had entered, and thereby taken on the obligation to obey the demands of Deuteronomy (23:1–3), the deuteronomist is in effect reminding his contemporaries that they have already undertaken to obey the law. The covenant made in the time of Josiah directly involves the present generation. Finally, in this connection, reference should be made once more to the fact that it is through deuteronomistic editing that the original Deuteronomy came to be seen in terms of a covenant document (see above). It is, however, only on the basis of its being understood in those terms that it could be referred to in the manner in which it is mentioned in 2 Kg. 22f. The book of the law is here Deuteronomy, edited by the deuteronomist to become a covenant document and introduced into 2 Kg. 22f. by the deuteronomist as such a covenant document.

If this is so, then the book of Deuteronomy, in any form, cannot be seen as basic to the reform of Josiah. It may have been in existence or in the course of preparation then, but there is no evidence of this. More likely the book originated in the period between Josiah's reform and the time of the deuteronomist in 598 BC and nearer to the latter date than the former. The book expresses the prophetic view that Israel's welfare in the land depends on her obedience to moral and religious obligations, a view which would be expressed in this way, in the form of a

written collection of laws, more probably after Josiah's tragic
death in 609 BC than in the euphoric atmosphere which would
have attended his moves towards independence including his
reform of temple worship in 621 BC. The book may to a certain
extent have been the deposit of that reform, in that Josiah's reform
measures, in so far as they may be deduced from 2 Kg. 23:4–20,
are reflected in Deuteronomy (17:3); but it was really only as a
result of the redactional work of the deuteronomist that the connection between Deuteronomy and the reform of Josiah became
firmly established.

(c) *The authorship of Deuteronomy*
Given the primary characteristic of the style of Deuteronomy,
that it is didactic, it is scarcely surprising that the three chief
teaching and preaching institutions in ancient Israel: prophecy,
wisdom, and levitical priesthood, have all been suggested as possible contexts of origin of Deuteronomy. It is a dominant aspect
of the book which has endured from its original to its present
form, that through warning and promise, through exhortation
and appeal, it seeks to persuade its readers to obey the demands
of the law of Moses.

The argument for prophetic authorship finds its strongest modern representative in Nicholson, *Deuteronomy*, 69f., 76, for whom
three points in particular support (northern) prophetic authorship
of Deuteronomy. In the first place, both Deuteronomy and the
northern prophets stand in the tradition of the old Israelite
amphictyony. This is to be seen in their common concern for the
observance of covenant law, their common involvement with the
holy war ideology, their attachment to charismatic leadership,
and their critical attitude to the monarchy. Secondly, there are
the contacts between Deuteronomy and Hosea especially. Several
writers have drawn attention to this (for example, Weinfeld,
Deuteronomy, 366ff., though Weinfeld does not support the idea of
prophetic authorship of Deuteronomy), and there can be no doubt
that there is an association with the thought of this prophet: with
both there is strong condemnation of the high places (cf. Hos.
8:11; 10:1, 8; 14:3, etc., and Dt. 12), and of idolatry (Hos. 13:2;
14:4 and Dt. 4:28); there is the same warning against forgetting
Yahweh as a result of satiety and pride (Hos. 13:6 and Dt. 8:12f.);
there is the same reference to God's love for Israel (Hos. 11:1–4;
Dt. 1:31; 8:5; 14:1), and the same threat of return to Egypt

(Hos. 8:13; 11:5; Dt. 17:16; 28:68). Thirdly, there is the portrayal of Moses in Dt. 18:15ff. as a covenant mediator; such an
office is understood to have existed in Israel's covenant cult,
and to have been held by a prophet, who, speaking in the name
of God, would proclaim the covenant law to the people. It is as
such a prophetic covenant mediator that Moses is here described.
To these points one might add that the general ethical concern
of Deuteronomy, and in particular the concern for the welfare
of the socially and economically weak, echoes strongly the teaching
of the prophets generally in the Old Testament.

Even though Dt. 18:15–18 is probably a post-deuteronomistic
addition to its context (see introduction to 18:9–22), and although
the office of covenant mediator is an institution which may be
inferred only with considerable uncertainty (see comment on
18:15), it remains true that the connections between Deuteronomy
and prophecy are strong, and any view of the authorship of
Deuteronomy must account for them. Yet the case for any exclusive connection with prophecy must be judged in the light of
the contacts which may be established with other areas, and
especially with wisdom. The arguments which are advanced
here are especially important because there is a broad similarity
to the case which is made for contact with prophecy.

In particular the studies of Malfroy, *VT* 15, 1965, 49ff.;
Weinfeld, *Deuteronomy*, 158ff., 260ff.; and Carmichael, *Laws*, 18ff.,
have made clear that connections between Deuteronomy and wisdom may be established in setting, in language and in content.
The setting is not precisely parallel: while Deuteronomy is in the
form of an address by Moses to Israel as a whole, in the wisdom of
Proverbs the setting is that of the teacher addressing his pupil.
Yet there is clearly a general similarity here: in both cases it is
a question of teaching, and the typical vocabulary and forms of
a teaching situation are used. The summons to 'hear' is a wisdom
form (see comment on 6:4); the 'teaching' which is imparted is
that of the wisdom teacher (cf. 32:2; the Song of Moses in particular has many wisdom elements, see introduction to 31:30–
32:44); other words found in Deuteronomy, which are chiefly
wisdom terms, are, for example: 'counsel' (32:28); 'wise' (1:13;
4:6); 'wisdom' (4:6; 34:9); 'fear' (2:25); '(do what is) good'
(6:18, 24). The injunction to lay the teaching on one's heart or
bind it to oneself is found in both Deuteronomy (6:8; 11:18) and
Proverbs (3:3; 6:21; 7:3). Other striking parallels in content

may be seen in a comparison of Dt. 4:2 and Prov. 30:5f.; Dt. 13:1 and Ec. 3:14; Dt. 19:14 and Prov. 22:28; 23:10; Dt. 25:13–16 and Prov. 11:1; 20:23, Dt. 23:23–4 and Ec. 5:1–5; Prov. 20:25; Dt. 23:16 and Prov. 30:10. Such parallels may be multiplied. Weinfeld, whose exploration of this aspect has been most thorough, suggests that Deuteronomy is in fact the work of scribes of the Jerusalem court who would have been familiar with this wisdom teaching. This is taken also to provide the best explanation for the clear influence from the treaties on Deuteronomy, for such scribes would have been familiar with treaty forms. Indeed it may be that Judah was at that time bound to Assyria by treaty, established through such a form (Frankena, *OTS* 14, 1965, 153, sees Josiah's covenant, understood as based on the original Deuteronomy, as a substitution for the former treaty between Judah and Assyria).

Thirdly, reference must be made to the proposal that the authors of Deuteronomy must be sought among the Levites. This view has had many supporters; it is associated particularly with von Rad, *Studies*, 66ff., and has in more recent years been strongly advocated with some refinements by Lindblom, *Erwägungen*, 42ff. For von Rad, Levitical authorship is indicated by the knowledge of old sacral tradition shown by Deuteronomy and by the freedom in dealing with these traditions in order to actualize them for the present. In Neh. 8 there is historical attestation of analogous Levitical activity, even though for later time than that of Deuteronomy. Von Rad also points, however, to the martial spirit which pervades the book and to the fact that the Levites were closely associated, through their function as keepers of the ark, with the old Israelite holy war (see Dt. 20). Lindblom has added to this the important point that Dt. 17:18ff.; 31:9, 24ff. (none of which can be claimed as an original deuteronomic passage) all presuppose a close connection between the deuteronomic law and the Levites not very long after its origin.

All three of these proposals show weaknesses, and it is doubtful that any of them may be accepted as it stands. The teaching of Deuteronomy certainly does show the influence of the prophets: this is clear not simply from the actual norms (which in many cases Deuteronomy and the prophets share with the wisdom writers) but rather from the context within which Deuteronomy presents these norms: that of the relationship between Yahweh and Israel. This is the behaviour which Yahweh demands of his people. Yet there are serious objections to seeing prophets as the authors of Deuteronomy. In the first place, Deuteronomy can scarcely be said to be enthusiastic about the institution of prophecy Dt. 18:15–18 (see comment) is a post-deuteronomistic addition; and Dt. 13:1ff. is very reserved. Secondly, the distinctive style of prophecy: oracular formulae, prophetic metaphor and poetic diction, is quite lacking in Deuteronomy. Thirdly, the book has no eschatology. The prophetic influence on Deuteronomy is clear, but prophetic authorship is most unlikely. A similar limitation applies to the theory of wisdom or scribal authorship. The influence of wisdom cannot be denied, but as Clements, *Prophecy*, 70ff., has noted, there are difficulties in the way of restricting wisdom forms and language to any single group or class. The chief point here is that contacts of this nature, even if not quite so extensive, may be established also between wisdom literature and the psalms or prophets. Wisdom thought and language were diffused throughout ancient Israel, and its presence cannot, therefore, indicate immediately the work of a single group such as the court scribes. Moreover, there are clear objections to deriving the book from such a class. If Proverbs is to be taken as representative of the wisdom by which such court officials were instructed, then one must point to the religious nationalism of Deuteronomy as something which distinguishes it sharply from such circles. There is here none of the internationalist outlook of Proverbs; the focus of attention is Yahweh and his relationship with Israel, and the teaching which Deuteronomy has in common with Proverbs is set in the distinctive context of Yahweh's election of and covenant with Israel. Secondly, scribal circles in the Jerusalem court, and the educational activity within that context were limited in their composition and range. They were centered on the training of potential court officials or royal advisers. It is difficult to link this with the content and range of Deuteronomy. Here Israel as a whole is addressed and the law is intended to cover the whole field of religion and morality within the context of Yahweh's covenant with Israel.

In the context of the theory of Levitical authorship questions also arise. Perhaps the most obvious is that through legislating for the abolition of the local sanctuaries, as Deuteronomy does, the Levites would seem to have been aiming to deprive themselves of their source of livelihood. In this context, however, the refinements to the theory which have been made by Lindblom (cf. also Cody, *Priesthood*) are relevant. One must distinguish among the

Levites between those who were priests, either of the high places or of the Jerusalem temple, and those who were not. The latter group, the non-priestly Levites, did not originate as a result of the abolition of the high places and the centralization of sacrificial worship to one sanctuary. The Levites in Deuteronomy are continually commended to the charity of Israelites (12:17ff.; 14:24ff., 28f.; 16:9ff., 13f.; 26:10f., 12f.), but not because of a sudden change in their economic status arising from centralization. Rather, they are included among the poor of the people because they are landless and have always been landless. This is a condition of the Levites presupposed throughout the Old Testament. Particularly significant are the narratives in Jg. 17–21 (cf. Cody, *op. cit.*, 52ff.), where individual Levites are depicted living as *gērîm* (see comment on 1:16) in the tribal areas of Judah and Ephraim (Jg. 17:7; 19:1); they have no status as priests simply by virtue of being Levites. However, these Levites did have a 'specialization' to which they laid claim: the priesthood. Even from early days (cf. Jg. 17:10) it seems to have been preferred to have a Levite as priest though their claim to that status was given no exclusive recognition.

Lindblom, *op. cit.*, 54ff., suggests that the authors of Deuteronomy should be sought among northern Levites, previously unconnected with the cult, who came to Jerusalem after the fall of the northern kingdom in 721 BC and there became members of the Jerusalem temple priesthood. The existence of such a specific group is difficult to prove; the northern associations of Deuteronomy have been widely argued for, especially because of the contacts with Hosea, but the argument assumes a completeness of documentation on southern belief that we do not possess and a degree of isolation between north and south in matters of faith which is quite improbable (cf. Lohfink, *Bib* 49, 1968, 109f.). That the authors of Deuteronomy were formerly Levites unconnected with the cult, now attached to the Jerusalem temple, is, however, a probable conclusion. The teaching activity which the book presupposes is one which is in many passages associated with the priests at the sanctuaries (Dt. 33:8ff.; 31:9ff.; Hos. 4; Mic. 3:11; Zeph. 3:4; Jer. 18:18; Ezek. 7:26; 22:26; 2 Kg. 17:27ff.; Mal. 2:7ff., etc.). That these authors were Jerusalem temple priests who had formerly been without connection with the cult explains the strong interest of the book in both non-priestly Levites and Levites who hold or claim priestly status at the central sanctuary (see introduction to 18:1–8). This background explains also the authors' independence over against the orthodox tradition of the Jerusalem temple, with its emphasis on the election of Zion and of the Davidic king, and their reflection of non-cultic norms and attitudes to be found among the prophets. At the same time this context of origin brings the book into an area in which it is not so surprising that it should be edited in a way which should show influence from the treaties, for it is in the capital in particular that knowledge of these treaties and the theological reflection implied in their use in the editing of Deuteronomy would be found.

E. OUTLINE OF CONTENTS

   (*b*) *Periodic obligations and institutions (14:22–16:17)*
       (i) The law of tithing (14:22–29)
       (ii) The law of release (15:1–11)
       (iii) The release of slaves (15:12–18)
       (iv) The law on firstlings (15:19–23)
       (v) The festival calendar (16:1–17)
   (*c*) *Officials in the theocratic state (16:18–18:22)*
       (i) Judges and the purity of Israel's worship (16:18–
          17:7)
       (ii) The supreme court (17:8–13)
       (iii) The king (17:14–20)
       (iv) The Levitical priests (18:1–8)
       (v) The prophet (18:9–22)
   (*d*) *Laws on capital cases and on war (19:1–21:9)*
       (i) The cities of refuge (19:1–13)
       (ii) Theft of land and false witness (19:14–21)
       (iii) Preparation for holy war (20:1–9)
       (iv) The conduct of war (20:10–20)
       (v) The case of unsolved murder (21:1–9)
   (*e*) *Laws on respect for life, especially in family relationships*
     (21:10–22:30)
       (i) Laws on family relationships and the treatment
          of a criminal (21:10–23)
       (ii) Laws on respect for different forms of life (22:1–
          12)
       (iii) Laws on marriage and sexual relationships
          (22:13–30)
   (*f*) *Laws on purity and humanitarian behaviour in the people of*
     Yahweh (23:1–25:19)
       (i) Membership in the assembly of Yahweh (23:1–8)
       (ii) The cleanliness of the camp (23:9–14)
       (iii) Laws on the fugitive slave and cultic prosti-
          tution (23:15–18)
       (iv) Laws on interest, vows, and the property of
          one's neighbour (23:19–25)
       (v) Divorce and remarriage (24:1–4)
       (vi) Humanitarian behaviour, especially to the
          needy (24:5–25:4)
       (vii) The preservation of the family (25:5–12)
       (viii) Laws on trade and on Amalek (25:13–19)
   (*g*) *Two liturgical confessions (26:1–15)*

        (i) Ceremony for the offering of first-fruits (26:1–11)

        (ii) Ceremony for the offering of the triennial tithe (26:12–15)

  D. The sealing of the covenant (26:16–27:26)

     (a) *The covenant formula (26:16–19)*

     (b) *The writing of the law (27:1–8)*

     (c) *Israel is the people of Yahweh (27:9–10)*

     (d) *Blessing and curse on Gerizim and Ebal (27:11–13)*

     (e) *Prohibited behaviour in the people of Yahweh (27:14–26)*

  E. Declaration of the blessings and the curses (28:1–68)

III Third Address of Moses to Israel (29:1–30:20)

  A. Exhortation to obedience to the covenant law (29:1–9)

  B. Present and future generations enter into the covenant relationship (29:10–15)

  C. Warning against idolatrous worship (29:16–21)

  D. Punishment for disobedience (29:22–28)

  E. Repentance and restoration (29:29–30:14)

  F. Choice between life and death (30: 15–20)

IV Appendix (31:1–34:12)

  A. Moses' provision for the future (31:1–13)

     (a) *The institution of Joshua by Moses (31:1–8)*

     (b) *The future reading of the law (31:9–13)*

  B. Yahweh's provision for the future, and the Song of Moses (31:14–32:44)

     (a) *Yahweh's institution of Joshua and command to Moses to write the Song (31:14–23)*

     (b) *Provision for the preservation of the law (31:24–29)*

     (c) *The Song of Moses (31:30–32:44)*

  C. Conclusion (32:45–34:12)

     (a) *Conclusion to the law (32:45–47)*

     (b) *Announcement of Moses' death (32:48–52)*

     (c) *Moses' farewell blessing (33:1–29)*

     (d) *The death of Moses (34:1–12)*

DEUTERONOMY

I. The First Address of Moses to Israel: 1:1–4:43

A. INTRODUCTION: 1:1–5

This is a deuteronomistic passage, but it has been considerably expanded through the addition of material which is intended to give more precision to the deuteronomistic statements of time and place. The original passage is to be found in part of v. 1 **(These are the words that Moses spoke to all Israel beyond the Jordan . . . in the Arabah)** and in v. 4. V.2, which in its present form seems wholly irrelevant to the introduction, came in by two stages. First, v. 2*a* was brought in to link the place and time of Moses' address (v. 1*a*) to Horeb, where Moses had received from God what he is to proclaim now to the people (see v. 6). The places mentioned in the expansion of v. 1 apparently give stations on this eleven-day journey from Horeb. Secondly, v. 2*b* was added on the basis of the association of Kadesh-barnea and Paran (one of the places mentioned in the expansion of v. 1) in Num. 13:26. V. 3 is in the style of the Priestly writer and v. 5 is an isolated addition which fits awkwardly with the picture of the function of Moses already given in v. 1 (see comment).

Lohfink (*BZ* 6, 1962, 32 n. 2) has argued that the passage is a structural unit displaying a chiastic form. However, not only does the determination of this form require the omission of v. 2 as a gloss, but the parallels and repetitions are scarcely close enough in order that the possible presence of the form should justify the conclusion that the passage is an original unit (for example, the precision of v. 3*a* is not a good parallel to the vagueness of v. 4); yet it may be that the attempt to produce a chiastic form influenced the way in which additions were made to the original passage.

1. all Israel: this is a favourite expression of Deuteronomy and the deuteronomist (cf. for example 5:1; 11:6; 13:12; 18:6; 21:21; 27:9; 29:1; 31:1, 7; 34:12), and suits well Deuteronomy's exclusive concern with this people. **beyond the Jordan:** the *AV* translation ('on this side Jordan') preserves the standpoint of the author of this verse as that of Moses himself—east Jordan—while the *RSV* translation sets the author in west Jordan. Gemser (*VT* 2, 1952, 349ff.) prefers the translation 'at the side, in the region of the Jordan' (so giving no hint of the standpoint of the writer or speaker) in the light of the use of the phrase in Num. 32:19; Jos. 22:11 and 1 Chr. 26:30. However, none of these passages is precisely parallel, and the sense of 'region across' is clearly preserved in 3:8, 20, 25; 4:41, 46f.; 11:30. So, both here and in v. 5 the reference is to the region 'beyond the Jordan', and the standpoint of the speaker or writer is west Jordan. **in the wilderness, in the Arabah:** these two statements of place are difficult to harmonize. The Arabah is the depression through which the Jordan flows, in which the Dead Sea lies, and which continues southwards to the Gulf of Aqabah. The reference to it here as the place of the people at the time of Moses' address coincides with the information of 3:29, **wilderness** is a more general term; it might indeed include the Arabah (at least in its southern part, but it is likely that the reference to it has been added here in order to accommodate the list of places mentioned in the secondary expansion of this verse. **Suph**: in 3:29 (see also 34:6) the place is defined as 'opposite Beth-peor'. There is no way of harmonizing that with the geographical location of Suph in this verse. **Suph**, which appears only here in this form, is probably to be identified with *chirbet sūfe*, a short distance south-east of Medeba in the mountains of Moab (see Noth, *Studien*, 28 n. 3). Together with the other places mentioned in the rest of the verse, it belongs to the secondary expansion of the verse listing the places on the eleven-day journey from Horeb. **Paran:** the wilderness of Paran is that which separates Horeb/Sinai from Kadesh (Num. 10:12; 12:16; 13:3, 26). It probably took its name from a particular site named Paran (cf. 1 Kg. 11:18), though the precise location of this is unknown. **Tophel:** referred to only here. Its location is unknown, but it is often identified with the modern *eṭ-Tafile* in Edom, about 15 miles south-south-east of the Dead Sea. Cazelles (*VT* 9, 1959, 412) points to the region of Diblathaim, north of Moab, as more suitable to the present context; but since the places mentioned here probably come from a list of wilderness stations their present literary context is an unreliable guide to their original location. **Laban:** this place is not referred to otherwise in the Old Testament, but it does occur in an Egyptian text from the time of Šošenq I and an Assyrian text from Sargon II; it is perhaps to be situated south of Raphia, near the Brook of Egypt (cf. Aharoni,

Land, 44, 139, 334). **Hazeroth:** it is mentioned in Num. 11:35; 33:17f., but is of unknown location. **Dizahab:** also unknown, but perhaps to be identified with *ed-dhēbe* in Moab.

2. It is eleven days' journey from Horeb by the way of Mount Seir: this addition is the basis for the expansion of v. 1*b*; it also links the event of Moses' address to Israel to the preceding account in Exodus-Numbers of the divine revelation on Horeb/ Sinai and the wilderness wandering. **Horeb:** this is the name given in E (Exod. 3:1; 17:6; 33:6) and Deuteronomy (1:2, 6, 19; 4:10, 15, etc.) to the mountain known as Sinai by J and P. They may have been originally two distinct mountains, or, more likely, Horeb was originally the designation of a region ('desolate place') in which Sinai lay, and gradually came to be understood as simply synonymous with Sinai. The Old Testament at any rate clearly identifies them as the one mountain of the revelation of God to Israel. The traditional identification of the mountain with Jebel Musa in the southern Sinai peninsula is perhaps still most widely favoured; yet it is far from certain and is in fact not easily accommodated to several Old Testament references. For a discussion of the possibilities, see Hyatt, *Exodus*, 203ff. **Mount Seir:** this is usually taken to refer to the mountainous region east of the Arabah. Bartlett (*JTS* 20, 1969, 1ff.) provides a detailed discussion which argues strongly in favour of its location west of the Arabah in the highland south of Beersheba, while its connections with the east through Esau and Edom are later developments. **Kadesh-barnea:** to be identified with 'Ain el-Qudeirat, a wilderness oasis about 50 miles south of Beersheba, and a traditional station of the wandering Israelites, whence they sent spies into the land (Num. 13f.).

3. This is a late verse with close parallels only in P, cf. Gen. 7:11; 8:13; Exod. 16:1; 19:1; 40:17; Num. 1:1; 9:1; 10:11; 33:3. The grammatical form for **eleventh** is also late (see GK, 290 n.1). This is the only such precise dating that we find in Deuteronomy; its object, like that of the list of places in vv. 1f., is to link Deuteronomy with what precedes. It derives, therefore, from the time of the connection of the deuteronomistic history with the Tetrateuch (see Introduction, p. 47).

4. On Israel's victories over **Sihon** and **Og** see Num. 21:21–35. The subject is alluded to fairly frequently in the deuteronomistic history (cf. Dt. 2:26ff., 3:1ff.; 4:46f.; 29:7f.; 31:4; Jos. 2:10; 9:10; 12:2ff.; 13:10ff.). The verse is a continuation of v. 1*a*,

being the original deuteronomistic introduction, analogous to
4:44, 46. On **Amorites** see comment on v.7. **Heshbon,** Sihon's
capital, lay about 15 miles east of the northern end of the Dead
Sea. **in Ashtaroth and in Edrei:** in Num. 2:33 Og is simply the
'king of Bashan', but in Jos. 12:4 he is described as living 'at
Ashtaroth and at Edrei'. In the present text there is no conjunction between 'Ashtaroth' and 'Edrei', so that **in Edrei** should
strictly be construed with **had defeated** (see *NEB* translation,
and also Dt. 3:1*b*). The *RSV* translation finds support in the LXX,
Syriac, and Vulgate, as well as in Jos. 12:4, but it is in fact most
likely that **in Edrei** is a simple addition to the present text, taken
from Dt. 3:1. **Ashtaroth** is named as the residence of Og in
Jos. 9:10; its location is uncertain. **Edrei** may have been a second
royal city; it is to be identified with the modern *Edreʿāt*, on the
southern border of Bashan, about 30 miles east of the Sea of
Galilee.

5. to explain: the verb used here is very infrequent, appearing
otherwise only in Dt. 27:8; Hab. 2:2. The meaning 'interpret' or
'explain' is derived mainly from the ancient versions and supported by reference to an Accadian root, to late Hebrew and
Jewish Aramaic. However, from its use in Dt. 27:8 and Hab. 2:2
it clearly cannot be separated from the notion of 'writing' or
'engraving', so that Moses is then presented here as the one who
made a first written record of his teaching. The verse is probably an isolated addition, based on and taking up terminology
from the deuteronomistic 1:1*a* and also 27:8; its intention is
to correct any impression that 27:8 might give that the written
form of the law only appeared after the settlement in the land.
In it Moses is presented as a scribe rather than as a proclaimer of
the law, which is his function otherwise (see Mittmann, *Deuteronomium 1:1–6:3*, 14f.). Moreover, as Plöger (*Untersuchungen* 117f.)
has indicated, the verse clearly presupposes that what follows is an
introduction to the giving of the law; but this is not the original
intention of the following section.

this law: the word *tôrāh*, which is here translated **law** is in
Deuteronomy confined to its framework (4:8, 44; 24:26; 27:3,
8, 26; 28:58, 61; 29:20, 28; 30:10; 31:9, 11, 12; 32:46) apart
from 17:11, 18, 19 (see comment). It refers to the law of Moses
as it actually exists within chs. 5–26. The word is probably to be
connected with the Accadian *tērtu*, 'oracle', so that 'teaching' or
'instruction' is perhaps a better translation than 'law'. Yet a

certain legalism is apparent in the use of the term in Deuteronomy, for it is in practice almost synonymous with 'the commandment and the statutes and the ordinances' used elsewhere (for example, 5:31; 6:1; cf. 12:1, etc.). More detailed discussion of these terms may be found in Braulik, *Bib* 51, 1970, 39ff.; Lindars, in *Words*, 117ff.

B. HISTORICAL REVIEW: 1:6–3:11

This section is a historical review of Israel's history from Horeb to the borders of the promised land. The unity of this section as the work of the deuteronomist is shown by its structure and content. A framework in 1:6–8, 19; 2:1, 8, 13*b*–15; 3:1, 8, uses the first person plural, refers regularly to the land as promised by Yahweh to Israel's ancestors, which the descendants of the present generation will possess, and provides a link between the elements of old tradition taken up by the deuteronomist. These elements are the traditional account of the appointment of judges, the sending of spies, and the beginning of the conquest. The deuteronomist has incorporated them, modifying them in some respects to suit his own viewpoint (especially in relation to his picture of Moses), but not obscuring his literary dependence on the older stories.

Baltzer, *Covenant Formulary*, 31ff., sees in this review the historical prologue of the covenant formulary, which then continued into ch. 4 with stipulations, sanctions, witness and blessing formula. However, the relationship of the present text to the covenant formulary is not a close or immediate one. 4:1–40 is in fact an independent unit; and chs. 1–4 taken together constitute a severely imbalanced version of the covenant formulary. The covenant demands, which otherwise are central, are here almost lost in exhortation. Chs. 1–3 and ch. 4 are certainly influenced by the covenant form, and it may be this which has brought them together; but they do not form an original unit conceived on that basis. Chs. 1–3 point beyond themselves as the introduction to an account of the settlement of the land west of Jordan. The dominant theme of the chapters (Israel the people of God, whose history is directed by the command and action of God) and the subsidiary themes (the place of the human leader, the holy war, acts of disobedience by the people leading to defeat in war) are continued into the book of Joshua, with which there is also clear stylistic affinity (compare 2:24 and Jos. 6:2, etc.). In other words, these chapters have been composed as an introduction to the deuteronomistic history, rather than to Deuteronomy. The concern with Israel's faithlessness and how it works itself out in her history is the basic deuteronomistic preoccupation.

(A) THE APPOINTMENT OF DIVISIONAL LEADERS AND THE CHARGING OF JUDGES: **1:6–18**

Vv. 6–8 form the first part of the deuteronomistic framework which brings together episodes from Israel's past history. This framework takes up again in v. 19. This does not mean, however, that vv. 9–18 are a late insertion into that context; the verses were in fact brought in here by the author of 1:6–8, 19, the deuteronomist. In 1:9–18 he is referring back to Israel's old traditions, and is using them to carry the particular impressions which otherwise come through in his own independent compositions. Within 1:9–18 two related subjects are treated (on the relationship see comment on v. 15): the appointment of divisional heads of the people and the charging of the judges. The main source in the older tradition is Exod. 18 where, at the suggestion of his father-in-law Jethro 'Moses chose able men out of all Israel, and made them heads over the people, rulers of thousands, of hundreds, of fifties and of tens. And they judged the people at all times; hard cases they brought to Moses, but any small matter they decided themselves' (Exod. 18:25f.). A second source is Num. 11, whence the deuteronomist has taken up and modified the theme of Moses' complaint of his inability to 'bear' the people alone, together with the title 'officers' for those appointed to assist him (Num. 11:16; Dt. 1:15). Supplementary material is derived from unknown sources (see comment on v. 17), while the whole has been expressed in a form suitable to the deuteronomist's own view.

There is a close literary relationship between Deuteronomy and its sources in Exodus and Numbers in this section (compare Dt. 1:9b. 10, 12 and Num. 11:14, 17b; Dt. 1:15, 17b, 18 and Exod. 18:20, 21b, 22a, 25, 26), close enough to justify the conclusion that the deuteronomist is making use of precisely these literary sources. There is no convincing evidence of the existence of a source independent of Exod. 18 and Num. 11 on which these passages and Dt. 1:9–18 depend. Such differences as exist between Deuteronomy and Exod. 18/Num. 11 (see Plöger, *Untersuchungen*, 31f.) concern matters on which the Exodus and Numbers accounts do not agree (for example, whether the event

took place before arrival at Sinai or at the time of departure
from there) or arise from an addition to the text of Deuteronomy
(see comment on v. 15), or are to be ascribed to the particular
concerns of the deuteronomist, on the basis of which he has
modified the information with which his sources supplied him.
His main concern is that Moses should be exonerated from all
blame for the disasters which overtook the people. So, while in
Num. 11 Moses is violent in his complaint to God, in Dt. 1:9ff.
this complaint is softened out of existence to the point that the
cause of it now becomes a reason for praise because of the fulfilment of the divine promise to the patriarchs. There now no
longer exists any sin on the part of Moses in this matter. So also
while in Exodus it is Moses himself who takes the responsibility
for choosing rulers for the people, here in Dt. 1:13ff. it is
the people themselves who choose their commanders and consequently bear the responsibility for their choice. This is particularly
relevant in the present overall context of the people's rebellion
against the commandment of Yahweh to take possession of the land.

6. The Lord our God: a very frequent phrase in Deuteronomy,
but seldom elsewhere in the Pentateuch (Exod. 3:18; 5:3; 8:6,
22, 23; 10:25, 26). Other forms of the phrase, such as 'the Lord
your God', are even more frequent in Deuteronomy.

7. hill country: this need not necessarily refer to actual
mountain territory. Much more generally it can be used simply
for 'land', as in 3:25; Exod. 15:17; Ps. 78:54; for Ugaritic parallels see Cross and Freedman, *JNES* 14, 1955, 249f. **Amorites**:
for the 2nd millennium BC this term is used in Accadian to denote
direction westwards, and designates the nomadic people of the
Syrian steppes. In Mari, 'Amurru' is a specific political state in
central Syria. There is no example of the use of Amorite from the
2nd millennium to include Palestine or Transjordan or any part
of them. After the end of the state of Amurru in the late 13th
century or early 12th century there was no longer any distinct
Amorite group. In the Old Testament Amorite is sometimes the
name of a state (e.g. Jos. 13:4), but not a state which includes
Palestine or Transjordan. A second Old Testament usage, however, is as a general designation of Syria and Palestine and of the
pre-Israelite population of this area; this usage too has extra-
biblical roots. It goes back to Assyrian texts of the 9th and 8th
centuries in which all the people of the west are regarded as
belonging to the country of Amurru. On the term see van Seters,

Abraham, 43ff; Liverani, in *Peoples*, 100ff. If the phrase **hill country of the Amorites** is then taken as a general designation of the whole land which Israel is to possess, then the rest of v. 7 should be understood as a closer definition of what this in fact includes. Grammatically this is perfectly possible, the conjunction following **Amorites** being taken as an emphatic *waw* (which could be left untranslated or rendered 'even' cf. Wernberg-Moller, *JSS* 3, 1958, 321ff.). In this case too the word translated **neighbours** would be better understood as 'inhabitants' as in Isa. 33:24; Hos. 10:5. This treatment of the verse conforms best with v. 19. **Arabah**: see comment on v. 1. **in the hill country:** here the reference must be specifically to the mountain territory of Palestine. **the lowland:** the term used is *sh^epēlāh*, which designates the low hill country between the mountains of Judah and the plain of Philistia, perhaps also including the plain; Jos. 15:33–47 lists the cities which lay in the *sh^epēlāh* (some of them being cities of the plain), and so gives an impression of its extent. **Negeb:** the word means 'south'; but it is clear particularly from Gen. 13:1 that it was also the proper designation of a particular geographical area. It denotes the pasture land or wilderness which lies between the southern hill country and the desert. **the land of the Canaanites:** the *NEB* translation takes this as a reference to the land of Canaan generally. This may be so, in which case this together with **and Lebanon** would be a summary description of what is meant by **the hill country of the Amorites.** Alternatively, **the land of the Canaanites** may be a reference only to **the seacoast.** Jos. 13:3f. seems to indicate that the coastal plains in particular were considered the **land of the Canaanites.** The extent of the land described here conforms broadly with 11:24 and Jos. 1:4. The basis of these descriptions, all of which belong in the context of the divine promise of land to Israel, lies in Gen. 15:18ff., the covenant of promise of land to Abram, which in turn probably reflects the extent of the Israelite empire under David (cf. 2 Sam. 8:3).

8. Behold, I have set the land before you: there is some evidence that the legal transfer of property was effected by means of presenting it in the sight of the new owner. If so, then the present passage should be understood in this context. The land is shown to Israel (in the form of the detailed description in the preceding verse), and Israel thus takes possession of it. It is now hers as the gift of Yahweh; cf. Lohfink, *Bib.* 41, 1960, 124ff., and,

further, comment on 34:1ff. **which the Lord swore:** since this
is still apparently divine speech, one would expect 'I swore' as in
the LXX. However. the *MT* reading should probably be retained as
the *lectio difficilior*. It cannot be explained as a fixed formula since
there is considerable variation in the form of expression of this
promise in Deuteronomy (cf. e.g. 6:18, 23; 8:1; 10:11). But
such inconsistency is not perhaps unexpected in a context in
which Moses is reporting a speech of Yahweh. For this promise,
which is of great significance for Deuteronomy (see Introduction,
pp. 79ff.), cf. Gen. 12:7; 15:18; 76:3; 28:13.

9. Moses' complaint is no longer addressed to God, as in Num.
11, but to the people. So immediately the possibility that Moses
might deserve censure for lack of faith is removed. **At that time:**
the time presupposed here, the point of departure from Horeb,
agrees with Num. 11 rather than with Exod. 18.

10. The deuteronomist's sources in Exod. 18 and Num. 11 give
two reasons for Moses' complaint. One is the great number of the
people with whom he must deal, and the other the burden of their
continual strife and murmuring. Both of these are taken up by
the deuteronomist. The first, which is more implicit than explicit
in the sources, is here given rather extended treatment. The
deuteronomist clearly wished to correct any impression that the
sources might give that the multiplication of the people is itself a
cause of complaint. It is God who has multiplied the people, so
that they have become **as the stars of heaven.** This phrase is
taken from the tradition of the promise to the patriarchs (Gen.
22:17; 26:4; Exod. 32:13; cf. Gen. 15:5), and, following v. 8, is
the second of the two promises which dominate the old patriarchal
traditions. V. 11 then explicitly links the multiplication of the
people to the patriarchal promise.

11. The view that v. 11 is an addition (Mittmann, *Deuteronomium
1:1–6:3*, 24) because it breaks into Moses' complaint, because it
speaks of the future rather than the past, and because it contains
a different divine title from that used elsewhere in the chapter
(v. 6, 10, 19f., 30, 32, 41, etc.; though cf. v. 21), is not convincing.
The deuteronomist's intention is to tone down Moses' complaint
as much as possible, in the process of exonerating him from all
blame for the misfortunes of the people. This process has already
begun in v. 10 where the clear allusion to the promise to the
patriarchs turns the multiplication of the people into an occasion
for praise rather than for complaint. The divine title **the Lord the**

God of your fathers belongs to this patriarchal tradition, and, while it is not typical of the deuteronomistic style, this style does appear at the end of the verse in the words **and bless you, as he has promised you,** cf. 6:19; 7:13; 9:3.

12. The reason mentioned here for the appointment of assistants for Moses is taken from Num. 11. However, of the three words used to characterize the people and their behaviour: **weight, burden** and **strife,** only one is in fact derived from Num. 11. This is **burden** together with its verb root 'to bear' (cf. Num. 11:11, 14, 17). By bringing in the other terms the deuteronomist has both strengthened the effect of the one derived from Num. 11 and has also vividly described what the attitude of the people really amounts to. **weight** (*ṭōraḥ*) is used otherwise only in Isa. 1:14 where Israel's festivals and cultic activities are described as a weight which Yahweh hates and is weary of bearing. Its sense is thus considerably stronger than that of **burden** (*massāʾ*), a word which can be used simply for the load borne by an animal (cf. Exod. 23:5; 2 Kg. 5:17; 8:9). **strife** (*rîb*) is a legal term which is used in general both for proceedings which lead up to a court case and for the court proceedings themselves (cf. Exod. 23:2, 3, 6; Dt. 21:5; 25:1; 2 Sam. 15:2, 4), and in particular, as the use of the verb in Jg. 21:22; Jer. 2:29; 12:1 shows especially, could be used for a speech of accusation. In the context of the sources on which the deuteronomist is drawing here, he is in effect showing Israel as accusing God and Moses of failure to provide for them in the wilderness. This verse is not, therefore, a simple explication of v. 9 indicating what the multiplication of the people involved as far as their leadership is concerned. Rather, it stands in stark contrast to v. 9: in spite of God's fulfilment of his promise to the patriarchs, Israel is a weight and a burden which responds only in accusation.

13. The qualifications given here which are required of those to be appointed differ from those given in Exod. 18:21. While there 'able men . . . such as fear God, men who are trustworthy and who hate a bribe' lays emphasis on their moral qualities (the first part of this description perhaps including also their military prowess), in the present passage it is on the basis of their wisdom that they are to be chosen. This change is perhaps indicative of the wisdom influence on Deuteronomy which is otherwise so marked (see Introduction, pp. 104f. **understanding:** this is not repeated with the other two terms in v. 15, and so may be an addition here. It is a frequent wisdom term (see, for example,

Prov. 1:5; 10:13; 14:6, and its use along with 'wise' to describe Joseph as minister of Pharaoh, Gen. 41:33, 39). **experienced:** this translation presupposes the active form of the participle of the verb *yāḏaʿ*, 'know', rather than the passive which is actually used here. The *NEB* translation '(of) repute' is) therefore, perhaps better (however, see also the discussion in Emerton, *JSS* 15, 1970, 175f.). The proposal to read the active participle form (so Bertholet; Weinfeld, *Deuteronomy* 244n. 2), to give the translation 'knowledgeable' or 'experienced', would yield a synonym of the preceding terms and finds some support in Job 34:2; Ec. 9:11. **as your heads:** the title has both military and judicial associations; see the study by Bartlett, *VT* 19, 1969, 1ff. For the translation of the preposition *bᵉ* by 'as' rather than 'at' (which is its translation in 1 Kg. 21:12), see GK, § 119 i (the *beth essentiae*).

15. In two respects this verse apparently presents some inconsistency with its context. Firstly, while in v. 13 it is the people who choose their own leaders, here it appears to be Moses. However, there is in fact no inconsistency here. V.15 is true to its source in Exod. 18:25 in describing how Moses **set** the heads over the people; but while Exod. 18:25 also ascribes the 'choosing' of these heads to Moses, Dt. 1:15 does not. Rather, Moses **took** those who had already been chosen by the people (v. 13). In vv. 13–15 the deuteronomist is clearly concerned to lay the responsibility for the choice on the people themselves, rather than on Moses. It must be the latter's function, however, to appoint those chosen. The second inconsistency cannot be resolved so easily. In v. 13 the criteria which determine the choice of the leaders is that they be 'wise, understanding and experienced' men. In v. 15, however, the situation is quite different: it is now on the basis of the position that they already occupy that the leaders are chosen; they are **the heads of your tribes.** The LXX felt this difficulty, and substituted 'from you', as in v. 23; this is not an original reading, but undoubtedly represents an attempt to ease the difficulty. Probably **the heads of your tribes** should be omitted as an addition, but the origin of it is not at all clear. If the addition suggests that the number of those chosen was twelve, then there is some conflict with Exod. 18 (where no number is given) and Num. 11 (which has seventy elders). **commanders:** as 1 Kings 4:2 indicates, this is a general term for 'officials'; however, the organization of the people to which they are appointed (**commanders of thousands, commanders of hundreds . . .**) suggests military associations in particular. On the other hand, the criteria on the basis of which they are appointed, along with what is explicitly stated in vv. 16f., indicate judicial functions also. The appointment of professional judges in Israel to take over from the elders the administration of justice belongs to the time of Jehoshaphat (cf. 2 Chr. 19:5ff., and comment on Dt. 16:18), and there is also evidence from about this time of the combination of judicial and military functions in one figure (a combination of which Exod. 18 gives an aetiological account), cf. 1 Kg. 22:26. See the discussion in Knierim, *ZAW* 32, 1961, 146ff. **officers:** the precise meaning of *šōṭ̥rîm* is difficult to determine. The term is apparently related to an Arabic root *saṭara* 'write'. In the Old Testament they appear with the elders (Num. 11:16) and the judges (Dt. 16:18; Jos. 8:33; perhaps this association explains the LXX reading 'as your judges' for **throughout your tribes**), as well as in particularly military contexts (Dt. 20:5, 8, 9; Jos. 1:10; 3:2). They are clearly administrative officials to be found in different contexts. The phrase **and officers throughout your tribes** appears quite superfluous in this verse. The organization of the people is already covered, and the phrase has no root in the Exod. 18 source. The deuteronomist has probably taken the word **officers** from his other source in Num. 11:16, but has included the whole phrase here primarily on the basis of the legal and military associations of the term in Dt. 16:18; 20:5, 8, 9. Perhaps the conjunction before **officers** should be taken as emphatic (as in v. 7) and left untranslated or rendered 'even'; then the **officers** would be a summary reference to all the commanders of the various divisions.

16. Vv. 16 and 17 apparently have little connection with the context since it is only here that **judges** are explicitly mentioned. However, clearly the criteria given for choice in v. 13 point to a judicial function, and this anchors vv. 16 and 17 firmly in their place. **brethren:** this, and the singular 'brother', appear frequently in Deuteronomy, and express the nationalistic focus of the book. The laws are designed for Israelites who are brothers; non-Israelites who may be living within the borders of Israel are specifically referred to when anything that might affect them is mentioned. **the alien:** the word *gēr* is also translated 'sojourner' (cf. 5:14; 14:29). The reference is to a landless and therefore economically weak individual, who, for some reason, is living either temporarily or permanently away from the land of his own tribe or people. In Deuteronomy he is a non-Israelite, though this is not an original characteristic. In older records there are Israelite *gērîm* living within Israel (see comment on 18:6). The *gēr* is regularly commended to the charity of Israelites (e.g. 14:29; 16:11, 14; 26:11), but for a long period he lived without the protection of the law (cf. 15:3; 23:21). In the deuteronomistic history it is possible to discern a tendency towards making him responsible before the law, and so also giving him the protection of the law (1:16; 29:10f.; 31:12); this process comes to full development in P, where the sentence 'there shall be one law for the native and for the stranger who sojourns among you' expresses P's view (Exod. 12:49; Lev. 24:22, etc., cf. Lev. 16:29; 17:8ff., etc.). See the discussion in de Vaux, *Ancient Israel*, 74ff.

17. V. 17a is in singular form of address in the LXX, in contrast to the plural address of the context. It is difficult not to accept the LXX version as the original, and the *MT* as a harmonizing modification. If this is so, then v. 17a is probably an addition here—a conclusion suggested also by the fullness of the description of the *functions* of the judges in a general context which is concerned rather with organization. If so, it is a free elaboration (based on Exod. 18:21 and Dt. 16:19) of the functions of the judges which is given in general terms in v. 16b. **the judgment is God's:** the judge administers the law which derives from God, and does so on behalf of God, cf. Exod. 18:15f.; 2 Chr. 19:6. It is unnecessary to translate the preposition *lᵉ* here as 'from' (so Loretz, *BZ* 2, 1958, 287) on the basis of the sense it sometimes has in Ugaritic. None of the Old Testament passages quoted in support (1 Sam. 17:47; 2 Kg 13:17; Pss. 81:5b; 85:9; Prov 16:11a) is convincing. Cazelles (*VTS* 15, 1966, 110f.) suggests that this is a formula deriving from the wisdom context. Its closest Old Testament parallel is to be found in Prov. 16: 33. The last part of the verse has its historical background in the right of appeal to the central court established by Jehoshaphat in Jerusalem; see comment on 17:8–13.

18. This summarizing verse, probably addressed to the people generally rather than to the judges specifically, has the intention of emphasizing that the people were fully provided for from Horeb onwards, so making their subsequent actions the more reprehensible.

(B) THE SENDING OF SPIES AND REBELLION AGAINST GOD: **1:19–46**
The character of the preceding section is to be found also here. After the framework v. 19 the deuteronomist takes up the story of

the spies in Num. 13f., but introduces some modifications in order to make the story more suitable to his overall theme. Apart from a few isolated additions brought in for various reasons (see comment on vv. 21, 24, 37f., 46), these verses are the work of the deuteronomist taking up older material.

As with the preceding section so here the literary dependence of the deuteronomist on earlier tradition may be established, while at the same time it is clear that the deuteronomist was not so bound to his source that he felt unable to adapt it more or less freely. A comparison of the following passages is sufficient to establish a literary link: v. 24a/Num. 13:17b, 23; v. 25a/Num. 13: 20b; v. 28b/Num. 13:28; v. 35/Num. 14:23a; v. 40/Num. 14: 25b; v. 42/Num. 14:42; and on vv. 41–45, see Num. 14:39–45. It is difficult to be certain about the precise nature of all points of contact; in Num. 13f. there is a basic J tradition which has had a P editing, so some contacts between Num. 13f. and Dt. 1 may be the result of P use of material in Dt. 1, rather than deuteronomistic use of J material in Num. 13f. However, the parallel passages in Num. 13f. quoted above are all generally recognized as J, and there is no doubt of the direction in which dependence lies. Moreover, in another important respect Dt. 1 shows clear dependence on the specifically J tradition of Num. 13f. This is in the fact that only Caleb is explicitly excepted from the 'evil generation' and promised admittance into the land (even if vv. 37f. are not an addition here, on which see comment, they mention Joshua only as the necessary successor to Moses as leader of the people and not as one bearing no blame for the disobedience of the people.) This is the case also in the J story of Num. 13f.; it is P which has brought in Joshua alongside and on the same terms as Caleb in Num. 13f.

The general viewpoint and concerns of the deuteronomist, already seen in vv. 9–18, are continued into this section: the misfortunes of the people are the result of the people's disobedience of the commands of Yahweh. Their leader, Moses, bears no individual responsibility. From a concern to show this there derive the general emphasis of the deuteronomistic story and the specific differences which may be established between these verses and the source in Num. 13f. So, in v. 22 it is the people who request that spies be sent (Num. 13:1f., which makes the sending of spies divine command to Moses, is P. However, J does emphasize that it is Moses who sent the spies in Num 13:27. This is not the case in Dt.

1). In v. 25, only the encouraging report of the spies is mentioned, while in v. 28 there is simply an allusion to those difficulties which, according to the source in Num. 13:28f., featured largely in their report. In this way the deuteronomist emphasizes the land as the good gift of Yahweh and the reaction of the people as distrustful and faithless disobedience. This disobedience is not, moreover, a matter of dispute between the people and Moses, as in Num. 13f.; rather, it is rebellion against the command of God (vv. 32, 43).

In one respect the deuteronomist's use of his source in this section shows a considerable difference over against 1:9–18. Whereas the deuteronomist's account in the latter section may be read independently as a self-contained and complete story, here that is not possible: here the deuteronomist not only uses a source but presupposes his readers' knowledge of that source. So, v. 28 refers to an aspect of the report of the spies which, though not excluded by what is told us of that report in v. 25, is not earlier hinted at; v. 36 excepts Caleb from the sentence of exclusion from the land, though no motivation for doing so is given here; v. 39 refers to an aspect of the people's fearful reaction to the adverse report of conditions in the land, though of this too there is no earlier hint in this chapter. In all three cases knowledge of the older tradition is presupposed, for it is here that the information is provided (see comment on vv. 28, 36, 39).

The general character of the story in Num. 13f. is that of an aetiological account concerned with Caleb's eventual possession of Hebron; this has secondarily become a story of an attempted settlement of the land by all Israel (for a study, see Noth, *Pentateuchal Traditions*, 130ff.). In Deuteronomy the primary concern of the story is with Israel and the problem of faith in her relationship with God. The aetiological concern of the old story does not appear (there is no reference to Hebron), and only the prominence of Caleb in the old story has forced the deuteronomist to make particular reference to him here (v. 36), even at the expense of creating some tension with his preoccupation elsewhere with the people in general (vv. 22, 26, 35, 39). This new emphasis on the part of the deuteronomist has its background in his historical situation: the present time of exile is the result of lack of faith and disobedience to the will of Yahweh. The promise of the land, which is a good land, remains in force, however, even if only for the next generation.

19. which you saw: the phrase does not fit well with its context which is in the first person plural style; but it has an emphatic function, serving to set v. 26 in strong contrast, and so also to emphasize the more the ingratitude and disobedience of the people.

20. On **the hill country of the Amorites,** here and in v. 19, as a general expression for the whole land which Israel is to possess, see comment on v. 7.

21. This verse uses the second person singular form of address while the context uses second person plural. The plural of the LXX here is undoubtedly a harmonizing change from the original singular. The phrases used have parallels either in v. 8 or elsewhere in the deuteronomistic literature (see v. 29; Jos. 1:6, 9). Apart from its use of the second person singular form of address, there are other reasons for taking the verse as an addition: it is redundant in its context; it portrays Moses as issuing the command whereas in v. 8 it is Yahweh. It may well be an addition brought in at this point on the basis of the order of events in vv. 7 and 8. Yet it is not untrue to the deuteronomistic view. Moses is here starkly contrasted with the faithless people.

22. Then: the *NEB* 'but' heightens the element of defiance of Moses and God on the part of the people even at this early point. This is in contrast to P (Num. 13:2), where it is at the divine command that the spies are sent into the land, and J (Num. 13:17, 27), according to which Moses himself sent the spies.

23. The only parallel to this in Num. 13 (v. 2) is a P passage; but it is probable that the original J narrative also had a similar process of selection.

24. Valley: *naḥal* is also translated 'brook' (e.g. 2:13; 9:21). Neither that nor **valley** is adequate to the true sense of the term. The word which perhaps best corresponds to it is the Arabic *wadi*: it is a valley gouged out by water, which in the rainy season may be filled with an impassable torrent but in the summer may be completely dry. The word denotes both the valley itself and the torrent of water which flows through it. **Eshcol:** the word means 'cluster', with reference to the fruits of this fertile valley; it was located near Hebron, according to Num. 13:22f. **and spied it out:** the word **it** is feminine, and has no antecedent, since **hill country** and **valley** are masculine nouns. The verb, moreover, is different from that used in v. 22 ('explore'), and the phrase has no counterpart in the parallel passage in Num. 13:23.

It should probably be taken as an addition (v. 25 then follows on more naturally), though its origin is not clear. The P account in Num. 13f. consistently uses a different verb (*tûr*, Num. 13:2, 17, 21, etc.).

25. Plöger (*Untersuchungen*, 50f.) has suggested that 1:20–32 has a concentric structure, based on the order of speakers: Moses speaks (vv. 20, 31f.), the people speak (vv. 22, 27f.), Moses reports (vv. 23ff., 26), the spies speak (v. 25). Prominence is thus given to the report of the spies as the centre and focus of the construction. Although the proposed structure contains only a part of the whole spy story, it may well be that it was deliberately used here in order to highlight the good gift of Yahweh, and contrast this with the ungrateful response of Israel. **and brought us word again:** this phrase is lacking in the LXX, and may be an addition here based on the P passage Num. 13:26.

26. In the spy stories of Jos. 2, 7 and Jg. 18, the report of the spies is immediately followed by the advance of the people into the land or area to be taken. In the present account, which even in the type of report delivered by the spies follows the model of these other spy stories, the pattern suddenly breaks down. A literary pattern, that of the spy story, is effectively used and then suddenly broken at this point to highlight the people's rejection of the leadership of Yahweh.

27. The expected course of events, following the report of the spies, is Israel's attack on the land in the form of a holy war under Yahweh (see comment on 20:1ff.). Israel's faithlessness is so incompatible with the intention of God that the sequel to the report of the spies is described in a reverse form to the holy war descriptions (cf. Buis; Buis-Leclercq). **in your tents:** the traditional order of demobilization may have been 'everyone to his tents, O Israel'. It is a cry used by Sheba in his rebellion against David (2 Sam. 10:1), and by the northern tribes in their revolt against Rehoboam (1 Kg. 12:16), and is referred to in a demobilization context in Jos. 22:4. **the Lord hated us:** so also 9:28, while in 7:8 (cf. also 4:37) it is because of his love for Israel that Yahweh brought them out of Egypt. **to give us into the hand of the Amorites:** the true purpose of Yahweh's leadership of Israel in war was to give Israel's enemies into her hand (2:24; 3:2, etc.). **to destroy us:** in the holy war it is the enemies who are to suffer this fate (7:23, 12:30, etc.).

28. This verse cannot be understood from the context of Dt.1. Only against a background of knowledge of what the source in

Num. 13f. contains concerning the report of the spies is it possible to reconcile what is said here with v. 25. **going up:** in contrast to 'the Lord brought us *forth* . . .', the formula 'the Lord brought us *up* . . .' is particularly associated with the theme of the settlement of the land and so also with the holy war (cf. Wijngaards, *VT* 15, 1965, 91ff.; see also 20:1). The inverted use of the holy war vocabulary is then continued in **our brethren have made our hearts melt,** for it is usually Yahweh who makes the hearts of Israel's enemies melt (Jos. 2:11; 5:1). Jos. 14:8 uses this phrase with reference to the same event as here, but it does not appear in Num. 13. This part of the verse seems rather to be modelled on the holy war regulation of 20:8, according to which, if the heart of the people melts the holy war cannot take place. The explicit complaint mentioned here does have its roots in Num. 13 (v. 28, where, though the precise expressions are rather different, the order of the three elements of the complaint is identical). **Greater and taller . . . great and fortified:** these words appear regularly in Deuteronomy as part of a confession of the power of Yahweh who dispossesses such peoples (4:38; 7:1; 9:1f.; 11:23). The situation here is reversed, and the words express the terrified anxiety of the faithless Israel (cf. Lohfink, *Bib* 41, 1960, 110f.). **the sons of Anakim :** a mixture of two expressions: 'the Anakim' and 'the sons of Anak'. These people formed part of the ancient population of Palestine, terrible in their gigantic stature, cf. Num. 13:33; Dt. 2:10f., 21; 9:2. They are referred to in the Egyptian execration texts from the early part of the second millennium (Wright), and in the context of Israel's actual settlement, in Jos. 11:21; 14:15; 15:13f. They are mostly connected with southern Palestine, especially Hebron.

29. do not be in dread: again in 7:21; 20:3; 31:6. Vv. 29 and 30 summarize the speech of the priest before battle, cf. 20:3f., but the actual roots of vv. 29–33 in fact lie in the Red Sea story of Exod. 13f.(cf. Exod. 14:13, 14). But then the people believed (Exod. 14:30f.) while now the people do not believe (v. 32.) Just as in earlier verses of this chapter holy war elements have been used in an inverted way, so here elements of the Exodus story have likewise been inverted (see Lohfink, *Bib* 41, 1960, 119f.). The Exodus, the primary event of Israel's history, was in the old tradition an occasion for faith; in the deuteronomistic history the first event of Israel's history is an occasion for faithlessness.

30. The beginning of this verse too uses phrases **(goes before**

you. . . will fight for you) from Exod. 13:21; 14:14, which are
rooted in the Exodus tradition. **before your eyes** as in v. 19
('which you saw') the deuteronomist is at pains to emphasize the
reality of the history for those he is addressing, even at the expense
of some inconsistency: according to the form of presentation this
is an address of Moses to a generation which had not experienced
the events to which he refers (cf. 2:16).

31. V. 31*a* is in second person singular form of address, breaking
the plural context. It is, moreover, superfluous in the continuity of
sense and content, and may be an addition aimed at elucidating
the phrase **in all the way that you went** with which in fact it is
synonymous. **as a man bears his son:** the father–son analogy
used by Deuteronomy (also 8:5) to describe the relationship
between Yahweh and Israel is a point of contact with Hosea (11:1).
The familial analogy does not exclude the expression of this same
relationship also in covenant terms. The covenant rite of sprink-
ling blood (Exod. 24) created a kinship relationship between
Israel and Yahweh (cf. McCarthy, *CBQ* 27, 1965, 144ff.; Sklba,
CBQ 34, 1972, 10ff.).

32. in spite of this word: that is, the speech of Moses recalling Yahweh's help and leadership from Egypt to the present.
For the translation **in spite of** for the preposition *b*[e], cf. Lev. 26:27;
Num. 14:11. **you did not believe:** the construction with the
participle indicates a continued state rather than a specific act of
unbelief: 'you continued not believing' (Driver).

**33. who went before you . . . in fire by night . . . in the
cloud by day:** in all three phrases there is contact with the Red
Sea story in Exod. 13:21 (see comment on v. 29). **to pitch your
tents:** Exod. 13:21 reads 'to lead them'; apart from the
suffix forms, the difference between the two unpointed texts is
slight (Dt. 1:33 *lḥnṭkm*; Exod. 13:21 *lnḥṭm*). The LXX follows the
reading of Exod. 13:21 here; this may be the original, the *MT*
of Dt. 1:33 originating from metathesis of the second and third
consonants, under the influence perhaps of Num. 10:31. The
possibility of influence from Num. 10 is increased by the fact that
just as here it is Yahweh who went before Israel **to seek out** a
place for them to encamp, so in Num. 10:33 the ark of Yahweh
went before them 'to seek out' a resting place.

34. At this point in Num. 14 comes Yahweh's vow to destroy
Israel and Moses' intercession. The latter element now appears in
the form of Moses interceding on his own behalf in 3:23ff.

35. this evil generation: the words are missing in the LXX and have no counterpart in Num. 14. They were undoubtedly added here in order to ensure that **these men,** to which they stand in awkward apposition, were not understood as referring only to the spies.

36. The exception of Caleb finds its justification not in this chapter but in Num. 13f., where the J tradition also refers only to Caleb in this connection. The deuteronomist was constrained to refer to Caleb here, not only out of fidelity to his source, but also as background for later material in his history (cf. Jos. 14:6-14).

37. Vv. 37 and 38 anticipate what is to come later in 3:26ff. They add little to the present context, and have probably been added in order to ensure that a full account of the fate of the whole people is given at this particular point. **on your account:** see comment on 3:26.

38. who stands before you: the phrase describes the role of a servant, and is synonymous with the designation 'minister' in Jos. 1:1.

39. your little ones, who you said would become a prey: the words are missing in the LXX, and conform with the priestly writer in Num. 14 (vv. 3, 31) rather than with J. Since **your children . . .** forms an adequate subject here, the words should be omitted as a late addition. **have no knowledge of good or evil:** knowledge of good and evil here (and also in Isa. 7:15) undoubtedly refers to moral discernment and responsibility: the children, having no moral discernment, cannot be judged faithless. In other contexts, however (for example, Gen. 2:9, 17; 3:5, 22; 2 Sam. 14:17), the phrase is perhaps more comprehensive than this, meaning universal knowledge.

40. the Red Sea: this is a translation of the LXX reading for the Hebrew *yam sûph.* The translation of the Hebrew as 'the Sea of Reeds' (cf. *NEB* note) depends on the use of the word *sûph* in Exod. 2:3, 5, of the reeds of the Nile or of one of the streams of the Nile delta. Originally 'the Sea of Reeds' was applied to a very limited area, the southern part of Lake Menzaleh near Baalzephon; later it was applied to the Gulf of Aqabah and perhaps also the Gulf of Suez, eventually coming also to apply to the Red Sea.

41. and thought it easy: the verb occurs only here in the Old Testament. It should probably be connected with the Arabic *hāna*, 'to be light, easy'. The *AV* 'you were ready' follows Rashi's view that the word is related to the interjection *hēn*, 'behold'. On the basis of a possible occurrence of the root in 'The Words of Ahikar', line 103, Grelot (*VT* 12, 1962, 198ff.) suggests that it is a synonym of *hgr* 'gird on', and proposes the translation 'equipped yourselves'.

42, 43. Traditionally, the presence of Yahweh was bound up with the ark, and in Num. 14: 42-44 when the ark remains in the camp Yahweh also is absent from the battle. The ark is not mentioned here, however, since for the deuteronomist the ark has a different significance; see comment on 10:1-5.

44. the Amorites: in Num. 14:43, 45 the enemy is 'the Amalekites and the Canaanites'. On the general use of 'Amorites' to include also these, see comment on v.7. **in Seir:** the common view that the preposition *bᵉ* should here be translated 'from' (following a Ugaritic usage) rather than the normal **in,** is in fact quite uncertain. The three Old Testament examples quoted by Loretz (*BZ* 2, 1958, 289f.) all refer to the special context of divine revelation and may more appropriately be translated 'through'. None of the examples quoted by Gordon (*Ugaritic Textbook*, 92f.) is in fact convincing in its context. If the meaning 'from' is required here (though both *RSV* and *NEB* translations are adequate), it is better to emend; the confusion of the letters *beth* and *mem* is fairly common, cf. Driver, *Samuel*, lxvii. **Hormah:** perhaps to be identified with *Tell el-Meshash*, near Beersheba; cf. Aharoni, *Land*, 378.

45. Just as the people did not listen to Yahweh (v.43) so Yahweh does not now listen to them. This verse forms the natural conclusion of the section.

46. That Israel should have **remained at Kadesh many days** is, in the light of v. 40, an unexpected and unlikely feature of the narrative. This verse is an addition which has the object of harmonizing the present account with the JE tradition that the period before passing through Edom was spent at Kadesh (Num. 20:1, 14ff.). **the days that you remained there:** this is an idiom to be found also in 1 Sam. 23:13; 2 Sam. 15:20; 2 Kg. 8:1; Zech. 10:8. It is simply a means of affirming the previous statement when that statement is vague and indefinite.

(C) ISRAEL'S JOURNEYS AND ENCOUNTERS WITH THE NATIONS: **2:1-3:11**
In this section Israel's fortunes begin to change as, at the command

of Yahweh, she undertakes her journey into the land. The account of her encounters with the east Jordanian nations goes on to 3:11. There is a certain pattern in the portrayal of these five encounters, in which the following elements frequently appear: the movement of Israel (2:1, 8*b*; 3:1); Yahweh's instruction (2:2, 9, 17, 31; 3:2); the pre-history of the settlement of the area (2:10, 12, 20; 3:11); the provision of food (2:6, 28); the departure of Israel or occupation of the land (2:8, 13, 24); cf. Sumner, *VT* 18, 1968, 216ff. However, there is little to show that this pattern belonged to any pre-deuteronomistic stage of the tradition; rather, it is due to deuteronomistic and post-deuteronomistic systematizing of varied material. In two cases (Edom and Sihon) there is literary contact between the deuteronomist and an older source (as in ch. 1); otherwise, there is deuteronomistic material with no older source (Og), or post-deuteronomistic material which also has no older source (Moab and Ammon).

From a historical and theological point of view a contrast is clearly drawn between Israel's encounters with Edom, Moab, and Ammon, on the one hand, and her encounters with Sihon and Og, on the other. In the former group there were no hostilities, while in the latter there were; in the former group these peoples possess their land as the gift of Yahweh, while with Sihon and Og this is not the case.

The full force of this contrast is, however, to some extent obscured by the addition to the deuteronomist's account of post-deuteronomistic material (2:9*aβ*–12, 18–23 have no background in the older tradition, are styled in second person singular form of address, and are clearly a secondary addition modelled on 2:4–6; in partial dependence on 2:4–6 the Sihon and Og traditions have also been expanded, again in second person singular form of address, in 2:24*aβ*–25, 30*b*, 31; 3:2, 9, 10*b*, 11. An isolated addition exists in 2:7; 2:29 is from the same hand as that responsible for 2:9*aβb*; and 2:37 from the same hand as 2:18f.). The deuteronomist had firmly linked his own material with the preceding section in 1:19–45 through the insertion of 2:14–16 in their present place. These verses also functioned to separate the two groups of deuteronomistic material in the present section, that dealing with Edom and that dealing with Sihon and Og, in such a way that Israel did not have the military help of Yahweh before the death of the rebellious generation (so there was no war with Edom) but did have this subsequently (so Israel defeated Sihon and Og).

This aspect of the nature of the deuteronomist's work has been obscured by the addition of 2:18-23 in their present place, for these verses present an encounter with Ammon of a form similar to those encounters with foreigners which took place before the death of the rebellious generation.

1. This verse is the sequel to 1:40.

4. the sons of Esau, who live in Seir: the sources used by the deuteronomist at this point, in Num. 20:14ff., refer to Edom rather than Esau. Edom and Esau came to be identified in the later centuries of Israel's pre-exilic period. This resulted from the expansion westwards of Edom into the land of Seir which was inhabited by the sons of Esau. The identification is, however, presupposed by the deuteronomist (this may be concluded from the fact that his source refers to Edom), yet the deuteronomist is in fact reflecting the original circumstances in referring to Esau rather than to Edom in connection with Seir. On this see Bartlett, *JTS* 20, 1969, 1ff., and the comment on 1:2.

5, 6. the sole of the foot to tread on: on walking over land as constituting the legal act of taking possession, see comment on **25:9. I have given Mount Seir to Esau as a possession:** the deuteronomist here expresses a thought which is taken up again in connection with Moab and Ammon in vv. 9, 19, viz. that the land of Esau/Edom has been assigned to it by Yahweh and so cannot become part of the promised land of Israel. This view does not appear in the deuteronomist's source in Num. 20:14-21 where, in fact, there is a quite different overall picture from the one provided here. According to the source, Edom refused permission to Israel to pass through its land, as a result of which Israel bypassed Edomite territory. In the present section, however, it is assumed that Israel did pass through the territory of Esau, from whom food and drink were also purchased for the journey (cf. also 2:28f.). Noth is undoubtedly right (*Studien*, 33f.) in thinking that the deuteronomist has a particular theory of Israel's settlement, according to which those powers which opposed her were defeated and their lands occupied. Since Edom's land was not occupied by Israel (and the same with Moab and Ammon), they cannot have opposed Israel in the course of her settlement. The deuteronomist has here given theological expression to his historical theory: the land is Esau's by divine promise.

7. This verse is an addition. Not only is it in second person

singular form of address, but its view has shifted from a wandering
to a settled people (see comment below), and it can be seen only
as a rather awkward general explanation of how it was that Israel
was provided for in the wilderness (cf. Mittmann, *op. cit.*, 66). **all
the work of your hands:** in deuteronomic language this phrase
belongs in an agricultural context (14:29; 16:15; 24:19; 28:12;
30:9). The author has a settled rather than a nomadic people in
view. **he knows:** the verb is *yāḏaʿ*; the *NEB* translation 'he has
watched' (i.e. he has looked on with concern) is justified by the
use of the verb in Gen. 39:6; Ps. 1:6. **forty years:** this is a
traditional period of time, the space of a generation (cf. Am. 2:10;
Ps. 95:10). The reference to the **forty years** of wilderness wandering at this point is rather premature. It belongs in the context
of a summary view of the wandering after its completion, see 1:3,
and comment on v. 14. **you have lacked nothing:** so there is no
economic need to justify Israel's conquering land not assigned to
her (Buis).

8. we went on, away from our brethren: the LXX presupposes the reading *ʾēṭ* rather than *mēʾēṭ* as *MT*. The LXX
undoubtedly preserves the original reading, and so the translation
should be: 'we crossed through (the territory of) our brethren'.
The prefixed preposition **from** in the *MT* is derived from Num.
20:21 and yields a sense which (implying that Israel avoided the
Edomites) conflicts with vv. 4ff., while agreeing with Num. 20:14–
21. See comment on v. 5. **away from the Arabah road:** the
preposition **from** also here is absent from the LXX. Here too it
may be a secondary addition made in order to avoid possible
conflict with the preceding statement once the preposition had
been added there. Without the preposition the translation is 'along
the Arabah road'. **Elath and Ezion-geber:** the point of origin
of the Arabah road. Probably these were successive names for the
same place on the Gulf of Aqabah (Wright). If the Arabah road
is understood to be a highway actually running through the
Arabah it is here presupposed that Israel, after wandering in the
region of Seir (v. 1), traversed that country, which lay to the west
of the Arabah (comment on 1:2), then followed the Arabah road
northwards before turning north-east into Moabite territory.

9. And the Lord said to me: the deuteronomist now followed
directly with v. 13. The rest of v. 9 is an addition modelled clearly
on v. 5. It has no background in older material. It is brought in
at this point (rather than, more appropriately, after the reference

to crossing the brook Zered in v. 13) because of the reference to
Moab at the end of v. 8, and reflects the desire to fill what was
felt to be an unacceptable silence on the part of the older tradition
on events between Israel's encounter with Edom and the arrival
at the border of the land. **Ar:** apparently the name of Moab's
capital city (used here for the country). Its identification is not
certain; v. 18 (though see comment; cf. also Num. 22:36) would
perhaps suggest a site in the valley of the Arnon. The attitude
towards Moab expressed here (see also vv. 28f.) is somewhat
different from that of 23:4; different times and political attitudes are reflected in these references. **the sons of Lot:** cf. Gen.
19:30ff.

10. Vv. 10–12 form an antiquarian notice; it is unlikely that
they were added at the same time as v. 9 (the interests of which
are not antiquarian), but its origin is uncertain. **Emim:** a giant
people, reputedly early inhabitants of (part of) Moab. In Gen.
14:5 they are said to have dwelt in Shaveh-kiriathaim, an area
which (if connected with the city of Kiriathaim) lay in Moab
north of the Arnon (Num. 33:37; Jos. 13:19; cf. Num. 21:26 for
Moabite territory extending to this area). **Anakim:** comment on
1:28.

11. Rephaim: not an ethnic term, but a general designation
for legendary pre-Israelite inhabitants of Palestine. These legendary heroes were apparently known by different names in different
areas: **Emim** in Moab (see also Gen. 14:5), **Anakim** in Judah
(Num. 13:33; Jg. 1:20), and Zamzummim in Ammon (see v.
20). Traditions of such figures are apparently common in coun-
tries having megalithic structures (Smith, 20). De Moor (*ZAW*
88, 1976, 323ff.) has noted the use of the term *rp'u* at Ugarit as an
epithet of the god Baal. It has the sense of 'Saviour' or 'Healer'.
It is also used at Ugarit of the spirits of dead men of eminence.
It is an honorific title in the context of the Canaanite cult of
heroes. Traces of this may be observed in the Old Testament
where the term Rephaim is used for the shades of the dead, see
especially Isa. 14:9, and Ps. 88:10; Prov. 2:18, etc.

12. Horites: the common identification of this people with the
Hurrians is not beyond question. The latter are not known
historically as early inhabitants of a region so far south, but rather
derived from the north and constituted a significant power in
Syria and northern Palestine for some time after the middle of
the second millennium. The Old Testament references to the

Horites, on the other hand, put their centre in Seir and do not know them outside this area (cf. Gen. 14:6; 36:20ff.; Num. 13:5; Dt. 2:12, 22; 1 Chr. 1:38f.). On the issue, cf. de Vaux, *RB* 74, 1967, 481ff.

13. The verse joins directly on to v. 9a*α*, vv. 9a*β*–12 being a post-deuteronomistic insertion. The verse follows the commandment-fulfilment scheme which has already appeared in the deuteronomist's work (1:40; 2:1). **the brook:** see comment on 1:24. **Zered:** referred to also in Num. 21:12, but its location is not certain. It is perhaps to be identified with the Wadi el-Hesa which flows into the south-eastern end of the Dead Sea.

14. Vv. 14–16 mark the real end of the history of ch. 1. As there so here there is inverted use of holy war and exodus motifs and vocabulary (see especially Moran, *Bib* 44, 1963, 333ff.): it is against rather than for Israel that Yahweh acts; but after the end of the rebellious generation Yahweh can once more act with and on behalf of his people in war. **thirty-eight years:** presumably the deuteronomist is working on the basis of an overall period of forty years in the wilderness (1:3), from which he deducts two years for the time taken to reach Sinai together with the period spent there and also at Kadesh (see the priestly chronology in Exod. 40:17; Num. 1:1; 9:1; 10:11ff.). **the men of war:** this seems to constitute a limitation on what was said in 1:35. However, the intention both here and in the reference to **the camp** is rather to provide a link with the essentially martial character of the earlier section through the use of holy war vocabulary.

15. the hand of the Lord: this phrase has two references, both of which are significant here. On the one hand, it is connected with plagues and pestilence sent by Yahweh (Exod. 9:3, 15; 1 Sam. 5:6, 7, 9, 11), which means that it takes up a part of the deuteronomist's source in Num. 14 not otherwise referred to here, viz. Yahweh's decision to destroy the people by pestilence (Num. 14:11ff.). On the other hand, the phrase also has holy war associations, particularly in the context of the exodus (cf. Exod. 15:6, 12, 17), so that here too there is an inversion of the normal use of holy war vocabulary, as in ch. 1. **to destroy them:** the holy war associations of this verb are clear (cf. Exod. 14:24; 23:27; Jos. 10:10; Jg. 4:15; 1 Sam. 7:10); it alludes to the divinely caused panic and confusion which creates havoc in the ranks of the enemy.

16, 17. These verses are clearly an introduction to a completely new phase in the history of Yahweh's relationship with his people.

The sequel to them is in v. 24 (compare vv. 9aα, 13). Vv. 18–23
are an insertion (18–19, like v. 9, having second person singular
form of address; 20–23 being an expanded antiquarian notice,
like vv. 10–12), with no background in old tradition.

18. the boundary of Moab at Ar: the sense of this phrase is
ambiguous since g^e*bûl* can mean either **boundary** or 'territory'
(cf. e.g. 11:24), and **at Ar** stands in apposition to what precedes
rather than as a prepositional complement. V. 9 indicates that
Ar can be used for the country; so the translation may be 'this
day you are to cross through the territory of Moab, that is Ar'.
The latter translation is probably preferable if the verse (which
is part of an addition) is to be compatible with its overall context;
for according to vv. 24f. the northern boundary of Moab at the
Arnon adjoined the territory of Sihon, not that of the Ammonites.

19. the sons of Ammon: Ammonite territory, apparently
lying eastwards of the route taken by Israel, did not have to be
crossed. The verse is clearly from the same hand as that responsible for v. 9.

20, 21. Vv. 20–23 are an antiquarian notice of the same type as
vv. 10–12, and undoubtedly come from the same hand. There is
a slight difference between the two sections in that while vv. 10–12
refer to the activity of Yahweh in connection only with the settlement of Israel, in v. 21 it is Yahweh who destroyed the Zamzummim in order to allow the Ammonites to settle. This type of
variation does not necessarily prove different authorship, but it
seems nevertheless that it was the cause of the even later addition of v. 22; see comment. **Rephaim, Zamzummim:** see on
v. 11.

22. This verse is awkward in its context: it seems to be a late
addition introduced in order to correct v. 12a in the light of v. 21.
It is Yahweh, not the sons of Esau, who destroyed the Horites.

23. the Avvim: referred to again only in Jos. 13:3; they were
evidently the original inhabitants of south-west Palestine, dispossessed by **the Caphtorim. Caphtor** is to be identified with Crete
(see the latest discussion in Strobel, *Seevölkersturm*, 101ff.). It is
from here, according to Am. 9:7; Jer. 47:4, that the Philistines
came. This indicates the reason for the presence here of this verse,
which otherwise appears quite irrelevant. The author of the addition of v. 22 also brought in v. 23 in order to contrast the
situation of the Ammonites and the Edomites (who were given
their land by Yahweh and so cannot be dispossessed by Israel)

with the situation of the Philistines (who took their land from the Avvim and so are themselves liable to dispossession by Israel).

24. The continuation of v. 17 is found in v. 24*aα* only, at which point a later addition interrupts the deuteronomistic account until v. 26. The addition stands in some tension with the deuteronomistic account in vv. 26ff., but is true to its general structure: its object is to emphasize that aspect of the deuteronomistic account which shows Israel successful in battle after the death of the disobedient generation.

25. The vocabulary used here (**dread, hear, tremble, anguish**) is derived directly from Exod. 15:14, 16, where also it is used of the fear of Israel in the course of their conquest which Yahweh sends on the peoples. It is the vocabulary of holy war, now used in the appropriate form.

26. Kedemoth: precise location is unknown. It is mentioned as a city of Reuben in Jos. 13:18. **Heshbon:** Sihon's capital (Num. 21:26, 34, etc.; see also on 1:4). In Jos. 13:17 it is a city of Reuben, but the Old Testament also indicates (Isa. 15:4; 16:8f.; Jer. 48:2, 34) that the city in time reverted to the Moabites to whom control of the area evidently belonged before the arrival of Sihon; see comment on v. 10. The negotiations with Sihon in vv. 26–30 are inconsistent with the tone of vv. 24*aβ*–25. Vv. 26–28 are the continuation of v. 24*aα*, the account of the deuteronomist. His presentation is in conformity with the war law of 20:10, and, as in ch. 1, literary dependence on older sources may be established. The deuteronomist is using material from Num. 20:17, 19 (concerning Edom); 21:21–23, and his own earlier passage in Dt. 2:5–6.

27. let me pass: the deuteronomist usually uses first person plural (2:1, 8*b*). The use of the first person singular derives from Num. 21:22 and shows deuteronomistic dependence on that passage. This makes less likely the view of van Seters (*JBL* 91, 1972, 182ff.) that Num. 21:21ff. is the later passage (dependent on Dt. 2:26–37 and a second deuteronomistic passage in Jg. 11:19–26). **by the road:** the repetition of this word in the *MT* may be taken to express emphasis and intensification, '*only* by the road', cf. GK, § 123e; alternatively, it should perhaps by emended (from *badderek* to *hammelek* as in Num. 21:22) to give the sense 'by the king's road'. **to the right nor to the left:** this phrase is taken from Num. 20:17.

28. This verse takes up both Num. 20:19 and Dt. 2:6.

29. The verse is an addition to the deuteronomistic story; it is intended to strengthen the ties of the addition on Moab (v. 9aβb) to its deuteronomistic context. There is a premature change within the verse from first person singular to first person plural form.

30, 31. Vv. 30b, 31 are in second person singular form of address. They come from the same hand as 24aβ–25, and their purpose is to lessen the tension between these verses and vv. 26ff. The deuteronomist's account continues from v. 30a to vv. 32ff. **hardened his spirit:** the phrase is reminiscent of the story of God's dealings with the Pharaoh at the exodus, cf. Exod. 7:3, 14; 8:15; 13:15; there is no fixed expression, though usually 'heart' rather than 'spirit' is used. **made his heart obstinate:** the verb is frequently used with the sense of 'strengthen' or 'encourage' (e.g. 3:28), but with the object 'heart' (also 15:7; 2 Chr. 26:13) it has the sense of 'make obstinate'.

32. The content of this goes back to Num. 21:23, but its expression is much closer to Num. 21:33b. The latter is, however, a post-deuteronomistic passage; see comment on 3:1. **Jahaz:** various proposals, all uncertain, have been made for the location of this city. Like Heshbon (v. 26) it is referred to as a city of Reuben which later came back under Moabite control. The Moabite capture of the city is referred to in the Moabite Stone, lines 19f.

33. and his sons and all his people: the expression is lacking in the deuteronomist's source in Num. 21:24, but is found in the post-deuteronomistic passage on Og in Num. 21:35.

34. utterly destroyed: the verb ḥāram is the technical term used for the extermination of the enemy in a holy war as well as for the exclusive reservation of certain things to Yahweh. The common factor is that the things so designated are not available for common use, being either the object of Yahweh's anger (as Israel's enemies in holy war, or even as Israel herself if idolatrous, cf. 13:16) or being sacred to him alone (cf. Lev. 27:21, 28). In war the application of the ḥērem ('ban') was not uniform in theory or practice. Sometimes it is a matter of the total destruction of people and property (Dt. 20:16ff.; 1 Sam. 15:3); sometimes property only is spared (Dt. 2:34f.; 3:6f.); and sometimes the male population only is destroyed (Dt. 20:10ff.).

35. The deuteronomistic presentation here conforms with neither of the regulations in Dt. 20:10–18; this is perhaps because the kingdoms of Sihon and Og, lying outside the promised land (understood as the land west of Jordan, cf. 3:25ff.; Jos. 1:1ff., etc.) and so 'very far from you' (20:15), are yet occupied by two and a half Israelite tribes in the course of Israel's journey to its land. Spoil is forbidden to Israel in her land (7:24ff.; 13:16f.), while in campaigns against cities distant from her land not only spoil but women, children and animals may be taken (20:14f.).

36. from Aroer, which is on the edge of the valley of the Arnon, and from the city that is in the valley: the source of this phrase is apparently the boundary description of the Reubenites in Jos. 13:16. The reference to the anonymous city in the valley is suitable in such a boundary context but not so here. **Aroer:** more than one site appears to have borne this name. Jos. 13:25 points to a location in the vicinity of Rabbah. The place mentioned here is perhaps to be located by the modern village of ʿAraʿir, three miles south-east of Dibon. **as far as Gilead:** Num. 21:24 gives Sihon's territory as extending 'from the Arnon to the Jabbok'. For the deuteronomist, however, east Jordan, consisting of 'the tableland and all Gilead and all Bashan' (3:8, 10a), all belonged to Sihon and Og; and since Og was known as 'the king of Bashan' (see comment on 3:1), the rest (so including land north of the Jabbok) must have belonged to Sihon. **into our hands:** unless this is simply a stylistic variation, the *RSV* is apparently following the reading of *Sam* (cf. also vv. 24, 30). The phrase in the *MT* appears also in v. 31, and is there translated 'over to you'.

37. This verse, reverting to second person singular form of address, is an addition from the same time and hand as vv. 18–19. It is added here because Ammonite territory extended along the eastern border of the kingdom of Sihon. **the river Jabbok:** the Jabbok, as the boundary of the Ammonites (cf. also 3:16; Jos. 12:2), runs in a north–south direction for part of its course; Ammonite territory lay east of this. **and wherever:** the LXX presupposes *keḵōl* rather than the *MT* *weḵōl*, which yields the preferable translation 'according to all' (see *NEB* translation), with specific reference to Yahweh's command concerning Ammonite territory (v. 19).

3:1. In contrast to the Sihon story, the Og story has no roots in old tradition preserved in Numbers. Og is referred to in Num. 21:33–35, and there is striking conformity between that passage and Dt. 3:1–3; but for a number of reasons the Numbers account must be seen as dependent on the deuteronomist and not *vice versa*: firstly, the language common to both passages **(do not fear, I have given him . . . into your hand)** is typical of the deuteronomist and not of JE; secondly, the JE tradition in Num. 22:2 refers to the victory over Sihon but not to that over Og; thirdly, the similarities between the Numbers and the Deuteronomic accounts of Og in contrast to the differences between their respective accounts of Sihon, together with the fact that the Deuteronomic accounts of each of these episodes follow the same pattern, is best explained by the view that the deuteronomist took up and expressed in his own way the Sihon story from Num. 21:21ff., and then formulated his own account of Og following the same pattern; the latter story was then at a later stage taken up and inserted in Num. 21:33–35 (cf. Driver; Noth, *Studien*, 35). **Bashan:** the appearance of the definite article with this name reflects its origin and use as a common noun ('fertile land'). It was an area lying to the north of Gilead, and was noted particularly for its rich pasture land and forests (Am. 4:1; Mic. 7:14; Isa. 2:13; Ezek. 27:6, etc.). **Og the king of Bashan:** although there is no preserved pre-deuteronomistic account of the battle against Og, his name and title were probably derived by the deuteronomist from Jos. 12:4. **Edrei:** see comment at 1:4.

2. This verse, in second person singular address, is in the style of the addition to the deuteronomist's account in 2:24*aβ*–25, 30*b*–31, and should be ascribed to the same hand. It interrupts the continuity of vv. 1, 3–8. **I have given:** this is a good example of the frequent use of the perfect in order to present the outcome of a future act as so assured that it may be described as accomplished, cf. GK § 106 m.

4. Argob: here, and in vv. 13f., this word is synonymous with Bashan. Its original application, however, was to a district within Bashan (1 Kg. 4:13); the extended application is the result of the addition of the (inaccurate) gloss at the end of this verse, **sixty cities, the whole region of Argob, the kingdom of Og in Bashan,** on the basis of the reference to sixty cities in 1 Kg. 4:13 (cf. Mittmann, *op. cit.*, 91f.).

5. unwalled villages: the word used here, *happerāzî*, is close to *happerizzî*, which is usually taken as an ethnic term, Perizzites, because of its occurrence in lists of peoples (Gen. 13:7, etc.). The nature of the connection between the terms is, however, uncertain (cf. Schnell, in *IDB*, vol. 3, p. 735). The sense of the word as used here is made particularly clear by Ezek. 38:11.

6. utterly destroyed: see comment on 2:34.

8. beyond the Jordan: see comment on 1:1. **from the valley**

of the Arnon to Mount Hermon: this summary description of
the land of Sihon and Og is derived from Jos. 12:1. **Mount
Hermon** formed a natural physical barrier at the northern limit
of Bashan.

9. Vv. 9 and 11 are antiquarian notices, probably deriving
from the same hand as 2:10f., 20ff. **Sirion:** in the Old Testament
only here and Ps. 29:6; the name is also found in the Ugaritic
texts. **Senir:** Ca. 4:8 and 1 Chr. 5:23 show that Senir and Hermon
are not identical. All three names, along with the fourth in 4:48,
would perhaps have been names for different peaks in the same
range of mountains in Anti-Lebanon.

10. the tableland and all Gilead and all Bashan: see
comment on 2:36. The tableland is the southern plateau extending
from Gilead to the boundary of Moab at the Arnon. **Gilead** is
the central area of east Jordan, divided in two by the Jabbok, the
division presupposed in references (as in vv. 12f.) to half of Gilead.
Salecah: of unknown location, but clearly at the northern limit
of Bashan (so also Jos. 13:11; 1 Chr. 5:11). **Edrei:** on Bashan's
southern border (see 3:1 and comment at 1:4); **and Edrei** must
be an addition here since it awkwardly reverses the south–north geographical direction of the first part of the verse. The rest of the verse,
which belongs with **and Edrei**, must also be part of this addition.

11. An antiquarian notice (see v. 9). **Rephaim:** see comment
on 2:11. **bedstead:** *'ereś* otherwise means 'couch' or 'bed' (Am.
3:12; Job 7:13, etc.), but it is probably best to translate it here as
'sarcophagus' (cf. Marti), in the sense of the last resting place,
and following the use of the word in Aramaic. **iron:** this probably
refers to black basalt (see *NEB* translation). **Rabbah:** the capital
city of the Ammonites, now Amman. The inconsistency between
the location of Og's sarcophagus at Rabbah and the site of the
battle at Edrei indicates the quite separate origin of these records.
Nine cubits . . . four cubits: that is, 13–14 feet by six feet. **the
common cubit:** literally 'the cubit of a man', that is, the ordinary
cubit. For this idiom in a different connection, cf. Isa. 8:1.

C. CONCLUSION. POSSESSION OF THE LAND UNDER
JOSHUA'S LEADERSHIP: 3:12–29

This passage completes the introduction to the deuteronomistic
historical work in three paragraphs. All of these include the phrase

at that time as part of their opening sentences: the first in vv. 12–13*a* has been supplemented by material of varied origins (some of it very old) in vv. 13*b*–17; the second paragraph lies in vv. 18–20, which has been later supplemented by vv. 21–22; and the third lies in vv. 23–28, with v. 29 forming the overall conclusion. The whole forms a transitional passage linking the preceding review (vv. 12–13*a* on the assignment to the tribes of the territory captured from Sihon and Og; vv. 23ff. alluding to events in Israel's history, including her rebellion recounted in ch. 1) with the account of the conquest in the book of Joshua (v. 18ff. on the gift of the land; v. 28 the appointment of Joshua to lead the conquest). Stylistic affinity with the book of Joshua (compare 3:18ff. and Jos. 1:14ff.) confirms this connection.

12. Vv. 12–13*a* form the basic part of the first paragraph, standing in some tension with the rest. This basis is derived from, and represents a summary and clarification of the description given in Jos. 13. **Aroer:** see comment on 2:36. **the edge of:** this is not in the *MT*. The *RSV* here follows a reading strongly supported in the ancient versions and also in the parallel passages in 2:36; 4:48. **half of the hill country of Gilead:** that is, the half of Gilead lying south of the Jabbok; see comment on v. 10.

13. V. 13*b* (including the phrase **all the region of Argob** transferred by the *RSV* to v. 13*a*) goes back to an antiquarian notice, analogous to 2:10ff., 20ff. It came in with reference to **all Bashan** in v. 13*a* (for the secondary identification of these, see comment on v. 4), and read originally 'all that region of Argob is called a land of Rephaim'. Since, however, v. 13*a* also referred to Gilead, the reference of the antiquarian notice in v. 13*b* was made more precise and accurate through the addition to v. 13*b* of the awkward gloss 'all Bashan'.

14. Vv. 14 and 15 supplement the first paragraph with information derived from Num. 32:39ff. They also have the object of resolving a conflict between vv. 12f. and Num. 32:39ff; for, whereas in the former the territory occupied by half the tribe of Manasseh is Bashan and the northern half of Gilead, in the latter the Manassites settled only Gilead. So v. 15 has Gilead settled by Machir, one son of Manasseh, and v. 14 has Bashan settled by another son of Manasseh, Jair. **Jair the Manassite:** the Hebrew is 'Jair the son of Manasseh' (also Num. 32:41). However, in 1 Chr. 2:21f. Jair is the great grandson of Manasseh's son Machir. This confirms better with Jg. 10:3–5 where Jair is a ruler in the

period of the judges. **the Geshurites and the Maacathites:**
these were two Aramean states, located immediately north of
Bashan. They were apparently still independent in the time of
David (2 Sam. 3:3; 10:6). **the villages:** this does not appear in
the *MT* which has simply 'them'. The latter has no antecedent
in the verse, and is a thoughtless copy from Num. 32:41. **Bashan:**
in the *MT* this appears awkwardly just before 'Havvoth-jair' (and
not as in the *RSV*); it is an addition presumably intended to
emphasize the new location given for Havvoth-jair. **Havvoth-
jair:** here located in Bashan, but in Gilead in Num. 32:41. This
geographical confusion arises from the attempt to harmonize vv.
12f. with Num. 32:39ff.

15. This verse is taken from Num. 32:39f., and conflicts with
vv. 12f. which it is intended to correct. No distinction is made
between the southern and the northern parts of Gilead. The verse
reflects an old historical situation before Gad's settlement of the
southern half of Gilead.

16. Here the substance of v. 12 is repeated, though revised in
the light of v. 15. **with the middle of the valley as a boundary:**
this translation is difficult to derive from the present *MT* which
is better rendered (as the *NEB* note), 'including the bed of the
gorge and the adjacent strip of land' (for *gᵉḇûl*, usually 'boundary',
as 'adjacent strip of land' cf. Num. 22:36; Jos. 13:23). The *NEB*
translation 'that is to the middle of the gorge; and its territory
ran' presupposes two slight changes: the first is a shift of the pause;
the second a minor re-division of the words (from *ûgᵉḇûl wᵉ'aḏ* to
ûgᵉḇûlô 'aḏ). **Jabbok:** see comment on 2:37.

17. as the boundary: better, 'and adjacent land' (as the *NEB*;
see comment on v. 16). **Chinnereth:** mentioned as a fortified
city of Naphtali in Jos. 19:35, it lay on the north-western side of
the Sea of Galilee and was used also as an alternative name for
that sea. **the Salt Sea:** the name 'Dead Sea' for this body of water
is not found in the Old Testament, but derives at the earliest from
the first or second century AD. **Pisgah:** see comment on 32:49;
34:1.

18. This, and the following two verses, are addressed to Reuben,
Gad and half the tribe of Manasseh; they summarize Num. 32.

19. many cattle: see Num. 32:1.

20. until the Lord gives rest: the promise of **rest** does not
appear in Num. 32, but is encountered first in Deuteronomy. It
is not just peace of mind, nor an eschatological state resulting from

radical change brought about by God in history, but rather the peace to which Israel will come when it settles the land, secure from the threat of enemies and from the threat of homelessness; see von Rad, *Problem*, 94ff. and comment on 12:9 **beyond the Jordan:** see comment on 1:1.

21, 22. Vv. 21 and 22 stand isolated in their context, and anticipate v. 28. They are an addition here brought in on the basis of the connection of the two subjects treated in vv. 18–22 to be found also in Jos. 1:12–18. In the latter passage, Joshua's reminder to the two and a half tribes of their undertaking to help in the conquest of west Jordan is immediately followed by the promise of these tribes to obey Joshua as Moses' successor. **I commanded:** the sense is 'commissioned' or 'installed as leader' (cf. Num. 27:19) the same verb is used in the imperative in v. 28: 'charge'.

23. The beginning of the last paragraph, containing Moses' intercession with Yahweh for permission to go into the land, is an adaptation of his intercession with Yahweh on behalf of the people in Num. 14:13ff. This was not taken up by the deuteronomist when he dealt with the theme of Num. 13f.; see comment on 1:34.

24. only: this word is not in the Hebrew, but its inclusion here is justified by the use of **begun.** This is not simply praise of God on the part of Moses: it is the basis of his plea to be allowed to enter the land. Only then will the full greatness of God be made apparent to him.

25. hill country: on the use of this with general reference to the land, see comment on 1:7.

26. was angry: the verb, different from that used in 1:37, denotes strong fury to the point of unrestrained rejection; cf. Ps. 78:59, 62; Prov. 14:16. **on your account:** this should not be taken to point to an idea of Moses having suffered vicariously for the people; there is no notion of Moses as a substitute. Rather, Moses was denied entry into the land because he, as leader, must suffer *with* Israel for the sin of rebellion (1:26ff.). The deuteronomist, having emphasized throughout the innocence of Moses (see the introductions to 1:6–18, 19–46), now addresses his own contemporaries, who, like Moses, may be individually innocent but nevertheless must bear the communal guilt (cf. Lohfink, *Schol* 35, 1960, 405f.). It is the priestly writer in Num. 20:12; Dt. 32:51 who, influenced by Ezekiel's polemic (ch. 18) against the idea that one could suffer for the sins of another, introduced the thought of Moses himself having sinned (cf. Bertholet).

27. Pisgah: see comment on 32:49; 34:1. **behold it with your eyes:** Daube has suggested that the legal transfer of ownership of property took place when the new owner looked it over; Moses, acting on Israel's behalf, takes possession of the land. However, see comment on 34:1. The present verse seems to be a free quotation of Gen. 13:14: Moses, like Abraham, is permitted only a view of the land.

28. charge: see comment on v. 21. The command to Moses to transfer the leadership of Israel to Joshua is not found before the deuteronomist. It seems to have been created by the deuteronomist (1:37ff; 3:21f., 28; 31:2-6, 7f., 14f., 23) and connected with the theme of the death of Moses. The task to which Joshua is commissioned is a twofold one: firstly, to conquer the land (expressed by the verbs 'enter' or, as here, **go over**), and, secondly, to allot the land to the tribes (expressed by the verb *nhl*, translated 'cause to inherit' or, as here, **put. . . . in possession**). See Lohfink, *Schol* 37, 1962, 35f.

29. Beth-peor: associated with Pisgah also in Jos. 13:20, but not located with certainty. The reference is undoubtedly to the same place as Baal-peor (see comment on 4:3), the latter being also the name of the particular manifestation of Baal worshipped there. The reference here, rounding off the deuteronomistic review and giving in more precise terms what has already been given in the basic deuteronomistic part of 1:1, is of considerable theological significance: it is just at the point of Israel's first encounter with the forms of Canaanite worship that she receives her own life order.

D. GENERAL COMMAND TO OBEY THE LAW:
4:1-40

This exhortation presupposes the existence of the deuteronomistic material in chs. 1–3 (see comment on v. 1), but is not the original continuation of that material, which is to be found rather in the account of the conquest of the land (see introduction to 1:6–3:11 and to 3:12–29). It is, therefore, a secondary deuteronomistic addition.

The whole section is a single unit (cf. now Levenson, *HTR* 68, 1975, 203ff.). Stylistically, the change from plural to singular forms of address breaks down as a criterion for distinguishing different layers or sources (see comment on v. 19); such a change seems to have become a characteristic of deuteronomistic writings (cf. Lohfink, *Höre Israel*, 90ff.), so that neither here nor in several other passages later in the book can it indicate the presence of secondary additions.

There is a corresponding unity of theme. The overall concern is to encourage obedience to the law in general and to the prohibition of images in particular. The uniqueness of Israel's God and the intimacy of his relationship with her find regular expression (vv. 7f., 19f., 32ff., 35ff.). In a certain sense the section is a patchwork, since the author has taken up many of the various deuteronomistic themes familiar to him; but these have been bound into a unity which is apparent not only in the themes but also in the general background which is presupposed. The concern for obedience to the law is particularly suitable for the exilic period, while the elaboration of the prohibition of images together with the positive emphasis on the uniqueness of God and also the uniqueness of Israel as the recipient of God's revelation point especially to the same background as that from which Second Isaiah emerged; see comment on vv. 28, 32, 35, 39.

Covenant thought dominates the composition, but a parallel to the form of extra-biblical treaties cannot be established. This is not a covenant or treaty document, but a speech which takes up elements—history, law, blessing and curse—which belong to the structure of such a document; cf. McCarthy, *Treaty*, 132ff.

1. And now: this is frequently found in covenant contexts where it functions as the turning point between a historical recital and the implications which may be drawn from the history in terms of laws governing present behaviour; cf. Exod. 19:5; Jos. 24:14, and Brongers, *VT* 15, 1965, 289ff. It is the link used by the author of the following verses to connect them with the already existing deuteronomistic material in chs. 1–3. **the statutes and the ordinances:** a common combination in Deuteronomy. Although the two terms are in Deuteronomy indistinguishable and used comprehensively for the whole law (see on 1:5), they originally had different connotations. The effect of Deuteronomy's generalizing of the terms for law so that they are practically synonymous is to bring civil and criminal law into the general context of religious instruction and teaching. **take possession of the land:** that obedience to the law is a condition of possession of the land is by no means typical of Deuteronomy as a whole. See above, Introduction, p. 78f.

2. You shall not add ... nor take from it: this formula as a general injunction is familiar from ancient Near Eastern texts both legal and wisdom. Old Testament usage conforms with this (cf. Dt. 12:32; Prov. 30:6; Ec. 3:14). In later Judaism and Christianity the formula received a strict interpretation, being referred to the immutability of a sacred text; cf. Leipoldt and Morenz, *Heilige Schriften*, 56f.

3. Baal-peor: here (see also Hos. 9:10) the name is that of a place. The reference is apparently to Num. 25:1–5 where, however, the name is that of the god (the local manifestation of Baal) worshipped at Peor. See comment on 3:29. V. *3b* may be an addition, in the second person singular form of address in a plural context, elaborating the allusion to Num. 25.

4. held fast: the same verb as that translated 'cleave' in 10:20; 11:22; 13:4; 30:20.

5. I have taught: the verb may also be translated by the present 'I teach', being an example of the declarative perfect; cf. Marti, and GK § 106i. This verse, in contrast to v. 1, understands the law as given to Israel as a rule of life in the land. The stylistic, thematic and vocabulary contacts between vv. 1 and 5 (initial imperative in singular address form, 'statutes and ordinances', 'teach', 'do', etc.) preclude different authorship of these verses, however.

6. your wisdom and your understanding: on the wisdom terminology see comment on 1:13. The explicit identification of the observance of covenant law with the possession and manifestation of wisdom is significant for late Israelite wisdom literature, where wisdom is a gift of Yahweh through which one receives life and the blessing of Yahweh (see especially Prov. 8f.). The idea that the collection and promulgation of law is a proof of wisdom is, however, ancient, and is to be found in the prologues and epilogues of ancient Near Eastern law codes; cf. for example, the Code of Hammurabi, *ANET*, 164f., 178.

7. near: this assertion of the nearness of God to Israel is distinctive in the context of a polytheistic world in which the distance separating the high god from man was filled with minor personal deities who could act as intermediaries; see Lohfink, *Höre Israel*, 101ff; cf. also Ps. 145:18.

8. this law: see comment on 1:5; 4:1. The identification of *tôrāh* with **statutes and ordinances** is especially clear in this verse. **righteous:** otherwise this adjective is found as a *personal* qualification. Its use here, to describe laws as conforming to what is just and right, is paralleled in the Code of Hammurabi. Wienfeld *School*, 150f., suggests that the claim of Deuteronomy that Israel's law is righteous should be taken as a polemic against the Code of Hammurabi, as well as being a challenge to claims by other peoples generally for the supremacy of their laws.

9. This verse, in singular address form, anticipates what follows, emphasizing the importance of the things seen rather than of the commandments received, which is the chief theme of its immediate context. In this the verse looks forward to vv. 32ff. **soul:** a generally unsuitable translation for the Hebrew *nepeš*, which, with its variety of particular meanings, does not carry any connotation of an indestructible element of man's being. The sense of the word is to be determined from its context: here the reference is to the individual person, and the translation 'yourself' is therefore preferable to 'your soul'. For a discussion of the various uses and meanings of the word, cf. Wolff, *Anthropology*, 10ff. **make them known to your children:** the transmission of the faith to the children is a recurrent theme of significance in Deuteronomy (cf. 6:7; 11:19); it has roots both in the wisdom setting of the 'father' instructing his 'son' (cf. Prov. 2:1; 3:1; 4:1, etc.) and also in extra-biblical treaty texts which sometimes demand that the vassal makes the treaty known to his children; for this in the Esarhaddon treaty, cf. Frankena, *OTS* 14, 1965, 141f.

10. Horeb: comment on 1:2. **my words:** v. 13 suggests that the reference here, as in 5:22; 9:10; 10:2, 4, is to the decalogue in particular, rather than simply to speaking or to the laws in general. In other passages, however, as 12:28, the reference is apparently to the laws in general; cf. Lindars, in *Words and Meanings*, 128. **fear:** the fear of Yahweh is a major Old Testament theme, to be found particularly in Deuteronomy and the wisdom literature (cf. Prov. 1:7; Job 28:28, etc.); it is man's proper response to God shown in reverence and obedience.

11. gloom: the Hebrew word is translated by the *RSV* elsewhere as 'thick darkness' (cf. Exod. 20:18; Dt. 5:22; 2 Sam. 22:10; Ps. 97:2). A more appropriate translation to most contexts is 'thick mist' (cf. *NEB*). On the subject of the verse, cf. Exod. 19:16ff.

12. form: the use here of the word *temûnāh* is the first hint of the particular concern of this chapter with the second commandment of the decalogue (where the word is translated 'likeness' by the

RSV). Although contrasted with 'voice' (see also Num. 12:8), the *t*e*mûnāh* is not the actual concrete image, but rather, in a less tangible sense, the form, shape or likeness of that which the image concretely represents.

13. covenant: the derivation of the Hebrew *b*e*rît* is still a matter of dispute. For example, Kutsch, *Verheissung*, 32ff., proposes that it comes from a root *bārā*, found only in 1 Sam. 17:8, in the sense of 'look' or 'choose', from which the noun could mean 'choice' or 'determination' and thence 'obligation'. Apart from the infrequency of the root, the rather awkward steps necessary in order to reach the sense of 'obligation' tell against this proposal (see also the discussion in Weinfeld, *Bib* 56, 1975, 120ff.). The various proposals made on the subject are of course, related to the meaning which *b*e*rît* is understood to have, and the development of that meaning, in the Old Testament. So Kutsch holds that it means 'obligation', while others emphasize rather the relationship to which the translation 'covenant' points. For a review of discussion see especially McCarthy, *Old Testament Covenant*, 2ff., 59ff. The diversity of ways in which *b*e*rît* is now understood is perhaps a reflection of the diversity of ways and contexts in which it could always be used. Even in Deuteronomy this variation is to be found: in the context of passages referring to the covenant at Horeb, the word often refers specifically to the decalogue itself rather than to the relationship between Yahweh and Israel of which the decalogue formed a part (see also 4:23; 9:9, 11, 15; 10:8). Otherwise, *b*e*rît* in Deuteronomy can also mean the divine promise made to the patriarchs (7:12; 8:18), or even the oath sworn in the ceremony establishing the relationship between Yahweh and Israel (29:12, 14), as well as the actual relationship itself (5:2, 3). On the covenant theology of Deuteronomy, see Introduction, pp. 64ff. **the ten commandments:** the phrase occurs only twice otherwise in the Old Testament, in Exod. 34:28 and Dt. 10:4, but not at all in immediate association with the actual decalogue itself, either in Exod. 20 or Dt. 5. This, together with the fact that there are different ways of numbering ten commandments in the decalogue, none of which is beyond criticism, might be taken to indicate that the collection was not originally intended as a decalogue. In view of the comparatively early date (sixth century BC), however, from which such an understanding of the intention of the collection derives, it seems more likely that the original intention was in fact to produce a decalogue, and that it is subsequent comment on and elaboration of the collection which has obscured its original numbering; cf. Nielsen, *Commandments*, 10ff., and comment on ch. 5. **two tables of stone:** extra-biblical treaty custom indicates that it is unlikely that the necessity for two tables arose from the amount of material to be inscribed. Rather, the one table was a duplicate of the other. In establishing treaties the sovereign had one copy of the treaty and the vassal the other, and each deposited his copy at his own sanctuary. In the case of Israel the sanctuary was at the same time the sanctuary of Yahweh and that of Israel, and so held the two copies of the treaty/covenant; cf. Kline, *Treaty*, 13ff.

14. statutes and ordinances: see comment on v. 1.

15. The second major theme of the chapter, hinted at in v. 12, is an exposition of the second commandment of the decalogue. It continues to v. 31. The second commandment originally referred to images of Yahweh, but in time came to be understood as referring to images of other gods (see comment on 5:8f.). The present passage goes beyond this later understanding of the second commandment; for, through anchoring the second commandment in the fact that Israel saw no form at Horeb, it clearly includes images of Yahweh in that commandment.

16. graven image: the *pesel* was originally a sculptured object of wood or stone (Exod. 34:1, 4; Dt. 10:1, 3; 1 Kg. 5:32), which could be overlaid with gold or silver (Dt. 7:25; Hab. 2:19). It came to have the general meaning of idol or image (Isa. 30:22; 40:19; 44:10; Jer. 10:14). **figure:** the Hebrew is of uncertain origin; an idolatrous statue of some form is suggested by Ezek. 8:3, 5; 2 Chr. 33:7, 15. **likeness:** the word *taḇnît* means 'structure' or 'construction' (from *bānā*, 'to build'), but it is used of the figure of an idol in the shape of a man (cf. Isa. 44:13) or animal (cf. next verse and Ps. 106:20; Ezek. 8:10).

17. The expansion of the list of possible likenesses in this and the following verse opens the way to include images of gods other than Yahweh, so leading on naturally to the forms of foreign worship mentioned in v. 19.

19. This verse, in singular form of address in a plural context, is a clear indication that change of address is on its own an uncertain criterion by means of which change of authorship may be established. The catalogue of objects of worship in vv. 16*b*–19*a* is an original list which corresponds, in reverse order, with the list of the elements of creation in Gen. 1. On the other hand, v. 19

belongs closely with v. 20 in that the latter contrasts the position
of Israel with that of the peoples described in the former. So v. 19
cannot be taken from its context in spite of the change of address.

The intention behind the verse is not to express either tolerance
or ridicule of the nations and their practices, but rather to prepare
the way for the contrasting picture of Israel's favoured status, in
the next verse. **the sun and the moon and the stars:** the astral
cults of Mesopotamia were familiar to Israel from the time of
Assyrian and Babylonian domination of her country (cf. 2 Kg.
21:5), but were a particular danger in the time of Israel's exile.

20. you: in the Hebrew the pronoun stands in the emphatic
position at the beginning of the verse, strengthening the contrast
between Israel and the peoples which has already been expressed
in v. 7. While the peoples have no direct and immediate contact
with God, such intimacy is the privilege of Israel. **the iron
furnace:** a designation of Egypt also in ɩ Kg. 8:51; Jer. 11:4
(cf. also Isa. 48:10); the image suggests a time of ordeal, of
testing and purifying. **to be a people:** in Deuteronomy, as also
in P (cf. Exod. 6:7), Israel is led out of Egypt by Yahweh in order
that she might become his people. With JE, on the other hand
(cf. Exod. 3:7f.). it is because Israel already is the people of
Yahweh that he leads them from Egypt; cf. Lohfink, in *Probleme*)
304. **his own possession:** the Hebrew word is *naḥᵃlāh*, which in
Deuteronomy is mostly used to describe the land as Israel's
'inheritance' (see, for example, vv. 21, 38). Here as in 9:26, 29,
the thought is of Israel, among the peoples of the world, as
Yahweh's inheritance. The idea is expressed in different terms in
7:6; 14:2.

21. on your account: see comment on 3:26. The subject of
vv. 21f. has little relevance to the context; probably the intention
of the author is to provide a link with the first three chapters where
the subject is treated. **inheritance:** *naḥᵃlāh* denotes the property
handed down within the family. It is Deuteronomy which has
generalized the term to apply to the land of Israel as a unified
whole. The land is, therefore, the inalienable possession of Israel.
However, it is also the gift of Yahweh; and it is only through
life in obedience to Yahweh that Israel may remain in the land;
cf. von Rad, *Problem*, 81ff.; Diepold, *Israels Land*, 83ff. Exiled
Israel is here addressed with the word that the land, though
conquered and occupied, is still Israel's possession.

22. that good land: Israel's inheritance is the land west of

Jordan, so that to cross the Jordan means to take possession of the land. This picture is somewhat blurred in some passages, however (see comment on 2:35; 3:28; see also 4:45ff.; 11:24), by a view of the land which includes also east Jordan, settled by some Israelite tribes.

23. This verse, with its supplement in v. 24, rounds off the paragraph beginning in v. 15.

24. This verse, in singular form of address, contains a solemn declaration parallel to that found in v. 31. The intention of the author here is to prepare for the contrasting positive picture which he provides in vv. 32–40. **a devouring fire:** apart from Deuteronomy (also 9:3), it is Isaiah who uses this phrase to describe Yahweh (Isa. 29:6; 30:27, 30). Fire, as a sign of the divine presence, is, however, frequent, cf. for example, Exod. 3:2; 14:24; Dt. 4:12. **a jealous God:** a formula from the decalogue tradition where too it is associated with the exclusive worship of Yahweh (5:9). It expresses Yahweh's exclusive claim on Israel and his absolute intolerance of her turning to other gods.

25. grown old: the root is rare; from the use of the adjective in passages such as Lev. 26:10 and Ca. 7:13, it is clear that staleness, as well as old age, is implied. Reference here, therefore, is to Israel's failure to keep fresh the memory of the land as the gift of Yahweh who demands Israel's obedience. **to provoke him to anger:** a phrase characteristic of deuteronomistic literature to describe the result of Israel's worship of other gods (cf. e.g., 1 Kg. 14:9, 15; 16:33; 22:53).

26. I call heaven and earth to witness: also 30:19; 31:28; 32:1. Heaven and earth are witnesses to the activity of Yahweh in different contexts. Outside Deuteronomy (e.g. Isa. 44:23; Pss. 69:35; 96:11f.) they witness the saving activity of Yahweh, especially in creation. Within Deuteronomy the reference is always to Yahweh's judging activity. The background here is again that of the extra-biblical treaties. Heaven and earth and other natural phenomena were part of the Hittite pantheon and functioned actively as treaty witnesses (cf. Moran, *Bib* 43, 1962, 318f.). They are not seen as divine beings in the Old Testament, however, and even in the Ugaritic texts 'heaven and earth' occurs as 'an antonymic pair signifying 'The Universe' (Gordon, *Ugaritic Textbook*, 491; cf. also Fisher, *Ras Shamra Parallels* 11, 411ff.). It is in this sense of the totality of God's creation that they are summoned to witness God's judgment on Israel. For a comprehensive discussion of their role, cf. von Waldow, *Hintergrund*, 15ff., and comment on 32:1.

27. few in number: it is incorrect to take this (cf. Bächli, *Israel*, 32f.n.15) as containing the positive idea of a remnant of Israel which will survive the divine punishment. The thought that governs the expression of both vv. 26 and 27 is that the curse which will follow on Israel's disobedience will be precisely the opposite of the covenant blessing: instead of being brought into the land to possess it, she will perish from it; instead of being led out of Egypt, she will be scattered among the peoples; instead of being made many in number, she will be decimated.

28. The verse describes, not what the exiles are forced to do by their captors, but rather what they will inevitably do when separated from Yahweh's land. The closest parallel to this scornful description of idols is to be found in Second Isaiah (Isa. 40:19f.; 44:19ff.; 46:6f.). The background of the verse, like that of its whole context, is clearly Israel in exile.

29. The curse and blessing of the covenant are presented not as alternative possibilities dependent on disobedience or obedience, but rather as successive periods of Israel's history in which the curse is followed by the blessing. A similar historicizing of the curse and blessing of the covenant into two successive periods is to be found also in the late section 30:1–10. In the latter passage the blessing is described in concrete terms of restoration to the land and prosperity; here, however, such a form of the blessing is at best implied. This is a prophetic attitude to curse and blessing (cf. Hos. 3:4f.; 5:5), to be found also in late deuteronomistic (e.g. 1 Kg. 8:46ff.) rather than deuteronomic passages (see also introduction to 29:29–30:14). **with all your heart and with all your soul:** a frequent phrase (6:5; 10:12; 11:13; 13:3; 26:16; 30:2, 6, 10). The functions of the heart and soul overlap considerably in Hebrew thought. Primarily, however, the **heart** is the seat of man's intellect and will (cf. e.g. Dt. 15:9). On **soul** see comment on v. 9. In the present context the reference is to the *nepeš* as the source of emotions, particularly of desire (cf. e.g., Isa. 26:8, 9). See Johnson, *Vitality*, 11ff., 75ff.

30. in the latter days: the phrase often has the general sense of 'days to come' (Gen. 49:1; Num. 24:14; Dt. 31:29); elsewhere, it has the more definite sense of a time in the future (Jer. 29:11; Prov. 23:18; 24:14), or particularly the sense of end of time as contrasted with the beginning (Isa. 46:10). A time of change or

a turning point is indicated in the present passage, as also in Hos.
3:5; Ezek. 38:8, 16, though the eschatological ideas present in
Isa. 2:2; Mic. 4:1 are not expressed. There is no thought here of
the establishment of God's universal dominion; it is a change
within history in the relationship of God and Israel.

31. a merciful God: the contrasting declaration to v. 24. **he
will not fail you:** the verb means to sink, and is often used of
the hands with the implication of losing heart (e.g. Jer. 6:24).
So here 'he will not abandon you to discouragement'. **the covenant with your fathers:** the covenant referred to is not that
with the Sinai generation but the covenant with the patriarchs,
the promissory covenant of land and posterity; see comment on
1:8.

32. since the day that God created man upon the earth:
the only allusion to creation in Deuteronomy, but a common
perspective in Second Isaiah (e.g. Isa. 45:18ff.; 46:9f). Moreover,
the conclusion to which the argument in this and succeeding
verses leads, viz. that Yahweh is God and besides him there is no
other (v. 35), is to be found also in Second Isaiah; here, however,
the emphasis lies equally on the fact that it is to Israel and not to
another nation that this has been revealed.

33. the voice of a god: it is unlikely that the word *ḥayyîm*
('living') should be restored in conformity with some of the
ancient versions and 5:26. Moreover, the twofold purpose of the
section, viz. to show that only Yahweh is God and that it is only
to Israel that this has been revealed, is best preserved by the
translation 'a god' rather than 'God' (*NEB*). No other God but
Yahweh has shown his existence, and only Israel has seen it. **and
still live:** the most frequently expressed thought is that no man
can *see* God and live (Gen. 16:13; 32:30; Exod. 3:6; 19:21; 33:20,
etc); here the reference is to God speaking to Israel at Sinai, in
the account of which in Exod. 20:19 it is hearing God speaking
which brings this danger.

34. attempted: a better translation is perhaps 'ventured', as
with the same verb in 28:56. **trials:** the reference is to the testing
of the Pharaoh through the plagues. **signs... wonders:** a sign
is any distinguishing mark, not necessarily of a strange or miraculous nature, which points beyond itself to the thing signified; a
wonder, on the other hand, is an unusual phenomenon requiring
explanation. The two terms are frequently coupled, sometimes
with the effect that they become synonymous (cf. Isa. 8:18).

Deuteronomy, in using the terms with reference to the plagues brought on Egypt (also 6:22; 7:19) conforms with the use in Exod. 8:23; 10:1, 2 (signs) and Exod. 7:3; 11:9, 10 (wonders). **a mighty hand and an outstretched arm:** a combination found in 7:19; 11:2; 26:8, and also in the decalogue in 5:15. The terms also frequently occur separately in other passages (e.g. 3:24; 6:21; 9:29).

35. The conclusion that the general background of the affirmation of this verse is also that of Second Isaiah, i.e. an exilic background, is unavoidable in view of the identity of thought between this passage and Isa. 43:10ff.; 44:6; 45:6f., 22. See also comment on v. 32.

36. discipline you: in view of the frequent use of the verb in the context of a parent training his child (8:5; Prov. 19:18; 29:17) or in the general context of correction (1 Kg. 12:11, 14; Jer. 10:24; 30:11, etc). the *RSV* translation is preferable to the weaker *NEB* 'your instruction'. At the end of the verse a good parallel to v. 33 is obtained by the transfer and slight emendation of the unnecessary word at the beginning of v. 37 (*wattehi* for *we͏taḥat*): 'and you lived', cf. Mittmann, *Deuteronomium 1:1–6:3*, 123.

37. he loved your fathers: otherwise this is mentioned only in 10:15, though elsewhere (e.g. 7:8) reference is made to God's love of Israel. **their descendants after them:** this follows the reading of the ancient versions. The *MT* has 'his descendants after him' (which, in view of its difficulty in the context, may well be the original reading), with reference perhaps to Abraham only. **with his own presence:** that is, Yahweh acted 'in person' (*NEB*) and not through an intermediary to deliver Israel; cf. Exod. 33:14; 2 Sam. 17:11.

38. nations greater and mightier than yourselves: it is not for Israel's power that God chose her (also 7:1; 9:1ff.), but because of his love for her ancestors. **inheritance:** see comment on v. 21.

39. there is no other: this is much more than a simple affirmation of Yahweh's exclusive claim on Israel; as in v. 35 and in Second Isaiah, it is an explicit affirmation of the uniqueness of God.

40. The conclusion repeats the basic theme of the chapter, the laws of Horeb which Moses is to teach the people, and expresses the blessing which will follow on obedience as a counterpart to the curse threatened in v. 26.

E. CITIES OF REFUGE IN EAST JORDAN: **4:41-43**

The deuteronomic law in Dt. 19 provides for three cities of refuge in west Jordan; and a post-deuteronomic addition in 19:8f. provides for three additional cities in the event of Israel's territory being extended. Ch. 19 makes no reference to the present passage, which is difficult to explain if 4:41-43 is the earlier of the two. If, on the other hand, the present passage is later than the law of ch. 19 and its addition, it may be conjectured that the author of the present passage understood the three additional cities as the Transjordanian cities of refuge mentioned in Num. 35:9-15 and named in Jos. 20:8; and assumed that these must have been established by Moses as soon as the conquest of east Jordan had been carried out. This would mean that 4:41-43 is very late, probably deriving from the one responsible for connecting the deuteronomistic work to the Tetrateuch.

41. three cities: on the cities of refuge see comment on 19:1ff. **beyond the Jordan:** see comment on 1:1.

42. manslayer: this is the participle of the verb translated **kills** later in the verse; see comment on 5:17, where the same verb appears.

43. The list of cities corresponds to Jos. 20:8. **Bezer:** referred to in the Moabite Stone, line 27, as having been rebuilt by the Moabite king Mesha. Its location is uncertain; Umm el-ʿAmad, some eight miles north-east of Medeba, is suggested. **Ramoth:** reference to this city in the context of Israel's wars with Syria (1 Kg. 22; 2 Kg. 8f.) presupposes that it was a border fortress in northern Gilead. The most probable location is Tell er-Ramith on the Wadi Shomer. **Golan:** of uncertain location; Sahem el-Jolan, about eighteen miles east of the Sea of Galilee, is possible.

II The Second Address of Moses to Israel: **4:44-28:68**

A. INTRODUCTION: **4:44-49**

The original part of this introduction lies in v. 45, composed in a form analogous to 12:1. It has been expanded in two stages: first, through the addition of vv. 44, 46 which, since they are in the style of 1:1a, 4, must be assigned to the deuteronomist who wished to have his own form of introduction represented at this point;

and, secondly, through the addition of vv. 47–49. These three verses are very similar to 4:41–43 (a common concern with east Jordan, the use of the phrase 'in the east beyond the Jordan'), and probably derive from the same, very late, author, taking up material from chs. 1–3; cf. Seitz, *Studien*, 26f.

45. testimonies: as Lindars (in *Words and Meanings*, 127) shows, the word *'ēḏôṯ* is derived from the primary idea of witness; the word has developed from denoting the act of witnessing to denote the thing which is witnessed, viz. the laws themselves. The word is used with general reference to the law here and in 6:17, 20. The parallel word used by the priestly writer (*'ēḏûṯ*; cf. Exod. 31:18; 32:15; 34:29; and Lohfink, *Hauptgebot*, 57f.) makes specific reference to the decalogue. With both words there is close connection with the Accadian *adē*, the technical term for a treaty, cf. Hillers, *Covenant*, 160f. Since it is precisely in the decalogue context that the word occurs also in Deuteronomy, it may be that it was in fact secondarily added here, with intentional reference to the decalogue, at the time of the deuteronomistic editing which introduced the decalogue.

46. For the places and people, see comment on 1:4; 3:29. **when they came out of Egypt:** the parallel here with v. 45 shows that this verse is not the original continuation of v. 45; rather it continues v. 44, in the style of the introduction to the book in 1:1*a*, 4.

48. from Aroer ... Arnon: see comment on 2:36. **Sirion:** the Hebrew text reads *śi'ōn*, a name not found elsewhere. The Syriac reading, from which the name Sirion is taken, is probably a correction in the light of 3:9 of what was felt to be a difficult text, rather than an original reading.

49. the Arabah ... the Sea of the Arabah: see comment on 1:1; 3:17.

B. EXHORTATION TO COVENANT FAITH: 5:1–11:32

Within the general structure of Deuteronomy, this section constitutes the statement of basic principle, immediately preceding the detailed laws of the covenant. The dominance of the parenetic over the historical material, and the subservience of what historical material there is to the aim of inculcating obedience to the demand for the exclusive worship of Yahweh, meshes this section in strongly with the beginning of the collection of laws proper, in chs. 12f., for there too the major concern is for safeguarding the purity and exclusiveness of Israel's faith. The connection between the two sections is so strong that it is clear that, in distinction to chs. 1–4 which are not an original preface to what follows, in chs. 5–11 we do have such an original preface. Although much of what is now contained in chs. 12ff. derives from very early time, as a collection of laws put together by the deuteronomic compiler (cf. Introduction, pp. 47ff.) there was always exhortation attached as a preface, which is now contained within chs. 5–11.

(A) THE TEN COMMANDMENTS GIVEN AT HOREB: 5:1–6:3

This section has the aim of introducing the decalogue at the head of the deuteronomic law. It is the first of two major deuterono-mistic expansions of the parenetic introduction to the deuterono-mic law (cf. also 9:7ff.). Deuteronomistic responsibility is indicated firstly by the fact that the form of the decalogue here finds its best explanation against a deuteronomistic background (cf. below), and, secondly, by the fact that outside the two deutero-nomistic additions, and some isolated insertions, the original par-enetic introduction to the deuteronomic law (to be found in the passages in singular form of address in 6:4ff.) does not refer to the decalogue or presuppose its presence (cf. Perlitt, *Bundes-theologie* 81ff.). Secondary deuteronomistic additions, deriving from the author of 4:1–40, are to be found in 5:1, 3, 4, 24, 26, 29, 32f.; 6:2f., and an even later isolated addition in 5:5 (see comment on the individual verses).

In the Sinai pericope of Exod. 19–24 the decalogue is a secondary insertion. It is not presupposed by Exod. 20:18–21 which follows directly on the theophany of Exod. 19. On the other hand, there is no support for the thesis (cf. Seitz, *Studien*, 45f.) that the decalogue is simply misplaced, its original position being after Exod. 20:18–21; there is no indication that it was ever considered to have been mediated to the people by Moses, which would be the case on this theory. The insertion of the decalogue in its present place is secondary. Its presence in the Sinai context is, however, presupposed by the deuteronomist who here follows the present general pattern of Exod. 19f., though how much earlier than this the addition was made is difficult to say. Nielsen, *Commandments*, 44ff., points to the period between 622 BC (the time of the original Deuteronomy which makes no reference to the decalogue) and 560 BC (the time of the deuteronomist who pre-supposes its presence in the Sinai/Horeb context) as the time when the decalogue was introduced. That *terminus a quo* is prob-able, though not for the reason stated. The original Deuteronomy was concerned not with the covenant at Horeb but with Moses' proclamation of the law to Israel on the eve of entry into the promised land. Its silence on the decalogue does not, therefore, presuppose that the decalogue did not as yet exist as a covenant document (cf. de Vries, *VT* 16, 1966, 530ff.).

Yet, it is clear that strong arguments exist against taking the decalogue as deriving from, or as a development of, an ancient collection of ten commandments. Certainly there are indications of the existence of some of the commandments of the decalogue in pre-deuteronomic time (cf. e.g. Hos. 4:2), but a distinction must be preserved between the history of the individual command-ments and the history of the collection. In any attempt to describe the latter the following may be proposed as guidelines: firstly, there is no indication that there ever existed a regular series of ten short prohibitions (as reconstructed by Nielsen, *ibid.*); secondly, it is unlikely that the decalogue was ever anything other than address of Yahweh (this does not depend on the elimination as secondary of all the material which refers to Yahweh in the third person; the decalogue is established as speech of Yahweh by the first two or three—see comment on v. 11—commandments); thirdly, in view of the fact that the Exodus version of the decalogue contains post-deuteronomistic material (see comment on v. 15), the Exodus version cannot simply be taken in its present form as an older version of the decalogue than Dt. 5. Both derive from a common prototype.

This common prototype cannot be established simply through working each individual commandment back to its shortest possible form through the omission of the motivating clauses. Such a procedure belongs within the context of the history of each commandment, not within the context of the history of the collec-tion. On the basis of the assumption that the decalogue is a collec-tion of commandments many of which had an earlier history (which is supported by the reference to some of them in Hos. 4:2), it is most probable that the occasion of the collection was also the occasion of the presentation of the commandments as speech of Yahweh and the occasion of the addition to them of motivating clauses.

For all their differences, both the Exodus and the Deuteronomic versions of the decalogue point to the deuteronomic milieu as the context of their collection and presentation. In the first place, from a form-critical point of view, the decalogue is late. Gerstenberger, *Wesen*, 86ff., has shown in general that series of ten or twelve cannot be seen as original compilations of apodictic law. Rather, such extended collections go back to original short series of two or three laws. With reference to the decalogue in particular, Gese, *ZThK* 64, 1976, 127ff., has argued that it consists of five pairs of commandments (the first and second dealing with the worship of Yahweh; the third and fourth with the cult; the fifth and seventh with the protection of the family; the sixth and eighth with the protection of the individual (see comment on the relevant verses for this possible original order of the commandments); and the ninth and tenth with the neighbour), and Alt, *Essays*, 117ff., has pointed to the intention of the decalogue 'to cover the whole field of apodeictic law', which indicates a date of compilation later than those series (such as Lev. 18:7ff.) which are concerned with a single subject. Finally, Schmidt, *VTS* 22, 1972, 201ff., has discerned a tendency towards generalizing within the individual commandments (for example, the first commandment being a generalization over against Exod. 22:20; 23:13; and the fifth being a generalization of an original specific prohibition, see comment on v.16). The decalogue, as a collection of such generalized law, would be a late compilation. This form-critical conclusion is not invalidated by arguments based on the supposed parallel between the decalogue and the form of the Hittite vassal treaties (cf. Beyerlin, *Origins*, 49ff.), which have attempted to show that the decalogue must derive from the time of currency of these treaty forms, viz. 1400–1200 BC. The parallel is far from close and really only gains any credibility from the general context within which the decalogue now stands. Moreover, the links which connect the Hittite with the later Mesopotamian treaty forms into one treaty tradition (see, in general, McCarthy, *Treaty*), together with the problems associated with Israel's adaptation of the treaty form, make any attempt to assign precise dates to any possible Old Testament parallels on the basis of the form extremely hazardous.

In the second place, there are particular links with literature deriving from the deuteronomic circle. These lie not only in the motivating clauses (see comment on the individual commandments) but also in the chief concern of the decalogue in its original form with the exclusiveness of Israel's worship of Yahweh. While it is not impossible that such a concern existed in pre-deuteronomic times it is from this time that it gets its closest parallel in the commands for the single sanctuary and for the abolition of all non-Yahwistic shrines and forms of worship in Dt. 12f. These connections between the decalogue and deuteronomic material cannot be explained (as Reventlow, *Gebot*, 1ff.) as a result of the dependence of both on an old tradition of preaching of the law. Rather, this is deuteronomic proclamation of a collection of law which takes its origin in a deuteronomic milieu (cf. Fohrer, *KuD* 11, 1965, 57ff.), and which was inserted by its deuteronomic compiler in the Sinai context in Exod. 20.

The decalogue was not, therefore, created by the later deuteronomistic editor responsible for its introduction into Dt. 5. It is a quotation here of an already existing document; it was composed in second person singular form of address and is now incorporated in a deuteronomistic context composed in the second person plural form of address. Yet the deuteronomistic editor responsible for its inclusion has contributed significantly to the form which the decalogue has in Dt. 5. Not only are there several additions and minor adaptations which may be identified as coming from this editor (see comment on the individual commandments), but the structure of the whole points to a late period as background.

This structure, as Lohfink, *BZ* 9, 1965, 17ff., has shown, is primarily one in which the original decalogue, which emphasized the importance of the first commandments simply through placing them first in the series, has been modified in two respects in particular in order to give prominence to the command to observe the Sabbath: firstly, a reference has been introduced into the Sabbath commandment to the exodus on the one hand and to 'ox and ass' on the other in order to provide catchword links with the beginning and end of the decalogue (see comment on vv. 14, 15); and, secondly, the sixth to the tenth commandments have been connected by the conjunction in order to bring them together as a single long unit, balancing the long unit formed by the first two commandments. Both modifications have the effect of pushing forward the Sabbath commandment as central to the decalogue, rather than simply as fourth commandment in a series of ten which is headed by the most important. Such an emphasis on the importance of the Sabbath points to a later rather than an earlier period of Israel's history, as the Sabbath began to assume increasing importance, though it is perhaps not necessary to go quite as late as the exile (as Lohfink does) in this connection.

Lohfink (*ibid.*, 28f.) argues, however, that this deuteronomistic decalogue is a replacement of an earlier decalogue which originally stood in this place. There certainly was an earlier form of the decalogue—and the phrase 'as the Lord your God commanded you' in 5:12, 16 refers back to it (it is only the decalogue which is given directly to the people by God)—but there is no sign that this earlier form of the decalogue originally stood in the place of the present one at the beginning of the parenetic introduction to the deuteronomic law beginning in 6:4. Rather, it is the deuteronomist who took the already existing decalogue from the context of the Sinai story in Exod. 20 into which an older deuteronomic editor had inserted it, and himself first brought it into its present context at the beginning of the Mosaic law. By so doing the deuteronomist effected a close connection between the decalogue and the deuteronomic law, which resulted in an enhancement of the latter so that it came to be seen as sharing in the authority which the decalogue already possessed (see also comment on 29:1).

1. The terminology of this verse **(hear, Israel, the statutes and the ordinances, this day)** finds its closest parallel in ch. 4 (cf. vv. 1, 4), and the verse should therefore be taken to derive from the author of that chapter.

2. This and the following verse use the first person plural form, as frequently in the deuteronomistic chs. 1–3. **made a covenant:** i.e. imposed an obligation (as already observed by Marti, 249).

3. The style links this verse with the preceding one, but the content is more closely associated with the author of ch. 4 than with the deuteronomistic author of chs. 1–3. Probably it comes from the former, but is influenced in style by the already existing v. 2. **our fathers:** the contrast with **us, who are all of us here alive this day,** indicates that there is no specific reference to the patriarchs here, but rather to the preceding generations generally. This means that strictly speaking there is a contradiction of chs. 1–3 with respect to the assertion there that the generation which had entered into covenant with Yahweh at Horeb died while wandering in the wilderness (cf. 2:14ff.); the contradiction should not be over-emphasized, however. The intention of the author of this late passage is to stress the continuing validity of the covenant law for his own generation (cf. 4:4ff.).

4. face to face: that the decalogue was given directly to the people is not stated in the complex structure of the Sinai pericope in Exod. 19ff. The late author of this verse makes this explicit, however (cf. also 4:13). However, his aim is also to prepare for and draw attention to the additional significant point that 'God (may) speak with man and man still live' (v. 24; see comment on 4:33). **out of the midst of the fire:** as in 4:12.

5. I stood between the Lord and you: the whole verse is incompatible not only with v. 4 but also with v. 22 which comes from the deuteronomist. Following Seitz, *op. cit.*, 49, it is best, therefore, to take the verse (except for the final two words) as a late correction to the deuteronomistic account on the basis of Exod. 34:10 which emphasizes the place of Moses as the one with whom Yahweh made the covenant. **He said:** this takes up v. 2 after the interruption caused by the addition of vv. 3f. and 5; cf. also Lohfink, *Hauptgebot*, 145ff.

6. I am the Lord your God: this is a self-revelation formula which occurs frequently in the Holiness Code particularly (cf. Lev. 18:2, 4, 5, etc. and Zimmerli, *Offenbarung*, 11ff.). An alternative translation here, which is perhaps more suitable in the immediate context of the service of Yahweh and Israel's exclusive allegiance to him, is 'I, Yahweh, am your God', cf. Noth. *Laws*, 20. **who brought you ... house of bondage:** this has been paralleled with the historical prologue of the Hittite vassal treaties; but the purpose here is perhaps rather to identify the speaker than to provide such a history. Its language is deuteronomic, especially the expression **house of bondage,** cf. Fohrer, *KuD* 11, 1965, 58.

7. before me: the phrase may mean 'in preference to me' (as with the same phrase in 21:16), or 'over against, in opposition to me' (cf. Gen. 16:12; 25:18), and the reference might be concretely to the setting up of an image in the sanctuary of Yahweh or simply generally to the worship of a god other than Yahweh. In any case, the attitude presupposed is not a monotheistic one; it is not the existence of other gods, but rather Israel's worship of them, which is repudiated.

8. The original prohibition was **You shall not make for yourself a graven image;** this has been extended and generalized by subsequent additions. **graven image:** see comment on 4:16. **any likeness:** see comment on 4:12. The reason for the prohibition is that the divine presence in the image made the image a source of power subject to human use and manipulation; it was, therefore, a limitation on divine freedom and sovereignty.

9. you shall not bow down to them or serve them: the antecedent to **them** is not image and likeness in v. 8, but 'other gods' in v. 7; it is only other gods which one serves and to which one bows down in the Old Testament (cf. Zimmerli, *Offenbarung*, 234ff.). This means, however, that the author of this verse must have taken the first two commandments together as one commandment and understood the image of v. 8 to refer to images of other gods, not of Yahweh. This cannot have been the original reference, since on this view the prohibition of the manufacture of images is quite superfluous once the worship of other gods has already been prohibited. The image of v. 8 must, therefore, originally have been understood as an image of Yahweh. A subsequent change in understanding is also indicated by the motive: **for I ... am a jealous God;** this can only be understood in the context o turning to the worship of other gods, not that of setting up an image of Yahweh (cf. Exod. 34:14, and comment on 4:24). **of those who hate me:** the phrase does not form an original part of the old formula **(visiting the iniquity of the fathers upon the children to the third and fourth generation)** which occurs in Exod. 34:7 and Num. 14:18. The additional phrase, which appears also in Exod. 20:5, apparently derives from the deuteronomic compiler of the decalogue; its purpose is to reconcile the old formula, according to which the whole family (the four generations being those generations living together as a family) bears communal responsibility for each of its members, with the later view of individual responsibility which is expressed in Dt. 24:16 (cf. Jer. 31:29; Ezek. 18), by describing the children as continuing the sin of the fathers in rejecting Yahweh.

10. steadfast love: see comment on 7:9. **thousands:** i.e. perhaps 'a thousand generations' (cf. 7:9). The old formula of Exod. 34:7, which is intended to show that the mercy of God is even more embracing than his anger (cf. Zimmerli, *Law*, 58), has again been amplified by the deuteronomic compiler of the decalogue. The words **those who love me and keep my commandments** modify once more the old formula in keeping with later views of individual responsibility.

11. the name of the Lord your God: the reference to Yahweh in the third person is out of keeping with a collection of laws purportedly spoken by Yahweh. Possibly the commandment originally read *šᵉmî* ('my name'), the last consonant of which was later taken as an abbreviation for Yahweh (that this could have happened is proved by Jg. 19 :18 where an original *beti*, 'my house', was later taken as *bêṭ YHWH*, 'house of the Lord'), which in turn allowed the addition of 'your God'. On the other hand, this kind of inconsistency is not without parallel in Deuteronomy; cf. 7:4; 11:14f.; 17:3; 28:20; 29:5f., where speech of Moses suddenly passes over into divine speech. Not all of these cases are open to the type of explanation which is possible in the present instance, and are perhaps best understood against a background of preaching and exhortation. **in vain:** for an empty and worthless purpose. Phillips, *Law*, 53ff., argues that the prohibition refers not to blasphemy nor to false swearing but to the use of the name of Yahweh for magical purposes; this would take place in the context of attempts to influence or harm another person.

12. Observe: Exod. 20:8 has 'remember'. The latter is probably original, and the change should be seen along with the use of the verb *'āśāh* at the end of the commandment (v. 15, 'to keep'; this does not appear in the Exodus version); for the two verbs together form a fixed idiomatic expression in Deuteronomy in the context of the proclamation of the law; cf. 5:32; 6:3, 17f., 25, etc., and Lohfink, *Hauptgebot*, 64f., 68ff., and the table on 300ff.

This and the following commandment are the only two positive commandments in the decalogue. The originality of their positive form has been widely questioned; but although it is possible to suggest suitable prohibitions to conform with the style of the rest of the decalogue (here: 'you shall do no work on the Sabbath day'), it is difficult to explain satisfactorily why only these prohibitions in the decalogue should have been changed into positive commandments (see also comment on v. 16). The case of the Sabbath commandment is considerably complicated by uncertainty with regard to the history of the Sabbath. The theory that it was originally a day of the month, derived from the Babylonian *shapattu*, on which it was unlucky to perform certain acts (for which then a prohibition would be particularly suitable), which in the context of Israelite faith was changed into a *festival* day (for which a positive commandment would then be more suitable) is possible (though cf. the reservations of Phillips, *op. cit.*, 65f.). Granted this possibility, however, it is still most likely that the change from a Sabbath prohibition to a Sabbath commandment took place before the decalogue originated and that the decalogue itself never contained any such prohibition.

14. your ox or your ass: this does not appear in the Exodus

version; it is taken from the last commandment in order to provide
a catchword link between the middle and the end of this deuteronomistic decalogue; cf. Lohfink, *BZ* 9, 1965, 23f. **the sojourner:**
see comment on 1:16. **that your manservant and your maid-
servant may rest as well as you:** this is an extension, apparently
based on Exod. 23:12, which is not found in the Exodus version
of the fourth commandment. Nor is the humanitarianism which is
expressed here, and in the next verse, even implicit in the Exodus
decalogue; humanitarian concerns are, however, prominent in
Deuteronomy, especially in its interpretation of some ancient
law (e.g. 20:5–7) and in its constant concern for the poor and
economically weak (e.g. 24:17, 19f.).

15. This verse has no counterpart in Exod. 20, where the Sabbath is rather associated with the priestly account of creation (cf.
Gen. 2:2f., Exod. 31:17). The reference to Israel's slavery in
Egypt as a basis for observance of the commandment is typically
deuteronomic, cf. 15:15; 16:12; 24:18, 22. Moreover, the reference
to it here provides a catchword link between the beginning of the
decalogue (v. 6) and the middle (see comment on v. 14). **a mighty
hand and an outstretched arm:** see comment on 4:34.

16. A proposed original prohibition is 'you shall not curse your
father or your mother' (cf. Exod. 21:17; Dt. 27:16), but, as with
the Sabbath commandment, it is unlikely that any such prohibition ever formed part of the decalogue (see comment on v. 12).
Even if the form-critical argument that positive commandments
originated from parenetic expositions of prohibitions (cf. e.g.
Lev. 19:18) is correct, such a process had undoubtedly already
taken place by the time of origin of the decalogue. For the compiler of the latter, then, there would have been available both
positive and negative forms of apodictic law. Gerstenberger,
Wesen, 43ff., points in particular to Exod. 20:8ff., 12; 23:7; Lev.
19:9f., 32; Dt. 25:13ff., in order to show, however, that while
prohibitions may greatly outnumber positive commands, the
latter are not secondary within the category of apodictic law.

The basic commandment here is **Honour your father and
your mother.** The remaining material derives from the deuteronomic compiler offering encouragement through the use of motive
clauses typical of the deuteronomic literature (cf. Dt. 4:40; 5:33;
6:2; 11:9; 22:7; 30:18; 32:47). **Honour** implies respect and
general submission to parents' authority (cf. 1 Sam. 15:20). Several
passages in Proverbs (1:8; 13:1; 19:26, etc.) indicate that this is a

traditional concern not confined to the religious context; yet, within Deuteronomy the chief object of the command is probably that of safeguarding the role of parents in the transmission of the faith to the children, cf. Dt. 4:9; 6:7, 20f.

17. kill: an adequate English translation of the verb is difficult to find. The *RSV* may be misleading since the killing of animals, capital punishment and killing in war are not covered by the verb. The *NEB* ('murder') is closer, yet does not cover the case of accidental homicide (as in Dt. 4:42) nor that of authorized killing within the community (cf. Num. 35:27, 30). The verb means simply to kill a man. Some scholars (cf. e.g. Reventlow, *Gebot,* 71ff.) wrongly associate the verb exclusively with the sphere of blood revenge. 1 Kg. 21:19 illustrates a quite normal use of the verb and cannot be taken as exceptional.

18. Neither: in distinction to the Exodus version of the decalogue, here this and the following commandments are all introduced by the conjunction. On the significance of this see, above, the introduction to this section. **adultery:** this concerned extramarital sexual relations on the part of a married woman, a betrothed woman being treated as though married (cf. Dt. 22:22ff.). Generally, in ancient Near Eastern lawcodes both the man and the woman involved were liable to the death penalty (cf. Schulz, *Todesrecht,* 15ff.). Dt. 22:22 conforms with this. Hos. 2:4; Jer. 3:8, on the other hand, would seem to indicate that the woman was punished with divorce rather than with execution. However, divorce should probably be taken as the normal practice in coping with a situation for which the law actually provided the ultimate punishment. The purpose of this prohibition was not simply to protect the husband's property, but rather to ensure the legitimacy of the children of the marriage. This general concern with the family connects the commandment with the fifth rather than the sixth, and it may be that the reverse order of the sixth and seventh commandments, given in some MSS of the LXX, the Nash Papyrus and Philo, is original; cf. Gese, *ZThK* 64, 1967, 134ff.

19. The proposal (cf. Alt, *Kleine Schriften* I, 333ff., anticipated by the Babylonian Talmud Sanh. 86a, and adopted by many scholars) that this commandment was concerned originally with kidnapping, arose from the observation that otherwise there is duplication with the tenth commandment which includes stealing (see comment on v. 21), and such duplication is unlikely within the context of a short series such as the decalogue. Furthermore, kidnapping is a subject of Old Testament law (cf. Exod. 21:16; Dt. 24:7). The same verb is indeed used for both theft and kidnapping (cf. Gen. 40:15; Exod. 21:16; Dt. 24:7; 2 Sam. 19:42), and it is therefore likely that kidnapping is in any event included in this commandment. However, that there ever existed an expressed object in the commandment, making kidnapping its exclusive interest, is unlikely. The verbs used here and in the tenth commandment are not synonymous, so in fact there exists no duplication to be explained; see comment on v. 21, and the study by Klein, *VT* 26, 1976, 161ff. Gese (see comment on v. 18) has pointed to the connection between the sixth and the eighth commandments (protection of one's life and freedom) which suggests that they originally stood together.

20. bear false witness: the verb ʿānāh is used as a technical term 'to testify, give testimony in a court' in Num. 35:30; Dt. 19:16, 18 so indicating that the concern of this prohibition is with a witness at law, not with lying generally (see the longer treatment of the subject in Dt. 19:15ff.). Although the *RSV* translation is the same in both Exod. 20:16 and here, there is a slight difference in the Hebrew. The Exodus version has ʿēḏ šeḵer (evidently the standard phrase, used also in Ps. 27:12; Prov. 6:19; 12:17; 14:5; 19:5, 9; 25:18), while the Deuteronomy version uses the phrase ʿēḏ šāw. There is no material distinction between the two. Although the latter only appears here there is an analogous phrase in Exod. 23:1, where šāw is similarly applied to the report or testimony which one makes. The change should be seen as a deuteronomic variation, perhaps under the influence of šāw ('vain') in v. 11.

21. The basis of the tenth commandment is 'you shall not covet your neighbour's house'. The remainder, as given in the Exodus version (Exod. 20:17), constituted a definition of what was meant by 'house', viz. it meant 'household' and included all the people and property connected with it. In time, however, the word came to be taken to refer to the building alone, so that the rest of the commandment was understood, not as a definition, but as the continuation of the list which was begun by 'house'. The deuteronomistic editor then reversed the order of the first two elements of the list to put 'wife' first; this change is probably based on the importance which the editor understood the decalogue to assign to marriage through its prohibition of adultery. **covet:** it has frequently been argued (cf. Stamm and Andrew, *Commandments*, 102f.) that the verb means not simply 'desire' but also 'take steps to appropriate' and therefore comes close to 'steal'. However, the case is by no means so clear as might at first appear. In almost all the passages quoted (cf. Dt. 7:25; Jos. 7:21; Mic. 2:2) an additional verb is required in order to convey the sense of 'appropriate for oneself', so that the verb translated 'covet' means just that. An exception is Exod. 34:24, but there the emphasis may be more on the fact that nobody will be left who might threaten the property of Israelites than on any feeling or action on the part of the enemies of Israel who may be left. That the deuteronomist understood the verb to mean 'covet' is clear from the fact that, apparently for the sake of variation only, he has substituted for the second occurrence of the verb in the Exodus version a verb meaning **desire,** which he takes to be synonymous. Moreover, covetousness is the object of widespread condemnation outside the Old Testament; see the Egyptian texts quoted in Hyatt, *Exodus*, 216.

22. these words: on the use of 'words' with specific reference to the decalogue, see the comment on 4:10. The term is also found outside the Old Testament used in treaties for the treaty stipulations, cf. Beyerlin, *Origins*, 53. **thick darkness:** see comment on 4:11. **he added no more:** the decalogue is distinguished by being the fundamental will of God made known directly to the people, cf. 9:10; 10:12. **two tables:** see comment on 4:13. **gave them to me:** the strict chronological order of events is not the main concern of the narrative. According to Exod. 19–34 the tablets containing the decalogue were not delivered to Moses until after he had mediated between Yahweh and the people and had received the additional covenant commandments, cf. Exod. 24:12; 32:15f.; Dt. 9:7ff. Through referring to the tablets at this point the author immediately completes the narrative of the decalogue.

23. all the heads of your tribes and your elders: this is a late gloss, unsuitable in a context which is consistently addressed to 'you'. Such a representative group does not otherwise appear (1:15 not being a parallel situation; and 29:10f. referring to them only in the context of a comprehensive list), cf. Mittmann, *op. cit.*, 137f.

24. The verse is from the author of ch. 4. It fits badly in its context in its understanding of the effect of God's speaking directly with man, and cannot justify the request of the people for a mediator (v. 27). **and man still live:** see comment on 4:33, which displays the closest parallel to the thought of this verse.

25. This verse rather than the preceding prepares for the request for a mediator. It is only with difficulty that vv. 24 and 25 may be harmonized (through the artificial distinction between the first and subsequent experiences of hearing the voice of God). They are in fact clearly from different hands: while the former is a declaration of praise and confident trust in the nearness of God (cf. 4:33f., 35f.), the latter expresses the pessimistic fear aroused by any contact with the divine.

26. This verse continues v. 24 rather than v. 25, and so comes from the late author of ch. 4. It expresses the exclusive privilege enjoyed by Israel in God's closeness (cf. 4:32ff.), rather than the fear of the danger which this closeness brings. **all flesh:** a late expression, used frequently by the priestly writer (e.g. Gen. 6:12, 13, 19), Second Isaiah (e.g. Isa. 40:5, 6), Jeremiah (e.g. 25:31; 32:27) and Ezekiel (20:48; 21:4).

27. Here v. 25 is continued. The substance of these two verses, with v. 23, is rooted in Exod. 20:18–21. It has been argued by Lohfink, *Hauptgebot*, 67f., that 5:27–6:3 constitute the literary form of a chiasm, so indicating the existence here of an original unit. However, the presence of this literary form does not of itself guarantee the existence of an original literary unit (see on 1:1–5), particularly when, as here, there is considerable imbalance between the two halves of the form (e.g. v. 28 in the first half has nothing corresponding to it in the second) as well as a difference in the style and the subjects of the characteristic verbs. The probability is, therefore, that the section has evolved through the addition of secondary material aimed at constructing such a literary form.

28. The divine approval of the request of the people is not found in the Exodus version of the Sinai event.

29. Two points suggest that this verse derives from the hand of the late deuteronomistic author of 4:1–40. Firstly, there are strong connections in terminology with 4:19, 40; and, secondly, the concern, expressed in **always,** for the possibility that with the passage of time the inclination to obey Yahweh will weaken also finds its closest parallel in ch. 4 (v. 25; see comment). **mind:** the Hebrew is the word usually translated 'heart'; see comment on 4:29. The importance of the inner disposition and attitude is a feature also of certain wisdom texts from Egypt, cf. Malfroy, *VT* 15, 1965, 63.

30. Return to your tents: a formula which belongs properly in the context of war; it is a demobilization command, see comment on 1:27 and also 16:7.

31. the commandment: this is used in the later parts of
Deuteronomy comprehensively for the whole law (cf. 11:22; 19:9,
etc., and Seitz, *op. cit.*, 37); that reference may be preserved here,
either by omitting the conjunction which immediately follows
(with *Sam*, and 6:1), or by understanding the conjunction as
pleonastic, see comment on 1:7. **the statutes and the ordinances:** see comment on 4:1.

32, 33. These two verses, belonging together in their concern to
inculcate obedience as the right **way** (so using wisdom thought
and terminology, cf. Prov. 10:29; 11:5, 20; 14:12, etc.), probably
derive from the author of ch. 4. The natural continuation of 5:31
is to be found in 6:1 (cf. Bertholet), and in referring to the law as
already delivered to the people there is close affinity with 4:5; for
the subject and expression of v. 33*b* see 4:40.

6:1. Here the deuteronomist, having completed his insertion of
the decalogue, leads back to the deuteronomic material already
introduced in 4:45.

2. This verse, in singular form of address, is awkwardly tagged
on to the end of v. 1 which reaches its own conclusion. Moreover,
the terms used for the law do not conform. It is a late addition,
probably from the hand of the author of ch. 4 (**you and your son
and your son's son** cf. 4:25; **his statutes and his commandments which I command you** cf. 4:40; **that your days may
be prolonged** cf. 4:40). **you and your son and your son's
son:** a familiar phrase from the extra-biblical state treaties.

3. As v. 2 so this verse is from the hand of the author of ch. 4,
who here takes up motifs and themes from the deuteronomic law
which now begins in v. 4, cf. 6:4, 18f.; 7:13, etc. As in ch. 4 so
here there is a sudden change of number (from the singular form
of address to the plural **you may multiply**). **in a land flowing
with milk and honey:** the Hebrew lacks the preposition 'in'.
The phrase stands in apposition, though these is nothing in the
verse to which it can stand in apposition. The antecedent in fact
is to be found in v. 1 of which the phrase was the original continuation (cf. the *NEB* transfer of the phrase to follow v. 1, and
the use of the phrase in 11:9; 26:9, 15; 27:3; 31:20), everything
between having been added by the author of ch. 4. This is a
fixed phrase, occurring, besides the Deuteronomic references given,
also in Exod. 3:8, 17; 13:5; 33:3; Lev. 20:24; Num. 13:27; 14:8;

16:13, 14. It has close parallels both in classical writers (cf. Knobel) and in the Ugaritic texts (1 AB iii 6–7, 11–12; cf. *ANET* 140; Gordon, *Ugaritic Textbook*, 168). Waterhouse, *AUSS* I, 1963, 152ff., argues that it does not simply express the contrast with the desert which would have been felt by a semi-nomad, but fairly reflects the lushness of the land in past years. Progressive despoliation of the land by indiscriminate economic use of its resources has led to its present relatively barren and sterile appearance.

(B) ISRAEL MUST SERVE YAHWEH ALONE: **6:4–25**

As Seitz, *op. cit.*, 70ff., has shown, the basis of this section is to be found in vv. 4–9, 20–25, into which vv. 10–18 have been subsequently inserted. Vv. 4–9, 20–25 (and not vv. 10–19, 20–25, as Lohfink, *Haupgebot*, 113ff.) are connected through the association of sign and question, the sign of the action described in vv. 4–9 and the child's question arising from this in vv. 20–25. This association exists in all other passages where the form of the child's question is used; cf. Exod. 12:24–27; 13:11–16, where the question is associated with ritual elements of the Passover, and Jos. 4:6f., 21–24, where it is associated with the sign of the stones set up at Gilgal. There is a further connection between the two passages in that each is associated closely with the context of a father instructing his son. This is explicit in vv. 20–25, but more implicit in vv. 4–9. In the latter, it is the presence of many wisdom forms and motifs which points to the father-son/master-pupil context developed in vv. 20–25.

Vv. 10–18, on the other hand, fall out of this context. They are (loosely) constructed in the literary form of a chiasm (cf Seitz, *op. cit.*, 72f., who points to the following corresponding elements: v. 10a = 18$b\beta$; v. 10b, 11 = 18$b\alpha$; vv. 12f. = 17f.; v. 14 = 16; with v. 15 forming the central point), to which v. 19 has probably been added. It is only in this section that an echo is found of the decalogue (vv. 14f.), though this does not mean that the author responsible for it is the deuteronomist responsible for the introduction of the decalogue itself. It is more likely, in fact, that vv. 10–19 are from the hand of the author of 4:1–40. As in that chapter, so here the author is concerned to inculcate a particular decalogue commandment: the prohibition of the worship of other gods; as there, so here there is specific reference to a situation which will obtain in the land where the law is to be obeyed (cf. 4:25ff.); as there, so here there is sudden switch from the singular to the plural form of address; and, finally, there is a considerable stock of common terminology (he swore, 4:31; fear, 4:10; the peoples, 4:19; a jealous God, 4:24; destroy, 4:26; diligently keep, 4:9; the commandments, 4:2; commanded, cf. 4:5; 5:33; that it may go well with you, 4:40; good land, 4:22).

4. This verse begins the parenetic introduction to the deuteronomic law code, which has its original heading in 4:45. **Hear, O Israel:** this summons, found also in 5:1; 9:1; 20:3 and 27:9, is probably modelled on the common wisdom introduction 'hear, my son' (cf. Prov. 1:8; 4:1, 10; 5:7; 7:24; 23:19; etc., and McKay, *VT* 22, 1972, 431f.). **The Lord our God is one Lord:** the variety of possible translations of this phrase (cf. Driver) may be reduced to a basic two: that given in the *RSV*, or, alternatively, 'The Lord is our God, the Lord alone' (for this sense of 'eḥāḏ, cf. Isa. 51:2; Ezek. 33:24; 37:22; Zech. 14:9; 1 Chr. 29:1). The *RSV* translation emphasizes the oneness of Yahweh in the face of the multiplicity of the manifestations of Baal, a translation which therefore fits with a dominant deuteronomic concern that Israel's sacrificial worship should be confined to one sanctuary (see on chs. 12f.), while the alternative emphasizes the exclusiveness of Israel's worship of Yahweh which is also a prominent deuteronomic theme (see, for example, ch. 13). Both translations thus find considerable support in Deuteronomy, but the alternative is perhaps the more probable, being more suitable to the immediate continuation in v. 5. In neither case is there an explicit monotheism.

The Shema, a title taken from the first word of this verse, is a text consisting of 6:4; 6:4f.; or 6:4–9, and sometimes including Dt. 11:13–21 and Num. 15:37–41. It is a text which the faithful are required to recite twice daily. For a study of the history of its use and interpretation in Judaism and the New Testament, cf. McBride, *Interp* 27, 1973, 274ff.

5. you shall love: love of God is an attitude which can be commanded. For Deuteronomy it is virtually synonymous with 'obedience', cf. 10:12; 11:1, 13, 22, etc. The root of the use of the word in the context of the relationship between Yahweh and Israel has often been traced to Hosea (e.g. 11:1), but the connection with the prophet is more indirect than direct. Hosea speaks of Yahweh's love for Israel but not of Israel's love for Yahweh. On the other hand, Hosea does use the father–son analogy to describe the relationship between Yahweh and Israel; and this image is to be found in the context of treaty making (cf. 2 Kg. 16:7) in which context there also often appears the command that the vassal should love his suzerain (for an Old Testament reference to love in a treaty relationship, cf. 1 Kg. 5:1 see further Moran, *CBQ* 25, 1963, 77ff. For the close relationship of the father-son and the treaty or covenant relationship, cf. McCarthy, *CBQ* 27, 1965, 144ff.). McKay, *op. cit.*, 432ff., has emphasized the wisdom associations of 6:4–9, which presuppose that Yahweh is seen in the position of wisdom teacher or father and Israel as pupil or son. **love** therefore means respect and filial obedience. **with all your heart and with all your soul:** see comment on 4:29. The expansion here: **with all your might,** is taken up also by 2 Kg. 23:25.

6. these words . . . shall be on your heart: close parallels to this may be found in biblical and extra-biblical wisdom texts; cf. Prov. 3:3; 4:4, 21; Amen-em-opet iii 10–11, xxvii 13 (*ANET*, 421, 424).

7. teach them diligently: the verb here is used in 32:41 in the sense of 'sharpen', and figuratively of 'sharp words' in Pss. 64:3; 140:3. This is the only occurrence of the term in a teaching context. It should in fact probably be derived from a second root *šnn* distinct from that translated 'sharpen', and found in Ugaritic and Accadian in the sense of 'tell', 'recite' or 'teach'; cf. Driver, *Canaanite Myths and Legends*, 151; Tsevat, *HUCA* 29, 1958, 125 n. 112. **your children:** see comment on 4:9. **when you sit in your house, and when you walk by the way:** this and the following phrase are to be seen in the context of the general Semitic idiom of using antonymic pairs in order to signify totality (see comment on 'heaven and earth' in 4:26). One should talk of the commandments at all times.

8. bind them: this command has parallels in wisdom literature (Prov. 3:3; 6:21; 7:3), where it is used figuratively of the command to the pupil to keep his master's teaching continuously before him. A figurative use of the same idea is found in Exod. 13:9, 16, where the reference is to rituals to be performed rather than to words to be remembered. The actual origin, however, probably lies in a religious custom of tattooing and of wearing amulets (Cazelles). The following verse suggests that Deuteronomy also has a literal understanding of the command in view, and it is as a literal injunction that later Jews have fulfilled the command, viz. through inscribing the texts of Exod. 13:1–10, 11–16; Dt. 6:4–9; 11:13–21, where the command appears, on scrolls which are then enclosed in small leather containers called phylacteries (cf. Matt. 23:5). These are bound on the forehead and left arm during the time of morning prayer; cf. Henton Davies, in *IDB* vol. 3, 808f. **sign:** see comment on 4:34. If the command is to be taken literally, then the short text is a 'sign' standing for the whole law; if it is figurative, then it is Israel's constant fulfilment of the commandments which is a 'sign' of her obedience to God. **frontlets:** the origin of the word is uncertain, though it is probably to be derived from a root which appears in Arabic with the meaning 'surround', so that the reference would be to bands wound around the head.

9. doorposts: the Hebrew is *mᵉzûzōt*, of which the singular *mᵉzûzāh* is the designation given by Jews to the small box containing the written text and attached to the upper part of the right hand doorpost. This has its background in the ancient widespread custom of inscribing sayings of good omen over the doors of houses (Smith); in the Israelite context, the command has an additional point in that the household gods were apparently found connected with the doorposts (cf. Exod. 21:6; Isa 57:8). The command, therefore, implicitly reinforces the preceding demand (v. 7) that the Israelite must give his whole allegiance to Yahweh. **gates:** if there is a real distinction here from 'doorposts' the reference must be to the entrances to the villages or towns rather than to the entrances to the individual homes.

10, 11. land ... cities ... houses ... cisterns ... vineyards ... olive trees: the remarkable correspondence between this list and those found in Jos. 24:13; Neh. 9:24f. indicates that in spite of slight variation there is a relationship between them. Baltzer, *Covenant Formulary*, 20f., suggests that they all go back to older prototypes consisting of fixed forms of property lists such as are to be found in some Ugaritic texts. This background clearly exists, though there is an additional direct or indirect relationship between the present passage and Jos. 24:13 in the relative clauses which connect the items of the list. The list refers to the distinctive elements of a settled civilization, taken over by the Israelites from their predecessors.

12. The danger that time and acclimatization to the culture of the land might bring forgetfulness of the God to whom Israel owes her prosperity, or might bring self-pride or even apostasy, is a regular theme of Deuteronomy (8:11ff., cf. 4:25; 5:29), and is one of several links which connect the deuteronomic tradition with Hosea (2:5ff.).

13. fear: the fear of Yahweh means comprehensively and generally religion; see also comment on 4:10. **the Lord your God:** this phrase appears in the emphatic position at the beginning of the sentence, strengthening the contrast with the prohibition of the next verse. **swear by his name:** there may be an allusion here to the third commandment of the decalogue, though the latter does not carry the meaning of this phrase (see comment on 5:11); to swear by the name of Yahweh is to acknowledge Yahweh as one's highest authority; cf. Isa. 48:1; 65:16; Jer. 5:7; 12:16. This verse is paralleled in 10:20, where, too, it is part of a late passage.

14. A late reformulation, in second person plural form of address, of the first commandment of the decalogue.

15. in the midst of you: this expression carries overtones of the help and saving presence of Yahweh with his people in war (cf. 1:42; 23:14). Here, however, the destructive potential of that presence for Israel herself comes to the fore. **a jealous God:** see comment on 4:24.

16. test: the same verb as that used in 4:34 ('attempted'). Here, however, the sense is that of testing or proving the faithfulness of God to his covenant, as, for example, through demanding signs (cf. Isa. 7:12). This motif is not otherwise found in Deuteronomy, but is associated with **Massah** also in Exod. 17:7; Ps. 95:8f.

17. testimonies: see comment on 4:45. The word is associated with the motif of testing God also in Ps. 78:56. **he has commanded you:** the law is understood as already imparted to the people; see comment on 5:33 and 4:5.

20. what is the meaning: in the light of the answer which is given to the question, the point of the latter is evidently: why is it that we must observe these laws? Such questions form a ritual part of the Jewish Passover festival, based on Exod. 12:21–27; 13:1–10, 11–16. That there is a background in actual practice in the present context is doubted by Lohfink, *Hauptgebot*, 113ff., who sees the question simply as a rhetorical device, and Weinfeld, *School*, 34f., who thinks that the deuteronomic author has taken the ritual dialogue from its original setting and used it in a literary way for instruction. However, when vv. 10–19 are seen as a late insertion, the connection with a specific ritual (in vv. 4–9), which may be the actual background of the use of the form here, is in fact preserved; cf. also Soggin, *VT* 10, 1960, 341ff. **testimonies:** see comment on 4:45. **which the Lord our God has commanded you:** in contrast to the immediate context, this is in

plural form of address. Possibly it is a late addition from the hand
of the author of vv. 10–19 (cf. v. 17b), made after the direct connection between the declaration of vv. 4–9 and the question and
answer of vv. 20–25 was broken.

21–25. The answer to the question has been isolated from its
context by von Rad, *Problem*, 5f., who suggests that this is a formal
unit which may be taken as an example of Israel's ancient creed,
other examples being found in 26:5–9 and Jos. 24: 2–13. Whatever may be the case on the question of Israel's having had such a
creed (see comment on 26:5–9), in the present instance there is no
justification for isolating vv. 21ff. (or vv. 20ff.) from their context
as an ancient independent liturgical text which has simply been
inserted here. The verses form an integral part of their context,
making an essential contribution to the answer to the question
posed, which itself belongs closely with vv. 4–9. In effect, the complete answer is that history shows that just as by law the one who
frees the slave becomes that slave's new master so now Israel,
having been freed from slavery in Egypt by Yahweh, must
acknowledge the overlordship of Yahweh through obeying his
law; cf.. Lohfink, *Höre Israel*, 68f.

22. signs and wonders: see comment on 4:34. The view of
Childs, *VTS* 16, 1967, 30ff., that **signs and wonders** has a
broader reference in Deuteronomy than in Exodus (e.g. 7:3; 10:1,
etc.), and is not to be confined to the actual plagues in Egypt, but
forms a bridge leading into the wilderness tradition, perhaps
suits some occurrences (e.g. 4:34; 29:3). Here, however, the
word **grievous** (a word often used in the ethical sense and translated 'evil'; here with the sense of what is injurious or harmful)
points directly to the plagues.

23. he brought us out: this expresses, in legal terms, Yahweh's
emancipation of Israel from Egypt; cf. Exod. 21:2ff., where the
verb is frequently used of a slave legally gaining his freedom. **he
swore to give to our fathers:** see comment on 1:8.

25. The verse is probably a later addition, taking up the later
clause in v. 20, and using **commandment** comprehensively for
the whole law; see comment on 5:31. **righteousness:** an extensive discussion of this term is provided by Jespen, in *Gottes Wort*,
78ff. The term denotes the state of being in the right, and in the
context of God's covenant relationship with Israel it refers to this
relationship as being in order (von Rad); see also Gen. 15:6; Ps.
106:31. Since a right relationship allows God's blessing to operate,

the two words 'righteousness' and 'blessing' may stand parallel.
cf. Ps. 24:5.

(c) THE NATIONS OF THE LAND AND THEIR CULTS MUST BE
DESTROYED: **7:1-26**
Two subjects are treated in this chapter: Israel is to destroy the
older inhabitants of the land, and she is not to worship their
gods. The two subjects are in fact treated quite separately. The
first one in vv. 1-3, 6, 17-24, and the second in vv. 4-5, 7-15,
25-26, are brought together in v. 16; this is a transitional verse,
and the abruptness with which it sets the two subjects side by side
(see comment) indicates their original independence. That these
are independent subjects is not contradicted by the many parallels
between the chapter in all its parts and Exod. 23:20-33. The
latter is itself not a uniform text, and the relationship between it
and Dt 7 is extremely complicated. It is unlikely that it is a matter
of literary dependence in either direction; both texts have been
edited, perhaps in part by the same hand. As a result of this
editing, however, the two subjects of Dt. 7 are in fact more closely
integrated within Exod. 23 than in the present chapter (see comment on v. 16, and the discussions in Lohfink, *Hauptgebot*, 172ff.
Seitz, *op. cit.*, 77ff.).
    Only in vv. 4-5, 7-15, 25-26 is there any reference to the law,
the decalogue; there is here too an irregular change from second
person singular to second person plural form of address, and there
is a direct link with ch. 4 in the concern with graven images (vv.
5, 25f.). It is probable, therefore, that the basic layer in vv. 1-3,
6, 17-24, which draws out the consequences for the peoples of the
affirmation that Israel is Yahweh's special possession (v. 6), has
been secondarily supplemented, as in ch. 6, by the author responsible for 4:1-40. Apart from the similarities and contacts
already mentioned, there is the same concern with the possibility
of Israel's defection to the service of other gods and with her possible worship of images, and there is the same clear dependence on
the decalogue; the latter is presupposed as already in its place in
ch. 5.
    Lohfink, *Hauptgebot*, 167ff., adopts a rather different division of
the text from the one followed here, distinguishing vv. 1-5, 13-16,
20-24, as a 'Gilgal covenant text' concerned with the destruction
of foreign cults, from vv. 6-12, 17-19, 21 (25f.), which were
secondarily added in order to bring in decalogue material. The

two are closely interwoven, especially in vv. 6–14 where a chiastic structure may be discerned, and in other places where the one responsible for adding the decalogue material edited the Gilgal covenant text. The chiastic structure may exist, but it is certainly too vague to be of great significance. It certainly does not obstruct the division given here (following mainly Seitz, *op. cit.*, 74ff.) which has the advantage of avoiding Lohfink's rather dubious separation of a Gilgal covenant text referring to other gods and graven images from decalogue material. However, in the most important point, viz. that the references to the decalogue (here including references to the worship of other gods and to graven images) do not belong to the basis of this chapter, Lohfink's presentation and the one given here are in agreement.

The basic text, in vv. 1–3, 6, 17–24, forms a good continuation of the basic text of ch. 6. The latter is a call to Israel to acknowledge only Yahweh as her God. Now this is further elaborated in terms of Israel as a holy people, chosen by Yahweh from all peoples. As a result, Israel must avoid all contact with the peoples of the land who must be utterly destroyed. The question-answer form of 6:20ff. is found also in 7:17ff., where too the answer is reinforced by reference to the exodus and the 'signs and wonders' in Egypt.

1. The list of peoples given here occurs with some variation in several passages in the Old Testament (Gen. 15:20; Exod. 3:8, 17; 13:5; 23:23; 33:2; 34:11; Dt. 20:17; Jos. 3:10; 9:1; 11:3; 12:8; 24:11; Jg. 3:5; 1 Kg. 9:10; Ezr. 9:1; Neh. 9:8; 2 Chr. 8:7). The number seven of the peoples mentioned is itself significant, since it carries connotations of totality (see comment on 28:7). The point here, therefore, is a theological and rhetorical one, rather than a geographical or historical; it is to indicate Israel's complete possession of the land and her existence in her land independent of all other peoples. **Hittites:** as in Gen. 23:10; 25:9; 49:29f.; 50:13; Num. 13:29, etc., so here the Hittites are understood to be inhabitants of Palestine. The reference is something of a problem, for the historical Hittite empire of the Late Bronze Age lay considerably north of Palestine. It should be understood either that there were in fact many Hittite migrants into Palestine (enough to justify Gen. 10:15, which lists Heth, from whom the Hittites descended, as a son of Canaan), or that the use of the term came to be very vague, as a result of a loose use of the name of the land of the Hittites to cover an area much more extensive than that to which it properly applied. **Girgas-hites:** practically nothing is known of this people who also appear in Gen. 10 (v. 16) as inhabitants of Canaan. **the Amorites, the Canaanites:** see comment on 1:7. **Perizzites:** frequently mentioned in the lists of pre-Israelite peoples who inhabited Palestine. No other details are given, however, which might help locate them precisely; see also comment on 3:5. **Hivites:** outside the lists of pre-Israelite peoples in Palestine little is known of this people. Accurate identification and description of their role is hampered not only by the lack of detailed reference to them but also by the strong probability that the Old Testament has itself confused them. This is true at any rate of the Horites (on whom see comment on 2:12) and the Hivites (cf. Gen. 36:2, 20, where Zibeon is in the one place listed as Hivite and in the other as Horite). The Hebrew consonants for Hittite, Hivite, and Horite differ only in their middle letter. **Jebusites:** known in the Old Testament particularly as the pre-Israelite inhabitants of Jerusalem who controlled that city until its conquest by David, cf. 2 Sam. 5:6f.

2. utterly destroy: see comment on 2:34. Basic to the word is the idea of 'devotion': the thing 'devoted' to the god is excluded from human use (cf. 13:17), which may involve its utter destruction. Had the command here been carried out or had it been intended that it should be put into practice, the following verse would be superfluous. However, the command represents rather an ideal: all forms of intermingling with non-Israelites are rejected. **make no covenant with them:** the intention is not simply that of preserving Israel's separateness and independence; rather it is that of safeguarding Israel's exclusive allegiance to Yahweh from compromise. Treaties made with other peoples necessarily involved a recognition of the gods of these peoples through calling on them as treaty witnesses.

3. There is some tension between this prohibition and the provisions of Dt. 21:10ff. See comment on 21:12, 13.

4. The same connection between intermarriage and apostasy is found in Exod. 34:16, cf. also Exod. 23:32f. The relative age of these texts is, however, difficult to determine, and in any case does not establish the original connection of vv. 3 and 4 in this chapter. V. 6 is in fact the most likely continuation of v. 3. **following me:** possibly the last consonant of the word *mē'aḥᵃray* should be taken as as abbreviation for YHWH to give the translation 'following the

Lord' (cf. *NEB*) to conform with the context which refers to Yahweh in the third person; however, see the comment on 5:11. Second person plural form of address appears in vv. 4*b*, 5 which, moreover, do not form a suitable basis for v. 6. They come from the author responsible for vv. 7–16.

5. The wording of this verse is almost identical to that of Exod. 34:13 with which there is clearly a close connection. **pillars:** the massebah was a stone monument of which examples have been found at Gezer and Hazor. It may originally have been a phallic symbol used in fertility worship (cf. Cazelles), and as such the counterpart to the Asherah. In the Old Testament the massebah is reinterpreted as a memorial stone indicating the place where a theophany of Yahweh occurred (cf. Gen. 35:14), and it seems that it was accepted as a legitimate element of cultic apparatus in Israelite worship (cf. Hos. 3:4). It came under condemnation, however, in Hezekiah's reform (2 Kg. 18:4), and is frequently classified among altars, images, and idols which are unacceptable (cf. Exod. 23:24; 34:13; Lev. 26:1; Dt. 12:3; 16:22, etc.). **Asherim:** a masculine plural form of the feminine singular 'Asherah'. The significance of the term has been obscure from early times. The confusion of the ancient versions is reflected in the *AV* translation 'groves' (this understanding—clearly erroneous, cf. 2 Kg. 23:6—apparently suggested by the use of the verb 'plant', as in Dt. 16:21, for the setting up of an Asherah). It is clear, however, from the use of the word in the Ras Shamra texts that it is the name of a Canaanite goddess. It appears as the name of a goddess in the Old Testament (e.g. 1 Kg. 18:19), but also as the designation of the object representing her (cf. Jg. 6:26, 28), and the distinction between the two is not always clear (e.g. Jg. 3:7). The form of the cult object is not certain; but since it is described as a man-made object of wood, which could be cut down and burned, and since it bore a designation which is also the name of the goddess it represented, it is probable that it was a carved wooden image of the goddess rather than simply an upright wooden pole. It represented the female principle in the fertility cult, and, in distinction to the massebah, seems never to have been an acceptable element of Israelite worship. **graven images:** see comment on 4:16.

6. This verse, which is repeated in 14:2, is the continuation of v. 3 rather than of v. 5, since it explains the demand for Israel's remaining separate from the peoples rather than for her destruction of their forms of worship. Both here and in ch. 14 the affirmation of Israel's holiness is the basis, not of a command to destroy pagan altars, but rather of a demand for total separation from pagans and their practices. **holy:** the idea of separation, which is basic to the word, is particularly clear in this context. **has chosen you:** first in Deuteronomy is Israel said to have been chosen by Yahweh; see Introduction, pp. 6of. **his own possession:** the application of the word *segullāh* to Israel as the special property of Yahweh is deuteronomic and later (Exod. 19:5 is certainly not earlier than Deuteronomy, cf. Perlitt, *Bundestheologie*, 168ff.). It appears elsewhere in Exod. 19:5; Dt. 14:2; 26:18; Ps. 135:4; Mal. 3:17. Outside the Old Testament it is used to describe the special relationship of the vassal to his overlord; so it belongs to the stock of treaty and covenant terminology. The basic meaning of the root is apparently 'to set aside' (so Weinfeld, *JAOS* 90, 1970, 195 n.103), and Lohfink, *ZKTh* 91, 1969, 545, suggests that the noun originally applied to private property, but that it early came to express the serfdom of a king or another man to a god or a great king.

The three terms used for Israel's relationship with Yahweh in this verse: **holy, chosen, possession,** together express the essence of deuteronomic election theology. Israel is set apart from the other nations to stand in a special relationship with God. It is in order to preserve and express this relationship that the law is given to her.

7. chose: the author of the later section in vv. 7–16 connects his addition to the existing material by taking up this key term. **love upon you:** in 4:37 the author writes of God's love for the patriarchs rather than for Israel. Only here, vv. 8, 13 and 23:5, is God's love for Israel expressed, as in Hosea (11:1ff.).

8. redeemed you: the verb is primarily used in the sense of ransom a person or animal from death through providing a substitute or by payment (cf. e.g. Exod. 34:20). From this comes the general meaning of 'set free' without any notion of payment or substitution being involved.

9. steadfast love: the word denotes the attitude of faithfulness, firmness, loyalty and kindness which one person has to another. On the term cf. Snaith, *Distinctive Ideas*, 94ff. Fox, *CBQ* 35, 1973, 441ff., rather overstates the case in holding that the word implies a one-sided boon or favour given by the one who has power to aid the recipient of the *ḥeseḏ*; so that in the context of God and Israel it could never describe Israel's attitude to God but only God's attitude and actions to Israel. In Hos. 4:1 (translated 'kindness'); 6:4 (translated 'love'), where the obvious interpretation puts the word in the context of Israel's attitude to God, it is at least presupposed that *ḥeseḏ* should be a characteristic of this attitude. When allied with the term *covenant*, as here, the two words should be brought together in the translation 'covenant loyalty'. **those who love him**: this phrase distinguishes what is said here from Exod. 34:6f., and shows that there is dependence on, or close association with, the decalogue; see comment on 5:9f. **a thousand generations**: an interpretation of the 'thousands' of 5:10 by the late author of this section.

10. those who hate him: see comment on 5:9. In contrast to the previous verse which speaks generally of those who love Yahweh, the Hebrew here speaks in individual terms of 'he who hates' (with the exception of the word *leśōneʾāw* where, however, the plural suffix has probably come in by attraction to the preceding verse and to *pānāw* which follows). So stress is laid on the fact that each individual evildoer is punished. **be slack**: i.e. delay (cf. *NEB*).

11. commandment: see comment on 5:31.

12. As noted above, Introduction, pp. 78f., there are two views of the laws in Deuteronomy: one that the laws were given to Israel to regulate her life in the land which God was giving to her in fulfilment of the promise to the patriarchs (cf. 6:23); for the second, Israel's obedience is the important factor, for it is on this that the fulfilment of the promise and hence also Yahweh's blessing depends. This is particularly clear in 7:12ff., where Israel's obedience to the law is the basis of the blessing of Yahweh manifest not only in possession of the land but also in fertility of both man and nature. The world of history and nature is seen as one creation in which is experienced the results of obedience or disobedience to the law. **because**: a better translation than 'if' (*NEB*). The word *ʿēḵeḇ*, which is used here is stronger than *ʾim* ('if'); it is a noun meaning 'consequence' or 'result', and so emphasizes the connection of blessing to obedience. **covenant**: only here and in 4:31; 8:18 is this word applied to the patriarchal promise in Deuteronomy; promise to the patriarchs and covenant at Horeb are thereby bound into one, so that the fulfilment of the promise is in fact now dependent on Israel's fulfilment of the Horeb covenant.

13. The fertility of man, animal and nature, which otherwise is seen to derive from Baal (cf. Hos. 2:5, 8), is the blessing of Yahweh. **your grain and your wine and your oil:** these three (found frequently together, cf. 11:14; 12:17; 14:23; 18:4; 28:51; Hos. 2:8, 22; for an example from Ugarit, cf. Gordon, *Ugaritic Textbook*, Text 126 III 13ff.) are the characteristic products of a settled, agricultural community. The words denote the products in their unmanufactured state (Driver), so emphasizing the immediate connection of blessing and natural growth: *tîrōš*, a fresh or new wine; and *yiṣhār*, fresh oil. **the increase of your cattle and the young of your flock:** another fixed expression, found again in 28:4, 18, 51. The words *šeger* and *ʿaštārōt*, here translated 'increase' and 'young', are, according to Fisher, *Ras Shamra Parallels* I, 305, originally the names of fertility deities, and appear together as such (in parallelism as here) in the Ugaritic texts. The second of the two terms appears as a deity also in the Old Testament (e.g. 1 Kg. 11:5). Its use as a common noun in Hebrew parallels not only the use of *šeger* but also that of *dāgān*, the word here translated **grain**, which appears (in the form *dāgôn*) as the name of a deity both in the Old Testament (e.g. Jg. 16:23) and in the Ugaritic texts.

15. the evil diseases of Egypt: this is ambiguous. The reference may be to the plagues brought by Yahweh on the Egyptians (cf. Exod. 15:26, which also indicates that terms such as that found here could be used for these plagues), or it may be simply to Egypt as a notoriously unhealthy place (in which case the phrase **which you knew** would refer to Israel's general experience of conditions in Egypt during her period of bondage there). Other references, similar to this verse (cf. 28:60; Am. 4:10), give no decisive information.

16. This is a transitional verse, bringing together the two subjects of the chapter: v. 16a commands the destruction of the peoples; quite independently, v. 16b prohibits the worship of their gods. The connection is smoother in Exod. 23:33, for there the independent prohibition of serving the gods of the peoples is formulated as a possibility which might arise if these peoples are not expelled. **destroy:** better 'devour' (as *NEB*); the verb is that normally translated 'eat'.

17-24. In this final paragraph of the deuteronomic parenesis in this chapter, motifs of the holy war ideology, as it is expressed for example in Dt. 20:1ff., are used in order to reinforce the demand made at the beginning (v. 2) for the utter destruction of the peoples.

18. you shall not be afraid of them: a typical holy war expression, cf. e.g. Jos. 8:1.

19. great trials: see comment on 4:34. **the signs, the wonders:** see comment on 6:22.

20. hornets: this translation of *sir'āh* is uncertain; it is based on the understanding of the word in the ancient versions. It occurs only in deuteronomic and deuteronomistic texts (Exod. 23:28; Dt. 7:20; and Jos. 24:12) in the context of the expulsion of the pre-Israelite inhabitants of Palestine from the land at the time of Israel's settlement. Köhler, *ZAW* 13, 1936, 291, derived it from the Arabic *ḍara'a* 'to submit', and suggested the translation 'discouragement'. Although there is no Semitic cognate known for the meaning 'hornet', there is a parallel in Greek, where *oistros* means basically 'gadfly', but is also used figuratively in the sense of 'madness, frenzy'. This meaning suits very well the context of the divinely inspired panic sent on Israel's enemies, which is so characteristic of descriptions of Israel's wars, cf. e.g. Exod. 15:14ff; Jg. 7:21f. This would tend to support the meaning for the word given in the ancient versions.

21. in your midst: for this as a holy war expression, see comment on 6:15.

22. The entire verse is a late addition based on Exod. 23:29f. It fits very awkwardly with its context which throughout presupposes the utter destruction of Israel's enemies on her entry into the land (cf. also 9:3). Moreover, the verse is clearly an abbreviated version of the parallel in Exod. 23:29f., where information essential for the understanding of the phrase is more clearly provided: the immediate expulsion of the enemies would leave the land deserted and so open to wild animals; the enemies will be driven out only in proportion to Israel's gradual expansion towards filling the land with her own numbers. **at once:** Exod. 23:29 has 'in one year'. **lest the wild beasts grow too numerous for you:** this is a rationalization of the obvious circumstance that Israel did not in fact completely replace the former inhabitants. Another explanation is provided by the deuteronomist in Jg. 2:20ff., viz. that Israel's enemies should be there to test her faith.

23. throw them into great confusion: the panic sent by Yahweh on Israel's enemies appears also in Exod. 14:24; 23:27; Jos. 10:10; Jg. 4:15; 1 Sam. 7:10.

24. stand against you: this phrase again only in 11:25.

25. The final two verses reintroduce (cf. v. 5) the subject of the late addition to this chapter. **the silver or the gold that is on them:** see comment on 4:16. **an abomination to the Lord your God:** this phrase is used in order to motivate obedience to several deuteronomic laws (cf. 16:21ff.; 18:10ff.; 22:5; 23:18f.; 24:4; 25:13ff.). In practically all cases in Deuteronomy it has a cultic sense, and expresses a strong anti-Canaanite sentiment and a Yahwistic exclusiveness. The cultic and nationalistic use of the phrase is not, however, its original sense, but represents a secondary adaptation of what was in origin a wisdom phrase. The wisdom origin is shown not just by its occurrences in Proverbs (3:22; 6:16; 11:1, 20, etc.), but by the fact that it has many close parallels outside the Old Testament in general ancient Near Eastern wisdom literature; see, for example, The Instruction of Amen-em-opet, xiii, 1f. (*ANET*, 423), together with the discussion of the phrase, its origin and significance, in Humbert, *ZAW* 72, 1960, 223f.; Merendino, *Gesetz*, 326ff.; and Weinfeld, *JBL* 80, 1961, 246f.; and comment on 18:12.

26. accursed: the word is *ḥērem*. Elsewhere the verb is translated 'utterly destroy', see comment on 2:34 and 7:2, and *NEB* translation 'under solemn ban'. Those who come in contact with that which is under ban are themselves subject to total destruction, cf. Jos. 6:18; 7:12. **detest:** the verb used in *šikkēṣ*, a late verb used primarily in the sense of treat as ritually unclean; cf. e.g. Lev. 11:11, 13 (*RSV* 'have in abomination'). **abhor:** the same root as that from which the noun 'abomination' (v. 25) is derived.

(D) IN THE LAND ISRAEL MUST REMEMBER YAHWEH: **8:1-20**

As in ch. 7 so here original deuteronomic parenesis has been later expanded through the addition of material relating that parenesis to the commandments and specifically to the decalogue. The distinction between early and late material is evident particularly in the use of the word 'forget'. The early sections of the chapter, in vv. 7-11a, 12-14, 17-18a, use it in the sense of the arrogant ascription to oneself of the power which is Yahweh's (see especially vv. 14, 17), while the later sections, in vv. 1-6, 11b, 15-16, 18b-20, use it in the sense of forget the commandments. The early and late material is now brought together, within the overall form of a chiasm (cf. Lohfink, *Hauptgebot*, 194f.), which,

as also in 7:6ff., is here the literary technique used for binding
material of varied origins.

The original parenesis in this chapter forms a good continuation
of 7:1–3, 17ff. The latter commands the destruction of the peoples
when Israel comes to the land and affirms the help of Yahweh in
carrying this out. Now Israel is warned not to think that the good
land of which she finds herself in possession has come to her as a
result of her own unaided power. The later additions to this parenesis show strong links in thought and vocabulary with the author of
4:1–40, who has already been seen at work in chs. 6 and 7. There
is the common concern with Israel's obedience to the commandments, and particularly to the decalogue, on which its prosperity
depends. There is the same switch between singular and plural
forms of address, the use of a literary scheme in vv. 2–6 which
otherwise appears in 4:35ff.; 7:7ff.(see comment on v. 2), and
the appearance of words and phrases otherwise characteristic of
this late section (see comment on vv. 1, 2, 4, 5, 11, 16, 19, 20).
Seitz, *op. cit.*, 79ff., proposes to divide these late passages between
two stages of redaction, a deuteronomistic one to which vv. 1, 19f.
should be assigned, and a pre-deuteronomistic one which brought
in vv. 2–6, 11*b*. However, the connections of thought between
these two stages are close, and their common connection to
material deriving from the late author in ch. 4 favours attributing
both to the one late author.

1. the commandment: on this as a late summary designation
for the whole law, see comment on 5:31.

2–6. These verses follow a literary pattern of argument from history, which is otherwise to be seen also in 4:35–40 and 7:7–11 (cf.
Lohfink, *Hauptgebot*, 125ff.; Buis). It consists of three elements:
(a) remember what Yahweh has done in history, vv. 2–4; (b)
know what this implies as far as faith is concerned, v.5; (c) apply
this knowledge to your behaviour through keeping the commandments, v.6. This is not, according to Lohfink, an independent
Gattung pointing to the original independence of the verses in
which it appears; rather, it is a form of speech used only within
wider literary contexts.

2. humble: the word appears again in vv. 3, 16; and although
it is elsewhere used of 'afflicting' Israel in punishment for sin (Isa.
64:11; Neh. 1:12; Lam. 3:33; cf. Pss. 90:15; 119:75), it is
particularly in the deuteronomistic 1 Kg. 8:35 and the late psalm
Ps. 119:71 that the use of the term to describe God's educative

disciplining of Israel finds its closest parallel. **testing:** see comment on 6:16. **to know what was in your heart:** i.e. to know what your attitude and true purposes were, cf. 1 Sam. 14:7; 2 Kg 10:30; 2 Chr. 32:31.

3. manna: the story of the divine feeding of Israel with manna in the wilderness (Exod. 16) may take its origin in the phenomenon, still observed in the wilderness, of the excretion by insects of an edible substance which is found especially on the tamarisk tree; cf. Bodenheimer, *BA* 10, 1947, 2ff. **everything that proceeds out of the mouth of God:** the idea of the creative power of the word, especially of the divine word, is widespread in the ancient Near East, and in Egyptian belief concerning the god Ptah 'man lives by what comes forth from his mouth' (cf. Brunner, *VT* 8, 1958, 428f.). This is not a contrast between the material and the spiritual as the basis of life, but rather a contrast between man's self-sufficiency (**bread alone)** and his dependence on God, exemplified in the feeding of Israel with manna. The reference is, therefore, not simply to the word of Yahweh (cf. LXX and *NEB*), perhaps understood in the sense of lifegiving commandments (30:15ff.; 32:46f.), but rather more generally to the divine utterance as the creative source of all forms of life, including manna.

4. The information given here appears also in 29:5 and Neh. 9:21, but not in any older source. There is no indication that it derives from old tradition, and so should be taken as a rhetorical description of divine care for the people deriving from deuteronomistic circles.

5. The father–son analogy, together with the motif of educative discipline, are prominent wisdom themes: cf. Prov. 3:11f.; comment on 1:31; 4:36; and Weinfeld, *Deuteronomy*, 316.

6. This verse forms the conclusion of the literary scheme begun in v. 2; see comment above on vv. 2–6.

7. This verse begins the original deuteronomic parenesis in this chapter. The first word, therefore, should be translated 'when' rather than **for**. This is indicated also by parallel constructions elsewhere; cf. e.g. 6:10ff., 20f., where the protasis is similarly introduced by *kî*, 'when' (cf. also Lohfink, *Hauptgebot*, 192). The apodosis then is to be found in v. 11*a*. **good:** the words 'and broad' are added here by *Sam* and LXX, apparently in dependence on the description of the land given in Exod. 3:8. **brooks:** see comment on 1:24. **springs:** the word is *tᵉhōmōt*, the plural of

tᵉhōm the word frequently used for the primeval waters of creation
(Gen. 1:2), though also simply of deep waters generally (Ps. 135:6);
see comment on 33:13.

8. olive trees: the Hebrew expression *zêṭ šemen* occurs only
here (though an analogy to it is to be found in 2 Kg. 18:32). The
NEB translation 'olives, oil' depends on the Syriac which separates
the two words, reading the absolute *zayiṭ* instead of the construct.
Driver takes the *MT* to refer to the cultivated olive as distinct
from the wild olive.

9. without scarcity: the Hebrew is apparently 'not in poverty'.
The word *miskēnuṭ* is found only here, but is connected with the
adjective *miskēn* which appears four times in Ecclesiastes with the
sense 'poor'. **whose stones are iron:** i.e. iron-ore. The description
is hyperbolical, but iron and **copper** were mined in the area of
the Arabah and elsewhere; cf. Winnet, *IDB*, vol. 3, 384f.

10. Against the syntax of the *RSV*, it should probably be
understood that the sentence begun in v. 7 continues through v. 10
to find its apodosis in v. 11a. Parallel constructions suggest this;
see comment on v.7.

It is difficult to understand precisely how v. 10b (**and you shall
bless ...** i.e. worship and praise) is to be properly integrated
into the overall construction. It apparently gives the first and
immediate result of Israel's taking possession of the land, while vv.
11a, 12ff. deal with a second possible result at a later stage of
Israel's living in the land. See Lohfink, *Hauptgebot*, 266, who also
points to the possibility that vv. 12ff. should be taken to refer to
the inner proud attitude towards the benefits of the land which
co-existed with the outward wholly correct attitude described in
v. 10b.

11. Take heed lest you forget the Lord: the same expression
as 6:12, where too it is a warning for the time when Israel shall have
taken possession of the land. The author of 6:10ff. has derived the
expression from 8:7ff. which uses it in the context of the original
deuteronomic parenesis. The general themes of 6:10ff. and 8:7ff.
are the same, but the expressions are different. The former, in its
identification of forgetting Yahweh with going after other gods
and not keeping the commandments of Yahweh (an original
identification in that section) is certainly later than 8:7ff.
where such an identification is secondary and only appears in
the late additions to the original parenesis in that chapter. The
one responsible for making this secondary identification is most

probably, therefore, the same as the one responsible for 6:10ff., **viz.** the late author of ch. 4. See also above, the introduction to ch. 8.

The apodosis to the sentence begun in v. 7 is found in v. 11*a*, which is then continued by vv. 12ff. V. 11*b*, on the other hand, is a late insertion (so also Steuernagel). It introduces the commandments into a context which otherwise makes no reference to them, and interprets the verb **forget** with reference to the commandments. Otherwise in this section (cf. vv. 14, 17) forgetting Yahweh means assigning to oneself the credit for enjoyment of wealth and prosperity; cf. Seitz, *op. cit.*, 79. **which I command you this day:** cf. 4:40.

12. lest: on this conjunction depends a long sentence which continues without break to v. 17 (vv. 15f. being a later addition to it, see comment).

14. To forget Yahweh is clearly here identified with pride and refusal to acknowledge dependence on Yahweh and what he has done. The thought, and to a notable extent the expression of it, are identical with Hos. 13:6 (cf. also Prov. 30:9). **out of the house of bondage:** a phrase connected particularly with the decalogue, see comment on 5:6. It does not, however, necessarily refer to the decalogue here; the decalogue probably took its origin in the same circles as those from which the deuteronomic law with its parenetic introduction came.

15. fiery serpents: the significance of **fiery** is not certain, though it is probably a reference to the burning inflammation which results from their bite. They are referred to also in Num. 21:6, while Isa. 30:6, speaks of the 'flying serpent'. The latter would suggest that some fabulous serpent is thought of here. **flinty rock:** i.e. the hardest rock. Exod. 17:6; Num. 20: 8, 11 refer only to 'the rock'. Deuteronomy's rhetorical addition uses a word which otherwise appears only in 32:13, Ps. 114:8; Job 28:9 and Isa. 50:7.

16. Vv. 14*b*–16 are sometimes taken as an addition (Steuernagel) largely on the grounds of their repetition of material already given in vv. 2ff., and the smooth connection of vv. 14*a*, 17 which they interrupt. It is probably true that vv. 15–16 at any rate are from the hand of the late author who supplemented the deuteronomic parenesis in this chapter. Not only is there repetition of information already given at the beginning of the chapter, but the use of the word **humble** has its closest parallel in the deuteronomist (see comment on v.2), while the end of v. 16 **to do you**

good in the end is very similar to the notion of curse and blessing as successive periods of Israel's history which was earlier identified in ch. 4 as late deuteronomistic rather than deuteronomic; see comment on 4:29.

17. Beware lest: these words are not in the Hebrew, which has a single long sentence from v. 12. **have gotten me this wealth:** the use of the phrase ʿāśāh ḥayil in the sense of gain wealth is paralleled in Ezek. 28:4. Elsewhere, however, it appears with the sense of 'do valiantly' (Num. 24:18; 1 Sam. 14:48). Common to both senses is the military context in which the phrase appears, a context which for both Deuteronomy and the prophets (Isa. 10:8ff; Ezek. 28:2, etc.) always holds the danger of man arrogantly claiming for himself the power that belongs to God.

18. his covenant which he swore to your fathers: the use of 'covenant' for the oath to the patriarchs, as in 4:31; 7:12 (see comment), indicates that with v. 18b the hand of the late author evident at the beginning of the chapter again appears. This is continued into the next two verses. **as at this day:** it is not presupposed that Israel is now in possession of the land with all its wealth and prosperity. The reference is rather to the covenant promise to the patriarchs that Israel should possess the land; it is this which is held out as a prospect to be confirmed **this day.**

19. other gods and serve them and worship them: an allusion to the first commandment of the decalogue where this vocabulary appears (5:7, 9). To forget Yahweh is therefore to forget the commandments, as in verses 1ff., 11b. The verse changes from singular to plural form of address with the words **I solemnly warn you,** a phrase which is found only in late passages in Deuteronomy (4:26; 30:19; 32:46). It is a legal phrase with the sense 'pronounce or testify in the presence of witnesses'. **you shall surely perish:** a phrase also found only in late passages, 4:26; 30:18.

20. If Israel joins the Canaanites in their religious practices then she may expect the same treatment as that which she herself is to mete out to the peoples, cf. 7:16. **because you would not hearken:** a construction found otherwise only in the late passage 7:12.

(E) THE COVENANT IS BROKEN AND RENEWED: **9:1–10:11**

The basic deuteronomic parenesis continues in 9:1–7a, taking up and expressing in different form themes already developed in earlier passages: the theme of the help of Yahweh to dispossess the inhabitants of Palestine, as in 7:17ff.; the warning against the false view that it is by virtue of her own ability or her own righteousness that Israel is being given the land, as already in 8:12ff.; other contacts with earlier deuteronomic parenesis being 'Hear, O Israel' as in 6:4, together with the absence of any reference to the law or to the necessity for obedience in order to gain possession of the land. It is because of Yahweh's promise to the patriarchs that Israel, in spite of her sinfulness, is being given the land. In order to reinforce his theme of Israel's own unworthiness the deuteronomic author then alluded briefly to Israel's rebellion against Yahweh in the wilderness. This is preserved in 9:13–14, 26–29; 10:10–11, verses which both in theme and expression (cf. 'stubborn' 9:6, 13, 27; 'destroy' 9:3, 14) form a good continuation of 9:1–7a. Only through the intercession of Moses was Israel preserved from destruction at the hands of Yahweh, so that the oath to the patriarchs might indeed be fulfilled.

This historical allusion in the deuteronomic account has been greatly elaborated by the deuteronomist, whose other major contribution to these chapters has been the introduction of the decalogue in ch. 5. The deuteronomistic account in the present context is to be found in 9:9–12, 15–19, 21, 25; 10:1–5. The following points indicate that the same deuteronomistic author is at work here as in ch. 5: (a) the use of the second person plural form of address in both places; (b) common vocabulary: 'out of the midst of the fire' 5:22 (cf. also 5:4, 24, 26); 9:10; 10:4; 'assembly' 5:22; 9:10; 10:4; (c) within chs. 5–11 it is only here and in ch. 5 that it is narrative rather than general parenesis which is the determinative characteristic; (d) the theme of chs. 9f., that of covenant breaking and renewal, presupposes an earlier account of covenant making, which is to be found in ch. 5.

As Lohfink, *Hauptgebot*, 207ff., has shown, there is a clear structure discernible within these chapters. Five sections may be distinguished as forming this structure; each of them begins with a reference to forty days and nights. These are 9:9–10, with the theme of covenant making; 9:11–17, the breaking of the covenant; 9:18–21, the measures taken to atone for breach of covenant; 9:25–10:5, the renewal of the covenant; and 10:10–11, the consequences of the renewal. In the order in which the sections appear there is a clear pattern and scheme, although within the sections there is chronological disorder: so, for example, 9:19 gives the impression that Moses' intercession is complete, so that 9:25ff. appear disruptive; 10:10–11 cannot fit after 10:5, but refer back to 9:25. This particular aspect of lack of harmony within chs. 9–10 does not necessarily indicate lack of original unity; however, there are, as Seitz, *op. cit.*, 51ff., has indicated, other obstacles which may not so easily, be accommodated. So, in particular, it is impossible to take 9:13–14 (which belong within one of the sections mentioned above) as a continuation of 9:12 (see comment on 9:13). But once this breach is made then other verses also fall out of the pattern; for 9:26–29 clearly presuppose and follow from 9:13–14.

This indicates that the structure discernible is not an original unit but incorporates material of different origins, and so confirms the view already mentioned that the deuteronomic 9:1–7a find their continuation in 9:13ff., 26ff. The deuteronomic account then concludes by reverting to its chief parenetic concern in 10:10f., which, like 9:1–7a, are in second person singular form of address. The deuteronomist, on the other hand, in line with the great importance he clearly attached to the covenant making at Horeb, has built on and greatly elaborated the deuteronomic account into an artistic scheme, following the order of events in the Sinai pericope in Exod. 19–34 with the significant change that the basis for the covenant renewal is the same collection of law, the decalogue, as that which was basic to the original covenant (see comment on 10:4).

A few late additions of unidentifiable authorship have been brought in: 9:2; 9:7b–8, 22–24 (see comment) and 9:20; 10:6–9 (see comment). Material is here incorporated which clearly disrupts what is basically an artistic deuteronomistic adaptation and elaboration of a deuteronomic account.

1. Hear, O Israel: see comment on 6:4, the beginning of the deuteronomic parenesis.

2. the sons of the Anakim: see comment on 1:28. **of whom you have heard it said:** presumably a reference to the report of the spies, cf. Num. 13:28. As in Jos. 11:21ff. the giants known as the Anakim are here spoken of as inhabiting the whole of Palestine before the Israelite settlement. Here the reference is incompatible with v. 1, which speaks of nations in the plural, and the whole verse should probably be taken as an addition, based on 1:28, and perhaps from the hand of the deuteronomist.

3. a devouring fire: see comment on 4:24. The use of the phrase in the present context, that of Yahweh acting in war against the enemies of Israel, is undoubtedly older than 4:24, where it is used of Yahweh's threatening presence within Israel in case of her apostasy.

4. righteousness and **wickedness** are legal terms originally (cf. e.g. Exod. 23:7): he who is in the right gains victory with the help of the gods, he who is in the wrong is defeated. That Israel should gain possession of the land through her righteousness, as a result of obedience to the law, finds expression in 6:18f., which stands in sharp conflict with what is expressed here (cf. Lohfink, in *Gott in Welt*, 436f.). That is not to say, however, that the present verse is a late correction of 6:18f. In fact, the thought here fits with the original deuteronomic parenetic warning against pride in 8:17. V. 4*b* (**whereas it is because ...**) is often omitted (so *NEB* following the LXX) as an unacceptable doublet to v. 5*b*. As it stands, with **before you** indicating that the direct speech of the people comes to an end with v. 4*a*, it does constitute a very awkward doublet. However, if Lohfink, *Hauptgebot*, 201f., is right in taking *mippānekā* as having been originally *mippānay*, 'before me', and its present second person suffix as the misplaced remnant of an original *kî*, 'for', introducing v. 5, then the direct speech of the people continues to the end of the verse; and 4*b* would then be no more of a doublet to v. 5 than v. 4*a*.

5. the wickedness of these nations: the view that the pre-Israelite inhabitants of the land lost possession of the land because of their wickedness finds expression also in Gen. 15:16 (JE). The legal language is carried on into this verse; but whereas the nations are deemed guilty there is no corresponding verdict of innocence passed on Israel, which would be expected in a law-court situation. The legal categories have to that extent broken down. Israel is also guilty, but is saved from the consequences of her guilt by God's promises to the patriarchs.

6. stubborn: the Hebrew is usually translated 'stiff-necked'. The image is presumably that of an obstinate animal, but it is always applied in the Old Testament to people cf. Exod. 32:9; 33:3, 5; 34:9, etc.

7. With the words **until you came** the verse changes from singular to plural form of address. The deuteronomistic narrative of the sin of the golden calf does not, however, begin until v. 9. Vv. 7*b*-8 are a later addition, corresponding to vv. 22-24, and introduced in order to set the specific event of the golden calf explicitly within the context of a whole history of Israel's rebelliousness. This is particularly clear if, following *Sam*, LXX and Syriac (see also Smith), the second person plural form of address is held to begin with **from the day you came out of Egypt.**

8. Even: Horeb is referred to not only because of the particularly serious form which Israel's rebellion took on that occasion, but also because it was here that the very basis of the whole law rested.

9. to receive the tables of stone: according to the deuteronomist's account in ch. 5, Moses has already received the tablets; however, as noted there (see comment on 5:22), chronological order is not the guiding principle of the narrative. This is particularly clear also in the structure of the present story; see above the introduction to this section. **the tables of the covenant:** see comment on 4:13. **I remained on the mountain forty days and forty nights; I neither ate bread nor drank water:** the source of this statement is apparently Exod. 34:28 (Exod. 24:18 is P) together with the deuteronomic account in 10:10; but there it belongs to the occasion of the renewal of the Sinai covenant after the rebellion of the people in the golden calf incident described in Exod. 32. Its original context of use is, therefore, the need for intercession for the sin of the people. The deuteronomist, however, has used it as a basic element in his artistic ordering of his material, a use which is historically unsuitable to the occasion described in v. 9, and which may indeed have partly caused the premature reference to the threatening anger of Yahweh in v. 8; see also above, the introduction to this section.

10. written with the finger of God: that the words are taken from Exod. 31:18 is unlikely since the latter, as the use of the word 'testimony' indicates, is probably to be ascribed to P. Other, earlier records do stress, however, that God wrote the commandments on the tablets, cf. Exod. 24:12; 32:16. **all the words:** this follows the reading of several of the ancient versions which omit the preposition 'according to' which appears before 'all' in *MT* (cf. *AV* translation). For **words** with specific reference to the decalogue, see comment on 4:10; 5:22. **out of the midst of the fire on the day of the assembly:** this takes up the vocabulary of 5:22.

11. This verse adds nothing new to vv. 9 and 10, and in fact directly repeats what is said in those verses. However, in the structure of the deuteronomist's narrative (see the introduction to this section) it begins a new section, which runs on to v. 17, and through the repetition is firmly linked with what precedes.

12. whom you have brought from Egypt: only here in Deuteronomy is Moses said to have led the people out of Egypt; otherwise Yahweh leads them out, or the people go forth. Exod. 32:7, 8*a*, where this is also found, is probably part of a deuteronomic redaction of that chapter. **the way:** the singular apparently refers to the decalogue (see also 5:33), though not the plural 'ways' (8:6; 10:12, etc.); here the reference is to the second commandment. **molten image:** the story in Exod. 32:4, 8, adds *'ēgel* 'calf', as in v. 16 of this chapter (see comment there).

13, 14. These verses are the original deuteronomic continuation of v. 7*a*. The new introduction at the beginning of v. 13 shows that it is not the original continuation of v. 12, on which v. 15 follows perfectly. The deuteronomist used the original deuteronomic general reference to Israel's rebellion as the base on which to build his detailed account.

13. Furthermore: not in the Hebrew, but an attempt by the English translation to get round the difficulty of a very obviously independent introduction to divine speech from that given in v. 12. **stubborn:** as in v. 6.

14. The closest parallel in the context of the story of the golden calf is Exod. 32:10, but Num. 14:12 provides the most striking similarity in expression. Deuteronomic influence is probable in both these passages. **let me alone:** the same verb as that translated 'fail' in 4:31 (see comment). **blot out their name:** cf. Exod. 32:32f., where reference is made to the 'book' in which the names of the living are written (Ps. 69:28; cf. Isa. 4:3; Mal. 3:16). Following on this verse, Moses' intercession is now expected, as in Exod. 32:11ff. The deuteronomist, however, has interrupted the older account at this point and the intercession does not appear until vv. 26ff.

16. molten calf: the calf or bull had obvious fertility associations, and it is on this account condemned in the Old Testament as a pagan cult symbol. That this was its original significance is, however, very doubtful. As a fertility symbol an agricultural context is presupposed; so if the story of the making of the golden calf is taken to have historical roots in the wilderness period its significance must have been different. On the other hand, it is likely that the purpose of the story is in fact to condemn an action which, according to 1 Kg. 12, was undertaken by Jeroboam I who erected golden calves at royal sanctuaries in Bethel and Dan. But even in this context the golden calf as a fertility symbol, and so associated with the worship of Baal, makes little sense. Jeroboam's aim was to rival the attractions of the Jerusalem sanctuary and its ark, which would suggest that his intention as far as the golden calf (Jeroboam having probably erected only one, at Bethel) was concerned, was to provide for his northern kingdom of Israel a parallel cultic symbol to the ark in Jerusalem (on which see comment on 10:1). This means that the calf was seen as a pedestal on which the invisible Yahweh stood or was enthroned, a function which has clear parallels outside Israel in the ancient Near East. A similar view of the function of the calf may hold good if the story of Exod. 32 is seen to have historical roots in the pre-settlement period; for here, as Dumermuth, *ZAW* 29, 1958, 85, suggests, the calf may have been a leadership symbol, parallel to the ark. However, in later time it did have close associations with Canaanite fertility rites and these are the reasons for its condemnation in the Old Testament.

17. broke them: this was not just an angry act of violence on the part of Moses; rather, such an action is referred to in a number of ancient treaty documents as the procedure by which breach of treaty is formally confirmed. The presence here of legal, diplomatic language is confirmed by **before your eyes**, for this phrase, which is not to be found in the Exodus account, points to a legal act carried out in the presence of witnesses.

18. This verse marks the beginning of a new section dealing with the measures for atonement necessary before the covenant may be renewed. **to provoke him to anger:** on this as a typical deuteronomistic phrase, see comment on 4:25. One would perhaps expect the account of Moses' destruction of the golden calf (v. 21) to precede vv. 18f., describing his intercession with Yahweh (Seitz, *op. cit.*, 54f., suggests that the verses were intentionally displaced when the deuteronomist's account, which referred to Moses' intercession *after* the destruction of the golden calf, was combined with the older deuteronomic account which also had a reference to Moses' intercession, vv. 26ff., in order to avoid having duplicate material in close proximity). However, the deuteronomist has apparently adopted a particular literary structure following which each section of his narrative is introduced by reference to forty days and nights spent by Moses fasting before Yahweh. See also comment on v. 21 indicating that

the present place of that verse is to be explained on the basis of
the deuteronomist's particular account of Moses' treatment of the
golden calf.

19. that time also: probably an implied reference back to
5:23ff.; cf. Lohfink, *Hauptgebot*, 218 n. 36.

20. There is no corresponding reference in Exod. 32 to Moses'
intercession on behalf of Aaron. The reference to it here comes late
after v. 19 which concludes with the information that Yahweh
hearkened to Moses, and the whole verse is generally admitted
to be an addition. See also comment on 10:6–9.

21. In Exod. 32:20 Moses mixed the dust of the golden calf
with water which the Israelites then had to drink, an action which
has certain resemblances to the ritual described in Num. 5:16–28,
and which had the purpose of bringing the guilty under curse for
their sin. Here, through scattering the dust of the calf on the
stream flowing down from the mountain, the object and so also
the curse which threatened because of the sin of making it were
carried away from the whole people. When understood in this
sense, it is clear that the way in which the deuteronomist has
chosen to describe Moses' action with the golden calf and its dust
could only come *after* his intercession on behalf of the people
and Yahweh's forgiveness of them. Now that they have been
forgiven the curse may also be removed. For a similar ritual, see
21:3ff.

22–24. As Seitz, *op. cit.*, 57, has observed, these verses belong
with v. 7*b* in language and content. In fact, vv. 7*b*–8 and 22–24
should not be separated. In content, language and form they
correspond: vv. 22f. correspond to v. 8 in the reference to Horeb
on the one hand and Kadesh-barnea on the other, and in the
declaration that Israel provoked Yahweh to wrath; v. 24 corresponds closely to v. 7*b* not only in the use of the term 'rebellious',
but also the phrase 'from the day you came out of the land of
Egypt until you came to this place' corresponds to 'from the day
that I knew you'. Vv. 7*b*–8, 22–24 are clearly a later addition
acting as a generalizing framework to the specific event narrated
in vv. 9–21.

22. Taberah: the site and the meaning of the name are unknown. The reference here is based on the isolated aetiology of the
name in Num. 11:1–3 which connects the name with the verb 'to
burn' and explains it with reference to the burning anger of
Yahweh at the murmuring of the people. **Massah:** see

comment on 6:16. **Kibroth-hattaavah:** as with Taberah, so
here neither the site nor the meaning of the name is known.
Num. 11:4–34 give the name the artificial sense 'graves of
craving' which is there explained through a story of Israel's
craving for meat in the wilderness and the death of many as a
result of a plague sent by Yahweh in punishment.

23. Kadesh-barnea: see comment on 1:2. The reference is to
the story in Dt. 1:19ff., Israel's refusal to enter the land at the
command of Yahweh after the report of the spies. **you rebelled
against the commandment of the Lord your God:** a verbal
repetition of 1:26*b*. **believe him:** i.e. trust Yahweh's promise that
Israel will possess the land.

24. I knew: that Moses should speak in these terms is strange.
Sam and LXX change the suffix to third person 'he (sc. Yahweh)
knew', though the latter is most likely an improved reading
(Cazelles, on the other hand, suggests that the *MT* wishes to
avoid an expression which would seem to limit the omniscience of
God; if this is the case it would support the originality of the
reading of *Sam* and LXX). Possibly the final consonant of *daʿtî*
should be taken for an abbreviation of YHWH, presupposing a
situation analogous to 5:11 (see comment) to give the translation
'the Lord knew' (cf. *NEB*). 'Know' is used here in the sense of
legal recognition, as found also in treaty texts where it is applied
to the overlord's recognition of his vassal and vice versa. Similar
uses of the verb are found in Gen. 18:19; Exod. 33:12; 2 Sam.
7:20; Isa. 45:3f.; Jer. 1:5; Hos. 13:4f.; Am. 3:2; cf. Huffmon,
BASOR 181, 1966, 31ff. (and, for relevant texts from Ugarit and
Mari, cf. Huffmon and Parker, *BASOR* 184, 1966, 36ff.).

25. The difficulty noted by Driver, viz. that the terms of the
intercession in the following verses are reminiscent of Exod. 32:11f.
(Moses' *first* intercession before his descent from the mountain)
but do not agree with Exod. 34:9 (Moses' second intercession on
the occasion of the renewal of the covenant) which in the present
form of ch. 9 represents the stage which the account has reached,
is resolved when it is recognized that vv. 26ff. connect directly to
vv. 13f. as the original deuteronomic account which made only
general reference to Israel's rebellion; the detail of the story,
bringing in Moses' ascents and descents, is deuteronomistic
elaboration of this account. V. 25, using second person plural
form of address, is deuteronomistic, leading into the deuteronomic
intercession.

26. thy heritage: the same word as that translated elsewhere 'possession'; see comment on 4:20. **redeemed:** see comment on 7:8. The terms in which Moses makes his intercession, referring to God's greatness and appealing to his honour, are familiar from some psalms (cf. Pss. 79:9f.; 106:8; 109:21, etc.), indicating that the deuteronomic author of this passage is in fact using traditional liturgical formulae.

27. Having referred to God's deliverance of the people from Egypt, the author now introduces a second reason for Yahweh's forbearance; his promise to the patriarchs. **Remember:** a word found in legal contexts where it may be used, as here, of a judge who 'remembers' in favour of (preposition l^e) someone; cf. Ps. 132:1; Jer. 2:2. Here the thought is of Yahweh favourably remembering the patriarchs and in particular his promise to them (Exod. 32:13), which will influence his actions towards Israel.

28. The third reason for Yahweh's forgiveness: that the Egyptians might interpret the destruction of Israel as an indication of Yahweh's inability to fulfil his promise and even of his hatred for Israel; cf. Exod. 32:12 and Dt. 1:27. **the land:** following *Sam* the *NEB* adds 'the people'. LXX prefixes 'the inhabitants'. However, for the construction here, see e.g. Gen. 41:57; 1 Sam. 17:46.

10:1 Hew two tables of stone like the first: so Exod. 34:1. **an ark of wood:** there is no JE account of the manufacture of the ark, it having probably been suppressed in favour of the P account which occurs in Exod. 37 *after* Moses had received the new tables of stone. There probably did originally exist a JE account in a place closely corresponding to the deuteronomistic account in Dt. 10:1-3. Beyerlin, *Origins*, 110, 114, points out that Exod. 33:7 probably contains a concealed reference to the ark, the JE account of the making of which may have originally immediately preceded. The word for ark, *'ārôn*, means 'chest' or 'box' (cf. 2 Kg. 12:9, 10, etc.); the ark was, therefore, clearly intended as a container. However, the phrase 'ark of the covenant' (10:8, 31:9, 25; Jos. 3:6, 8; 4:7, 18, etc.) is deuteronomistic, and the emphasis with which the deuteronomist elsewhere (1 Kg. 8:9) insists that the ark had nothing in it but the two tables of stone, makes it likely that the connection between the ark and the decalogue (which, as indicated in the introduction to ch. 5, is a deuteronomic compilation) is deuteronomistic. Deuteronomistic insistence on the ark as a simple container also suggests that the attempt is being made here to counter a more elaborate view of the ark held earlier. The historical time and place of origin of the ark are uncertain; it is widely understood to have functioned as a desert sanctuary, with which origin its later movements from one site to another in the immediate post-settlement period are thought to conform. However, all references to it before its appearance in the temple at Shiloh (1 Sam. 3:3) are of doubtful historical value, and it has in fact been suggested by Maier, *Ladeheiligtum*, 58ff., that it was originally the symbol of an anti-Philistine alliance of Israelite tribes and may have contained the covenant document or the covenant symbol of that tribal alliance. Under David it also functioned as a war palladium (cf. 2 Sam. 11:11), though after having been installed in the temple at Jerusalem by Solomon (where it is rightly referred to by the deuteronomist in 1 Kg. 8; cf. 2 Sam. 6; Ps. 132), it is probable that it became more and more closely associated with the Jerusalem kingship, perhaps becoming a dynastic symbol of the covenant between Yahweh and the Davidic king, cf. 2 Sam. 7. Consistently, however, the ark seems to have been understood as the throne or pedestal of the invisible Yahweh; see especially Num. 10:35f.; 1 Sam. 4:3, 6f. It is this view, probably elaborated in the Jerusalem temple, which is countered in the sober deuteronomistic evaluation of the ark as a simple container for the law tablets. In this evaluation the deuteronomist is not proposing something wholly new, for although his association of the ark and the decalogue in particular is apparently his own work, the ark was, to judge from its name, made as a container. Moreover, as 1 Sam. 10:25 indicates (cf. also Dt. 31:9ff.; Jos. 24:26), the deposition of law at sanctuaries is not a deuteronomistic invention; and indeed in the extra-biblical treaty context the copies of the treaty were deposited at the sanctuaries of the treaty partners; cf. Phillips, *Law*, 6. For general discussions of the ark, reference may be made especially to Nielsen, *VTS* 7, 1960, 61ff.; de Vaux, *Bible*, 136ff. See also comment on 31:14.

2. Except for v. 2*b* this verse repeats Exod. 34:1*b*. The P version of the making of the ark, which apparently suppressed the older account, does not appear until Exod. 37.

3. acacia: Hebrew *šittîm* (cf. *AV*), a hard, durable, orange brown wood, still common in desert regions of Palestine.

4. as at the first writing: in all the first four verses of this chapter the deuteronomist has insisted that the renewed covenant is on the same basis as the original one which was broken: not only are the tablets 'like the first', but their words are the words

that were on the first tablets. This is in contrast to the Sinai
pericope where it is the 'cultic decalogue' which is found in
Exod. 34, rather than a repeat of the 'ethical decalogue' of Exod.
20. The background of this is very complex. The collection of
laws in Exod. 34 is undoubtedly earlier than the deuteronomic
compilation of the decalogue found in Exod. 20, which was
placed in the Sinai pericope at a secondary stage. The deuteronomist is carrying this process a stage further by insisting that the
laws of the renewed covenant were not those of Exod. 34 but a
repeat of the original ones and were again written by God himself.
he wrote: in Exod. 34:28 it is Moses who writes the laws. The
deuteronomist here conforms with Exod. 24:12; 31:18 which
ascribe the writing of the original covenant laws to God.

5. and there they are: this should be taken as a rhetorical
statement in the context of the deuteronomist's insistence on the
ark as only a box containing the law tablets, and, moreover,
tablets containing the original covenant laws, rather than as an
indication of either the date of the author of this verse or the
place and condition of the ark in the time of the deuteronomist.

6–9. V. 5 obviously finds its continuation in v. 10, where the
first person singular speech of Moses appears once more; so the
intervening verses are secondary. They are not all from the same
hand, however; vv. 6f. are the late fragment of an itinerary, close
to the priestly writing both in style and in the reference to the
Aaronide priesthood. Yet they are probably earlier than P since
they do not insist on exclusive Aaronide priesthood and since
neither the itinerary nor the place of Aaron's death given in verse 6
conform with the information given by P in Num. 20 and 33.
Vv. 8f. give information which is found elsewhere in Deuteronomy
(cf. 31:9ff., 25f.), but is out of place here. The addition, which
derives its material for the most part from the deuteronomistic
18:1*, 2, 5 (see comment), was probably caused by the reference
to the deposit of the tablets of the law in the ark in v. 5, for in the
view of the deuteronomist the Levites were both the bearers of
the ark and the expounders of the law; cf. Cody, *Priesthood*, 138
and n. 27. Vv. 8f., therefore, were added before vv. 6f., and
originally followed immediately on v. 5. The reason for the
addition of vv. 6f. may simply have been the desire to emphasize
the continuity from Mosaic times of the Aaronide priesthood, in a
context which referred to the institution of a Levitical ministry
from the time of Moses, a desire which would have arisen in

post-exilic times when Aaron was regarded as the ancestor of the genuine priesthood.

6. from Beeroth Bene-jaakan to Moserah: *Sam* follows the reverse itinerary given in Num. 33:31. Beeroth Bene-jaakan, or 'the wells of the son of Jaakan', is the name of an unknown site; el-Birein, about twelve miles north of Kadesh, is often mentioned. **Moserah:** this site is unknown, but there is no reason for supposing that it is an alternative name for Mt Hor which in Num. 20:22ff., is the place of Aaron's death.

7. Gudgodah: presumably the same as Hor-haggidgad in Num. 33:32. Its site is unknown. The differences between the forms of some of these names as given in 10:6f. compared with Num. 33:31ff. indicate that there is no direct relationship between these two passages. **Jotbathah:** unknown, but sometimes identified with *et-Taba* in the southern Arabah.

8. at that time: although this and the following verse are additions here, this phrase is appropriately used since, according to Exod. 32:26–29 to which reference is undoubtedly being made, it was at Horeb that the Levites displayed their special zeal for Yahweh, justifying their being set apart for particular functions. **to carry the ark of the covenant of the Lord:** the deuteronomist consistently assigns this role to the Levites (cf. 31:9ff.; Jos. 3:3, etc.). **to stand before the Lord:** this is synonymous with **to minister** (cf. 1 Kg. 10:8); for the Levites to minister to Yahweh means that they have priestly status. This is not acceptable to the priestly writer for whom the Levites never minister to Yahweh but only in the sanctuary, at the altar, or to the Aaronide priests (cf. Smith). **to bless in his name:** again for the priestly writer this is a priestly duty, carried out by Aaron (Lev. 9:22; Num. 6:23).

9. inheritance: see comment on 4:20, 21. The meaning here is that just as the inheritance is the means of livelihood passed down within the family, so Yahweh (i.e. the offerings made to Yahweh) is the means of livelihood for the Levites through their generations. **as the Lord your God said to him:** as with the phrase 'the Lord set apart' in v. 8, so here there is no record of this in the older sources in Exod. 32. Perhaps, as with the account of the making of the ark (see comment on v. 1), the older story has been suppressed in favour of the priestly account of the consecration of Aaron, which is given in detail in Exod. 28f. On the Levites, see further on 18:1ff.

10. This verse cannot follow directly either on v. 9 or on v. 5, but is clearly the continuation of the intercession of 9:26–29 (von Rad). It takes up the basic deuteronomic account once more (using the second person singular form of address). It has been modified through the addition of the words **as at the first time** (which are not found in the LXX) and **that time also** (repeated from 9:19), in order to accommodate more smoothly the deuteronomistic material already incorporated.

11. In this transitional verse the deuteronomic account leaves its very brief historical retrospect to take up the exhortation once more in the words of 9:5.

(f) ISRAEL MUST OBEY THE LAW WHICH CARRIES BOTH CURSE AND BLESSING: **10:12–11:32**

The extent of the unit following 9:1–10:11 is debated. Lohfink, *Hauptgebot*, 219ff., takes 10:12–11:17 as a unit composed of six commandments, each provided with its justification, and followed by blessing and curse, so giving the form of the covenant formulary. Seitz, *op. cit.*, 81ff., on the other hand, takes 10:12–13 as the conclusion of the basic deuteronomic account which precedes, 10:14–22 as being of late origin, and ch. 11 as basically deuteronomistic, to which vv. 13–15, 18–21, 26–30 have been later added, while vv. 31f. belong with what follows in the next chapter. The deuteronomistic basis follows the pattern of the treaty or covenant formula: v. 1 is a transitional verse connecting it to what precedes; vv. 2–7 form the historical prologue; vv. 8–9 the statement of basic principle; vv. 10–12 the land description (a part of the treaty form which usually, however, follows directly on the historical prologue); vv. 16–17, 22–25 conditional curse and blessing. However, attractive as this view is, it remains difficult to omit any of the suggested sections as secondary; they betray features common to the rest of 10:12–11:32 (see comment on vv. 13–15) and even vv. 18–21, almost generally understood to be secondary, share with the remainder of the whole section the purpose of bringing together in summary form the most important elements of all that has gone before.

Although additions are probably to be found in 10:19, 22; 11:29f. (see comment), attempts to carry through a division on the basis of the change from singular to plural form of address do not appear to be successful. To take 10:15*c*–19 as a plural addition to the singular context (cf. Minette de Tillesse, *VT* 12, 1962, 37) is possible, but it would seem better to understand that the command to fear God in v. 20 and the description of what God has done in v. 21 presuppose the description of the nature of God in v. 17. In ch. 11 the sudden changes between singular and plural form of address in vv. 8, 10–12, 14f., 19ff. do not admit of explanation along these lines.

In fact, this irregularity in forms of address is one of several points which connect this whole section with 4:1–40. There too it is impossible to use it as a basis for literary division. Other contacts with 4:1–40 and with material deriving from the author of that section are to be found in the use of common vocabulary and expressions (see comments on 10:12, 13, 15, 16, 20, 21; 11:2, 12f., 16, 17, 21, 23). As with ch. 4, so here the whole section is connected to already existing material through the use of *we‘attāh* 'and now' (see comment on 4:1; 10:12). Again as in ch. 4 this section is a speech which takes up various familiar themes, and, while its overall structure does not follow the covenant or treaty form, it uses elements of that covenant form: history, law, blessing and curse. Moreover, allowing for many differences, there is also a discernible common overall form in ch. 4 and 10:12–11:32. Both begin (4:1–8; 10:12–22) with a general reference to the command-ments, to part of Israel's history and to Israel's worship of Yahweh alone; this is followed (4:9–14; 11:1–7) by a section in which a historical recitation leads up to covenant and law; then (4:15–24; 11:8–17) a general warning against disobedience is combined with a reference to the land; the next section (4:25–31; 11:18–25) is concerned with obedience to the law in the future and carries the promise of (curse and) blessing; finally (4:32–40; 11:26–32), there is a conclusion with general exhortation to obey the law.

It would seem, therefore, that 10:12–11:32 should be taken as a single section deriving from the author of 4:1–40; and just as in the latter chapter this author opened the general parenetic intro-duction to the law, so now he closes it, and at the same time presents the covenant context of blessing and curse within which the following law is to be understood.

12. And now: this phrase establishes the connection between what precedes and what follows. The commandments which follow have been collected here as the necessary practical conse-quence of the history which precedes; see also comment on 4:1. As Lohfink, *Hauptgebot*, 229, has noted, however, the particular historical narrative in 9:9–10:11, as a story of covenant breaking, is not precisely the type of account one would expect as a historical prologue preceding the commandments (nor is any part of that history, such as 9:22–24, any more suitable). The connection between the two is, therefore, not original; and it is more probable that the commandments have been brought in here as the continuation of the already existing history than that the history should have been joined later to the commandments. So 10:12ff is from a hand later than the deuteronomistic author of the preceding section. This is confirmed by other connections which may be established between what follows and 4:1–40 or other material known to derive from the late deuteronomistic author of that section.

what does the Lord your God require of you: the question and its answer are reminiscent of Mic. 6:8. However, the use of a different verb in the question, and the different answer, indicate that there is no possibility of direct dependence. The answer in Deuteronomy uses expressions and ideas which have already appeared: **to fear,** cf. 5:29; 6:13; **to walk in all his ways,** cf. 5:33; **to love him,** cf. 6:5; **to serve,** cf. 6:13, **with all your heart and with all your soul,** cf. 6:5. Although no other examples of this particular question and answer form are found in the Old Testament, probably the connections between Deuteronomy and Micah are to be explained by their common use of a general speech form.

13. The vocabulary and thought here are to be found in slightly different formulation in 4:40.

14. the heaven of heavens: the Hebrew expression properly denotes the superlative (cf. GK §133 g–i), and so a more suitable translation would be 'the highest heavens' (cf. *NEB*, and also 1 Kg. 8:27; Ps. 148:4). God's universal dominion is here affirmed in order to provide a sharp contrast with the next verse.

15. yet: an adverb which (variously translated) is frequently used in deuteronomic and deuteronomistic writings (cf. 12:15; 20:16; 1 Kg. 3:2, 3; 8:19, etc.) in order to restrict and limit something previously expressed. So here it means 'in spite of this (sc. God as Lord of the universe) God loved your fathers . . .'. **set his heart in love upon your fathers:** using the thought and vocabulary of 4:37; 7:7. Vv. 14 and 15 together affirm in the strongest terms the favour which God bestowed on the patriarchs and on Israel, as a basis and reason for the already given and again following demand to fear and love him.

16. circumcise: circumcision was probably originally a rite associated with marriage and was performed at puberty (cf. Gen. 17:25; 34:14ff.; Exod. 4:25; note also that the Hebrew word for 'father-in-law' means also 'one who circumcises'). As such it signified also full membership of the community. In Israel where the rite was at some uncertain stage transferred to infancy, this meant membership of the covenant community. Circumcision, as a sign of such membership, was then spiritualized to signify inner dedication and openness to Yahweh (as in Jer. 4:4; cf. also Jer. 6:10). Along with Sabbath observance, circumcision assumed great importance for Jews from the exile onwards, as a distinctive religious custom. An insistence on the necessity for an inner change of heart (see also Dt. 30:6) would be most suitable in the context of emphasis on the importance of physical circumcision. **be no longer stubborn:** the result of inner conversion, using terminology already used in the previous section (9:6, 13).

17. God of gods and Lord of lords: as in v. 14, the Hebrew construction is that of the superlative: 'the supreme God and Lord'. Although possibly having a polytheistic background, it is clearly here used simply as an honorific title. It is an expression of praise expected in the type of liturgical setting in which Ps. 136:2f. uses it. In the present context it is an assertion of Yahweh's kingship, and it is in the light of his kingship that the following terms should be seen. **the mighty:** the word may be translated 'warrior'. Here, and in the words **the great** and **the terrible** there is allusion to Yahweh's action in the exodus (cf. Exod. 15:3) as well as to his performing the general royal function of leadership in war. **not partial:** the Hebrew idiom is 'does not lift up faces', i.e. does not give special regard to; a similar expression, using a different verb, is used of human judges in 1:17. **takes no bribe:** the association of royal and judicial roles is common, and in particular the responsibility of the king for the maintenance of justice is widely presupposed throughout the ancient Near East; see the Old Testament and extra-biblical material quoted in Johnson, *Sacral Kingship*, 4ff. This quality of kingship is then transferred to Yahweh, also in Pss. 96:10, 13; 99:4, etc.

18. To help the poor and oppressed is also a royal function; see the claim of Hammurabi in the epilogue to his lawcode (xxiv 50ff.) 'In my bosom I carried the peoples of the land . . . I have sheltered them in my strength. In order that the strong might not oppress the weak, that justice might be dealt to orphan (and) to

widow ... I wrote my precious words on my stela ... to give
justice to the oppressed' (*ANET*, 178). **the fatherless and the
widow, and ... the sojourner:** this is the traditional group of
weak and poor, particularly open to economic and judicial
oppression; cf. 24:17, 19, 20, 21; 27:19; also Exod. 22:21f. To this
group Deuteronomy also adds the Levite in 16:11, 14; 26:12, 13.
sojourner: see comment on 1:16.

19. Though probably an old formulation (there is a similar
command in 24:17f.; cf. also 5:15; 15:15; 16:12), this verse is a
secondary addition to the present context. The context is concerned with Israel's behaviour towards God, and motivates its
demands by reference to the greatness of God. This verse is
concerned with Israel's attitude to the sojourner only (though
other members of the group of poor are mentioned in the previous
verse), and motivates its demand by reference to Israel's status in
Egypt. The verse is a late gloss which came in by association with
v. 18; see also Lohfink, *Hauptgebot*, 223 and n. 14.

20. See comment on 6:13 where this verse is closely paralleled.
Here a fourth element, not found in 6:13, is added: **and cleave to
him.** This is synonymous with love (cf. Gen. 34:3; 1Kg. 11:2) or
devotion to a leader (2 Sam. 20:2). In the Pentateuch it is only
Deuteronomy which uses the word in connection with the
relationship of God and Israel (cf. also 11:22; 13:4; 30:20, and
also the deuteronomistic passages in Jos. 22:5; 23:8).

21. He is your praise: according to Smith this may mean
either that God is the object of Israel's praise (cf. Ps. 109:1) or
that he is the cause of Israel being praised, by reason of the **great
and terrible things** which he has done on her behalf. That
Jer. 17:14 justifies the latter understanding is doubtful, but if true
it would fit well with the general thought of 4:6–8. **great and
terrible things:** cf. 4:34 'great terrors'. **which your eyes have
seen:** cf. 4:9.

22. seventy persons: the translation misses the emphatic
presentation of these words in the Hebrew where they come first
in the sentence. The number seventy signifies totality; cf. the
seventy elders of Exod. 24:1, 9; Num. 11:16, 24f., etc.; and, outside the Old Testament, the seventy sons of the goddess Asherah
(Gordon, *Ugaritic Textbook*, Text 51:VI, 46). Seventy as the
number of those who went down to Egypt is otherwise found in the
priestly passages in Gen. 46:27 and Exod. 1:5. It is not easy in this
instance to determine the direction of dependence, if any; but the

probability is that this verse is a late addition to Deuteronomy, and dependent on the priestly passages. This is because of the use of *nepeš*, which is a favourite word in P for 'person', and also because the verse is apparently a secondary interpretation of v. 21 which in fact refers, however, not to the multiplication of Israel in Egypt but to the events accompanying Israel's exodus from there. **as the stars of heaven for multitude:** see comment on 1:10.

11:1. V. 2 begins a new section, so 11:1 should be taken as the conclusion of the preceding verses, taking up the two main elements of 10:12ff.: the commands to love God and to keep his commandments. **his charge:** in all instances of the use of this word with regard to the commandments of Yahweh, in P (Lev. 8:35; 18:30; 22:9; Num. 9:19, 23), in the deuteronomistic historical work (Jos. 22:3; 1 Kg. 2:3), and elsewhere (Gen. 26:5; Mal. 3:14), it has a general comprehensive sense with reference to the will of Yahweh. This comprehensive sense is rather obscured here through the use of the conjunction (in Hebrew) between **charge** and **his statutes.** However, one may understand the conjunction as pleonastic (see comment on 1:7), or it may be taken as dittography of the suffix at the end of the preceding word (cf. *Sam*).

2. The scheme of vv. 2–8 follows the literary pattern of argument from history which in its purest form appears in 8:2–6 (see comment). As noted there, this does not separate the verses as an independent unit; this is a form used only within wider literary contexts. Here it brings together two elements (history and commandment) of the more general covenant form (see, above, the introduction to this section).

There is an anacoluthon in v. 2. It is often understood (as *RSV*) that the words *kî lō' ... lō' rā'û* stand in parenthesis, and that *'eṭ mûsar* is the object of *wîḏa'tem*. However, even with this awkward understanding a verb must be supplied in order to make sense of the words in parenthesis (*RSV* **I am ... speaking**), and, as Bertholet notes, it is in fact much more natural to take *'eṭ mûsar* as the object of the immediately preceding verb *lō' rā'û*. Since v. 7 indicates that the intention here is to emphasize that it is the present generation which has witnessed the great works of Yahweh and not the generation which is to come, one may refer to 5:3 (apparently from the same late author), where there is the same care to emphasize the present generation as the one immediately responsible before God, and supply here the words (cf. Seitz, *op.*

cit., 85): *kāraṭ 'ªdōnāy eṭ habbᵉrît hazzōᵗṭ.* The translation of the verse would then be: 'and know this day that the Lord did not make this covenant with your children who have not known and who have not seen the discipline . . . (v. 7) but your eyes have seen . . .'

4. Red Sea: see comment on 1:40. The summary of the saving history in vv. 2–6 refers to four elements: the plagues in Egypt, the deliverance at the Red Sea, the leading through the wilderness, and the divine punishment of Dathan and Abiram exemplifying the punishment brought by God on Israel for its murmuring. Of these elements the second, mentioned in this verse, and the last, in v. 6, do not otherwise appear in the Deuteronomic summaries of Israel's saving history (6:21ff.; 26:5ff.). The power of Yahweh over nature, which these references demonstrate, is referred to again later in the chapter (vv. 10ff., 13ff.).

5. until you came to this place: the same phrase in the deuteronomistic 1:31, and the late passage in 9:7*b*.

6. swallowed them up: *Sam* adds 'with all the men of Korah'. The point of the addition is to bring the verse into line with the story of Num. 16, according to which Korah, along with Dathan and Abiram, was punished in this way for opposing the authority of Moses. The JE story there, however, knew only Dathan and Abiram, and it is this which the *MT* in this verse follows. The references to Korah are additions, apparently from the hand of the priestly writer, and it is in keeping with these that the *Sam* version has made its addition here. **living thing:** an infrequent word, otherwise used only in Gen. 7:4, 23, where it includes both men and animals.

7. for: in view of the different syntax proposed (see comment on v. 2) for the sentence which extends from v. 2 to v. 7, it must be understood that this verse provides a contrast to what has already been said; in which case a better translation here is 'but'. **your eyes have seen:** so also in 10:21. **all the great works of the Lord which he did:** the same phrase appears in the deuteronomistic Jg. 2:7.

8. the commandment: on the late comprehensive use of this term for the whole law, see comment on 5:31. On obedience to the commandments as the condition of possession of the land, see comment on 4:1. The verse is a good illustration of the point (see comment on 8:2–6) that the literary pattern of argument from history is not an independent unit, but is used within larger literary contexts. V. 8 provides the conclusion of the argument form but it is also the statement of basic principle in the covenant form and, moreover, along with v. 9, it forms a transitional section leading over into a description of the land.

9. The divine promise to the patriarchs is subordinated to the demand for obedience to the law, as in 7:12. **a land flowing with milk and honey:** see comment on 6:3.

10. This and the following verses are particularly important in that they extend the favoured position of Israel to the very land which she is to occupy: it is a land specially cared for by Yahweh. Therefore, it is not only in history, but also in nature, that it can be seen how Israel is a chosen people; cf. Lohfink, *Höre Israel*, 51f. **watered it with your foot:** the significance of this is not entirely clear. It is sometimes taken as an allusion to the irrigation channels which are hollowed out by foot in soft earth, or to a way of regulating by foot the flow of water in such irrigation channels, or to a water wheel turned by the foot, or even as a metaphorical allusion to physical labour. *BHS* suggests an emendation of $beragle\underline{k}\bar{a}$ ('with your foot') to $bedoly^e\underline{k}\bar{a}$ ('with your bucket'); cf. Num. 24:7). Whatever the precise sense, however, it is clear that the intention is to contrast Palestine, which is made fruitful by the rain sent by God, with Egypt, where fruitfulness is achieved only as a result of constant human effort.

11, 12. Different points are emphasized in these verses: the land is one of **hills and valleys,** and so not suitable for the form of irrigation possible in Egypt; it is therefore dependent on the rain, and to that extent dependent also on Yahweh who sends the rain. Furthermore, it is Yahweh on whom Israel and the land depend, not Baal, the fertility god worshipped by those already in the land. This prepares the way for the particular form of the blessing which appears in vv. 13ff. **cares for:** the verb usually means 'to seek'; here, as in Isa. 62:12; Jer. 30:17; Job 3:4, with the sense of 'seek carefully after'.

13–15. The conditional blessing in these verses is expressed in terms of the blessings of nature; a further conditional blessing in vv. 22–25 is expressed in terms of Yahweh's giving Israel possession of the land. Seitz, *op. cit.*, 87ff., thinks that the first of these conditional blessings is probably later than the second: it is mostly made up of formulae: **with all your heart and with all your soul** (cf. 4:29; 6:5; 10:12; 13:4; 30:2, 6, 10); **your grain and your wine and your oil** (cf. 7:13; 12:17; 14:23; 18:4; 28:51); **and you shall eat and be full** (cf. 6:11; 8:10, 12; 14:29; 26:12;

31:20). Further, the verses use both first and third persons of
Yahweh. In contrast to vv. 10-12, where the well-watered nature
of the land is part of the description of Palestine as it is, here it is
the content of conditional blessing. Finally, the plural **commandments** is used, rather than the singular, as in vv. 8, 22. These
objections to the originality of the verses have considerable
strength, especially if, with Seitz, the chapter is taken to be basically deuteronomistic. However, for reasons already given (see,
above, the introduction to this section), it seems best to see the
chapter as part of the single section 10:12-11:32, and deriving
from the same late author as 4:1-40. The use of words and phrases
common elsewhere is a familiar element of this author's style;
moreover, the use of the well-watered nature of the ground as a
conditional blessing is not so out of keeping with vv. 10-12 if these
verses are understood as implying the dependence of the land on
Yahweh (see comment on vv. 11, 12). The variation in use of
first and third person of Yahweh is a problem whatever the authorship. Furthermore, in favour of the originality of the verses in their
context there is the fact that the fruitfulness of the land is a strong
feature of its description, so that a blessing referring to that is to
be expected; also, the form of the conditional curse in v. 17,
referring to Yahweh's withholding rain, demands a corresponding
blessing.

13. my commandments: not an impossible construction in
the context of a speech of Moses, since it is he who is imparting the
commandments to Israel (cf. e.g. 7:11; 11:8, where Moses speaks
of the commandments 'which I command you'). Nevertheless,
Moses usually refers to 'the commandments of the Lord your
God' or 'his commandments' (4:2, 40: 6:17); so probably (and
particularly in view of the following verses) the suffix should be
taken as referring to Yahweh.

14. he will give: this reading, referring to Yahweh in the third
person as would be expected in a speech of Moses, has some
support in the ancient versions and the Qumran texts; it is clearly,
however, a correction of the more difficult 'and I will give' of the
MT. This is one of several such inconsistencies in Deuteronomy,
some but by no means all of which are open to explanation on
textual grounds. See the comment at 5:11. **the early rain and
the later rain:** or 'the autumn rain and the spring rain' (Jer.
5:24). These rains mark the beginning and end of the rainy
season, October/November-March/April, and are particularly

mentioned because in the one case they signify the end of the summer dryness, preparing the ground for ploughing, while in the other they are the last rain before the onset of the dry season, and bring the greenness of spring to the whole country.

15. he will give: again the *MT* here has the undoubtedly original reading 'I will give'. In this case *Sam* reads 'he will give', while mss of the LXX vary between 'he will give' and 'you will give'; Targ and Vulg simply omit the word. The variations illustrate the difficulty which the reading of the *MT* caused. **grass:** the word is the same as that translated 'plants' in Gen. 3:18; it denotes the food of both man and animal.

16. Take heed: so 4:23 and, in singular form of address, 4:9 **be deceived:** so also in Job 31:9, 27, etc. Other passages, such as Hos. 7:11, Job 5:2, suggest the sense of 'simple', or (if the word is to be closely associated with the root *pāṭāh* 'to open') 'open-mindedness' (cf. Craigie), so that the warning is against being so open to the culture of the land that the worship of the fertility gods is accommodated to Yahwism along with the new way of life. See also Hos. 2:5ff.

17. Although this particular expression of the curse resulting from disobedience is found only here, the theme—that the rain will be withheld—is not infrequent in curse texts, cf. Lev. 26:19f.; Dt. 28:23f.; see also the deuteronomistic 1 Kg. 8:35. **fruit:** i.e. general produce. The word may be used even of one's material possessions generally (Job 20:28). **and you perish quickly:** the same expression, in slightly varied form, in 4:26.

18–20. Vv. 18–20 take up 6:6–9 (see comment on these verses). **these words of mine:** the definite article has been accidentally dropped from the demonstrative pronoun in *dᵉḇāray 'ēlleh*. This suggests the possibility that two other letters also may have been omitted, a restoration of which, to read *haddᵉḇārim hā'ēlleh*, 'these words', would bring the expression into line with 6:6; cf. Seitz, *op. cit.*, 87 n. 105.

21. that your days ... may be multiplied: cf. 4:40; 6:2; 11:9; where, however, a different verb is used. **as long as the heavens are above the earth:** i.e. for ever, cf. also Job 14:12. The stability and eternity of the universe is frequently alluded to in this way in the royal psalms, cf. Pss. 72:5, 7, 17; 89:29.

22. For the expressions used in this verse cf. 5:31; 6:5; 10:12, 20.

23. For the expressions here cf. 4:38; 9:1.

24. Every place on which the sole of your foot treads: the

foot is a symbol of power, so that, for example, to put under foot
means to subjugate (cf. Ps. 110:1), while to walk over an area of
land is the act of taking possession of that land; see comment on
25:9. **territory:** for this meaning of the word *gᵉḇûl* see comment
on 2:18. **and Lebanon:** the *NEB* translation, 'to the Lebanon',
presupposes a change in the Hebrew text which finds no support
in the versions or in the parallel verse in Jos. 1:4. The phrase **from
the wilderness and Lebanon** could still possibly be taken as a
reference to the southern and northern limits of the land respec-
tively; but it is better to take it along with what follows: **from
the River, the river Euphrates,** as a list of three reference
points covering the boundaries to the north (Lebanon), and north-
east (Syrian wilderness) and east (Euphrates), corresponding to the
western border formed by the Mediterranean; cf. Diepold, *Israels
Land*, 31f. See also comment on 1:7. **western sea:** the Hebrew
is 'the sea (lying) behind'. This way of referring to the Mediterranean (cf. also 34:2; Zech. 14:8; Jl 2:20; in the last two passages
the Dead Sea is referred to as 'the sea in front') presupposes the
natural direction of orientation being eastwards (cf. Driver)

25. The verse takes phrases from 2:25 and 7:24. The vocabulary
is that of the holy war, found also in Exod. 15:16.

26–32. In this concluding paragraph there is, as Lohfink,
Hauptgebot, 233f., has shown, a unit which, apart from the addition
in vv. 29f. (see comment), is held together in form and content.
Vv. 26 and 32 open and close the unit using the same phrase: **I set
before you this day.** In content, it consists of a uniform blessing
and curse combined with commandments; as in 4:5f., it opens
with the imperative **Behold,** which is followed by a statement and
completed by commandments (see also 30:15ff.; 1:8; 1:21; 2:24;
2:31). These verses are intended as a conclusion to the whole of
chs. 1–11, in that after all the history and the exhortation they
bring Israel to the point of decision. The verses are also a prelude
to what follows, since the decision which is now set before Israel
concerns obedience or disobedience to the law which is now to be
proclaimed. The context in which Israel is addressed is, therefore,
the historical context of the eve of entry into the land, and the
theological context of decision for blessing or curse, life or death.

28. turn aside: as in v.16. **the way:** apparently a reference to
the decalogue (see comment on 9:12), the first commandment of
which is indicated also by the reference to **other gods. which
you have not known:** gods with whom Israel has had no contact

in her history, with whom she has had no covenant (on the covenant or treaty context of use of the verb 'know', see comment on 9:24).

29. Vv. 29 and 30 stand out from their context, not simply by reason of their formulation in singular form of address in a plural context, but chiefly because of their content. Their particular geographical concern is outside the scope of interest of this chapter, and they form a very unsuitable prelude to vv. 31f., where the point of the section is reached: the commandments which carry with them the blessing and the curse. The schematic reference to blessing and curse in vv. 26–28 provided the occasion for the introduction of the verses which in fact anticipate and are based on ch. 27 (cf. 27:12f.). They have been brought in here so that with ch. 27 they may act as a framework to the deuteronomic lawcode in chs. 12–26. See also comment on ch. 27, and L'Hour, *RB* 69, 1962, 166f. **you shall set:** on the form of ceremony directed here, see comment on 27:12f. **the blessing on Mount Gerizim and the curse on Mount Ebal:** it is usually supposed that the background to the association of these two mountains with blessing and curse is a covenant ceremony near Shechem in the valley between Gerizim and Ebal. Gerizim is chosen as the mountain of blessing because, lying on the south and therefore the right-hand side (see comment on v. 24), it was the place of good fortune; Ebal, on the other hand, lay on the north, the left-hand side and so is associated with misfortune. This explanation should be complemented with that of Bülow, *ZDPV* 73, 1957, 105ff. (cf. also Smith), who points out that because of their different geological structures Ebal and Gerizim present starkly different appearances: the latter being fruitful and the former bare and barren. This would have been ascribed to the action of Yahweh: fruitfulness being the result of blessing, and sterility the result of his judgment and curse; so the curse is associated with Ebal and the blessing with Gerizim.

30. west of the road, toward the going down of the sun: the road intended is not clear; it is not mentioned elsewhere, but it is perhaps a reference to the route followed by the Israelites in their penetration of the land west of Jordan. **over against Gilgal:** the general obscurity of this verse has been focussed on this phrase. That it should be omitted as an addition (cf. Neilsen, *Shechem*, 42f.), or that the Gilgal referred to should be identified with a place near Shechem (for proposals of various possible sites named

Gilgal near Shechem, cf. Driver and Smith), really does not help, since with the phrase **who live in the Arabah** the verse is still apparently localizing Ebal and Gerizim in or near the Jordan valley. The most probable explanation (cf. L'Hour, *RB* 69, 1962, 167f.; and also the discussion by Eissfeldt, in *Proclamation*, 90ff.) is that the author of this verse was in fact intentionally bringing together the covenant tradition of Shechem (see Introduction, p. 68) with Gilgal, the sanctuary lying on the border of the promised land and the probable place of transmission of Israel's conquest traditions, in order to make the moment of entry into the land the moment of entry into the covenant with its law, blessing and curse. See, further, the introduction to 26:16–27:26 and the comment on 27:2. **the oak of Moreh:** the reference is probably to an oracular tree (the *MT* reads the plural 'oaks'; for the singular, and for the location of this tree near Shechem, cf. Gen. 12:6). **Moreh:** derived from the same root *yārāh* as that from which *tôrāh*, 'teaching', is derived; the word is probably an appellative, and should be translated 'the teacher' or 'the diviner'. Jos. 24:26 and Jg. 9:37 may refer to the same place.

31. For: this translation arises from the mistaken view that the verse has the function of justifying vv. 29f. However, apart from the fact that these preceding two verses are additions, it is clear that the verse should in fact be taken as the protasis of an independent conditional sentence (of which the apodosis is in v. 32), and that the first phrase should therefore be translated 'When you pass over . . .' The *RSV* translation indicates the need for finding a protasis in this verse through the insertion of **when** later in the verse, although it does not appear there in the Hebrew. The final two verses, therefore, describe the giving of the law **as a** prelude to entering the land where it is to be obeyed; for this, see also 4:5; 6:10ff.

C. THE LAW OF THE COVENANT: 12:1–26:15

Within the structure of Deuteronomy as a whole this section is the presentation of the detailed law of the covenant. It falls into seven major sections: (a) 12:1–14:21, on the unity and purity of Israel's worship; (b) 14:22–16:17, on periodic obligations and institutions; (c) 16:18–18:22, on officials in the theocratic state, their responsibilities and the responsibilities of Israelites towards them; (d)

19:1–21:9, on war and death; (e) 21:10–22:30, on respect for life particularly in the context of family relationships; (f) 23:1–25:19, on purity and humanitarian behaviour; and (g) 26:1–15, on first-fruits and tithes.

A certain correspondence can be seen between the order of subjects treated and the order of the decalogue commandments (cf. Schulz, *Das Todesrecht im alten Testament*, 67): section (a) corresponding to the first three commandments; section (b) to the fourth; section (c) to the fifth; section (d) to the sixth; and section (e) to the seventh; but the correspondence is not consistent and close, and clearly breaks down in the later sections. Furthermore, the sections are not always clearcut. There are strong bonds between some of them which blur the distinctions. So, for example, the false witness law in 19:15–21, section (d), is connected with the laws on the administration of justice in section (c), and the laws on marriage and descendants in 25:5–12, section (f), are connected with the marriage laws of 22:13ff. in section (e). For further discussion of the arrangement of the laws, see Introduction, pp. 49ff.

(A) THE UNITY AND PURITY OF ISRAEL'S WORSHIP: 12:1–14:21

Various divisions of the law into sections have been suggested (see the table in Seitz, *op. cit.*, 92f.), and none is free of objection. The reason for this is that the laws have not been subjected to a uniform process of editing. This is particularly clear in that the parenesis of the introductory chapters is strongly represented in the earlier parts of the law and almost completely absent in the later parts. This parenesis has brought into a single section laws which at the stage of development reflected in later sections of the law would have been separate. This is particularly so in the first section marked out here, consisting of 12:1–14:21. 12:1–28 demands Israel's worship of Yahweh at a single sanctuary, and is concerned with the consequences which arise from that demand. 12:29–13:18 has as its subject the possibility of Israel's serving gods other than Yahweh. It is a fairly distinct section with that as its concern. These two sections have, however, been closely linked, especially by the late author whose hand appears in 12:1–7, through the insertion of 12:32 into the first part of what was earlier a separate section (see also Seitz, *op. cit.*, 107f.). So the two themes of cultic unity and cultic purity have been closely joined. The theme of cultic purity is continued into 14:1–21. Although that section is clearly independent in treating the subject from the point of view of foods which are clean and unclean, the very basis for the distinction, which is a judgment made from the point of view of Israel's status as the people of Yahweh, brings the section into the general context of concern for the purity of Israel's relationship with Yahweh.

(i) *The centralization of worship* 12:1–28

The structure and origin of ch. 12 have been widely discussed. While source criticism as such is not capable of dealing adequately with the repetitions and variations within the chapter, it is not adequate either to explain these (cf. Carmichael, *Laws*, 36f.) as a reflection of the setting of instruction from which the material emanated. Reventlow, in *Gottes Wort*, 174ff., has adopted a strict form-critical approach, following which he takes the apodictic law of v. 2 as the oldest kernel of the chapter which has then been gradually enriched and developed in the context of preaching. However, the very basis of this explanation is faulty, in that even if apodictic is to be taken as the oldest Israelite legal form it cannot follow that every example of apodictic law is therefore old. Others have suggested a 'supplementary theory', following which an original short written text has been gradually supplemented in a literary process. So Merendino, *op. cit.*, 48ff. (cf. also Nebeling, *Schichten*, 26ff.), suggests an original short catechetical text (to be found within vv. 14, 17, 18), fixing the offerings to be brought to the central sanctuary, which was supplemented in five stages. The resulting text was then given a parenetic framework by the deuteronomic redactor in vv. 1, 8–12, 28, and later by the deuteronomist in vv. 1, 2–5, 6f., 12, 29–32. The chief problem here lies with the process of growth of what is taken as the central section in vv. 13–27. The theory of a literary development of a kernel by five distinct stages is an imaginative exercise involving an analysis into literary layers too minute to be probable, and an unlikely assignment of duplicate material to a single layer (e.g. vv. 15, 20, 22 are seen to be the result of the fourth stage of development). Moreover, it underestimates the significance of the clear distinction between vv. 13–19 as a single whole and the new paragraph beginning in v. 20 (see Seitz, *op. cit.*, 209ff.).

The original deuteronomic law of the central sanctuary is to be found in the passage 12:13–19, composed in singular form of address. Apart from the addition in v. 16 (see comment) these verses form a unity not only in content but also in their chiastic form (see comment on v. 19). This unit was edited by the deuteronomistic historian whose hand appears in vv. 8–12 (see comment on vv. 8 and 9 particularly); the purpose of this editing was primarily that of emphasizing the historical situation of Israel still not in possession of its 'rest' and 'inheritance'. Finally, the second deuteronomist responsible for 10:12–11:32 contributed also 12:1–7. This is indicated by the chiastic structure which binds 12:1 to the end of ch. 11 (see comment on 12:1), as well as by the regular appearance in these verses of terminology known already from this late author (see comment on vv. 2,3). 12:32 derives from the same hand. The purpose of this editing was to link up with material already supplied by this editor, but also to clarify a possible ambiguity in the original centralization law (see comment on vv. 5, 14).

At some uncertain stage after the origin of the deuteronomic law on centralization, the latter was given a new and somewhat limited interpretation. This is now to be found in 12:20–28 (see comment on v. 21). This is probably a pre-deuteronomistic addition, however, since the deuteronomist seems to have used material contained in it for his insertion of v. 16 into the deuteronomic law (see comment on v. 16).

1. As Seitz, *op. cit.*, 39f., has shown, this verse is very closely connected with the end of ch. 11 through a chiastic construction. The mid-point of the construction is formed by the final clause of the preceding chapter, in which reference is made to the law as promulgated to the people. The present verse then repeats in reverse order the significant elements and grammatical forms of 11:31f. This, together with the sudden change from plural to singular form of address, points to common authorship here and in ch. 11. **statutes and ordinances:** a combination most frequent in ch. 4 (vv. 1, 5, 8, 14). This, together with the formula **you shall be careful to do,** which likewise appears in late sections (5:1, 32; 6:3, 25; 7:11; 8:1; 11:22, 32, etc.) confirms the existence of the hand of a late author here. **has given:** the perfect is not otherwise used in this phrase in Deuteronomy (cf. Jos. 18:3).

2. The verse is composed of phrases which go back to deuteronomic parts of the book (**you shall surely destroy, the nations**

whom you shall dispossess: cf. 7:1ff. 9:1ff.) and to the terminology of the deuteronomistic historian (**upon the hills and under every green tree:** cf. 1 Kg. 14:23; 2 Kg. 16:4; 17:10). The deuteronomic law in vv. 13ff. is indeed concerned with Israel's worship of Yahweh 'at the place which the Lord will choose'; the late author here, however, has elaborated this in terms of the necessity for the utter destruction of all other places of worship. **green tree:** the translation of the versions, together with Ezek. 6:13 where the phrase is parallel to 'leafy oak', suggest that the reference is to a luxuriant tree, thick with leaves, rather than simply a green tree (cf. *NEB* 'spreading tree', and D. Winton Thomas, *VTS* 16, 1967, 387ff.). Trees, like mountains, frequently had sacred associations, though the cool shade offered by a densely leafed tree would perhaps have been reason enough for its choice as the site of a sanctuary,

3. **pillars ... Asherim:** see comment on 7:5. **the graven images of their gods:** the same phrase in 7:25. **destroy their name:** what is not named has no existence (Bertholet), and to call on the name of means to acknowledge.

4. The verse is found in a rather different context in 12:31. Here it apparently means that the worship of Yahweh is not, like that of the gods of the Canaanites, to be utterly rooted out of the land.

5. **you shall seek:** the verb is that used for visiting a sanctuary for a religious purpose; cf. Gen. 25:22; Dt. 18:11; 1 Sam. 9:9; Am. 5:5. The *NEB* perhaps comes closer in translating 'you shall resort to'. **the place which the Lord your God will choose:** this is the basic formula used to indicate the one sanctuary at which Yahweh should be worshipped. The full formula here, with the addition of the words **out of all your tribes** finds parallels in the deuteronomistic history (1 Kg. 8:16; 11:32; 14:21; 2 Kg. 21:7), where it is clear that the deuteronomist understood the formula to have reference to Jerusalem and only to that city. This deuteronomistic form is distinct from the form of the formula as it appears in v. 14. The latter is possibly, though not actually, ambiguous, in its expression, since it could admit the existence of more than one sanctuary; it is this possible ambiguity which lies behind the change which the deuteronomist has made. See comment on v. 14. Pss. 78:68ff.; 132:13ff. suggest that the notion of Yahweh's having 'chosen' was attached specially to Zion and the Davidic dynasty, and it is probable that the present formula

has its roots in the context of such beliefs. The deuteronomic school, however, has brought a sense of exclusiveness to that idea which is not original to it. Merendino, *Gesetz*, 382ff., has outlined a possible history of the formula within Deuteronomy in which it was first used with reference to the three great festivals: Mazzot, Weeks, and Tabernacles (16:16), whereas less significant cultic actions could be carried on at any sanctuary; next it was applied to Passover, and finally to all sacrificial acts. This last stage of the tradition is the one reflected in ch. 12. Merendino's rather atomistic treatment of the text, however, makes his outline rather uncertain; on the historical background of centralization, see Introduction, pp. 61ff. **will choose:** when this verbal form occurs, the *Sam* regularly reads 'has chosen'. The intention of the change is probably to guard against any possible interpretation of the phrase with reference to Jerusalem; rather, it is an already existing (patriarchal) sanctuary which Yahweh has chosen. **to put his name:** a formula (found also in 12:21; 14:24) synonymous with 'to make his name dwell there' (12:11; 14:23; 16:2, 6, 11; 26:2). De Vaux, in *Wort*, 219ff., has interpreted it in the light of a similar Accadian expression found twice in the Amarna letters: 'the king has established his name on . . .', and thus understands the phrase as a simple affirmation of ownership (see also comment 28:10). The idea of Yahweh as owner of the sanctuary is found elsewhere, cf. Exod. 15:17; Ps. 78:54; what is new in Deuteronomy is that it is integrated into an election theology: Yahweh has chosen the sanctuary as his possession. De Vaux finds that it is not until the deuteronomist (cf. 1 Kg. 8:19; 2 Kg. 23:27) that one finds in the phrase a 'name theology' as such, i.e. the view that Yahweh himself is not present in the sanctuary since his dwelling is in heaven; rather, he is permanently available to his people at the sanctuary through the presence there of his name. However, as Weinfeld, *Deuteronomy*, 194f., has noted, the notion of a symbolic presence of the person who establishes his name is not to be divorced from the idea of claiming ownership: ownership is in fact claimed and established through the symbolic presence of the person in his name. The origin of the idea in the Yahwistic context is obscure. It is not confined in its application to Jerusalem (cf. Jer. 7:12, where it is used of Shiloh,), and so is unlikely to be of deuteronomic origin. Dumermuth, *ZAW* 70 (NF 29), 1958, 70ff., has suggested that it arose in the north out of concern for the problem of the presence of Yahweh after the ark, the throne of the invisible Yahweh, had been lost to the northern tribes when taken to Jerusalem (see also Nicholson, *Deuteronomy*, 55f., 71ff.). Whether or not this is so, it is true that the basic idea is an affirmation of the real and actual presence of Yahweh at the sanctuary; the primary concern is not with the problem of how God can dwell in heaven and at the same time be present with his people (a question which may have influenced the deuteronomist in 1 Kg. 8:27–30). **and make his habitation:** the Hebrew is 'for his habitation', using a noun which never otherwise occurs. A slight change in pointing, from *lešiknô* to *lešakkenô*, gives a verbal form with the meaning 'to make it dwell', which is found frequently elsewhere (cf. 12:11; 14:23; 16:2, 6, 11; 26:2; Jer. 7:12).

6. This verse confirms the cultic significance of the verb 'seek' in the previous verse. One seeks Yahweh's 'place' in order to sacrifice there. **burnt offerings:** the offering that was wholly (except for the hide) devoted by fire to Yahweh. According to Levine, *Presence*, 22ff., the purpose of this offering is to ascertain the attitude or disposition of the deity and specifically to evoke a favourable response in a situation in which the deity is felt to be deaf to the entreaties of his worshippers. As such it preceded the **sacrifice,** a general term which would apply to a number of cultic actions which have in common, however, that they were a communion meal; they were shared by the deity and his worshippers, the blood and the fat being assigned to the deity, and the purpose was to strengthen fellowship among the participants. Before the legislation of Deuteronomy, every slaughtering of an animal was a sacrifice (*zebaḥ*); but with the restriction of such actions to a central cult site provision had to be made for profane slaughter (vv. 15f.) which could be carried out without recourse to the sanctuary. It is for this profane action that the deuteronomic law in v. 15 reserves the verb *zābaḥ*; the later editor has here, however, used the root also of cultic acts at the central sanctuary. For a description of the significance of and the rituals involved in the sacrifices and offerings mentioned here, see de Vaux, *Studies*, 27ff. **tithe:** see comment on 14:22. **the offerings that you present:** (*AV* 'heave offerings of your hand'; *NEB* 'contributions'). The term is primarily used by P and Ezekiel; apparently the reference is to what is raised or lifted off and separated from a larger mass. So in Exod. 25:2f. it denotes a proportion of precious articles and materials set apart for sacred use. In the context of sacrifice it denotes the portion which is set apart as the priest's due

(Lev. 7:14, 32, 34). **votive offerings:** an offering made in fulfilment of a vow; see especially Jg. 11:30, 39. **freewill offerings:** a
general and fairly comprehensive term, distinct from the votive
offerings, but could include the burnt offering and peace offering
(Ezek. 46:12). **firstlings:** see comment on 15:19ff.

7. you shall rejoice: the general purpose of sacrifice and
offering in Deuteronomy is twofold. Firstly, humanitarian:
offerings should provide food, especially for the poor and destitute
in Israelite society (cf. 14:26f.; 16:11; 26:11), so that all may
rejoice. Secondly, it has a private purpose, that of fulfilling a
religious obligation undertaken in the form of a vow (cf. vv. 11,
17, 26; 23:21-23). The notion that offerings belong in the context
of expiation for sin is generally foreign to Deuteronomy; expiation
is the function of prayer and confession. It is, therefore, no accident
that the list of offerings and sacrifices, apparently intended to be
comprehensive, makes no reference to the sin and guilt offerings
(Lev. 4:1ff.). See the discussion in Weinfeld, *Deuteronomy*, 210ff.
in all that you undertake: the use of this phrase in 15:10;
23:20; 28:8, 20, suggests that it belongs primarily in the context
of curse and blessing. Its use here and in v. 18, in conjunction with
the verb 'rejoice', is a secondary application of the phrase, which
has attracted, as a probable addition, the rather awkward phrase
in which the Lord your God has blessed you; see also
Merendino, *op. cit.*, 26.

8. The second section, the deuteronomistic vv. 8-12, includes
the prescriptions of vv. 5-7, but emphasizes the historical situation
of Israel still on the way to its 'rest'. **doing whatever is right in
his own eyes:** a phrase used by the deuteronomistic historian in
Jg. 17:6; 21:25, to describe the morally reprehensible life of Israel
before the foundation of the monarchy; so the morality of the law
now to be presented is emphasized.

9. rest: see comment on 3:20. The verse points generally to
settlement in the land as the time when Israel will have rest.
However, in conjunction with the previous verse and also with
1 Kg. 5:4; 8:56, it is clear that the specific period intended is that
of Solomon and the foundation of the temple. **rest,** therefore, is
here not merely the state of peace and security in the land, free of
threat from enemies (though the association here with **inheritance**
shows that simple possession of the land is certainly included), but
also involves the realization of Israel as a single people centered
around a single sanctuary. **inheritance:** see comment on 4:21.

11. The list of sacrifices and offerings here is the source of the slightly expanded list in v. 6. **all your votive offerings:** the Hebrew refers rather to 'all the choicest of your votive offerings' (cf. *NEB*).

12. maidservants: usually a servant whose primary attachment was to the mistress of the house, cf. Ps. 123:2; Isa. 24:2; Prov. 30:23, with Dt. 5:14, 21; 12:18; 15:17; 16:11, 14. In some places, however, the word means 'concubine', cf. Exod. 21:7; 23:12, and the discussion in Jepsen, *VT* 8, 1958, 293ff. **Levite:** on the background of the regular inclusion in Deuteronomy of the Levite among the poor recommended to the charity of the Israelite, see comment on 18:1. **that is within your towns:** a phrase characteristic of Deuteronomy; in Exod. 20:10 it is used of the resident alien who, like the Levite, is a landless and so economically weak member of Israelite society (see comment on 1:16).

13. Take heed: the opening of the original deuteronomic law of the central sanctuary uses a formula also to be found in the deuteronomic parenesis (8:11a, see comment), from which it has been taken also into later layers (e.g. 6:12).

14. in one of your tribes: a possible ambiguity exists in the Hebrew of this phrase. In the light of the use of the phrase 'one of' in 15:17; 16:5; 17:2; 18:6; 19:5, 11; 23:16, the translation here could be 'in one or other of', i.e. the reference need not be an exclusive one to a single place. This was how it was understood by Oestreicher, *Grundgesetz*, 106, who also took the definite article in **the place** in a distributive sense, translating it 'every place'. From a grammatical point of view this is possible, but within the literary context of the deuteronomic law in vv. 13–19 it is a most unlikely interpretation. The contrast with 'any of your towns' in v. 15 suggests that a single place is intended here, and had the intention been a number of legitimate sites the expression would undoubtedly have been clearer (e.g. 'at the places which the Lord will choose in your tribes'; cf. Nicholson, *Deuteronomy*, 27, 54). The possible ambiguity was, however, recognized also by the later editor who eliminated it in v. 5; cf. Minette de Tillesse, *VT* 12, 1962, 66f.

15. slaughter: the verb used (*zābaḥ*) is that otherwise translated 'sacrifice'. Originally all slaughter was in fact sacrifice, and through treating it as such man was safeguarded from the dangers accompanying this violent incursion into the animal world. The sacrificial ritual consisted of offering the blood on an altar, while the flesh could be eaten (cf. 1 Sam. 14:32ff.). Since the abolition of the local sanctuaries made this procedure impracticable, two possible consequences followed: either the killing of animals and eating of meat apart from sacrificial ritual at the one sanctuary should be completely forbidden (as proposed in the Holiness Code, in Lev. 17:3ff.); or the slaughtering of animals should be 'secularized' (cf. Weinfeld, *IEJ* 23, 1973, 230f.), so that it could take place quite independently of the cult-ritual sphere. It is the latter course which Deuteronomy adopted. **the unclean and the clean may eat of it:** since the killing of the animal was no longer a sacrificial act, the requirements relating to ritual cleanliness need no longer be observed. **as of the gazelle and as of the hart:** the gazelle and the hart, as species of game, were not acceptable for sacrifice; animals acceptable for sacrifice may now be treated in a similar way; cf. also 15:22.

16. you shall not eat the blood: the blood is the bearer of life, and so belongs to God, cf. Gen. 9:4; Lev. 17:10ff. The law given here, however, while emphasizing that blood is not open to human consumption, also partially divests it of its original taboo significance. It is no longer offered to God on the altar (cf. 1 Sam. 14:32ff.), but is poured out like water on the ground. The verse is formulated in plural form of address in a singular context. Either this is a fixed form of prescription (though unlikely in view of 15:23), or, more probably, the original deuteronomic law made no reference to the blood. This was added later by the deuteronomist on the basis of the special reference to the blood in vv. 23, 27; cf. also 15:23.

17. You may not: the use of the verb *yākōl* in this prohibition, rather than the simple imperfect of the verb, gives particular emphasis. For this verb with a sense of duty and even legal liability, cf. Gen. 43:32; Num. 9:6. **your grain ... your wine ... your oil:** see comment on 7:13.

18. The tithe is included in vv. 6f. among those things which the Israelite shall eat at the sanctuary. In vv. 17f. there is specific reference to it as eaten by the offerer. This is a further aspect of the process of secularization in Deuteronomy to which Weinfeld has pointed (see comment on v. 15). The tithe is not given to Yahweh or to the priesthood, but is eaten by the offerer himself together with his household and the Levite. **you shall rejoice:** Merendino, *op. cit.*, 34, points to the connection of rejoicing with the feast of Tabernacles (16:14; Neh. 8:17), and suggests that this may have been the occasion and context of the tithe; see also on 14:23. **all that you undertake:** see comment on v. 7.

19. Take heed: the basic deuteronomic centralization text of this chapter closes with the words with which it began in v. 13. The whole forms a chiasm in which a correspondence also exists between v. 14*a* and v. 18*a* (reference to the place which Yahweh will choose), v. 14*aβb* and v.17 (the offering at the central sanctuary), v. 15*a* and v. 17*a* (reference to your towns), with v. 15*b* forming the centre point (v. 16 being omitted as a later addition).

20. When the Lord your God enlarges your territory: this has been widely thought to be an allusion to the expansion of the kingdom of Judah under Josiah into the territory of the former northern kingdom (2 Kg.2 3:15ff.). However, on the historical background in general and the use of 2 Kg. 22f. in particular in the reconstruction of this background, see above Introduction, pp. 81ff. The phrase occurs again in 19:8 where it is set against the background of the promise to the patriarchs.

21. It is not possible to accommodate this verse to the law of vv. 13–19 by saying (as Bertholet) that those who live close to the sanctuary are not necessarily excluded from the provision here, nor by holding (cf. Buis) that there was no need to legislate for those living near to the sanctuary since ritual slaughter was retained. The verse, and the whole of the section vv. 20–28 to which it belongs, is a clear restriction on what has been already provided for: profane slaughter is now permitted only when the central sanctuary is too far away for ritual slaughter to be a practical possibility. This limited permission is not implied, but is in fact probably excluded, by the basic deuteronomic law (cf. v. 15 'within any of your towns'). **to put his name there:** as in v. 5, rather than v. 11 'to make his name dwell there'.

22. See comment on v. 15.

23. be sure: the verb appears only here in this particular sense. Otherwise, it is frequent in the combination 'be strong (sure) and of good courage' (e.g. 31:6). **the blood is the life:** see comment on v. 16.

25. that all may go well: the Hebrew 'that it may go well', as in 5:16, 29; 6:18; see also 4:40.

26. the holy things: not necessarily just sacrificial animals (cf. Lev. 22), but probably including all the different gifts brought to the sanctuary, such as tithes and firstlings; see Nebeling, *Schichten*, 29.

27. offer your burnt offerings: the use of the verb 'āśāh in this context is found with the deuteronomist (Jg. 13:16; 1 Kg. 8:64, etc.), Ezekiel (43:27, etc.) and the priestly writing (Lev. 9:7 etc.). This verse clearly illustrates the difference between **burnt offerings** and **sacrifices;** see comment on v. 6.

28. This verse is evidently the conclusion of the section beginning in v. 20. It follows a pattern found elsewhere (see v. 25; 13:17f.), consisting of (a) command or prohibition; (b) statement of the consequence; and (c) condition. Seitz, *op. cit.*, 106ff., argues that it should be taken rather as the opening of the following section, and, with 13:17f., as forming a framework for that section. However, there is no clear example of such a form with an introductory rather than a concluding function (4:1; 6:2f.; 8:1 do not offer close parallels). **Be careful to heed:** Sam and LXX add another verb, 'and do', which is accepted by the *NEB* and several commentators. However, that reading probably represents an addition on the part of *Sam* and LXX on the basis of the common combination in Deuteronomy of the verb ῾*śh* ('do') with *śmr* ('keep') or *śm῾* ('heed') or both; see the table in Lohfink, *Hauptgebot,* 300ff.

(ii) *The problem of apostasy* **12:29–13:18**

In subject 12:29–31 belong with and serve as a general introduction to ch. 13, for the common concern here is with the problem of apostasy. This subject appears again later in the law corpus, in 17:2–7, and it is frequently conjectured (cf. e.g. Smith, Wright, Buis) that 17:2–7 properly belongs in the context of ch. 13. However, the subject of the latter is consistently the *enticement* to apostasy, which is not the case in ch. 17.

The formulation of ch. 13 is not that of law; it is a preaching style, similar to the conditional form of casuistic law, but using the direct form of address characteristic of parenesis (see above, Introduction, pp. 51, 73. The whole section is of deuteronomic authorship, with deuteronomistic editing in vv. 3*b*–4 (see comment), and some further additions (comment on verses 2, 5, 6, 7, 13, 16, 17, 18) the sources of which cannot always be identified.

29. The historical introduction in this verse to the command which follows shows close connection in form and content with the deuteronomic parenesis in 7:1; 9:1. The form including this and the following commandment is one which is frequent in the parenesis of Deuteronomy. It consists of a protasis which refers to

Israel's settlement of the land, followed by a command which is to be observed in the new situation; cf. 11:29, 31f.; 12:20; 17:14f.; 18:9; 19:1f.; 26:1f.; 27:2, and the study by Lohfink, *Hauptgebot*, 113ff.

30. be ensnared: the Hebrew here is *tinnāqēš* (from the verb *nqš*, 'strike'), which may be a mistake for *tiwwāqēš* (from the verb *yqš*, 'lay a snare'; used in 7:25). **inquire:** the verb is the same as that translated 'seek' in v. 5 (see comment). **How did these nations serve their gods:** although the ostensible background here is that of Israel about to settle the land and so anxious about the proper form of worship customary in the land (cf. 1 Sam. 26:19; 2 Kg. 17:25ff.), the actual background is the considerably later one of the worship of Assyrian gods in the territory of the former northern kingdom after 721 BC or in Judah particularly during the reign of Manasseh.

31. The first part of the verse has already appeared in v. 4 (see comment). Here its meaning is that the rites by which the gods were worshipped were not to be used in the worship of Yahweh. **abominable thing:** see comment on 7:25. There is a general allusion here to the *tôʿēbāh* ('abomination') laws which appear later in Deuteronomy, though this is not a precise example of the form; see comment on 17:1. **they even burn their sons and their daughters in the fire to their gods:** this is a reference to the rite of offering children in sacrifice to gods, known in Palestine from the beginning of the second millennium and practised in Judah in the time of Ahaz and Manasseh (2 Kg. 16:3; 21:6). Reportedly abolished by Josiah (2 Kg. 23:10), the rite reappeared before the exile (cf. Jer. 7:31; 19:5; 32:35). In Judah it was practised especially in the valley of Ben-hinnom outside Jerusalem. Lev. 18:21 refers to it in the midst of a list of sexual crimes, which may indicate a connection of the rite with cultic prostitution; if so, the children so sacrificed may at times have been the offspring of cult prostitutes (Phillips). However, references such as 2 Kg. 3:27; 16:3, would suggest that the practice was not confined to that context; see also de Vaux, *Studies*, 87 n. 137; and comment on 18:10.

32. It is very doubtful whether this verse is the close of what precedes or the opening of what follows. The relatively late Hebrew chapter divisions make it the first verse of ch. 13; however, the Massoretes clearly took it as a concluding formula (see the *peṭuḥa* at the end of the verse). In vocabulary and in the

plural-singular change of address within the verse there is close
connection with the beginning of ch. 12 (cf. v. 1), which indicates
that it derives from the late hand responsible for vv. 1–7. **you
shall not add to it or take from it:** on this so-called 'canonical
formula', see comment on 4:2.

13:1. dreamer of dreams: dreams were considered a normal
and acceptable source of prophetic enlightenment (cf. Num. 12:6),
but in time came to be considered a source of self-deception and
false guidance (cf. Jer. 23:25–32). **a sign or a wonder:** these two
terms are often used synonymously (see comment on 4:34). Here
they clearly have different senses; the **sign** here is a sign of what
the future holds (cf. also Isa. 7:11), while the **wonder** is a miracle
(cf. also Exod. 4:21) proving the power of the prophet or dreamer.
The words are part of a late addition to the case described (see
comment on next verse).

2. and if he says: the Hebrew word ('saying') is awkwardly
distant from v. 1a ('. . . dreamer of dreams') to which it is immediately relevant. It is probable that v. 1b and v. 2a to this point are a
later addition making the case an extreme one of a prophet
apparently validated by his words and actions. **which you have
not known:** see comment on 11:28. The clause does not occur
immediately after 'go after other gods' in the similar contexts of
6:14; 17:3, and may here be an addition from the hand of the
late author apparent also in 11:28. The addition emphasizes the
contrast between Yahweh and the gods of the peoples.

3. Vv. 3b, 4 are in plural form of address in a singular context.
They are undoubtedly an addition and probably derive from the
deuteronomist. The immediate cause of the addition was the
earlier addition of vv. 1b, 2a, for the latter apparently indicated
that the prophet in question was a true prophet of Yahweh (this
would be the case following the criteria for distinguishing false
from true prophets in 18:22). The only possible explanation for a
true prophet enticing Israel to serve other gods is that Yahweh
is **testing you.** For this specific idea, cf. 1 Kg. 22:22, and for
the general theme of God's testing Israel, cf. 8:2, 16; Jg. 3:4.
whether you love: the Hebrew is more emphatic—'whether you
do love' (Driver), see also comment on 6:5. **with all your heart
and with all your soul:** see comment on 4:29.

4. The *RSV* translation does not bring out the emphasis present
in the Hebrew of this verse, where all the objects precede their
respective verbs in the emphatic position. **You shall walk after**

the Lord your God: this is the only place in the law corpus where the phrase 'walk after' is used with Yahweh as object; otherwise it is 'other gods'. It is the contrast between Yahweh and other gods which demanded the use of the phrase of Yahweh here, as also in 1 Kg. 18:21. However, 2 Kg. 23:3 (and also Hos. 11:10) shows that it could also be used of Yahweh apart from this contrast. It is a phrase familiar also from treaty contexts where it is used of the obedience of the vassal to his overlord; cf. Moran, *CBQ* 25, 1963, 82f. n. 35, and Weinfeld, *Deuteronomy*, 83f., who points especially to the Esarhaddon treaty for the background of **walk after, fear, obey his voice, serve** and **cleave.**

5. In this verse there is a long addition **(because he has taught ... commanded you to walk)** composed first in the plural and then in the singular form of address, and probably deriving from the late deuteronomistic author of several earlier passages. It is mainly composed of stock phrases (cf. 5:6; 6:12; 7:8; 8:14) and **the way** is probably intended as a reference to the decalogue (see comment on 9:12). **he has taught rebellion against the Lord:** the same phrase occurs in Jer. 28:16; 29:32. **to make you leave:** the same verb as that translated 'draw away' in vv. 10, 13. It is on the latter context that its use here is based. **So you shall purge the evil from the midst of you:** this formula is found also in 17:7; 19:19; 21:21; 22:21, 24; 24:7, and, with 'from Israel' instead of 'from the midst of you', in 17:12; 22:22. In all cases (except 19:19) it follows on the death penalty and describes the consequences of its being carried out. It is not found outside Deuteronomy, but its existence is apparently presupposed in Jg. 20:13. Its origin and background of use are very obscure. That all the laws to which it is attached originally belonged together as a series is by no means certain. Apart from the problem of how such a series then came to be split up, there is no clear unity either of form or content in these laws apart from the formula; and the probability must be admitted that while a series of laws including this formula may once have existed, the particular examples now to be found in Deuteronomy may in some cases be secondary imitations of the form rather than original parts of the series. For the question of background, therefore, the formula should be treated apart from the particular laws to which it is attached. It is clearly not a legal formula; with its direct form of address it points to a situation of instruction or teaching of the law. In itself, however, the formula does not point to a cultic background and makes no reference to Yahweh. Seitz, *op. cit.*, 131f., points to a possible background in the ancient Israelite amphictyony, while Merendino, *op. cit.*, 342ff., argues that the form with 'from the midst of you' is the original, that it referred to an individual family, tribe or small group of tribes, and that it was used originally outside the context of the worship of Yahweh in regulations dealing with relations between men. 24:7 belongs to the oldest stage of the tradition while the use of the formula in the present context is traditio-historically late and secondary. In the present context it would then be an example of deuteronomic composition applying an existing formula to a new context, that of apostasy. See further the comment on the relevant passages.

6. your brother: *Sam* and LXX now add 'the son of your father or', an addition which is widely accepted (cf. also *NEB*). However, it is unlikely that these words were accidentally omitted from the Hebrew text; more probable is the view (cf. Seitz, *op. cit.*, 144f. n. 160) that the text of this command originally referred only to **your brother,** which was understood, in the way common in Deuteronomy (cf. e.g. 15:2f.), as 'your fellow-Israelite'. Later, the word **secretly** being understood to imply 'within the family', **your brother** was taken literally, and so defined as **the son of your mother** (cf. Gen. 27:29; Ps. 50:20); this in turn encouraged the addition of **or your son ... your friend who is as your own soul** in order to provide a more complete enumeration. The singular 'him' in v. 8 also suggests a singular object here originally.

7. This verse, giving a closer definition of 'other gods', varies between singular and plural address form. It may well be a later addition, based on clauses in 20:15; 28:64; at least the final clause of the verse has little actual relevance to the case in hand (Israel's form of worship within her own land), and the *NEB* translation which attempts to meet this ('at one end of the land or the other') finds only doubtful support in Jer. 12:12; the reference is, as the *RSV*, to **the earth** rather than to the land.

9. but you shall kill him: as Weinfeld, *Deuteronomy*, 94f., remarks, this reads like lynch law. The difficulty which the words cause is also revealed by the fact that Merendino, *op. cit.*, 67, feels that the rest of the verse must then be an addition with v. 10 as the original immediate continuation. In fact, however, a slight change in the consonants of the Hebrew gives a better text: *haggēd taggîdennú* 'you shall surely report him' (presupposed by the LXX). For this legal sense of the verb *ngd* in the Hiphil, cf. e.g. Jos, 2:14,

20. What follows in the verse, as 17:7 clearly shows, demands an earlier reference to a public trial (which the suggested original text would allude to), and not a reference to killing. **your hand shall be first against him:** this is not because the family of the one enticing to apostasy must demonstrate that it is not involved (so Buis-Leclercq)—as noted above on v. 6 the case originally referred only to the fellow-Israelite and not specifically to a member of the family—but because in law it is the witnesses who must be first in the stoning of one condemned to death (cf. 17:7).

10. You shall stone him: also 17:5. For an example of the application of this method of execution, cf. 1 Kg. 21:13. By this method all direct contact with the guilty was avoided, and at the same time every member of the community contributed to the elimination of the evil from its midst.

11. A number of contacts exists between the case described in vv. 6–11 and those cases which end with the formula 'you shall purge the evil from the midst of you'. Death by stoning is mentioned in Deuteronomy only here and in 17:5; 22:21, 24, in which contexts the formula also occurs. The expression 'your eye shall not pity' (v. 8) is connected with the formula in 19:13, 19–21. The phraseology of v. 11 is found again in 17:12f.; 19:20f.; 21:21, also in connection with the formula. This has suggested to L'Hour, *Bib* 44, 1963, 10 n.3, that the old formula 'you shall purge the evil from the midst of you' should be restored in the present passage. However, in the light of the comment above on v. 5, one should perhaps rather understand that the whole case as described in vv. 6–11 is a deuteronomic composition, in which use has been made of various expressions which also occur in older examples of laws which use this formula. There is no indication of an older, pre-deuteronomic law here to which the formula would have originally belonged.

12. The third and final case of the chapter presents a certain awkwardness in structure. Since the case is one of incitement to apostasy the apodosis is to be found in v. 15. However, the form of the protasis in v. 12 puts the apodosis in v. 14, so making the basis and framework of the whole case the secondary element of hearing and enquiring. This is a structural awkwardness resulting from the adaptation of a casuistic form to a parenetic expression in direct address. **in one of your cities:** a certain vagueness in the expression leaves it uncertain if the city is the place where the report is heard or where the enticement to apostasy took place;

for the latter interpretation, cf. Smith, and, in support, compare the construction in 31:29.

13. base fellows: *AV* 'children of Belial', *NEB* 'miscreants'. The origin of the word $b^e liyya^c al$ is obscure. It is often taken to mean 'worthlessness' (cf. *BDB*, 116, deriving it from $b^e l\hat{i}$, 'not', and $ya^c al$, 'worth'). However, Dahood, *Psalms* I, 105, prefers the suggestion that it derives from the root bl^c, 'swallow', and means 'the swallower'. This suits well the occurrence of the word in Ps.18:4 (*RSV* 'perdition') in the context of the overwhelming power of death and Sheol which threaten to 'swallow up' the psalmist. By New Testament times the word had become a proper name, synonymous with Satan (cf. 2 Cor. 6:15). **among you:** the Hebrew is rather 'from your midst', emphasizing that the enticement to apostasy comes from within. **the city:** the Hebrew is 'their city', so again indicating that the enticement is from within Israel. **which you have not known:** in plural address. The words are perhaps an addition based on v. 6.

14. you shall inquire: the verb is frequently found in Deuteronomy in the sense of 'visit a sanctuary' (e.g. 12:5), but with the legal sense only here and 17:4; 19:18, i.e. with laws using the formula 'you shall purge the evil from the midst of you'. This also applies to the word **diligently** when used with the verb **inquire or ask,** cf. 17:4; 19:18. **make search:** the verb does not otherwise occur in Deuteronomy. Elsewhere it denotes both the legal process and enquiry of God, cf. Prov. 18:7; 25:2; Job 13:9; 28:27; Ps. 44:21; Jer. 17:10. **abominable thing:** see comment on 7:25; 12:31.

15. The laws of the holy war are applied to a city in which this crime has been found. **destroying it utterly:** see comment on 2:34; 7:26.

16. V. 15 brings the case to a fitting conclusion. V. 16 is a late supplement, using ideas and phraseology which are late and, in part, not easily compatible with what has already been said. Although the burning of a city which has been put under ban is known also from Jos. 6:24; 8:28, etc., the reference to it here is caused by the desire to present the destruction as an expiatory sacrifice for sin. It is described as **a whole burnt offering** (for *kālîl* in this sense see especially 33:10; 1 Sam. 7:9; against Merendino, *op. cit.*, 69, there can be no doubt that here the word must be a sacrificial term, as shown by its combination with **to the Lord;** otherwise, e.g. Exod. 28:31, the word can have the sense simply of 'entirety'), offered in order to atone for a sin for which the whole community is regarded as responsible. Not only is this application of holy war terminology and ideas unique (there is another possible but by no means clear or certain example in Jg. 20:40, where *RSV* translates 'the whole of the city'), but the notion of the purpose of sacrifice which it reveals is not otherwise found in Deuteronomy (see comment on 12:7). **a heap:** Hebrew *tēl*, a mound made up of the ruins of previous habitations of a site and itself either still occupied (cf. Jos. 11:13) or deserted (cf. Jos. 8:28).

17. Vv. 17 and 18 bring this collection of cases of enticement to apostasy to a close, using a form which has already appeared as a concluding form in 12:28 (see comment there), and which should therefore be ascribed to the post-deuteronomic editor responsible for 12:20-28. V. 17 has clearly been extended by an even later hand; probably only the first motivation **(that the Lord may turn from the fierceness of his anger)** is original. Only it is really suitable to the context of the ban being carried out on a city because of Yahweh's anger (cf. Jos. 7:26). The remainder of the verse has the intention of affirming that Yahweh will build up the people again after the decimation caused by the destruction, cf. Seitz, *op. cit.*, 149. **devoted things:** the *ḥērem*, see comment on 2:34; 7:2. **turn from the fierceness of his anger:** although not otherwise in Deuteronomy, the phrase is found in Exod. 32:12; Num. 25:4; Jos. 7:26; Jer. 4:8; 30:24; 43:12. **multiply you:** a phrase found otherwise in late parts of Deuteronomy (cf. 1:10; 7:13), but only here in combination with **as he swore to your fathers.**

(iii) Israel is holy to God and must avoid what is unclean **14:1-21**
Here the deuteronomic law has been extensively supplemented with the list of clean and unclean animals in vv. 4-21 and also with v. 1. Because of the plural form of address the hand of a deuteronomistic editor may be suspected in these additions, and the general interest in the law which is presupposed suggests the work of the second deuteronomist. The deuteronomic law in vv. 2f. is continued in v. 21 (see comment).

There is a close connection between 14:4-21 and Lev. 11. The most likely explanation is that both texts ultimately go back to a common source from which each developed independently. However, while this accounts in principle for both similarities and

differences between the two, there are also direct influences of
one text on the other. With regard to 14:12–18, Moran, *CBQ* 28,
1966, 271ff., has shown that these verses have been secondarily
extended. Originally, they constituted a list of ten unclean birds,
corresponding to the list of ten clean animals in vv. 4*b*–5. This
list was later supplemented by a further ten birds taken directly
from Lev. 11:18ff., where a total of twenty is given. The original
list can be distinguished from the supplementary group in Dt. 14
by the use of the sign of the direct object, '*et*, which appears before
the names of only ten birds; it is used, however, before the names
of all twenty birds in Lev. 11. The Dt. 14 list was supplemented
from Lev. 11 at a time when the latter was accepted as a fixed
text. Along with the names of the ten birds, the supplementer of
Dt. 14 also took the phrase 'after their (its) kind(s)', which is
priestly terminology appropriate to Lev. 11.

The background to this list is catalogues of priestly teaching
concerning clean and unclean animals. So, although v. 3 is not
the original heading of the list it does not distort its intention. The
background to the priestly teaching is not altogether clear. The
basis for the classification of some animals as clean and some as
unclean may not indeed be uniform. In some cases the basis is a
cultic one: for example, birds such as the vulture (v. 12) are
unclean because of the fact that they feed on carcasses, themselves
impure. In other cases other reasons may explain the classification
(see comment on vv. 7, 8, 9f.). But whatever the ultimate origin
of the classification it is clear that the lists as such were drawn up
in the context of priestly teaching, and it is in order to illustrate a
religious law that the list was introduced here.

1. You are the sons of the Lord your God: see also 32:5, 19;
Isa. 1:2–4; 30:1, and for the people as a whole as the son of
Yahweh, cf. Exod. 4:22f.; Dt. 1:31; 8:5; Hos. 11:1; Ps. 103:13.

That the mourning rites mentioned here were normal practice
in pre-exilic Israel, as with her neighbours, is clear from Am. 8:10;
Isa. 15:2; 22:12; Jer. 16:6; 41:5; Ezek. 7:18. It was only very
late in Israel's history that the customs were prohibited (cf. also
Lev. 19:28; 21:5). Here the prohibition is a deuteronomistic
addition to the deuteronomic law, as shown also by its plural form
of address; see also Horst, *Gottes Recht*, 61. To explain the prohibition by reference to Israelite respect for the body as God's creation
(Thompson, Wright) does not really account either for the specific
form of introduction to the prohibition in v. 1*a*, or for its place

immediately following on the laws dealing with apostasy. It is, therefore, best to refer to 1 Kg. 18:28 and also to certain texts from Ugarit (collected by Craigie), as illustrating at the least the custom of self-laceration as part of the ritual by which the death of the fertility god Baal was mourned. Israel's status as the sons of Yahweh means that her participation in rites proper to the worship of any other god must be considered apostasy. It is probably on the basis of this understanding of the mourning rites referred to that the deuteronomist introduced the prohibition at this point.

2. The addition of v. 1 brought in also the word **for** in v. 2, so making the latter a second motivation to the prohibition of v. 1. Such duplication is not original, however, and this verse in fact continues the deuteronomic law, giving the basis for the prohibition in v. 3. On the terminology **holy, chosen, his own possession,** see comment on the deuteronomic parenesis in 7:6.

3. abominable thing: see comment on 7:25. By this verse the following list of clean and unclean animals is explicitly stated to be a religious classification: it is on the basis of their acceptability to the worship of Yahweh that the animals are distinguished. The reason for the decision in each particular case is by no means certain.

4. The present list is generally more positive than its counterpart in Lev. 11, where there is no corresponding list of clean animals; there only the type of clean animal is defined (Lev. 11:3), while the emphasis lies on the unclean.

5. the hart, the gazelle: these have already been mentioned together (12:15, 22; cf. also 15:22) as common kinds of game which may be eaten. **wild goat:** only referred to here. **ibex:** only here. The *NEB* translation 'white-rumped deer' is based on the LXX. **mountain sheep:** only here; the meaning is quite uncertain, and the versions give various translations.

6. Only very slight differences exist between this verse and Lev. 11:3. In both places the phrase **and has the hoof cloven in two** must be a secondary explanatory gloss on **parts the hoof.**

7. V. 7*b* brings together Lev. 11:4*b*–6, where these animals (in slightly different order from Dt. 14:7) are each referred to along with the reason for its being unclean. The similarities and differences between Deuteronomy and Leviticus on this point arose as the result of the independent formulation of a tradition which was already fixed in its essential elements, cf. Merendino, *op. cit.*, 85. **the hare and the rock badger:** it is argued by Albright,

Yahweh, 154f., that the reason for the prohibition of these animals is that they are both disease carriers; see also comment on next verse.

8. but does not chew the cud: the full form of the phrase is not present in the Hebrew, but should probably be restored with *Sam*, LXX and the parallel passage in Lev. 11:7. The versions and Lev. 11:7 before this phrase also have the additional 'and is cloven footed', which too may have been accidentally omitted here (in this case by homoioteleuton). Albright, *op. cit.*, 154, argues strongly that in the case of the pig too the reason for the prohibition is nothing to do with the fact that the pig was sacred in certain non-Israelite cultures and religions, but that it has a hygienic background: insufficiently cooked pork is a danger to health. It is very difficult to be certain on the matter. On the one hand, Albright's argument that it is irrational to propose a cultic background for the prohibition of the pig when large and small cattle, reckoned clean for Israelites, were even more generally sacred, has a certain force; but it takes no account of the significance of the *particular* cultic contexts in which the pig may have been used. So, for example, de Vaux, in *Bible*, 252ff. (cf. also Stendebach, *BZ* 18, 1974, 263ff.), concludes that the cultic use of the pig was not the general rule; it was a rare custom, restricted to certain magical and mystery rites (the secret and mysterious nature of the rites is suggested also by Isa. 65:4f.; 66:17). It may have been such a particular association, rather than general cultic usage, which led to the prohibition. Moreover, the strength of the prohibition in this verse, reinforced by **their flesh you shall not eat** (a phrase used in Lev. 7:18, 21, of the eating of the flesh of a sacrificed animal), and the absolute **their carcasses you shall not touch,** suggests something more than a simple health regulation.

The general classification on the basis of whether or not an animal divides the hoof and chews the cud gives no reason for characterizing the one category as clean and the other as unclean, and in fact clearly lies at the end of a process in which it gradually became clear that certain animals, for other reasons judged as clean or unclean, belonged to one or other of these categories. As far as the pig is concerned, in the light of the clear evidence adduced by de Vaux and Stendebach for its association with particular cultic contexts in Palestine, Babylon, Egypt, among the Hittites and in the Greek world, it must be concluded that this prohibition in the Israelite context is most probably to be fully explained by reference to the use of the pig in cultic practices considered incompatible with Yahwism. This fits not only the present context of the prohibition but also all other references within and outside the Old Testament to the use of the pig in cultic rituals.

9, 10. Fish featured in mythological and magical contexts in Egypt, where Seth was worshipped in the form of a fish, and in Assyrian religion, where the priest occasionally functioned dressed in a garment like a fish skin. Here again Albright, *op. cit.*, 155, proposes a health background for the distinction between fish with scales and fins and those without: the former are normally free swimming, while the latter are usually mud-burrowers and so the carriers of possibly lethal parasites.

11. No definition of **clean birds** is given, nor any particular examples. There must have been available to the deuteronomistic editor only a list of unclean birds, which he gives in vv. 12ff., while he composed v. 11 simply in order to provide a balance and to correspond with the earlier references to clean and unclean animals and fish. The verse has no parallel in Lev. 11.

12. The list of unclean birds has been secondarily extended from a basic list of ten birds to the present list of twenty, by material taken from Lev. 11 (see the introduction to this section). The birds mentioned in this verse belonged to the basic list. The major work on the identification of the birds has been done by Driver, *PEQ* 87, 1955, 5ff., who believes that his identifications show that the unclean birds are those which are flesh-eating; except in the case of the hoopoe and bat which are reckoned as unclean perhaps because their flesh is distasteful or because of their dirty habits. Flesh-eating birds are unclean because they eat either flesh with the blood or carrion, and in neither case has the blood, the bearer of life, been properly disposed off; see comment on 12:16. **eagle:** Driver, *op. cit.*, 8f., suggests rather the 'griffon-vulture' (cf. *NEB*), as the most easily and often seen of the great birds of prey (the vulture is certainly indicated by Mic. 1:16; Job 39:27–30); the word, however, is a comprehensive one and can also mean eagle. **vulture:** either the ossifrage (*AV*) or the black vulture (*NEB*). **osprey:** the ossifrage or the bearded vulture (Driver, *op. cit.*).

13. The Hebrew text has three terms in this verse: *rāʾāh*, *ʾayyāh* and *dayyāh*. The first is unknown, and should be taken as an

orthographic error for *dā'āh*, the hawk or kite (*NEB*), which
appears in this position in Lev. 11:14. The second is the buzzard
or falcon, and the third should be omitted as an original correction
to the erroneous Hebrew form of the first; it does not appear in
Lev. 11:14. The second term (along with the phrase **after their**
(Hebrew 'its') **kinds**) is a supplement, taken from Lev. 11, and
added to the original basic deuteronomistic list.

14. The verse is a supplement taken from Lev. 11:15.

15. The whole verse is a supplement taken from Lev. 11:16.
ostrich: the *NEB* (following Driver's proposal, *op. cit.*, 12f., that
the first two terms here refer to species of owl) translates 'desert
owl'. The Hebrew means 'daughter of greed' or 'daughter of the
wilderness', and is mentioned in the Old Testament as a symbol
of loneliness and as living among ruins or in the desert (Job 30:29;
Isa. 13:21; 34:13; 43:20; Jer. 50:39). **night hawk:** *NEB* 'short-
eared owl' is based on Driver, who suggests that the basic meaning
of the word is 'robber'. **sea gull:** only from its place in the list
may it be conjectured that in fact another owl is intended here; so
NEB 'long-eared owl'. **hawk:** the term *nēṣ* is a generic name and
includes the kestrel and the hawk.

16. The first two are derived from Lev. 11:17. **little owl:**
referred to in Ps. 102:6 as inhabiting ruins. Driver (and *NEB*)
'tawny owl'. **great owl:** where this word occurs in Lev. 11:17 the
RSV translates 'ibis'; this bird is out of place at this point and is
indeed practically unknown in Palestine. **water hen:** the translation is completely uncertain; the place in the list suggests perhaps
another species of owl (cf. *NEB*).

17. The second and third of the birds mentioned are derived
from Lev. 11:17f. **pelican:** this translation does not suit the
description of the bird as inhabiting the wastes (cf. Ps. 102:6;
Isa. 34:11; Zeph. 2:14). So Driver, *op. cit.*, 16, suggests another
species of owl. **carrion vulture:** identification is again uncertain.
Driver suggests the osprey (so *NEB*), since some of its habits
suggest an affinity with owls which have just been mentioned,
while as a fish eating bird it has connections also with the birds
that follow. **cormorant:** this bird is named in Lev. 11:17
between the little owl and the great owl, which suggests that it
may be yet another species of owl; so *NEB* 'fisher owl'.

18. heron: identification is quite uncertain. *NEB*, again
following Driver, translates 'cormorant'.

19. The parallel in Lev. 11:20 is slightly differently formulated and more limited. The general prohibition here is probably a redactional addition to the preceding list of birds, which was later in Leviticus given more specific application.

20. If the word '*ōp* refers to the winged insects of v. 19, rather than to birds generally (in which case it would simply repeat v. 11) then it is paralleled in Lev. 11:21f., where, however, it is much more explicit and detailed.

21. anything that dies of itself: the blood of such an animal has not been poured out, and so its flesh cannot be consumed; see comment on 12:16, and also Lev. 17:10ff. In Lev. 22:8; Ezek. 44:31 the prohibition is applied only to priests, but in Lev. 11:40; 17:50 to everyone. The deuteronomic law of v. 3 is continued in what follows. The **foreigner,** as distinct from the **alien** (on whom see comment on 1:16), was not settled in Israel; see also comment on 15:3. In Lev. 17:15, reflecting a later situation when the *gēr* was more integrated into Israel, this prohibition applies also to the alien. **you shall not boil a kid in its mother's milk:** the origin and background of this prohibition have defied complete clarification. Probably even in the time of Deuteronomy the original reason for it was no longer known, and the prohibition was preserved only out of respect for tradition. In its present context it is understood as a dietary regulation; however, in Exod. 23:19; 34:26 it stands in a sacrificial context, and its original significance is probably to be sought in that sphere. Daube, *JTS* 37, 1936, 289f., believes that behind it is a distinction between milk sacrifice, as practised by nomads, and (later) sacrifice of living animals, the prohibition being directed against maintaining the two forms of sacrifice together. Others (see especially Kosmala, *ASTI* 1, 1962, 50ff.; followed by Fisher, *Ras Shamra Parallels* I, 30ff.) point to a Ugaritic text (Gordon, *Ugaritic Textbook*, Text 52, line 14) which in a fertility context contains the line: 'cook the kid in milk, the lamb in butter'; possibly reference is made here to a fertility rite in which the milk was then sprinkled on the fields (cf. also Smith). It must be noted, however, that the text requires restoration and its interpretation is uncertain; moreover, neither proposal explains why the prohibition specifies its mother's milk.

(B) PERIODIC OBLIGATIONS AND INSTITUTIONS: **14:22–16:17**

The second section of the deuteronomic law has a general concern with periodic obligations and institutions. Tithes, remission of

debts, release of slaves, firstlings, pilgrimage festivals, are all recurrent events in the life of the people of Yahweh, and because of this
characteristic they are here grouped together. It is, of course,
probably true that the deuteronomic legislator whom we recognize
as ultimately responsible for this collection (especially through the
regular appearance of the centralization formula in 14:23; 15:20;
16:6, 11, 15, as well as through such parenetic formulae as 14:29*b*;
15:10*b*, 18*b*; 16:15*b*, 17*b*, and the references to the poor and needy
among the family of the Israelite in 14:26f., 29; 16:11, 14) is not
alone responsible for the present connection of all the laws which
are now grouped here. For example, 14:22-29 and 15:1-18 are
related through being social laws as well as laws relating to
periodic institutions; similarly 16:1-17 is concerned with the
three pilgrimage feasts which are grouped together already in the
older festival calendars. So the collection contains smaller collections of laws which existed as such before the deuteronomic edition
(for a detailed reconstruction of the processes which led to the
bringing together of these collections, see Merendino, *op. cit.*,
104f., 121ff., 138ff.). As a whole, however, the section holds
together as a single catechetic text gathering together regulations
relating to regularly recurrent obligations laid on the Israelite.

(i) The law of tithing 14:22-29

The deuteronomic law of tithing here brings an old law into a new
context and gives it a new meaning. Tithes in general are referred
to in Gen. 28:22 and Am. 4:4 for the pre-deuteronomic period,
and with particular royal associations in Gen. 14:20 and 1 Sam.
8:15, 17. It has been suggested that tithes in fact originated as a
royal taxation designed for the upkeep of royal sanctuaries, and
these only subsequently were paid to the sanctuaries generally.
However, sanctuaries would always have required some form of
support, and even if the system of tithing was the form this took in
association with royal sanctuaries, the offering of a part of the
produce—perhaps in the form of first-fruits with which the tithes
are closely connected in Dt. 26—is practically a universal custom.

Within Deuteronomy there is considerable obscurity on the
precise relationship between tithes and first-fruits. While 26:1-15
would permit a general identification of the two, this is not allowed
by a comparison of 14:22-29 with 18:4, for in the latter passage
the first-fruits are the priest's due while in the former the tithe is
eaten by the offerer with his household. Three points should,

however, be remembered: firstly, particularly if 'tithe' means 'tenth' (though see comment on v. 22), it is unlikely that it would be entirely eaten by the offerer and his household; the emphasis of 14:22–29 on the eating of the tithe may in large part be ascribed to the particular deuteronomic view of the significance and purpose of offerings (see comment on v. 23). Secondly, both tithes and first-fruits must ultimately have the same general significance: the offering of a portion of the produce at the sanctuary and its consequent removal from common use. Thirdly, differences in emphasis and formulation may well be in large part due to the fact that the customary regulations of different sanctuaries are here brought together by the deuteronomic legislator.

In 14:22–29 the deuteronomic editor has taken up an old law of tithing (v. 22) and given it a particular expression in the light of the new conditions prevailing as a result of the centralization of worship to one sanctuary (v. 23–27). To this he has then appended in vv. 28f. his own law regarding the humanitarian use of the tithe every third year for the relief of the poor and destitute.

22. The custom of tithing is certainly older than Deuteronomy; cf. Gen. 28:22; Lev. 27:30f.; Am. 4:4. There is nothing in this verse specifically deuteronomic and it may, therefore, represent the old law. **tithe:** that the verb comes from the same root as the numeral ten, to give the meaning 'take the tenth of', is not entirely certain. Gordon, *Ugaritic Textbook*, 462, notes a second root *'šr* with the sense 'to pour out a libation', 'give to drink', which suggests the possibility of a root with the more general sense of 'offer' as the origin of the word translated 'tithe'; cf. also Cazelles, *VT* I, 1951, 131ff. On the custom see also the introduction to this section.

23. The deuteronomic law in this verse has been supplemented by the words **the tithe of your grain, and of your wine, and of your oil, and the firstlings of your herd and flock.** The law in v. 22 refers only to seed, and the list provided here, which does not harmonize with this, is probably taken from 12:17. The offering of firstlings was indeed probably connected with tithing, but it is not dealt with until 15:19ff. V. 23*b* (**that you may learn . . .**) connects the offering of the tithe at the central sanctuary with the reading of the law. This in turn strengthens the possibility that the tithe was to be brought at the feast of Tabernacles (cf. 31:12f., and Merendino, *op. cit.*, 98, 104); see comment on 12:18. **you shall eat the tithe:** that the tithe was to be eaten by the one who brought it was scarcely the case originally, since its purpose seems to have been to provide for the upkeep of the sanctuary and its personnel. Moreover, particularly if 'tithe' means 'tenth' it is most unlikely that even in the present context it is intended that the whole of it should be consumed by the worshipper and his household. The deuteronomic emphasis and formulation of the law here is in line with his humanitarian view of the purpose of sacrifice which is primarily that it should provide food, especially for the poor. See comment on 12:7.

24. The verse is awkwardly overloaded, and the long phrase **because the place ... to set his name there** may well be an addition taken from 12:21.

26. That the money must be reconverted into food and drink clearly indicates that for the deuteronomic legislator the primary purpose of the tithe is not the upkeep of the sanctuary. The priest may indeed have a share in the meal (cf. 18:3), but its essential object is that the offerer himself and his household should eat before Yahweh.

27. Levite: see on 18:1.

28. all the tithe of your produce: clearly the intention is not to impose an extra tithe in the third year, but rather to put the annual tithe in that year to a different use. That this was an additional tithe, as supposed in post-exilic times (cf. Tob. 1:7; LXX on Dt. 26:12; Josephus, *Antiquities* iv. 8.22), is an erroneous understanding which arose as part of an attempt to harmonize the law on the tithes in Deuteronomy with the priestly legislation in Num. 18 where the purpose of the tithe is the support of the priests. The law of vv. 28f. is found in no older source and should be seen as a deuteronomic innovation. It is unlikely that it arose out of the new situation created by the abolition of the local sanctuaries (so supposedly depriving the poor of their former annual share in the tithe), for there is no evidence that before Deuteronomy the tithe was devoted to the welfare of the needy. The deuteronomic law here conforms with the humanitarian concern so evident elsewhere in Deuteronomy, e.g. 12:18f.; 16:11.

29. sojourner: see comment on 1:16. On the general concern of ancient Near Eastern law and also wisdom with the deprived elements of society, cf. Fensham, *JNES* 21, 1962, 129ff.

(ii) *The law of release* 15:1–11
The law of release applied originally to the agricultural context:

the land lay fallow for one year in every seven. The custom is known outside Israel; its ultimate origin is probably to be sought in a time of common ownership of land, when individuals were permitted to work it for their own benefit for a limited period only. The application of the law to debts rather than to agriculture is found only in Deuteronomy, while there is no reference in Deuteronomy to leaving the land fallow. A connection between the two applications may exist in the sense that the year in which the land lay fallow would also necessarily be the time when the poor, dependent on the land for their income, would not be in a position to repay a debt. However, that should not lead to the conclusion that the law of Deuteronomy prescribes only a *suspension* of the debt in the seventh year (so Craigie, following several earlier commentators). The following verses, and particularly the conjunction of the law with the law of release from slavery in 15:12ff., suggest that 'release' means something more than simply delay in repayment. Deuteronomy demands rather the cancellation in the seventh year of debts previously incurred.

The new application has brought with it some other changes in the original law besides its new reference to debts. The original law referred to the seventh year of a seven-year cycle; in the present context the reference is to the end of the seventh year (cf. *NEB* translation of v. 1). The original law scarcely referred to a simultaneous fallowing of the land throughout Israel; rather, there would have been some system of rotation. The present law, however, refers to a fixed period simultaneously valid throughout Israel (cf. v. 9).

The old law of release (v. 1) was already before Deuteronomy interpreted with reference to remission of debts (see comment on v. 2). This aspect of it the deuteronomic legislator has expanded in vv. 3, 7–11. In vv. 4–6 there is a later addition (perhaps from the hand of the second deuteronomist here emphasizing the connection between obedience to the law and prosperity) which, even if it can be harmonized with the law by understanding that it presents an ideal while the law deals with actual conditions (cf. Driver, Wright), is still a secondary interruption of the link between vv. 3 and 7.

1. you shall grant a release: the root of the word translated 'release' means 'to let fall', and is figuratively applied to the land in Exod. 23:11 with the sense of 'leave uncultivated' (Driver). The year of release was originally the seventh year in which the land lay fallow (Exod. 23:10f.). Thereby Israelites were reminded that ownership of the land was theirs only through the gift of Yahweh.

2. While v. 1 uses the second person singular form of address, the formulation of v. 2 is in third person singular. The verse is a secondary interpretation of the original release law of v. 1, applying it to debts (cf. Horst, *Gottes Recht*, 79f.). The Hebrew of the verse is difficult: **every creditor** is apparently the translation of the anomalous phrase *kol baʿal maśśēh yāḏô*, 'every holder of a pledge of his hand'. The best solution (cf. also *BHS*) is to assume the accidental omission of the words *maśśeh ʾeṭ* after *baʿal*, which would give the translation 'every holder of a pledge (shall release) the pledge of his hand'. In this case the following relative clause would have to be taken as the subject of the next clause (so ignoring the *MT* punctuation): 'he who lends to his neighbour shall not exact it of his neighbour'; see the discussion in Merendino, *op. cit.*, 108f. **his brother:** so following *Sam.* The *MT* reads 'and his brother'. The words are a gloss on **his neighbour,** and were added by the deuteronomic editor who shows a marked preference for the word 'brother'. This indicates that the verse, and so also the application of the release law to debts, is pre-deuteronomic; cf. Seitz, *op. cit.*, 167f.

3. foreigner: it is clear from 14:21 that the foreigner is distinct from the alien or sojourner. The foreigner is one who passes through Israel, perhaps on business; he is not integrated into the community, nor is he recommended to the charity of Israelites. **your brother:** the use of this word, rather than 'neighbour' as in v. 2, and the contrast drawn with the foreigner, indicate deuteronomic authorship here; see also comment on 1:16.

4. V. 3 finds its continuation in v. 7. The intervening verses are clearly a late addition making explicit here what is elsewhere promised in Deuteronomy, viz. that the blessing of Yahweh will follow on obedience to the law and this blessing brings with it prosperity to every Israelite. However, the verses contradict the context which presupposes the existence of the poor in Israel. The thought of this addition harmonizes with 7:12f., and consequently it may be from the hand of the late deuteronomistic editor; cf. also the use of the word **inheritance** here and in 4:21.

5. which I command you this day: cf. 4:2, 8, 40.

7. This verse continues from v. 3 the deuteronomic expansion of the law of release, using typical deuteronomic words and phrases: **in any of your towns, which the Lord your God gives you, brother.** On the phrase **harden your heart** see comment on 2:30.

8. As Seitz, *op. cit.*, 169f., has shown, vv. 8–11 have a chiastic structure showing a consciously formed unit here. V. 8*a* corresponds to v. 11*bβ*, v. 9*aα* to v. 10*b*, v. 9*aβ* to v. 10*aβ*, and v. 9*aγ* to v. 10*aα*. **lend:** the verb used in this section means to take or give in pledge; here the Hiphil form—so *NEB* 'lend on pledge'.

9. Take heed: so also the deuteronomic law of centralization in 12:13 is introduced. **base:** see comment on 13:13. **your eye be hostile:** in 28:54, 56 this phrase is translated by the *RSV* 'will grudge'; see also the next verse. V. 9*b* appears again in 24:15*b*, and its counterpart: 'and it shall be righteousness to you', appears in 24:13.

10. in all that you undertake: see comment on 12:7.

11. to the needy and to the poor, in the land: in the Hebrew the pronoun 'your' appears with all three nouns, so emphasizing that it is to the community of Israelites living in their own land that the law applies.

(iii) *The release of slaves* 15:12–18

The slave law in this section is a modified form of Exod. 21:2–6. Four major modifications concern the inclusion in the law of the Hebrew woman on an equal footing with the man, the understanding of the Hebrew as a fellow Israelite, the provision that released slaves are to be given the means of establishing their independence in society, and also the reckoning of the period for which the slave should serve.

In order to formulate his law the deuteronomic legislator has made free use of the Exodus law (cf. Horst, *Gottes Recht*, 99; and for the structure of the law see comment on v. 18), so producing a law appropriate to his time and place. It is suggested by Weingreen, *From Bible*, 132ff., that the deuteronomic formulation arose from the attempt of the legislator to harmonize Exod. 21:2ff. with the slave law of Lev. 25:39ff. which prohibits the enslavement of a fellow Israelite and permits only that he should serve 'as a hired servant and as a sojourner'. However, this view simply assumes that the law of Leviticus is older than that of Deuteronomy—or at least that aspect of it prohibiting the enslavement of a fellow Israelite—whereas in fact the relationship is probably the other way around. The law of Deuteronomy speaks of a Hebrew

(= Israelite) slave, and v. 18 makes it quite clear that his status is not that of a hired servant. The differences between the deuteronomic law and its Exodus counterpart may be adequately explained by reference (a) to the fact that by this time 'Hebrew' had come to be understood as 'Israelite' (see comment on v. 12); (b) to the social change which set the woman on an equal footing with the man (see comment on v. 12); and (c) to the general humanitarian concerns of the deuteronomic legislator for the poor and deprived elements of society, cf. 12:18f.; 14:27, 29, etc.

One other major modification deserves special notice. The Exodus law laid down a period of six years' service for each slave who was then freed in the seventh. There are three considerations, however, which indicate that the case is not the same in Dt. 15:12–18. Firstly, the slave law is associated in this chapter with the law of release, which, as noted above, in its deuteronomic formulation was understood to function on the basis of a fixed and generally valid seven-year cycle. Secondly, the most common reason for a person's being reduced to slavery was debt (cf. 2 Kg. 4:1; Am. 2:6; 8:6; Isa. 50:1; Neh. 5:5; Prov. 22:7), and it is this which is the subject of the law of release at the beginning of the chapter. Clearly the deuteronomic legislator sees the slave law not as independent of what precedes but as a particular, though common, example of its application. Thirdly, Jer. 34:8ff. recounts how in the reign of Zedekiah a general simultaneous release of slaves took place, and this was understood to be in fulfilment of the 'covenant with your fathers'. Unless this action is to be seen as a fulfilment of the slave law, it is a particular event which has no precedent or basis in law (see the study by Sarna, in *AOAT* 22, 1973, 143ff.). These considerations point to the conclusion that for the deuteronomic legislator the period for which a slave should serve was regulated according to the fixed seven year cycle, and consequently six years was the maximum for which a slave might serve. With the abolition of debts in the seventh year there came also the abolition of slavery, this being a condition arising from debt. This would always have been the case with a Hebrew slave; slaves of foreign origin, for example prisoners of war, are not considered by the deuteronomic legislator.

12. Hebrew: the term has a history. Its use here is required by its appearance in the slave law of Exod. 21:2ff., the source of the present law. However, for the deuteronomic legislator the important term is not this but rather **your brother.** The Hebrew is the

fellow Israelite. This identification is not made in Exod. 21:2ff.,
and indeed is not presupposed in other uses of the term Hebrew
in the Old Testament. It may be used to designate Israelites, but
its connotation is not a clearly ethnic one. Moreover, assuming
that the identification of Hebrew and ḥabiru is correct, the term
also appears outside the Old Testament in widely different times
and places. The term originally had social significance and
application, referring to the legal position of an individual who
sells himself into slavery, cf. Alt, *Essays*, 93ff. As such it was
appropriate for Israelites also in certain situations, and in time
came to be used, as here, in the sense of Israelite. **a Hebrew man
or a Hebrew woman:** the law of Exod. 21:2 legislates only for a
Hebrew man. The extension of its application to cover also the
Hebrew woman reflects the changed status of women in Israelite
society by the time of this law. The woman could inherit property
(cf. 2 Kg. 8:3) and so held an independent position of responsibility before the law, which carried with it the possibility of being
reduced through debt to slavery. **is sold to you:** alternatively,
'sells himself to you' (so *NEB*). Both translations are possible, both
in grammar and as far as the law is concerned. **free:** the term is
ḥopši, a legal term which refers specifically to the status of a
released slave or one who has discharged his obligations. Lemche,
VT 25, 1975, 140ff., describes a particular social status which the
ḥopši held in ancient Near Eastern law, being subordinate to a free
citizen but above a slave.

13. At this point the deuteronomic legislator goes beyond the
provisions of Exod. 21:2ff. The slave is not to be simply freed from
a state of bondage to a state of indigent insecurity, but is to be
provided with the means of establishing himself as a full and
independent member of Israelite society.

14. furnish him liberally: the verb means 'to make a neck-
lace for', i.e. to honour or enrich.

15. The reference to Israel's slavery in Egypt as the motive for
obedience to the law appears in almost the same words in 5:15;
16:12; 24:18, 22; cf. also 10:19 .In the present context the
reference is particularly appropriate in that on this occasion,
according to Exod. 3:21f.; 11:2; 12:35f., the Israelites left slavery
in Egypt enriched with gifts given them by the Egyptians. Daube,
Studies, 49f., explains this by saying that the law whereby a
released slave may not depart empty-handed has influenced the
form of the story of Israel's release from slavery in Egypt, from

which, then, there has been reciprocal influence on the expression of the law.

16. The case of the slave who wishes to remain in the security of his master's service is treated in Exod. 21:5f.

17. If the purpose of boring through the ear was to attach a tag to the ear (cf. Mendelsohn, in *IDB* vol. 4, 385), the tag must have indicated something more than slave status or ownership of the slave. Rather, the slave electing to remain in his master's house may well have been accorded a preferential status over other slaves (the debt which led to his slavery having been discharged), this being indicated by a tag fixed to his ear. For the ceremony the slave was brought to **the door** of his master's house. Exod. 21:6 refers also to bringing the slave 'to God', a probable reference to the household gods found at the home entrances. This was passed over in silence by the deuteronomic legislator who clearly would have seen such cults as illegitimate in the light of the requirement of a single sanctuary. **bondman for ever:** the Hebrew phrase is ʿeḇeḏ ʿôlām. It occurs again in 1 Sam. 27:12; Job 41:4 and on several occasions in the Ugaritic texts, cf. Gordon, *Ugaritic Textbook*, 452. It is apparently a technical term, marking out the perpetual slave as different from, and probably preferred over, the other slaves.

18. The verse is awkward after v. 17, and so Seitz, *op. cit.*, 172, takes vv. 16f. as a later addition, even though they correspond in content with Exod. 21:5f. However, this does not solve the difficulty, for this verse fits no better as a continuation of v. 15 which clearly concludes the preceding section. In fact, v. 18 is better seen as an overall conclusion to the slave law, which is composed of two subsidiary sections with corresponding structure: vv. 12–15 and vv. 16–18. Both sections have a law in casuistic style (though using second person singular form of address rather than the impersonal style typical of casuistic law), completed and concluded by a general exhortation. The clear correspondence in structure means that v. 18 should be left as the conclusion of vv. 16f., even though in content they do not fit well. **half the cost of a hired servant:** the *RSV* translation is apparently intended to imply that the cost of keeping a slave was only half of the wage of a hired man. The *NEB* translation 'his six years' service to you has been worth twice the wages of a hired man', apparently implies that a hired man would have to be paid double the usual rate to get from him the amount of work that the slave has done. It is unlikely that this implication is intended, just as in Jer. 16:18 the *RSV* translation of the same word ('doubly') produces an unintended characterization of divine justice as vindictive. Tsevat, *HUCA* 29, 1958, 125f., points to a treaty text from Alalakh where the cognate term *mištannu* occurs four times to describe what is given by the owner of a runaway slave when his slave is returned. Both there and here the sense of 'equivalent' is clearly required (cf. *NEB* note): 'equivalent to the cost of a hired servant'.

(iv) The law on firstlings 15:19–23

The law on firstlings here has a transitional function. The eating of the firstlings would have taken place at the time of a pilgrimage festival (probably the feast of Tabernacles; see comment on v. 20), and in Exod. 34:18–24 the law on the firstlings is set in the context of the festival calendar. Thus, there is clear connection not only with the festival calendar which follows in ch. 16, but also with the law on tithes in 14:22–29, for tithes too were probably brought at this same festival (see comment on 14:23). Tithes and firstlings are also connected in that they both constitute a separation from profane usage of a part of the produce.

The most ancient part of the law is probably the prohibition of v. 19b, of which the positive implications are then drawn out in vv. 19a, 20. Similarly, the ancient law of v. 21 is expanded positively in v. 22. It is particularly in the positive elaboration of the older material (the latter not necessarily, however, being preserved in its original form and wording) that the work of the deuteronomic legislator may be seen.

19. The law of the firstlings applied originally to all males, animal and human; cf. the old law of Exod. 22:29f.; 34:19f. Seitz, *op. cit.*, 190, suggests that since male and female are not distinguished in Num. 18:15; Exod. 34:19, the law on firstlings may well have originally not distinguished between them.

20. The earlier law of Exod. 22:30 stipulated that the firstling must be offered on the eighth day. The deuteronomic centralization law would have made this impracticable, since it would have involved frequent visits to the central sanctuary. So the law is modified to allow the offering to be made at any time during the year. It may be intended that the offering should be made at the time of the offering of the tithes, i.e. probably at the feast of Tabernacles; see comment on 14:23.

21. The old prohibition of 17:1 is here applied by the deuteronomic legislator to the sacrifice of the firstlings. This has led to his using the verb *zbḥ* as a cult technical term for 'sacrifice', whereas in deuteronomic usage this verb usually means profane slaughter; see comment on 12:6, 15.

22. The firstling animal unfit for sacrifice is treated in the manner of those animals which the Israelite may eat outside the cultic context; see comment on 12:15f. Since the eating of a blemished firstling is here presented as a profane act, it must also be assumed that the legislation of v. 19*b* does not apply to such an animal, i.e. a blemished firstling may also be worked as an ordinary animal.

23. On not eating the blood, see comment on 12:16.

(*v*) *The festival calendar* **16:1–17**

Within the festival calendar vv. 1–8 in particular have been much discussed. They are clearly not an original unit: v. 8 contradicts v. 3, and there are clear traces of a process of growth in the text in the course of which two separate festivals, Passover and Unleavened Bread (Mazzot), have been combined. V. 8 is probably a late addition (see comment) attached to a unit which has a chiastic form (cf. Halbe, *ZAW* 87, 1975, 154): vv. 1 and 6*aβb*, 7 correspond in dealing with Passover and the time of its celebration; v. 2 and vv. 5, 6*aα*, in dealing with Passover and the place of its celebration (at the central sanctuary); vv. 3*aα* and 4*b*, the ritual of Passover; vv. 3*aβ* and 4*a*, the seven day feast of Mazzot; and the remainder of v. 3 with its reference to the saving history forming the central point. However, this unified structure conceals a very complex situation in which regulations relating to Passover and Mazzot have been intertwined. V. 1 is now presented as a Passover regulation, but this is as a result of an addition to the original form which was a Mazzot law (see comment). V. 3 apparently refers only to the eating of unleavened bread; but one of these references is to the eating of unleavened bread as part of the Mazzot festival and the other to the eating of it in the context of Passover (see comment). The regulations relating to Mazzot are to be found in vv. 1*aαb* (without 'by night'), 3*aβ*–4*a*, while the remainder deals with the Passover and its centralization. The fact that it is to the Passover theme that the centralization motif is attached, and not to Mazzot, indicates that it is Passover in particular with which the deuteronomic legislator is concerned.

The Mazzot regulations could, then, be either the basis to

which the deuteronomic editor has added Passover (cf. e.g. Plöger, *Untersuchungen*, 74f.; Merendino, *op. cit.*, 137f.), or a later addition to an original deuteronomic text (cf. von Rad; and also Seitz, *op. cit.*, 196ff.). That the former alternative is correct is indicated primarily by the fact that in the older festival calendars of Exod. 23 and 34 (and Dt. 16:16) it is Mazzot, not Passover, which is the first of the three major festivals, the other two being Weeks and Tabernacles (Exod. 23:14ff.; 34:18ff.). This is confirmed, moreover, by the fact that it is possible to reconstruct a credible course of events by which Passover was later secondarily combined with Mazzot, whereas it is difficult to see why Mazzot should have been secondarily incorporated in Passover regulations.

Mazzot has been commonly understood as an original Canaanite agricultural and harvest festival, adopted, like the feasts of Weeks and Tabernacles, by Israel after settlement. However, Halbe, *ZAW* 87, 1975, 324ff., has shown that for a number of reasons this is unlikely. Firstly, Mazzot does not have the character of a festival (cf. also Kutsch, *ZThK* 55, 1958, 28f.): the eating of unleavened bread cannot be the basis of a pilgrim festival; there is no dancing or rejoicing associated with it, nor is anything offered to Yahweh (Exod. 23:15; 34:20 can specify nothing). Secondly, it is difficult to explain the connection between eating unleavened bread and harvest. Thirdly, the month of Abib (March–April) is probably too early for a harvest festival. Fourthly, Mazzot as a seven-day festival is a most unlikely event at the beginning of harvest. Finally, of the three major festivals it is only Mazzot which has apparently an original connection with the exodus, in the sense that reference to the exodus as a reason for celebrating the festival is original with Mazzot but not with the other two festivals which *are* harvest festivals adopted from the Canaanites.

Mazzot as a seven-day festival certainly belongs to the post-settlement period, but it has a history which goes behind this. Important in this connection is Jos. 5:10–12, recording the celebration of Passover and Unleavened Bread at Gilgal. These verses have been edited by the priestly writer (especially in the addition of vv. 10*b*, 11*a*, 12*a*), but particularly in not referring to a seven day festival the verses also clearly contain older tradition. Unleavened bread is here eaten within the framework of Passover. This is the case also in Exod. 34:25 and the J story of the Passover in Exod. 12:29–39 (cf. Nebeling, *Schichten*, 96).

Passover bears all the signs of having been a semi-nomadic festival of apotropaic character: it is celebrated without priest or altar and the blood of the sacrificed animal is sprinkled on the tent entrances in order to ward off evil and destructive influences. Since it is associated also with the eating of unleavened bread, the food of wanderers, and with departure 'in haste' (cf. Exod. 12:33), it may be surmised that the time of its celebration was the occasion of the seasonal migration of semi-nomads from the desert into the cultivated area (cf. Kraus, *Worship*, 45ff.). According to 2 Kg. 23:21f., however, Passover was not celebrated by Israel from the days of the judges until the time of Josiah, and apart from Jos. 5:10–12 (and a reference in 2 Chr. 30 for the time of Hezekiah), no reference is made to it for the post-settlement period until Josiah's reform. It was a festival that belonged to a different context of life from that of Israel settled in Palestine. Jos. 5:10–12 also indicates, however, that the eating of unleavened bread had begun to establish itself as a custom in a measure distinct from Passover: it is here eaten with 'parched grain', the produce of the new agricultural mode of life, and so now connected with that form of existence rather than its original semi-nomadic setting.

As Halbe has shown, *op. cit.*, 324ff., it is, therefore, very probable that after settlement in the land the Passover festival, since it was a festival proper to the semi-nomadic way of life, ceased to be celebrated, or perhaps became a private family affair. On the other hand, one aspect of it, the eating of unleavened bread, gradually detached itself as an independent custom preserved to commemmorate the exodus from Egypt. Under the influence of the form and duration of the feast of Tabernacles it became a seven-day celebration in its own right, but it never acquired the distinctive traits of a totally independent festival. The deuteronomic legislator in 16:1–8 is in fact, then, reverting to old custom in bringing together Mazzot and Passover, and in introducing Passover as the chief element. However, because Mazzot had by this time been long established as a seven-day celebration, that aspect of it, which is not original to Passover, had to fix the framework for the whole.

Older legislation on the other two festivals, the feast of Weeks and the feast of Booths or Tabernacles, is easier to abstract from its present deuteronomic context. The feast of Weeks, regulated in vv. 9–10*a*, appears in the older calendars as the 'feast of harvest' (Exod. 23:16) and 'first fruits' (Exod. 23:16; 34:22). The present reference is the oldest information on how it was fixed chronologically, although Exod. 34:22 in using the term 'feast of Weeks' presupposes this method of reckoning. It is still more precisely determined in the later Lev. 23:15f. as being on the fiftieth day (hence the name Pentecost) from the sabbath after the first sheaf was offered. This is a purely agricultural festival, with no original connection with Israel's saving history (see comment on v. 12); it was derived from the Canaanites, and apparently lasted only one day. Its essential character as a pilgrimage festival (see comment on v. 10) would have been strengthened by the deuteronomic provision that it must now be celebrated at the central sanctuary rather than at the local shrine.

The feast of Booths or Tabernacles has its basic legislation in vv. 13, 14a, with deuteronomic elaboration in vv. 14b, 15. In the oldest calendars this was known as the feast of 'ingathering'; it was held at the end of the agricultural year in the autumn (Exod. 23:16; 34:22). As a harvest festival it also was of Canaanite origin (cf. Jg. 9:27), but since it is only in Deuteronomy and later legislation (cf. Lev. 23:39, 41f.) that it is a seven-day festival known as the feast of Booths, it is likely that at least in these characteristics it received a distinctive stamp in the Israelite context. It was the most important of the Israelite festivals, being referred to simply as 'the feast' in 1 Kg. 8:2, 65; Ezek. 45:25, and 'the feast of Yahweh' in Lev. 23:39. Its significance for Israel is apparent in its duration, and also in the fact that it was this festival which was prescribed for the reading of the law to the assembled people every seven years (though the historical connection between the law and this feast is doubtful; see introduction to 31:9–13).

The whole section is at present in deuteronomic formulation, and it is only occasionally that pre-deuteronomic expressions may be discerned with some confidence (see comment on, for example, v. 16). In general the deuteronomic legislator has taken up the older material, preserving its substance but adapting it to the new contexts into which he has brought it.

1. Abib: the first month (March–April); it is referred to otherwise only in Exod. 13:4; 23:15, in connection with the observance of the feast of Unleavened Bread (Mazzot). It is sometimes suggested that **month** here means 'new moon'; however, it is not in fact until post-exilic texts that there is any precision in the date of Passover, and there it is given as 14th/15th of the first month, which may be a date based on the solar cycle rather than the lunar phases; for a discussion, cf. McKay, *ZAW* 84, 1972, 435ff.

and keep the Passover to the Lord your God: the phrase appears otherwise in priestly texts in Exod. 12:48; Num. 9:10, 14. It does not appear in the old festival calendars which in Exod. 23:15; 34:18 use the verb **observe** in connection with Mazzot. The phrase has been interpolated here in the course of bringing Passover and Mazzot regulations together. To this interpolation belongs also the end of the verse, **by night.** At present it stands in its precision in strange contrast with the general reference to the month Abib (with no date given). Moreover, the motif of a nocturnal exodus is not otherwise connected with Mazzot (cf. Exod. 13:4; 23:15; 34:18, where Mazzot is connected with a simple reference to the exodus). Rather, the reference to night serves the purpose of linking Abib, and so also Mazzot which was celebrated in that month, to the Passover; cf. Halbe, ZAW 87, 1975, 154f.; Merendino, *op. cit.*, 127f. **Passover:** for a brief review of some proposals on the etymology of the word cf. Kraus, *Worship*, 45f., who concludes that the most reasonable interpretation is that which in the light of Exod. 12:23 sees here the idea of 'the merciful passing over' of a destructive power.

2. This is the beginning of that part of vv. 1–8 demanding the centralization of the Passover sacrifice (cf. vv. 5f.), and clearly derives from the hand of the deuteronomic legislator. **from the flock or the herd:** the later priestly writer in Exod. 12:3–6 restricts the Passover sacrificial animal to a lamb. **the Passover sacrifice:** the same word *pesaḥ* means both the sacrificial animal and the festival itself.

3. you shall eat no leavened bread with it: this is a Passover regulation; **it** refers to the Passover sacrificial animal. Leaven was not permitted with the Passover sacrifice (cf. Exod. 23:18; 34:25), nor could it provide the material of any meal offering (cf. Lev. 2:11; 6:17). **seven days you shall eat it with unleavened bread:** with the reference to the seven days and to unleavened bread there is here a regulation of the feast of Unleavened Bread (Mazzot), which continues into the beginning of the next verse. The regulation was inserted here because of the catchword connection with the immediately preceding Passover regulation from which the word *ʿālāw*, 'with it', has been secondarily repeated in the Mazzot regulation. **bread of affliction ... hurried flight:** probably a late addition, using priestly motifs and unnecessary in its anticipation of the immediately following reference to Egypt. **hurried flight:** hurry mixed with alarm

(Driver), cf. 20:3 where the verbal form is translated 'tremble'.

4. V. 4*b*, prescribing that the Passover sacrifice must be consumed in one night, stands in some conflict with the reference to seven days in the first half of the verse, and in sharp conflict with the present form of v. 3 where, with the addition of *'ālāw*, both Unleavened Bread and the Passover sacrifice are eaten over a period of seven days. V. 4*a* is clearly a Mazzot regulation, and its connection with the Passover regulation in v. 4*b* is not original.

5. Vv. 5, 6*a* continue the deuteronomic centralization text of v. 2.

6. in it: this is not present in the text, and presupposes the addition of the word *bô*; Sam and LXX add *šām*, 'there', cf. 12:11. The reference to the evening in v. 6*b* connects the verse with the Passover reference in the word 'night' in v. 1*b*.

7. This is a Passover regulation, referring to the one night Passover festival; with the reference to the central sanctuary it is also clearly in deuteronomic form. **you shall boil it:** possibly the verb *bšl* would be more accurately translated 'cook', cf. Num. 11:8; 2 Sam. 13:8. Exod. 12:9 (P) expressly forbids cooking (*bšl*) 'in water', i.e. boiling, and demands that the lamb be roasted; cf. Thompson. **go to your tents:** the use of this phrase probably goes back to the context of war where it is a demobilization command meaning 'return home'. That it should have this sense here (cf. Kutsch, *ZThK* 55, 1958, 13) is, however, unlikely. This is a deuteronomic formulation of a Passover regulation in the context of his bringing Passover and the seven-day Mazzot festival together. It should be taken literally as a reference to the tent encampments of the pilgrims to the central sanctuary for the celebration of the seven-day festival.

8. This verse contradicts the Mazzot regulation of v. 3, which prescribes the eating of unleavened bread for seven days; it is probably a late addition in which the whole period of the festival is presented as a single whole leading up to the **solemn assembly.** This is a characteristic expression of the priestly author; cf. also Exod. 12:16, and Halbe, *ZAW* 87, 1975, 148f., 341ff.

9. You shall count seven weeks: the seven-week period from the beginning of the harvest to the festival is stipulated presumably to allow sufficient time to bring in the whole harvest. Conditions would have varied in different parts of the land; but by allowing a seven-week period it would then be possible to hold a festival at the same time for the whole country.

10. feast: *NEB* 'pilgrim-feast'. The Hebrew is *ḥag*, which is cognate to the Arabic *ḥajj*, the pilgrimage to Mecca required of every Muslim at least once in his lifetime. There were three such *ḥaggim* in Israel, the three mentioned in this chapter, and here too they have the character of pilgrimage festivals. **Weeks:** so called because of the way in which it was chronologically fixed. In the older festival calendars it is called 'the feast of harvest' (Exod. 23:16). **tribute:** the word *missaṯ* is of obscure origin. It is found only here in the Old Testament, but occurs in Aramaic with the sense of 'sufficiency'. The translation 'tribute' is apparently based on a (questionable) connection with the word *mas*, 'forced service'. The word may be a corruption of *kᵉmatteᵉnaṯ*, which appears in v. 17 (with *yāḏô* translated 'as he is able'), though there is no support in the versions for this. As it stands the translation is 'the sufficiency of the freewill offering', i.e. as much as possible in relation to the total harvest.

The old law of the feast of Weeks is not continued beyond v. 10*a*. From v. 10*b* **(as the Lord your God blesses you)** it is deuteronomic material (cf. also v. 17) relating the law to the blessing of God, to the requirement to observe the festival at the central sanctuary along with one's household and the poor, and to Israel's slavery in Egypt.

11. you shall rejoice: this motif is otherwise found with the feast of Booths, cf. 14:26; 16:14. It is not associated with the feast of Weeks in earlier calendars or in Lev. 23:15ff., and is probably not an original characteristic of the regulations relating to this festival; cf. also Merendino, *op. cit.*, 135. On the **sojourner** see comment on 1:16, and on the centralization formula in v. 11*b* see comment on 12:5.

12. The reference to Israel's slavery in Egypt does not appear any earlier than Deuteronomy in connection with the feast of Weeks; moreover, it does not even here explain the observance of the festival, but rather why the Levite and the poor should be invited to join in it—in itself a deuteronomic recommendation. So the reference to Egypt in the context of this festival is of deuteronomic origin at the earliest. V. 12*b*, **you shall be careful to observe these statutes,** uses deuteronomic language; but it is strange in its occurrence at this point before the regulations relating to the three festivals have been completed. That it marks a stage in the growth of the festival calendar which did not include the feast of Tabernacles is unlikely in view of the regular association of all three festivals from pre-deuteronomic times.

13. The pre-deuteronomic law on the feast of Booths is to be found within vv. 13-14a. **feast of booths:** called the 'feast of ingathering' in the oldest festival calendars (Exod. 23:16; 34:22). The name 'booths' or 'tabernacles' is first found in Deuteronomy (also 31:10; cf. Lev. 23:34; Zech. 14:16, 18f.; Ezr. 3:4; 2 Chr. 8:13), and probably derives from the custom observed by farmers of living in temporary dwellings set up in the fields during the time of the harvest, cf. Lev. 23:42; Neh. 8:14, 17.

14. you shall rejoice: on rejoicing as a characteristic of the feast of Booths, see comment on 12:18. The list of participants in the festival is a typical deuteronomic expansion emphasizing the nature of the festival as one to be enjoyed by both the family and the needy within Israel.

15. As with the first two festivals so the feast of Booths is appointed by the deuteronomic legislator for celebration at the central sanctuary. **all the work of your hands:** a phrase which has particular reference to the agricultural context; see comment on 2:7.

16. The appearance in this verse of the centralization formula, **at the place which he will choose,** points to the hand of the deuteronomic legislator. Otherwise, however, the verse does not harmonize with the deuteronomic festival calendar, and would seem to be an old summarizing command. It makes no reference to Passover, which in Deuteronomy is the chief of the three festivals, but to Unleavened Bread; it restricts the validity of the command to **all your males,** whereas the deuteronomic law extends it to include both male and female (vv. 11,14). Apart from the centralization formula the verse is a pre-deuteronomic compilation using material from Exod. 23:15b, 17; 34:20b, 23. **shall appear before:** in its two occurrences in this verse the verb is Niphal, fitting very awkwardly with the direct object *eṭ penê,* 'the face of', which immediately follows. Probably here, as in 31:11; Exod. 34:23f. (cf. Driver for further cases), the word should be revocalized to Qal, and the phrase translated 'shall see the face of', in the sense of 'have access to', 'have an audience with', as in royal contexts (cf. 2 Sam. 3:13; 14:28, 32; 2 Kg. 25:19). The change in vocalization was introduced because the literal understanding of the phrase was felt to be objectionable.

(G) OFFICIALS IN THE THEOCRATIC STATE: **16:18-18:22**
The third section of the law corpus is chiefly concerned with the

institutions of Israel the people of Yahweh. These are the offices of judge, king, priest and prophet. The deuteronomic legislator has made use of old material (a model for judges and some cultic laws) to formulate a law on the local administration of justice by judges, whose primary responsibility is now presented as the purity of Israel's faith. Although the law on the central tribunal may have its roots in the judical reform of Jehoshaphat, the formulation of that law shows no pre-deuteronomic material, while in some respects, particularly in the appearance of the judge alongside the priest, there is no pre-deuteronomic tradition. The introduction of the judge at the central tribunal is apparently the consequence of the deuteronomic legislation on the king, the former court of appeal, who in the deuteronomic view is severely limited in his powers and presented simply as a member of the covenant people, not above his brethren. Pre-deuteronomic material rooted in prophetic circles is taken up in this royal law. Old material is also present in the laws on the priest and the prophet. For the former, the deuteronomic legislator made use of old law detailing the priests' dues. This he has applied specifically to the Levitical priests whose claim to priestly status at the central sanctuary is acknowledged. In the law on the prophet the deuteronomic law is in fact limited to a prohibition of all forms of divination, which takes up an older law on this subject describing it as an abomination to Yahweh.

The presentation of the function of the judge as that of ensuring the purity of Israel's faith meant that a good connection already existed between this collection and the preceding. This connection has, however, been strengthened by subsequent late deuteronomistic editing. Particularly the deuteronomistic contribution to 17:2–7, which turned a general law into a specific one dealing with apostasy, constituted a conscious linking with ch. 13. A similar contact was established through the addition of the purging formula to the end of 17:12 and through 17:13 (cf. 13:5, 11). Otherwise, the chief contribution of the post-deuteronomic additions is in the royal law, where the king is explicitly subjected to the divine law; the law on the priests, where the special position of the whole tribe of Levi is stressed; and the law on divination, which has been extensively supplemented by a section dealing with the prophet of Yahweh as the true source of guidance for Israel. An even later addition to this supplement is concerned with the problem of true and false prophecy, a subject of concern particularly to Jeremiah and Ezekiel.

(i) Judges and the purity of Israel's worship **16:18–17:7**
A clearly distinct section is contained here. In large part, however,
it is frequently understood to be misplaced or secondary. So 16:18
has been understood as the basis of 17:8ff., while everything in
between has been added (Seitz, *op. cit.*, 201); rather similarly,
16:21–17:7 has been taken as an intrusion which originally stood
elsewhere (Driver); 17:2–7 has been noted to be of similar form
to the laws on enticement to apostasy in ch. 13, to which context
it is then frequently assigned (see introduction to 12:29–13:18).

Pre-deuteronomic material is to be found in the section, in
16:19, 21–17:1a (see comment). Only in v. 19 has this material a
close connection with the context of administration of justice
where it is now to be found. Otherwise, the older material is
cultic, concerned with the purity of Israel's worship and its being
free of contamination by Canaanite practices. The deuteronomic
legislator has brought the material into its present context, and
indeed supplemented it in order to emphasize the significance of
its new context. The context is that of the local administration so
justice, and the judges are seen by the deuteronomic legislator af
being primarily responsible for ensuring the purity of Israel's faith
and worship. So, the law relating to the appointment of the judges
is followed by three prohibitions which are anti-Canaanite in
character (see comment on 17:1), and then by a wholly deuteronomic composition (later supplemented by the deuteronomist) in
17:2–7, which in comprehensive terms puts before the judges the
task of dealing with those who do 'what is evil in the sight of the
Lord your God'. The verses have the casuistic form of the laws of
ch. 13, but it is only as a result of deuteronomistic editing in vv. 2
and 3 that a particular reference to apostasy has been incorporated
(see comment). This casuistic form, using the direct form of
address, is deuteronomic (see introduction to 12:29–13:18), and
its use does not indicate the existence of a particular collection in
this form.

The historical background of the law on the appointment of
local judges may be the judicial reform of Jehoshaphat, who
reigned in Judah 873–849 BC. The reform is mentioned only in
2 Chr. 19:5, and not in the books of Kings. It is, however, strongly
argued by Phillips, *Law*, 18ff., that the Chronicler's account is
historically trustworthy, and that Jehoshaphat was in fact
responsible for replacing the old traditional judicial authority of
the elders with a system of official appointments. See also Knierim,

ZAW 32, 1961, 162ff., who notes that Isa. 3:2; Mic. 3:1, 2, 9–11 presuppose the existence of judges already in their time, and points to Exod. 18:13ff. as an aetiological story justifying Jehoshaphat's reform.

18. judges: it is unlikely that this means simply 'elders', those traditionally responsible for the administration of justice in the community. There would be no need for a law such as this to deal with local administration of justice by the elders. The wording **you shall appoint** (rather than simply 'you shall have') suggests, rather, official appointments from a centralized authority. That the judges envisaged exercised a purely judicial function may be a too narrow interpretation of their office. In some Old Testament contexts (e.g. Am. 2:3; Dan. 9:12) the root from which the word translated 'judge' is derived is better given the sense of 'rule', and the same word has, moreover, an instructive parallel in the office of the Carthaginian 'suffetes', which was a general ruling office rather than a narrowly judicial one (see Hayes–Miller, *History*, 321f.). So in the present context, particularly against the background of Jehoshaphat's reform, the reference may be to the appointment of local governors generally responsible for the affairs of their districts. **officers:** see comment on 1:15. In the present context the 'officers' should be taken as administrative assistants to the judges. **righteous judgment:** the Hebrew phrase is *mišpaṭ ṣedeq*, 'judgment of righteousness'; both words are legal terms (cf. *NEB* 'true justice'). The legal connotations of the second word are especially clear in the verbal form of the root, as used particularly in 25:1.

19. The first three clauses have a common form and are widely taken to constitute a 'model for judges' or part of such a model (cf. von Rad, Seitz, *op. cit.*, 201 n. 312), i.e. a series of apodictic prohibitions addressed to the judges as a basic text by which their performance of their functions is guided. However, it is only the regular form of the series of prohibitions which suggests this. The first and third of them are in fact found separately in an older collection (cf. Exod. 23:6, 8), while the second, **you shall not show partiality,** has no parallel earlier than Deuteronomy, and may well be a secondary prohibition modelled on the other two. In view of the concern of biblical wisdom with partiality (cf. Prov. 24:23; 28:21) and of the many wisdom contacts in Deuteronomy (see Introduction, pp. 104ff.), the clause may perhaps best be seen as the result of the deuteronomic adoption of a wisdom theme.

The measure of the deuteronomic legislator's dependence on older material is indicated by the way in which the motive clause is almost a verbal repetition of Exod. 23:8*b* (**the eyes of the wise** being substituted for 'the officials'). **and subverts the cause of the righteous:** for a number of reasons the translation of the *NEB*, 'and (makes) the just man give a crooked answer', is to be preferred. Firstly, the word translated **cause** means 'words'; secondly, the previous clause pointed to the effect of bribery on those normally wise and upright; so here reference is to the effect of bribery on those normally just and innocent: they are dishonest in their speaking. The verb means to 'twist' and 'pervert' as well as to 'subvert'.

20. Justice: on the repetition of the word for the sake of emphasis and intensification, see comment on 2:27. **inherit:** the verb *yāraš* is usually translated by the *RSV* 'possess' (cf. 1:8; 2:24, 31; 3:12; 4:1; 5:33; 6:1, 18; 9:23, etc.).

21. Asherah: see comment on 7:5. **the altar:** in the deuteronomic context this indicates the single altar permitted at the central sanctuary. However, Exod. 20:24 shows that even in its present form this prohibition may be pre-deuteronomic, the reference being to any altar rather than to the single altar. That the law, in this form, is pre-deuteronomic is, moreover, suggested by the probability that as a deuteronomic formulation it would undoubtedly have included the phrase 'at the place which the Lord your God will choose'.

22. pillar: see comment on 7:5. **which the Lord your God hates:** this relative clause refers to both v. 21 and v. 22, the Asherah and the pillar, which belong together. 'Hate' is not sentimental antipathy, but rather it has a legal sense, and means 'reject' or 'break relations with', as in Jg. 11:7. It is, therefore, an antithetic parallel to 'love' (see comment on 6:5), and like it is used in a treaty or covenant context; see L'Hour, *RB* 71, 1964, 487 n. 30.

17:1. This general law on sacrifice has a specific practical application in 15:21. **any defect whatever:** this does not appear in the parallel law of Lev. 22:20f. It may be a deuteronomic contribution to an older law, though there is no pre-deuteronomic occurrence of the law. The Hebrew phrase *dābār ra'*, 'an evil thing', is here used of a physical disfigurement. **an abomination to the Lord your God:** it is particularly through this phrase that the law of 17:1 takes on the anti-Canaanite character evident in the laws of 16:21, 22; it is precisely such a character which attaches to those laws where the phrase is otherwise found; see comment on 7:25; 18:12.

2. The verse uses language familiar in deuteronomic and deuteronomistic contexts: **in any of your towns which the Lord your God gives you:** cf. 15:7; 16:5, 18. **who does what is evil in the sight of the Lord your God:** cf. 4:25; 9:18. The expression **in transgressing his covenant** is probably deuteronomistic; it occurs only here in Deuteronomy. It goes back to Hos. 6:7; 8:1, and is found in the deuteronomistic history in Jos. 7:11, 15; 23:16; Jg. 2:20; 2 Kg. 18:12. In its use here 'covenant' means the decalogue; cf. 4:13, and Kutsch, *Verheissung*, 137.

3. As the last phrase of the previous verse, so all of this verse is probably of deuteronomistic origin. **served other gods and worshipped them:** this phrase appears in slightly varying forms only in late passages in Deuteronomy (4:19; 5:9; 8:19; 11:16; 29:26; 30:17). **the sun or the moon or any of the host of heaven:** grammatically this phrase is awkwardly related to the previous words. Otherwise it occurs in 4:19 and the deuteronomistic history 2 Kg. 17:16; 21:3, and Jer. 8:2. **which I have forbidden:** again a deuteronomistic phrase, which does not otherwise occur in Deuteronomy. It depends on Jer. 7:31; 19:5; 32:35, where it appears in the same context of idolatry; cf. L'Hour, *Bib* 44, 1963, 14; Merendino, *op. cit.*, 173.

4. The deuteronomic law takes up again in this verse, using expressions which have already appeared in 13:14 and in 19:18.

5. that man or woman: in its second occurrence the phrase is omitted by LXX, Vulg (and *NEB*). The *RSV* makes it the object of **and you shall stone:** in the *MT*, however, the object of the verb is 'them', and the phrase is clearly an accidental repetition from its first occurrence in the verse. **you shall stone:** see comment on 13:10.

6. The verse anticipates 19:15; but the latter is an addition based on this verse (see comment on 19:15).

7. The witnesses take responsibility for their action to its ultimate consequences. False witnesses, therefore, could find themselves liable for wrongful execution. **So you shall purge the evil from the midst of you:** see comment on 13:5.

(ii) The supreme court **17:8-13**
The deuteronomic formulation of the law on the supreme central

tribunal is clear from the use of the centralization formula in vv. 8–10*a* (see comment). The rest of the section is composed of deuteronomistic additions, probably from the hand of the second deuteronomist. Although there may be contact here too with the judicial reform of Jehoshaphat, the deuteronomic legislator is responsible for one important modification: the introduction of the judge beside the priest in the court (see comment on v. 9). No pre-deuteronomic formulation of the law can be traced here, although it was by no means an innovation in deuteronomic times that difficult cases should be submitted for decision to the priests. The passage does not state whether it was the parties to the dispute or the judges who would bring the difficult case to the attention of the central court. Exod. 18:13ff. suggest that it was the function of the judges to do this.

8. one kind of homicide and another: i.e. whether murder or manslaughter, cf. Exod. 21:12–14. **one kind of legal right and another:** apparently this translation understands the law here to refer to uncertainty with regard to the precise law under which a case should be judged. However, the word used (*dîn*) does not otherwise have such a sense, but refers rather generally to 'judgment' or 'strife' which is subject to judgment, or specifically to the particular 'cause' or 'plea' which comes to judgment. So here the issue is perhaps one of conflicting testimony, cf. 19:16ff. **one kind of assault and another:** different forms of assault or personal injury are dealt with in Exod. 21:12ff. **any case:** for *rîb* in the sense of case or dispute, cf. 21:5 and especially 25:1. **within your towns:** the word translated 'towns' means also 'gates' as the place where justice is administered (cf. v. 5). The reference here may be to the gates (cf. Merendino, *op. cit.*, 178 n. 28) as the place of local administration of justice even after the appointment of judges, or more generally to the cities where the judges were based, as in 16:18. In any case, there is a contrast drawn between the local courts in the cities and the central appeal court at **the place which the Lord your God will choose. which is too difficult for you:** the Niphal of the verb *pl'* is used here. It often denotes a divine action which is 'wonderful' in the eyes of men, and Horst, *Gottes Recht*, 133, argues that here it points to a case in which human processes are inadequate and which must, therefore, be submitted to God for decision (viz. through trial by ordeal or some other means). This would suit a context which mentioned only the priest (see comment on v. 9), but in the present context it is more likely that reference is being made generally to the submission of complex and difficult cases to a supreme court.

9. to the Levitical priests and to the judge: in the attempt to find a pre-deuteronomic form of this law, one or other of the two parties mentioned here is frequently omitted as secondary. Some omit the reference to the priests as a deuteronomic innovation, on the grounds that priests had no judicial function in early Israel and only got this at the time of centralization (cf. Phillips, *Law*, 22). Others omit the reference to the judge as inappropriate in a context which deals with an intractable case being decided by divine pronouncement (cf. Seitz, *op. cit.*, 202). Yet others think in terms of the combination in these verses of two judicial traditions, that of the sanctuary and that of the city-gate (cf. Weinfeld, *Deuteronomy*, 235, following Steuernagel). It is unlikely that any simple literary-critical operation on the text will be successful, for there is no pressing indication of secondary additions to the text here. On the other hand, there are four indications in particular that traditio-historically the reference to the judge is secondary in this context. Firstly, the judge is not explicitly referred to in the context of Jehoshaphat's judicial reform in 2 Chr. 19:8–11, whereas 'Levites and priests' are referred to; it has already been seen that this reform, in so far as it affected the local administration of justice, may be reflected in 16:18ff. Secondly, the section as a whole presupposes that it is at the central sanctuary that the decision is to be made; had there existed in pre-deuteronomic times a lay appeals procedure to a supreme court (apart from the king; cf. below), in which context the judge would have belonged, it would not have been located at the sanctuary, and reference to such a lay court would have been preserved here. Thirdly, there is enough evidence to suggest that judicial decisions were on occasions delivered by God (through his priests) in pre-deuteronomic times; cf. Exod. 22:8, 9, and also the trial ordeal in Num. 5:11ff. which is undoubtedly only one precise example of a practice which was more general. Finally, pre-deuteronomic records indicate that the functions of the supreme court were exercised by the king (cf. 2 Sam. 12:1ff.; 14:2ff.; 15:1ff.). The deuteronomic legislator does not see this as a royal function in 17:14–20, and it must, therefore, be considered probable that it is precisely as a consequence of the king's having been deprived of this function by the deuteronomic legislator that the judge makes his appear-

ance in vv. 8–13. The introduction of the judge is, then, a deuteronomic innovation, and the reference to the priests should be seen
as resting on old traditional practice. **you shall consult them:**
the verb is that translated 'inquire' in 13:14. Though occasionally
used in a legal context, the verb is frequently used of consulting
the oracle or visiting the sanctuary; see comment on 13:14. **declare:** the same verb with this sense of 'solemnly pronounce' is
used of the decalogue in 4:13; 5:5.

10. Vv. 10*b*, 11 are superfluous after vv. 9*b*, 10*a* (cf. also Seitz,
op. cit., 202). They repeat as additional encouragement what has
already been said, using expressions already found in later parts
of Deuteronomy. **you shall be careful to do:** cf. 5:1, 29; 6:3,
25; 7:11, etc., a phrase associated with deuteronomistic sections
of the parenesis. **they direct:** the verb is used also in 33:8–10;
2 Kg. 17:27 for the instruction of the Levites and priests. From
the same root comes *tôrāh* in the next verse.

11. instructions: this is the translation of *tôrāh*, elsewhere
translated 'law' or 'teaching' (see comment on 1:5; 11:30).
Though used here in its old sense (the answer of a priest to a
specific enquiry), the word appears in a context which is late. **the
decision:** *NEB* 'the precedent'; at any rate, the word *mišpāṭ*
refers to the pronouncement of the judge rather than of the priest.
**you shall not turn aside ... to the right hand or to the
left:** also in v. 20. The expression is used (in plural form of
address) in the late 5:32.

12. Vv. 12 and 13 should be taken as a late addition to the
deuteronomic law. They constitute a second independent law
rather than a part of the law on cases to be brought to the supreme
court; in making a clear threat they are out of keeping with the
tone of encouragement adopted in earlier verses. They are a
relatively late addition taking up expressions from other contexts,
and were added in order to bring 17:8ff. into line with other units
dealing with judicial cases (cf. Merendino, *op. cit.*, 177; Seitz, *op.
cit.*, 203). **you shall purge the evil from Israel:** cf. 17:7; 21:21,
etc. and comment on 13:5.

13. and all the people shall hear, and fear: cf. 13:11; 19:20;
21:21.

(iii) The king **17:14-20**
The law on the king follows naturally on and is closely connected
with the law on the supreme court. The functions of the latter,

in so far as they involved appeals to a lay judiciary, had formerly been exercised by the king (see comment on v. 9). The deuteronomic legislator, however, is concerned here to mark out the limits of the monarchic institution, limits which are determined by his view that the king is a member of the covenant people (chosen from the 'brethren', v. 15), who is not to see himself or be treated as superior to his people (v. 20).

In order to put forward his law the deuteronomic legislator has used a series of prohibitions which, if they did not exist earlier in precisely the form they now have, are certainly well rooted in tradition. Gerstenberger, *Wesen*, 67f., proposes that basic to the royal law is a series of three demands: he shall not multiply horses for himself; he shall not multiply wives for himself; he shall not multiply silver and gold for himself, which constitute a sort of 'model for the king' (see comment on 16:19). Such a model might conceivably have had a setting in prophetic circles critical of the monarchy, a possibility which is strengthened by the clear identity of concern between these demands and Isa. 2:7ff.; Mic. 5:10ff. (see comment on vv. 15–17).

The view of kingship expressed in the law is often thought to fit better in the context of the northern rather than the southern kingdom (cf. Alt, *Kleine Schriften* II, 263ff.; Galling, *ThLZ* 76, 1951, 133ff.; von Rad, Buis-Leclercq, etc.). It is indeed true that distinctively southern conceptions of the king as standing in a covenant relationship with Yahweh and as the member of a dynasty which will endure for ever, do not come to expression here; and it is with northern rather than with southern prophets that the criticisms of the monarchy implicit in the laws are to be associated (e.g. Hos. 7:3–7; 8:4; 10:7). However, this northern connection may be exaggerated. It is important that the specific terms of the basic demands of the law find their parallel not with northern prophets but with Isaiah and Micah (see above); moreover, v. 20 presupposes a dynastic form of monarchy (see comment), and any specific historical allusions that exist in the text fit a southern as well as (and perhaps better than) a northern context (see comment on vv. 15, 16). Furthermore, in general it should be noted that the purpose of the deuteronomic law is not to pass judgment on the monarchy (cf. Lindblom, *Erwägungen*, 50ff.), but rather to put over the characteristic deuteronomic view of Israel as a whole, including her king, being 'brothers' bound together as the people of Yahweh.

The deuteronomistic historian supplemented the law of the king through the addition of vv. 18f., and the later deuteronomistic editor added a note in v. 16, and a phrase in v. 20, by which he drew out what was for him the consequence of the king being simply a fellow-Israelite, viz. that just as his people so the king was subject to the divine law.

14. The style of the opening of the deuteronomic law, with its reference to the future and specifically to taking possession of the land, followed by a commandment, is typical of the deuteronomic parenesis; cf. 6:20ff.; 7:1ff.; 8:7ff. **I will set a king over me:** so the monarchy originated on the basis of a desire of the people, not as a divine ordinance, as in 1 Sam. 8. **like all the nations:** apart from this passage, the phrase occurs only in 1 Sam. 8:5, 20. The contacts between verses 14*b*, 15*a* and 1 Sam. 8:5, 20; 10:24 are not accidental. In 1 Samuel the deuteronomist is making use of the deuteronomic law in his edition of the story of Saul's election as king.

15. The relative clause **whom the Lord your God will choose** is frequently taken as a deuteronomistic addition (cf. e.g. Boecker, *Beurteilung*, 49 n. 1). It stands in some tension with the previous verse where the emphasis lies on popular desire as the basis of the monarchic institution, and, moreover, it makes the rest of the verse more or less superfluous. Furthermore, if it is correct to see the deuteronomistic reference to Yahweh having chosen *Israel* as a new application by the deuteronomic author to the people of a concept which belonged to the monarchy originally (see comment on 7:6), it is unlikely that the same author would have created a rather problematic tension by using the term also in its original sense and context. Caquot, *Semitica* 9, 1959, 25, suggests that divine choice was a fundamental requirement of kings both north and south, but that we should perhaps think here of the background of regicide and usurpation of the throne which characterized the northern kingdom after 743 BC. However, a specific historical background such as this is not demanded by the law; its general concern is with the possibilities of apostasy inherent in the monarchy as an institution. The particular reference to the king's election by Yahweh is best taken as an independent element introduced at a secondary stage. **you may:** see comment on 12:17 for the notion of duty implicit in this verb. **foreigner:** see comment on 15:3. Various suggestions have been made to provide a historical background to the prohibition of making a foreigner

king. So, for example, Omri and Ahab do not have pure Hebrew
names, and through Ahab's wife Jezebel foreign influence was
particularly strong in Israel (cf. 1 Kg. 16:31-34). Reference might
also be made to Isa. 7:6, according to which it was proposed to
instal an Aramean named Tabeel as king in Judah in place of
Ahaz. However, the main purpose here is not to recall a specific
incident, but rather to strengthen the positive demand that the
king must be a member of the covenant people.

16. A background in royal policies pursued by Solomon in
particular has been suggested for the prohibition of multiplying
horses (and wives and wealth referred to in the next verse).
However, the aim of building up an effective army of horses and
chariots was undoubtedly pursued by more than one king, both
north and south, and it must remain doubtful that a particular
individual is in view. The important aspect is the religious one,
for multiplying horses (in the context of establishing and strengthening a professional army) had definite religious implications.
These are drawn out by the prophets, particularly Isa. 2:7-9 and
Mic. 5:10ff., where horses along with wealth (cf. v. 17) are seen
as the things which lead to pride, to a loss of awareness of the need
to trust in Yahweh, and so to unfaithfulness and apostasy. **cause
the people to return to Egypt:** the precise point of this is
uncertain. Some think in terms of the sending of Israelite slaves
to Egypt in return for horses (cf. Steuernagel, Galling, *op. cit.*, 136,
Rennes); others take it metaphorically in the sense of a return to
dependence on Egypt through alliances involving the sending of
ambassadors (cf. Horst, *Gottes Recht*, 139; Caquot, *op. cit.*, 28;
Buis-Leclercq). The latter proposal gains considerable support in
the condemnations of Isaiah (30:1-7; 31:1-3) concerning Israel's
reliance on Egypt, where a link is also made with her reliance on
horses and wealth. **the Lord has said to you. 'You shall never
return that way again':** this is in plural form of address in a
singular context, and is probably to be seen as a late deutero-
omistic comment on the actual command in this verse that the
people must not be brought back to Egypt. No word of Yahweh
on the subject has been preserved, though a reference to it is
given also in 28:68, and its existence would add greatly to the
impact of Hos. 8:13; 9:3.

17. Isa. 2:7ff. and Mic. 5:10ff. connect horses and wealth with
idolatry; here the connection is with **wives.** But the intention is
the same here as with the prophets, for, as the verse goes on to

indicate, the danger of many wives is precisely that it leads to apostasy from Yahweh to the religions of the wives; cf. also 1 Kg. 11:1ff.; 16:31–33, and Seitz, *op. cit.*, 234f. **nor shall he greatly multiply for himself silver and gold:** as Caquot, *op. cit.*, 29f., remarks, this represents the application to the king of the deuteronomic parenesis in 8:13f.

18. Only in vv. 18 and 19 is a positive task assigned to the king, that of writing a copy of the law and of keeping it by him throughout his life. Not only for this reason, but also because the existence of Deuteronomy as a fixed and known entity, for which the word *tôrāh* (see comment on 1:5) is appropriate, is apparently presupposed, and also because v. 20 follows naturally on v. 17, it is very likely that these verses are a deuteronomistic addition. They harmonize well with the expression of the deuteronomistic Jos. 1:8 and also with the deuteronomistic view of both king and people as subject to the divine law, a subject treated at length in 1 Sam. 12 (see above the introduction to this section). **when he sits on the throne:** i.e. immediately on his accession, cf. especially 1 Kg. 2:12; 2 Kg. 13:13. **a copy of this law:** the ungrammatical LXX rendering *to deuteronomion touto*, from which the title 'Deuteronomy' is derived, presupposes *mišnēh hattôrāh hazzeh*, 'this repetition (or copy) of the law', and clearly understands Deuteronomy not as an independent entity but in relation to other older collections of law. This understanding is implicit also in the rabbinic title of Deuteronomy as *mišnēh tôrāh*, a title which is of uncertain date (but certainly not contained in Deuteronomy itself) though evidently based on this verse. The rabbinic title sees Deuteronomy not simply as a copy of the law, but as an official and authorized exposition of the law (see the discussion in Weingreen, *From Bible*, 145ff.). This may indeed have been the way in which the deuteronomic law was originally understood, but that cannot be concluded from the present verse. The Hebrew here (and in Jos. 8:32) can mean only 'a copy (or duplicate) of this law', with reference to Deuteronomy as an independent entity, not to Deuteronomy as an official exposition of law in Exodus-Numbers; see also Introduction, p. 27 **from that which is in charge of:** the *NEB* 'at the dictation of' apparently presupposes *mippî* instead of *millipnēy*.

19. The word *tôrāh*, 'law', is feminine, and is the subject of the verse; the word translated **in it** is masculine and refers to the book containing the law. **and these statutes:** probably an addition to this deuteronomistic verse; the word 'statutes' never otherwise appears along with *tôrāh*, which is the comprehensive term for the law.

20. This verse follows well on v. 17 and explains why the king should not multiply his wealth. **and that he may not turn aside from the commandment, either to the right hand or to the left:** a late deuteronomistic addition; in the deuteronomic basis there is no reference to the law which the king is to obey. **commandment** is a comprehensive term used in late parts of the parenesis (see comment on 5:31), and **to the right hand or to the left** is likewise found in late sections (see comment on v. 11). **he and his children:** Galling, *op. cit.*, 137, and von Rad take this expression as an addition accommodating the law to dynastic kingship, and so of Judean origin. The presupposition of this, viz. that the royal law has an exclusive northern background in a charismatic understanding of the monarchy, is, however, doubtful; see above the introduction to this section.

(iv) *The Levitical priests* **18:1–8**

Three stages in the growth of the law on the dues of the priest may be distinguished. The oldest law is to be found in vv. 3f., detailing the priests' dues at the sanctuary. The deuteronomic legislator has taken up this law and applied it specifically to the Levitical priests (v. 1), emphasizing also that these priests at the central sanctuary shall have equal rights no matter what their individual private means may be (see comment on v. 8). This exhortation should be seen against the background of the right of any Levite from any part of the country to claim priestly status at the central sanctuary if he is really determined to do so (see comment on v. 6). The latest layer is related to the post-deuteronomistic section in 10:8f. (see comment on 10:6–9). Either both are post-deuteronomistic additions or in the present text there is deuteronomistic material which served as the source of the addition in 10:8f. To this layer belongs the reference to 'all the tribe of Levi' in v. 1, along with vv. 2, 5. It is concerned to emphasize how the whole tribe of Levi is set apart by Yahweh and has its livelihood from the offerings made to Yahweh.

The deuteronomic legislator preserves to some extent the position which always existed in Israel. The tribe of Levi had no share in the land of Palestine; but from very early days the Levites were closely associated with the priesthood, being particularly desirable as priests (cf. Jg. 17f.) and claiming priestly functions (cf. Dt. 33:8–11; 1 Sam. 2:27f.), even though it was never the case that all priests had been Levites. The deuteronomic legislator *recognizes* this Levitical claim to the priesthood; but in commending the Levites to the charity of their fellow-Israelites (12:18f.; 14:27, 29, etc.) he also recognizes that priestly status will not be the condition of most Levites, so that just as before (and so not just as a result of centralization) they will belong to the deprived elements of society.

The primary intention of the deuteronomic law is not to demand that every Levite should be allowed to minister at the central sanctuary (even though their right to do so is admitted), but to regulate what the priests' dues are to consist of and their fair distribution. In practice, then, the law is concerned with that very small minority of the tribe which would find employment at the central sanctuary. For the later priestly legislator (cf. Num. 3f.) this minority within the tribe is fixed and limited to the sons of Aaron; as priests, they are distinguished from the Levites to whom subordinate non-priestly duties are assigned. On the history see particularly Cody, *History*.

1. that is, all the tribe of Levi: it is argued by Wright, *VT* 4, 1954, 325ff., that the translation of the *AV*: 'and all the tribe of Levi', is preferable (and permissible on the understanding that asyndeton explains the omission of the conjunction in Hebrew), since otherwise **Levitical priests** and **all the tribe of Levi** are identified. This, according to Wright, is not possible since only a very small minority of the tribe could have been priests (there being only one legitimate altar in the deuteronomic view), while the vast majority, called by Deuteronomy simply 'the Levites', were non-priestly members of the tribe who had the function of teaching. The case is, however, not quite so straightforward. On the grammatical point, Emerton, *VT* 12, 1962, 133f., has noted that asyndeton is very rare in Hebrew, while apposition is very common; on Wright's view of the relationship between Levites and Levitical priests a conjunction is necessary here. Moreover, the simple use of 'Levite' in vv. 6f. (cf. also 27:9, 14) indicates that for Deuteronomy the term does not only refer to non-priestly members of the tribe. On the other hand, the deuteronomic legislator does, as 12:18, etc. indicate, use 'Levite' also with reference to non-priests. Through the use of the term 'Levitical priests', and particularly through vv. 6f., the deuteronomic legislator expresses his belief that all Levites have the right to function as priests; on the other hand, he does not use this terminology in order to distinguish between priestly and non-priestly Levites.

Vv. 1f. are certainly overfull; they have been expanded by a late editor (deuteronomistic or later) who wished to emphasize that the whole tribe of Levi was set apart and had no land inheritance with their fellow-tribes. This editor is responsible for **all the tribe of Levi** here (see the introduction to this section). **the offerings by fire:** for a thorough study of the word *'iśśeh*, cf. Hoftijzer, *VTS* 16, 1967, 114ff. It does not denote a particular form of sacrifice among others, since it is missing in the catalogue of sacrifices in Lev. 7:37f. It designates the edible parts of a sacrificial offering, which were sometimes burnt on the altar, but which also could be handed over to be eaten by the priests (cf. Lev. 2:3, 10; 6:10; 7:30, 35; 10:12f.; 24:7, 9). The translation **offerings by fire** depends on an etymological connection (which cannot be proved) between *'iśśeh* and *'ēś*, 'fire'; if such a connection exists it must, however, be concluded that the word has undergone great change in meaning in view of its application to offerings which clearly were not burnt. The translation 'gift' is better, not only in view of the Old Testament contexts but also in view of the contexts of use of the cognate Ugaritic term (for which cf. Fisher, *Ras Shamra Parallels* II, 152). **his rightful dues:** the RSV apparently means by this 'the offerings which are rightfully due to Yahweh'. However, the word *naḥᵃlāh* is not otherwise used in this sense. It means 'property' or 'inheritance' as the source of livelihood passed down within the family (cf. 4:20, 21). and then in a metaphorical way it is used to describe Yahweh (i.e the offerings made to Yahweh) as the source of livelihood of the Levites (cf. 10:9). It is undoubtedly in the latter sense that the term is used here, in which case the pronoun 'his' must refer to the tribe of Levi (see comment on next verse, where this pronoun is used), not to Yahweh. However, the word is then very awkward in the context, and so one should understand it as an addition by the late editor who is already responsible for 'all the tribe of Levi' in this verse, and also for the following verse; alternatively, it may be a marginal gloss on **the offerings by fire to the Lord,** which was subsequently erroneously incorporated into the verse. The *NEB* 'their patrimony', follows the LXX reading (which is scarcely original) of *naḥᵃlātām* for the *MT* *wᵉnaḥᵃlātô*.

2. The Hebrew here is in third person singular: 'He shall have

no inheritance among his brethren; the Lord is his inheritance as
he promised him'. The antecedent can be only the late addition
'all the tribe of Levi' in v. 1; consequently, all of v. 2 is also late.

3. In referring simply to the **priests** rather than the 'Levitical
priests', this verse may be a direct quotation by the deuteronomic
legislator of an older law. The age of the law is, however, uncertain.
1 Sam. 2:13f. indicates that in the time of Samuel the priests'
dues had not yet been fixed with the precision given here, while
Lev. 7:32–34, in prescribing even choicer parts of the sacrificial
animal for the priest, is later priestly legislation. **the priests' due:**
the word *mišpāṭ* has a wide variety of precise meanings: most
frequently 'judgment, justice' or 'ordinance'; also 'manner' or
'fashion' (cf. 2 Kg. 17:33); and, as here, 'custom', 'manner' or
'due'; cf. also 1 Sam. 2:13.

4. In distinction to the previous verse, the second person
singular form of address appears here. The verse cannot, however,
be separated from v. 3 as the reference to 'him' indicates. It should
be seen as an addition to that verse by the deuteronomic redactor
who is undoubtedly using older material. **first fruits:** the word is
rē'šīt which, in its second occurrence in the verse, is translated
simply **first.** For the translation 'best' cf. Smith, and Eissfeldt,
Erstlinge, 40. The word is synonymous with *ḥēleḇ*, 'choicest', 'best',
in Num. 18:12; and Exod. 34:26 refers to the *rē'šīt* of the first
fruits, clearly meaning the 'best'. **your grain ... your wine ...
your oil:** see comment on 7:13. The first or best of the fleece is
mentioned only here as due to the priest; the others occur also
in the priestly legislation in Num. 18:12.

5. The verse is clearly the source of, or from the same hand as,
the addition to the deuteronomistic work in 10:8. **to stand:** *Sam*
adds 'before the Lord your God' as in 10:8 (cf. also *NEB*) to
indicate that the sense is 'to stand in attendance on'. **him:** not
the priest of verses 3f., but 'all the tribe of Levi' in the addition to
v. 1. **minister in the name of the Lord:** this expression is
influenced by the deuteronomic v. 7. In 10:8 the phrase 'to
minister to him and to bless in his name' undoubtedly caused the
addition by *Sam* of 'and to bless' before 'in the name of the Lord' in
the present verse. **him and his sons:** this is probably an addition.
The verse is otherwise concerned with the tribe as a whole. The
addition was made in order to include the priests of verses 3f. in
the divine election; cf. Merendino, *op. cit.*, 188.

6. The work of the deuteronomic legislator is clearly recogniz-

able in the expression **all your towns** as well as in the centralization formula. Moreover, the general construction of this and the
following verses—a reference to a future historical situation, introduced by *ki*, 'when', 'if', followed by a commandment—is a
deuteronomic construction; see comment on 17:14. **where he
lives:** the verb is that from which the noun *gēr*, 'sojourner', 'alien'
is derived (see comment on 1:16). The Levite in early time was
considered a *gēr* since his tribe had no settlement area of its own
(cf. especially Jg. 17:7f.; 19:1). In the course of time, however,
the *gēr* came to be seen as a non-Israelite; this is the case in
Deuteronomy, cf. von Rad, *Gottesvolk*, 45f. Although the same verb
'to sojourn' is used of the Levite in the present verse as in Jg. 17:7f.;
19:1, it is clear from those passages where the Levite is mentioned
separately from the *gēr* (14:29; 16:11, 14; 26:11f.) that he is no
longer seen as belonging to that category. See the discussion in
Cody, *History*, 54ff., where it is concluded that while the Levite
is not a *gēr* in Deuteronomy, the view that he has that status is
not far below the surface. **he may come back when he desires:**
the intention is not to give any Levite complete and unquestioned
liberty to do as he wishes in this matter (so *RSV*), but rather to
discourage Levites from coming to claim priestly rights at the
central sanctuary unless it is their deepest longing to do so (cf.
NEB).

7. In the *RSV* the apodosis of the sentence begins with this
verse, whereas the *NEB* translation (cf. Driver) treats it as a
continuation of the protasis begun in v. 6; the apodosis then begins
in v. 8. The effect of the difference is that whereas the *RSV*
commands that any Levite who wishes to do so may minister
at the central sanctuary, the *NEB* states only that *if* a Levite
comes and *if* he ministers at the central sanctuary, then he shall
enjoy an equal share with the priests already there. Since the
context concerns the portions due to the Levitical priests, the *NEB*
translation is preferable. However, both translations at least
presuppose that any Levite may in fact claim priestly rights at
the central sanctuary. In both cases it must also be emphasized
that there exists no simple connection of this passage to 2 Kg.
23:9. It is widely thought that the latter passage represents one
aspect of Josiah's reform where it was found impossible to fulfil
the demands of the lawbook (i.e. Dt. 18:6f.). However, one should
probably distinguish between the priests of the high places in 2
Kg. 23:9 (which is probably part of the deuteronomistic redaction

of this chapter; see Introduction, p. 97 who would have been
considered contaminated from a cultic point of view and so unfit
for service at the central sanctuary, and the Levites of Dt. 18:6ff.,
of whom it is not said that they were formerly priests of the
country shrines (cf. Lindblom, *Erwägungen*, 30; Würthwein, *ZThK*
73, 1976, 417). Deuteronomy in fact has in mind simply Levites
who are not priests but who aspire to become priests.

**8. besides what he receives from the sale of his patri-
mony:** this presupposes a slight change in pointing, reading
mimmᵉkārāw instead of the *MT mimkārāw*, since **besides** is
properly a translation of *lᵉbad min* rather than *lᵉbad* alone. The
remainder is, however, very obscure. The *RSV* translation is
unlikely since the sale of the patrimony was not permitted.
Driver, *Syria* 33, 1956, 77f., argues that the Hebrew phrase
corresponds to the Babylonian *makkūr bît abim*, 'property derived
by inheritance'; and Airoldi, *BZ* 18, 1974, 99f., points to Num.
20:19; Prov. 31:10 and Neh. 13:16, in support of the translation
'goods' for the plural of *meker* which, with the repointing given
above, appears here. The expression *ʿal hāʾābôt* remains obscure,
but there is probably here a reference to family inheritance; if
so, the *NEB* translation 'besides what he may inherit from his
father's family', should be followed. The verse then affirms that
the Levites at the central sanctuary should all be treated equally
with regard to the priestly rights and dues, and that no account
should be taken of inherited property which each individual
Levite may bring with him.

(v) *The prophet* 18:9–22

Several stages in the growth of the law on the prophet may be
distinguished. The oldest part is to be found in vv. 10–12a,
prohibiting all forms of divination as an abomination to Yahweh.
This has been edited by the deuteronomic legislator in vv. 9, 12b.
Vv. 15–18, for which v. 14 is a connecting transitional link, form
a late addition to the law. It points to Israel's legitimate source
of knowledge, prophecy, and validates the succession of Israel's
prophets by tracing their continuity from Moses. Moses is here
understood not as the archetypal prophet but as the measure or
standard by which the validity of the prophetic word may be
judged (see comment on v. 15). The section has links with the
deuteronomistic presentation of the Horeb event (5:23ff.; 9:9ff.),
but the differences between the two indicate that the present

passage is a secondary interpretation of, and therefore later than, the deuteronomistic presentation (see comment on v. 16). In its view of the prophets as 'raised up' by Yahweh, the section also closely resembles the deuteronomistic presentation of the judge (cf. Jg. 2:18). The final stage consists of vv. 19–22 in which the question of distinguishing false from true prophecy is treated. The section has some contact with the late 17:12–13 in its harsh demand for obedience, and with the deuteronomistic history in Kings in its understanding of the function of prophecy (see comment on vv. 21, 22). V. 13 is an isolated later addition to the section.

9. On the deuteronomic structure of this verse see comment on 17:14.

10. burns his son or his daughter as an offering: the Hebrew is 'makes his son or his daughter pass through the fire'. Interpreted as a reference to child sacrifice the phrase is quite out of place here, for the context is solely concerned with forms of divination. It is probably a simple addition, caused by the use of the term **abominable practices,** for it is this which describes the burning of children in 12:31. Driver's suggestion that the rite was a kind of ordeal in which an omen was derived from observing whether or not a child passed through the fire remained unharmed, is an attempt to fit the reference into the context of divination, but has in fact no support in any reference to the practice in the Old Testament. The following terms (for which cf. especially Seitz, *op. cit.*, 236 n.460; Smith), referring to various types of divination, were distinct originally, but by the time of the deuteronomic legislator may well have been synonymous. They are all brought together simply to emphasize the absolute exclusion of all forms of divination. **practice divination:** reference is sometimes made to Ezek. 21:21 in order to show that this refers to the practice of shaking arrows in a quiver and deciding the answer to a question by the first arrow drawn out (cf. Buis-Leclercq, Thompson). However, even there 'divination' is probably a general designation for the different methods mentioned. So here it is a summary designation (it is the only one of the series not separated by the conjunction from the one which follows). It is mentioned as a prophetic activity in Mic. 3:11. **soothsayer:** two Arabic roots have possible connections with this word: one, meaning 'to appear', suggests a practitioner of a form of magic for the noun here; the other, meaning 'to speak

through the nose', suggests one who divines from noises or prac-
tises incantations. **augur:** Gen. 44:5 suggests that the reference
here is to a form of divination involving the reading of dregs in
a cup or perhaps the observation of reflections on the water in a
cup. **sorcerer:** the precise meaning is uncertain. The Akkadian
cognate, *kišpu*, is apparently a general term for magic.

11. **charmer:** one who binds through casting a spell. **medium
. . . wizard:** the Hebrew is 'he who consults a *'ôḇ* or a *yiddeᶜōnî*';
the two terms are frequently found together, cf. Lev. 19:31; 20:6,
27; 1 Sam. 28:3, 9; 2 Kg. 21:6; 23:24; Isa. 8:19; 19:3. In neither
case is the precise meaning absolutely clear. Eichrodt, *Theology* II,
215, suggests a connection of the word *'ôḇ* with the Arabic root
'wb, 'to return', and translates 'revenant'; so here, 'one who
consults a revenant'. Then *yiddeᶜōnî*, 'knowing one', would here
refer to the spirit as that which possesses hidden knowledge (cf.
also *NEB* 'ghosts and spirits'). Yet 1 Sam. 28:3 indicates that
the words may on their own refer to those who consult revenants
and spirits as well as to the revenants and spirits themselves.
necromancer: he who consults the dead. This is a summary
designation, and Isa. 8:19 indicates that it includes the previous
two terms. It is intended to include every other type of activity
similar to but not covered by the previous two terms.

12. **an abomination to the Lord:** see comment on 7:25; 17:1.
That all the laws to which this phrase is attached originally
belonged together as a single collection (16:21ff.; 18:10ff.; 22:5;
23:17f.; 24:4; 25:13ff.; cf. L'Hour, *RB* 71, 1964, 481ff.) is very
doubtful. As with the phrase 'so you shall purge the evil from the
midst of you' (see comment on 13:5), it is more likely that there
is secondary application of the phrase by the deuteronomic
legislator to laws where it did not originally belong. In the present
context the absence of the appositional 'your God' after **the Lord**
indicates a pre-deuteronomic usage, whereas the combination of
the two (7:25; 17:1; 22:5; 23:18; 25:16) indicates deuteronomic
authorship (on this stylistic characteristic of deuteronomic authorship, cf. Driver, lxxixf.). See also the discussion in Seitz, *op. cit.*,
185ff. V. 12*b* (**and because of these. . .**) has close connections
with the deuteronomic parenesis in 9:1, 4f. So vv. 9, 12*b* function
as a deuteronomic framework taking up older material in vv. 10–
12*a*.

13. **blameless:** *tāmîm* denotes a man without moral blemish.
Apart from the present verse and Ps. 18:23, 25, the word is used

of men only in P (Gen. 6:9; 17:1). In general it is a favourite
term of P and Ezekiel. Since also the verse has a summary character with no particular connection to what precedes or what follows,
it may be a late addition.

14. That this verse is of deuteronomic authorship and connected immediately to v. 12*b* (cf. Seitz, *op. cit.*, 240) is uncertain. V. 12*b* completes the preceding section, while v. 14 takes up
the end of that section in order to introduce a new theme. The
contrast between the nations and Israel in this verse provides a
transition to the new section on the prophet in vv. 15ff.

15. will raise up: Steuernagel has shown that the verb here,
and in v. 18, is to be understood in a distributive sense (i.e. will
raise up from time to time), and does not refer to a single future
act. However, this does not necessarily mean that the passage
should be interpreted with reference to an institutional 'office',
as Kraus, *Verkündigung*, 14ff., has proposed. There is no indication
of the existence of a prophetic office of covenant mediator,
through which the law would have been proclaimed to Israel in
her covenant cult. The verse is rather a general reflection on the
history and significance of prophecy in Israel, in which the prophets
are understood in relation to Moses and legitimated through connection of their proclamation with the law that was given through
him; cf. Perlitt, *EvTh* 31, 1971, 588ff.; Clements, *Prophecy*, 11ff.

16. The appeal to the events at Horeb does not establish any
unity of authorship with any part of that narrative. There are
important differences between these verses and 5:23ff.; 9:9ff.,
which preclude such unity of authorship. In particular, while
5:23ff.; 9:9ff. understand the appointment of Moses as mediator
between God and people as a unique event, here the request of
the people on that occasion is interpreted as having reference to a
series of successors to Moses in the future.

17. Cf. 5:28.

18. The divine answer to the people's request in 5:31 is differently formulated since there Moses is understood as the unique
mediator and so the recipient of 'all the commandment and the
statutes and the ordinances'. The messianic interpretation of this
promise, referring it to a single individual, arose in later Judaism,
and was the accepted interpretation in New Testament times, cf.
Jn. 1:21, 45; 6:14; 7:40; Ac. 3:20ff.; 7:37, etc.

19. The verse, beginning with *weḥāyāh*, 'and it shall come to
pass', is the start of a new section dealing with the problem of

false prophecy and how it is to be recognized. **I will require it of him:** for the use of this phrase with reference to divine punishment, cf. Gen. 9:5; Ezek. 33:6; 34:10.

20. The prophet who entices to apostasy is to be put to death, according to 13:1ff. Here the concern is with the prophet who falsely and deliberately claims that what he says is the word of Yahweh or the prophet who speaks what he claims is the word of other gods. On false prophecy, cf. Jer. 23:9–32, where both types are mentioned (vv. 13, 21), and Ezek. 13.

21, 22. The criterion for distinguishing true from false prophecy which is expressed here reveals an understanding of the nature and function of prophecy similar to that of the deuteronomist, especially in the books of Kings: the task of the prophet is to declare in advance what is to happen; the true prophetic word has within it the seeds of its own fulfilment, and consequently the legitimacy of the prophet will be demonstrated by the fulfilment of what he has predicted. See the study by von Rad, *Problem*, 205ff.; and McCurley, in *Light*, 305f. **presumptuously:** the only other occurrence of the term in Deuteronomy is in 17:12, part of a late addition to the law on the central tribunal; the verb is used in v. 20 and in 1:43.

(D) LAWS ON CAPITAL CASES AND ON WAR: **19:1–21:9**
The first and last sections of this collection, in 19:1–13 (on the cities of refuge) and 21:1–9 (on the unsolved murder), hold the whole together. They are both concerned with judicial cases of murder or manslaughter and, as the common elements in 19:13 and 21:9 indicate, they have both been edited in the same way by the deuteronomic legislator. However, the relation of the remainder of the collection to these laws is less clear. The law on false witness in 19:15–21 probably originally concerned false witness in a capital crime, and its deuteronomic editing in v. 19 provides a further link with the laws on cities of refuge and unsolved murder. V. 14, however, on the removal of the neighbour's landmark, in spite of the various proposals which have been made to account for its position, stands in remarkable isolation.

The war laws in ch. 20 are likewise only loosely related to their context. They interrupt the clear connection of ch. 19 and 21:1–9, and indeed it is sometimes proposed (e.g. by Driver) that ch. 20 originally followed 21:9. However, while its content certainly connects the chapter with the laws of 21:10ff., the present order is the original deuteronomic one. It seems to have come about because the deuteronomic legislator in his introduction of the subject of ch. 19 referred to a holy war situation, that of Yahweh's cutting off the nations in the course of Israel's settlement. Moreover, a connection of the war laws to the beginning of the law of 21:1–9 was also suggested by the phrase 'slain, lying in the open country' in 21:1, for this phrase uses the words *ḥālāl* and *nōp̄ēl*, two words frequently found together in texts dealing with war (cf. Jg. 9:40; 1 Sam. 31:1; Jer. 51:47, 49, etc.).

(i) The cities of refuge 19:1–13

The deuteronomic law on the cities of refuge (a description which is not used in Deuteronomy but which occurs in Num. 35:6, 11) appears in the direct form of address in vv. 1–3, 7, 13. This acts as a framework to the pre-deuteronomic law on this subject which still preserves its impersonal, casuistic formulation in vv. 4f., 11f. The law received post-deuteronomic supplements in v. 6, which supplements the older law in the light of v. 3, and in vv. 8ff., permitting the establishment of further cities of refuge in the event of Israel's territory being enlarged. The latter must be dated earlier than 4:41–43 since otherwise that passage could not have been ignored here; it is most unlikely that the three cities of refuge in vv. 8f. are tacitly intended as additional to those mentioned in ch. 4. On the relationship, see also comment on 4:41–43.

It has often been supposed that the law on the cities of refuge originated as a result of the abolition of the local sanctuaries following the deuteronomic law of centralization of worship (cf. e.g. Bertholet). For a number of reasons, however, this is unlikely. Firstly, there is no indication in the law of ch. 19 that this is the case. The sanctuary was always understood to be a place of asylum (cf. Exod. 21:12–14), and this notion was carried over also to the central sanctuary (cf. 1 Kg. 1:50f.; 2:28ff.; Neh. 6:11), but there is no indication that it was the loss of the local sanctuaries which resulted in the establishment of the cities of refuge (see also comment on v. 6). Secondly, it is clear from the form of presentation of the law that the deuteronomic legislator has taken up an older law on this subject (see comment on vv. 4, 11). Thirdly, Hos. 6:8f. is best understood as an allusion to Gilead and Shechem as cities of refuge; it is precisely their status as such cities which is being ignored. Finally, it would have been impossible for a law presenting the elders as exercising judicial functions (as here in v. 12) to have originated as a deuteronomic law. For the deuteronomic legislator justice is administered by professional judges (cf. 16:18ff.). If these go back to the judicial reform of Jehoshaphat (see introduction to 16:18–17:7), then the law on the cities of refuge must be earlier than this.

It is best to see the law on cities of refuge as being of high antiquity. It is not explicable as a monarchic innovation, for the latter would have relied on centralized judicial authority to enforce the aims for which the cities of refuge were established, viz. to provide the means for ensuring a fair trial for the manslayer who claimed he had acted unintentionally. The law is rather an inevitable development of the provision of asylum at the local sanctuary, for the latter could offer only temporary protection rather than the more lasting refuge which a manslayer would have required; cf. Greenberg, *JBL* 78, 1959, 125ff. If this is the case then the institution of asylum at the local sanctuary and the institution of the cities of refuge may be seen as two parallel and connected institutions. The abolition of the local sanctuaries would have entailed a certain secularizing of the institution but it is not only to these circumstances that the origin of the cities of refuge is to be traced. On the other hand, it is not so clear that the provision of three or six such cities is so old. It presupposes a certain degree of centralized organization, since it works on a regional rather than a tribal basis, and may be the result of a certain systematizing of the institution in the course of the monarchic period.

1. For the clear deuteronomic pattern of this introduction to the law see comment on 12:29; 17:14.

2. The deuteronomic law in direct second person singular form of address appears in v. 2 and again in v. 7, so acting as a framework to the older law.

3. You shall prepare the roads: the *RSV* apparently understands the Hebrew to mean that roads affording quick and easy access to the cities of asylum should be established. Steuernagel is perhaps too sensitive in objecting that this means that equally easy access would then also be provided for the 'avenger of blood'. Nevertheless, the context does seem rather to suggest the notion of the even distribution of the cities throughout the land, so that the sense here would be that of measuring the distances and determining precisely where each city should be located, rather than marking out the roads (cf. also *NEB*). **the area of the land:** for *geḇûl* in the sense of 'area' or 'territory' see comment on 2:18; 3:16. **manslayer:** the word is the active participle of the verb used in the sixth commandment of the decalogue, and translated 'kill' by the *RSV*; see comment on 5:17.

4. Vv. 4f. preserve an impersonal, casuistic style which is quite distinct from the direct apodictic style of the context. The corresponding asylum law in Jos. 20 is also impersonal and casuistic, and has many other contacts with Dt. 19:4f. indicating a common tradition (cf. Seitz, *op. cit.*, 111ff.). It is in these verses that the original law on cities of refuge may be found. Yet the verses have been secondarily elaborated. This has taken place primarily through the addition of the description of a typical case of un-intentional manslaughter, but also through the addition of the awkward first relative clause in v. 4, which anticipates the end of v. 5. The pre-deuteronomic law would have read: 'This is the provision (the same introduction as that given in the pre-deuter-onomic 15:2) for the manslayer: if anyone kills his neighbour (the deuteronomic legislator uses the term *'āḥ*, brother; see comment on 15:2) unintentionally without having been at enmity with him in time past, he may flee to one of these cities and save his life.'

5. Instead of describing a case the corresponding law of Jos. 20:4f. prescribes that the manslayer is to state his case to the elders of the city of refuge, who will then admit him. **the head slips from the handle:** *NEB* 'the head glances off the tree'; *'ēṣ* can mean both 'tree', as in the previous clause, and also a piece of wood.

6. avenger of blood: Hebrew *gō'ēl haddām*. This is usually taken to refer to the next-of-kin of the slain man who has the duty of avenging his kinsman by killing the one responsible. The situation is therefore understood to be one involving the wide-spread custom of blood revenge, in which the individuals within the kinship group are responsible for one another's lives; if one is killed then the members of his kinship group must avenge his death on the killer or on some other member of the killer's kinship group. So the *NEB* translation 'the dead man's next-of-kin who had the duty of vengeance'. It is, however, argued strongly by Phillips, *Law*, 102ff., that this distorts the true picture. While the term *gō'ēl* does designate the kinsman responsible for the protec-tion of his relative, it is only in the context of killing that the term is qualified through the addition of another word. This in itself indicates that the *gōʾēl haddām* is someone different from the individual otherwise known simply as the *gōʾēl*. Furthermore, it is only in connection with the cities of refuge (except for the case of 2 Sam. 14:4ff., where, however, since it is a case of a murder within a family, there can anyway be no question of a blood revenge situation arising) that the term *gōʾēl haddām* is used. Phillips takes the term as the title of an official. It may be translated 'the protector of blood', and it designates the official appointed by the elders of a killer's city to recover the killer from the city of refuge and execute him. The official would be despatched only after the elders had decided that the case was one of murder, not of involuntary manslaughter. **in hot anger:** this suits the context of blood revenge, but not that of the action of an official as described above. However, the phrase may denote eagerness (cf. Ps. 39:3), and here refer to the zeal with which the official carries out his duties. **because the way is long:** 14:24 suggests that this phrase should be taken to refer to the central sanctuary; however, there is otherwise no allusion to the central sanctuary in this section. The phrase may, therefore, be intended to reinforce the earlier command to establish cities of refuge evenly throughout the land, ensuring that they are accessible to everyone. This interpretation is perhaps supported by the fact that compared with Jos. 20:5 this verse is quite elaborate, having been secondarily extended through additions apparently derived from earlier parts of the law. So, lack of previous enmity is referred to again as in v. 4, and the reference to the way is then probably derived from v. 3. If this is so, then v. 6 presupposes v. 3, though its authorship and time of origin are otherwise unclear.

8–10. These verses are a post-deuteronomic addition. The expressions and ideas are those of deuteronomistic passages in Deuteronomy. That the land is given to the fathers rather than simply promised to them, is found only in the late 1:8; 11:9, 21; 30:20. Possession of the whole land on condition of obedience to the law appears in the late 11:22f.

10. Although it is not stated that the shedding of innocent blood will lead to loss of the land, the general context in which the warning against shedding innocent blood is put is that of possession of the land. This connection may be paralleled by reference to Gen. 4 where Cain's shedding of the blood of Abel leads to Cain's sentence to be a wanderer and a fugitive. **the guilt of**

bloodshed: the same word, *dāmîm*, means bloodshed and also the guilt which the shedding of blood brings with it. For the latter, cf. also Exod. 22:2; 2 Sam. 21:1; Ps. 51:14.

11. Vv. 11f. correspond to vv. 4f. in having an impersonal formulation and being in casuistic style. They are the counterpart of vv. 4f., describing the case of intentional homicide in relation to the cities of refuge and are probably part of the pre-deuteronomic law; cf. Seitz, *op. cit.*, 111ff.

12. and hand him over: better 'and they shall hand him over', for, following the view outlined above (see comment on v. 6), the subject of the verb is not the elders of the killer's city but the elders of the city of refuge to which the killer fled. **so that he may die:** cf. Exod. 21:14. This is not the exercise of blood revenge, but judicial execution for murder, carried out by the community through its representative, the *gō'ēl haddām*.

13. This is the deuteronomic conclusion to the law on the cities of refuge, using expressions which have already appeared in 13:5, 8. The motive clause **so that it may be well with you** is probably a late deuteronomistic supplement to this; cf. 4:40.

(ii) Theft of land and false witness **19:14-21**
The place of v. 14 continues to defy adequate explanation. It has a connection with the preceding law in referring to the *rē'a*, 'neighbour' (cf. vv. 4, 11), rather than the *'āḥ*, 'brother'. It may be connected to the following as a capital crime, the removal of the landmark being understood as an attack on the owner's life since it is on his land and its produce that his life depends, and vv. 16ff. may be interpreted as an accusation of a capital crime (see comment on v. 16). We may explain it against the background of the connection of the whole chapter with the curses of Dt. 27 (Merendino, *op. cit.*, 218), since the latter chapter, in v. 25, curses the one who takes a bribe to slay the innocent. This corresponds to the concerns of 19:15-21, and in 27:24 there is a curse upon the one who slays his neighbour in secret, corresponding to vv. 1-13 of the present chapter whilst 27:17 curses the one who removes his neighbour's landmark. Or, we may interpret the verse in the sense of stealing, and refer to the decalogue order of murder, theft, and false witness to explain the order of the laws in this chapter. None of these explanations, however, is free of objection and adequate in itself. At any rate, the law is an ancient one, here taken up by the deuteronomic legislator.

The original law in vv. 15-21 is preserved in the impersonal, casuistic form of vv. 16ff. It probably concerned a witness to a capital crime (see comment on v. 16), in which judgment was given by divine decision, the local elders having failed to resolve the issue. An attempt has been made to bring the law into line with deuteronomic law on judicial procedure (17:8ff.) through the addition of reference to the priests and judges in vv. 17f., and through the addition of v. 15 taken from 17:6. That this is deuteronomic editing is not certain, however, since the correspondence is not complete. The law in 17:8ff. refers to the Levitical priests and the judge, rather than priests and judges. The hand of the deuteronomic legislator is, however, clear in vv. 19-21a, where phrases from earlier deuteronomic passages appear. Finally, the *lex talionis* in v. 21b was added here as an isolated addition, as also in its other occurrences in the Pentateuch.

14. men of old: or 'forefathers'; cf. Lev. 26:45. The reference is of course to the remote Israelite ancestors of the present possessors of the land. The prohibition is concerned with what was evidently a longstanding and widespread problem, that of the fraudulent acquisition of land; it is alluded to in Dt. 27:17; Hos. 5:10; Isa. 5:8; Job 24:2; Prov. 23:10, and a form almost identical to the prohibition here appears in Prov. 22:28. Outside the Old Testament the problem is given extensive treatment in the sixth chapter of the Instruction of Amen-em-opet, cf. *ANET*, 422. There too the removal of the landmark is understood as a violation of the divine order. In the present context, the language used indicates that deuteronomic editing is responsible for the clause **In the inheritance ... gives you to possess.** It would not, however, have been only as a result of the work of the deuteronomic legislator that the law received a sacral basis in Israel; the land was always understood as the gift of Yahweh, and so the misuse of it was a violation of the sacral order.

15. The verse does not harmonize with the law of vv. 16ff. either in form or in content: it is apodictic while vv. 16ff. are casuistic; it demands two witnesses for all cases whereas vv. 16ff. deal with a case involving only one witness. So the verse is an addition. **for any crime or for any wrong:** the words 'āwōn and ḥaṭṭā't occur only here in the law corpus, but are found in 5:9; 9:18, 21, 27. The source of the addition is 17:6, and its purpose is apparently to make a general principle applicable to all cases from a rule which in the source applied only to capital crimes.

16. malicious witness: also in Exod. 23:1; Ps. 35:11. Literally 'a witness of violence'; this refers, however, not to someone who witnesses violence, but rather to someone who by his witness promotes violence, in the form of the execution of an innocent person, cf. Phillips, *Law*, 144f. **to accuse him:** on the technical use of *ʿānāh* see comment on 5:20. **wrongdoing:** except for the doubtful case of Isa. 59:13, there is no example of *sārāh* having the general sense of 'wrongdoing', whereas it is used of apostasy in Dt. 13:6; Isa. 1:5; 31:6; Jer. 28:16; 29:32. Apostasy was a capital crime.

17. before the priests and the judges who are in office in those days: this is a later addition, attempting to bring the old law, which provided that the case should be submitted to divine judgment, into line with the deuteronomic legislation on the central court (see comment on 17:9). See the discussions in L'Hour, *Bib* 44, 1963, 18 n.1; Seitz, *op. cit.*, 114f. The original law, then, provided that the case should come only **before the Lord,** i.e. that it should be tried at the sanctuary, perhaps by means of an oath or trial by ordeal.

18. V. 18*a*, **the judges shall inquire diligently,** is an addition to the original law which came in with the reference to the priests and judges in v. 17. The last part of the verse, **and has accused his brother falsely,** is also a late addition. It is superfluous, it uses the deuteronomic term *'āḥ*, 'brother', and is clearly directly based on the ninth commandment of the decalogue (in its Exodus form); see comment on 5:20.

19. The use of the direct second person form of address in this verse, together with *'āḥ*, 'brother', and the same concluding formula as that found in 13:5 (cf. also 19:13), clearly indicate deuteronomic work in this passage. Yet the pre-deuteronomic law must have had some conclusion, and the demand in this verse is closely paralleled in extra-biblical laws for the case of false witness (cf. the Code of Hammurabi, *ANET*, 166, paras. 1–4). It is likely, therefore, that the present verse is simply a deuteronomic version of a similar conclusion to the old law which would have had an impersonal form.

20. The language of this verse is that of the deuteronomic parenesis in 13:11.

21. Your eye shall not pity: a deuteronomic phrase, cf. 7:16; 13:8. The rest of the verse constitutes the *lex talionis*, which appears on two other occasions in the Old Testament (Exod.

21:23–25; Lev. 24:18–20). It is a quotation in all three passages with no essential connection with its context. There are some differences among its occurrences, in that it has a fuller form in the Exodus and a slightly different form in the Leviticus passages. The example here is probably the original, the Exodus version being a simple extension of it and the Leviticus version being a broken example. The law probably has a nomadic background; and, as Daube, *Studies*, 120ff., suggests, the idea behind it is that of restoration: a wrong committed by one person on another upsets the balance in the relationship between them; it is in order to restore this balance that the law operates. The principle embodied in the law is reflected in certain provisions of the Code of Hammurabi (*ANET*, 175f., paras. 196, 197, 200, 210, 230) and the Middle Assyrian Laws (*ANET*, 184f., paras. 50, 52). See the discussions in Phillips, *Law*, 96ff., and Wagner, *Rechtssätze*, 3ff.

(iii) Preparation for holy war **20:1–9**
The deuteronomic law on the holy war is in this section concerned with those who are to be exempted from service. In formulating his law the deuteronomic legislator made use of a series of three ancient regulations which exempted those who had just built a house, planted a vineyard, or married a wife. According to primitive belief throughout the Semitic world such persons were taboo and particularly subject to demonic influences, and it is in order to ward off such influences from the army that they are excluded from service (for the parallel religio-historical material, cf. Schwally, *Krieg*, 75ff.; and for Ugarit in particular, cf. Herrmann, *ZAW* 70, 1958, 215ff.). These demonic ideas do not appear in Deuteronomy, however, where it is rather out of a humanitarian concern that the regulations are now applied. There may be here also ideas of keeping property within the family and of ensuring that a family is not brought to an end through the husband being killed in battle and leaving no posterity (cf. Bertholet); but the primary emphasis is on the individual himself, and his right to enjoy the blessings of Yahweh. It is a man's inability to enjoy precisely these blessings which is reckoned as a curse in 28:30.

V. 8 adds a criterion for exemption which is rooted in Israelite tradition in particular rather than in Semitic belief generally. It was probably brought in here by the deuteronomic legislator (see comment). On the other hand, vv. 2–4 are a later addition (see comment on v. 2), which is probably due to the same late

deuteronomistic hand as that which also introduced the reference
to priests in 21:5. The section presupposes and builds on the
deuteronomic parenesis in 7:17ff.; 9:1ff. in a manner similar to
that of the second deuteronomist in the earlier chapters.

1. an army: the word used is *ʿam*, usually translated 'people'.
The army here envisaged is an army of the people rather than a
professional army distinct from the people. This is fundamental to
the deuteronomic understanding of Israel's wars with her enemies.
The Israelite army too is Israel the people of Yahweh, defending
itself under the leadership of Yahweh and opposing her enemies
with the help of Yahweh. Von Rad, *Krieg*, describes this as a holy
war, which he believes to have been a cultic institution of the
early period of Israel's history. However, there was no fixed
pattern to Israel's wars as they were actually practised, and von
Rad has to think in terms of the holy war ideal which never came
completely to appearance historically. But in fact it seems best to
see the whole theology of the holy war as a deuteronomic creation;
it is first now that a pattern comes to dominate the accounts of
Israel's wars, so that the holy war is more a matter of an interpretation of past events and a schematization of accounts of them
than an actual method of waging war. The deuteronomic
theology is built on various ancient traditions and ideas, such as
the traditions of Yahweh's leadership in war and regulations such
as those in vv. 5-7 relating to those exempt from military service.
However, it is as a result of the systematizing of Deuteronomy
that these traditional ideas have first been brought together into
a holy war ideology. See now the studies by Stolz, *Kriege*; and
Jones, *VT* 25, 1975, 642ff. **who brought you up:** the verb *ʿālāh*
in the Hiphil is used here; otherwise Deuteronomy uses the Hiphil
of *yāṣāʾ* in this phrase. Although the differences between the two
are slight, they do seem to have belonged to two different traditional contexts originally. The latter refers strictly only to the
leading out of slavery in Egypt, whereas the former, used here,
belongs in holy war contexts and includes the notion of leading
into the land (see also 1:28); cf. Wijngaards, *VT* 15, 1965, 91ff.

2. Beginning with *wᵉhāyāh*, 'and it shall come to pass', this verse
opens a new section (see comment on 18:19). This continues to
v. 4 and constitutes a late post-deuteronomic intrusion into the
text. It is in the second person plural form of address, whereas
the context is singular; it introduces the priest who otherwise
makes no contribution to the proceedings; it is in fact clearly out

of place anyway, for in being addressed to an army about to go into battle it presupposes that the exemption procedure, referred to in vv. 5ff., has already been carried through. The section is a summary of the war speeches in 7:16ff.; 9:1ff.; and 31:3ff. See von Rad and Seitz, *op. cit.*, 158.

3. do not fear ... or be in dread: cf. 1:29; 3:22; 7:21, etc.

5. This verse follows directly on v. 1, but whereas the latter is the deuteronomic introduction to the law it is in this and the next two verses that the deuteronomic legislator quotes old material. **officers:** see comment on 1:15. There is no other reference in the Old Testament to the dedication of a private house (cf. 1 Kg. 8:63 of the Jerusalem temple), so nothing is known of the rituals which it may have involved.

6. enjoyed its fruit: the Hebrew means strictly 'profaned it'. The first produce of the vineyard was sacred and could not be used by the owner. Only the second harvest could be 'profaned' by being put to ordinary, common use; cf. Jer. 31:5 and the law of Lev. 19:23-25.

7. According to 24:5 a newly married man was exempt for a year.

8. The new introduction shows that the criterion of exemption advanced here is an addition to the previous ones. That it is the deuteronomic legislator who made the addition is not certain, but likely in view of the use of the term 'brothers' (*RSV* **fellows**). Although additional here, the criterion does, however, feature in Israelite tradition (the story of Gideon in Jg. 7:3), and it was undoubtedly because of its appearance there that it was added here. Buis notes that besides the religious motive for the addition (fear reveals a lack of faith), there is a good psychological reason: nobody would declare himself to be afraid, and so all are obliged to prove how courageous they are.

9. commanders: i.e. the commanders of thousands, hundreds, etc. (see comment on 1:15). However, the expression *śārê ṣeḇā'ôt* used here is unusual, appearing also in 1 Kg. 2:5; 1 Chr. 27:3.

(iv) The conduct of war **20:10-20**

The deuteronomic law on war continues in the same style as before: introduced by *kî*, 'when', and formulated in the second person singular form of address. It falls into two major parts: the first in vv. 10-17 is concerned with the attitude to be adopted by Israel to the cities she attacks, and the second in vv. 19-20 is concerned specifically with prohibiting undue devastation of the country. In the first part there are two subsidiary sections, in only one of which is it likely that traditional material is taken up by the deuteronomic legislator. In vv. 10–14 Israel is commanded to offer terms of peace to a besieged city; if they are accepted the inhabitants of the city are to be put to forced labour; but if they are rejected then the male population of the city must be slaughtered, the women, children and property being taken as spoil. This represents a form of warfare widely practised in the ancient Near East (cf. Stolz, *Kriege*, 27), and is known also from Old Testament records (see comment on vv. 10, 13). But while it characterized also Israel's attitude to her Canaanite enemies in the land (cf. Jg. 1:27ff., and comment on v. 11) and thus had a firm place in Israel's tradition, it did not agree with the deuteronomic ideal already expressed in 7:1ff. Therefore, the deuteronomic legislator has restricted this form of warfare to Israel's treatment of cities outside her borders; to those cities within her borders, however, she must show no mercy. Only complete extermination will free her of the danger to faith which these cities pose.

The whole of this law is, however, in deuteronomic formulation, so that it is only on the basis of what may be concluded on forms of war from other sources that it is possible to see older tradition behind vv. 10–14, which the deuteronomic legislator has modified through vv. 15–17. V. 18 is an addition in second person plural form of address, giving the reason for the measures demanded in vv. 15–17. The deuteronomic law takes up again in vv. 19–20, where, however, there is probably no pre-deuteronomic basis (see comment on v. 19).

10. On the deuteronomic opening of the law see also v. 1 and comment on 12:29; 17:14. **a city:** no distinction exists here between cities in the land and cities outside the land. **offer terms of peace to it:** such dealings are alluded to in Jos. 10:1, 4; 11:19; 2 Sam. 10:19; see also the negotiations described in 2 Kg. 18:19ff.

11. forced labour: the Hebrew word *mas* is not an abstract concept, but a collective noun denoting those people conscripted for forced labour. There are twenty-three occurrences of it in the Old Testament, four of which are in Jg. 1:27–36. There it is referred to the Canaanites within the territory occupied by Israel whom the Israelites reduced to forced labour. This probably alludes to the situation which came about under David, for it was then that the Canaanite enclaves mentioned in the passage came under Israelite control. David, moreover, is said to have had a superintendent of the *mas* among his officials (2 Sam. 20:24). Solomon extended this institution to include Israelites themselves, though apparently in their case it was a temporary measure, perhaps related to the building of the temple, while the permanent state of servitude was reserved for non-Israelites. See the comprehensive philological and historical review by Mettinger, *Officials*, 128ff.

13. gives it into your hand: this is a common deuteronomic and deuteronomistic expression in this context, cf. e.g. 3:3; 7:24. That only the males should be killed but everything else taken as spoil is but one variation in the conduct of Israel's wars. See also Jos. 8:25-27; 11:11, 14; 1 Sam. 15:8f., for different variations, and the comment on 2:34. The deuteronomic legislator in particular emphasizes the necessity for total extermination and destruction of the enemy and all that belonged to them; cf. 13:15ff. It is only from the time of the deuteronomic legislator that a definite pattern in a theory of the conduct of war begins to emerge.

15. Only now is a distinction made between cities of enemies outside the land and cities of enemies within the land. By this means a transition is made to the deuteronomic law of vv. 16f. Blenkinsopp, *CBQ* 28, 1966, 207ff., points out that this deuteronomic distinction between distant cities and cities of the land is basic to the present form of the story of the Gibeonite covenant in Jos. 9. He argues, however, that this account originally told simply of a covenant with the Gibeonites without being unfavourable towards them, and that it is as a result of 'proto-deuteronomic' editing that the account has been transformed into an anti-Gibeonite story of how the Gibeonites succeeded only by underhand means in making this covenant, in the course of which the deuteronomic laws for the holy war were violated.

16. that breathes: the same expression appears in Jos. 10:40; 11:11, 14; 1 Kg. 15:29 and Ps. 150:6. Although the word *nešāmāh* is chiefly used of the breath of life in man (only Gen. 7:22 uses it of animals), and although Jos. 11:14 seems to use the expression of human beings only and not of animals, the *NEB* is undoubtedly correct in translating 'any creature' in the present context. Explicit reference is made to the peoples only, but since the context is one of sharp contrast with Israel's attitude to those cities from which she may take spoil, it is clear that the intention here is one of the utter and complete destruction of the enemy.

17. utterly destroy: see comment on 2:34. The list of peoples seems to have been secondarily added here in apposition to the object **them.** For the peoples mentioned see comment on 7:1. There, however, the Girgashites are also included, which is undoubtedly the reason for the addition of them here too by LXX and *Sam* (at different places). Otherwise, the *MT* here and in 7:1 correspond in the peoples listed and in the order in which they appear. *Sam* reads the first three here, however, as 'Canaanites, Amorites, Hittites', an order which may be original in its distinctiveness, the *MT* being a secondary harmonization to 7:1.

18. The verse expands the reason for destroying the peoples. It is formulated in the second person plural form of address, which connects it with vv. 2–4, so suggesting that it is an addition. Because of its emphatic concern with the danger of apostasy which the existence of these nations posed to Israel, the verse has close connections with passages in the parenetic introduction to the law which have already been seen to be late (6:16; 7:4f.; 7:25; 8:19f.; 11:16f.; see also Minette de Tillesse, *VT* 12, 1962, 42f.). It should be ascribed, therefore, to the second deuteronomistic editor.

19. That there is any pre-deuteronomic law in vv. 19–20 is doubtful. At least its present structure (see v. 10) and its expression in second person singular direct form of address is deuteronomic. It is not presupposed as known earlier than Deuteronomy in Israel; cf. e.g. 2 Kg. 3:19, 25, which reveal that Israel shared with many others in the common practice of destroying the natural sources of life in the country invaded by her armies. The prohibition here is a deuteronomic protest against a practice considered unnecessarily destructive. **to take it:** for the verb *tāpaś* in the sense of 'capture a city', cf. also Jos. 8:8; 2 Kg. 14:7; 16:9; 18:13, etc. The verb means generally 'to lay hold of', and can be applied even to skilful use, e.g. of a bow (Am. 2:15) or of the law (Jer. 2:8). **Are the trees in the field men:** this presupposes repointing the *MT hā'ādām* to *he'ādām* (the interrogative particle rather than the definite article), following LXX. As it stands the *MT* means 'men are the trees of the field', which, with considerable effort, may be interpreted to mean that men live on the trees of the field (cf. *AV* which depends on Ibn Ezra 'for the lives of the sons of men are the trees of the field'). But even this leaves the rest of the verse unintelligibly isolated.

20. siegeworks: the precise form which siegeworks took in Israelite war is uncertain, but wooden battering rams and siege towers and ladders are known from sculptures to have been employed in Near Eastern warfare.

(v) The case of unsolved murder **21:1–9**
The interpretation of this section is complicated by the fact that it clearly consists of old material which has been edited in at least two stages. Vv. 1* and 9 are deuteronomic, acting as a framework to the law. The same editor has probably also added the reference to the judges in v. 2 in order to connect the law with judicial practice as already stipulated in 16:18ff. On the other hand, vv. 5 and 8 are post-deuteronomic. As in 20:2–4 so in these verses the one responsible is probably the second deuteronomist; there is the same concern to bring to the fore the role of the priest. V. 5, which may in fact have come in by two stages, uses a late expression in referring to the priests. V. 8 contains a prayer which it was probably intended should be spoken by the priests. In any case, it is quite out of place, since it refers to Israel as a whole rather than to the specific community which bears responsibility for the crime. It is this post-deuteronomic editing which explicitly gave the ritual a quite new purpose: it is no longer a self-efficacious ritual; rather God must forgive before the guilt of bloodshed and the threat which that carries is removed.

The deuteronomic editing seems to have been primarily concerned with giving the law at its beginning and end a formulation comparable to other laws in the deuteronomic collection. Otherwise, the older elements are retained. These elements—the breaking of the neck of the animal, the washing of the hands and the declaration—belong not to an expiatory sacrifice but rather to a ceremony with magical overtones. The ceremony combines both judicial and sacral ideas (cf. McKeating, *VT* 25, 1975, 62f.): judicial in that, as usual in the ancient Near East, the city nearest the scene of the crime must bear responsibility and consequently must perform the ritual including the oath of exculpation; and sacral cleansing in that the murder has brought the guilt of bloodshed on the community and this must be removed. The washing of the hands over the animal was designed to transfer this guilt from the community to the animal (see particularly Elhorst, *ZAW* 39, 1921, 58ff.). The killing of the animal was not a sacrificial act, but rather the means of ensuring that, bearing the guilt of bloodshed, it could not come once more into contact with the community.

1. The deuteronomic editor has modified the original law through the introduction of the phrase **in the land which the Lord your God gives you to possess;** otherwise, the verse preserves a pre-deuteronomic impersonal casuistic statement of the case.

2. your elders and your judges: it is the elders alone who function in verses 4, 6; the judges have no real place in this pericope, and historically it is unlikely that they would have appeared alongside the elders, whose functions they rather took over (see the introduction to 16:18–17:7). They have been introduced here in order to connect this law with 16:18ff. The *Sam* reading, 'your officers' (followed by the *JB*; cf. Buis-Leclercq, Cazelles), may be a simple erroneous reading of *šōṭᵉrekā* for *šōpᵉṭekā*, although it is perhaps more likely that it reflects the view that the particular task which is given them here, that of measuring distances, was more appropriate to the 'officers' as assistants to the judges (see comment on 16:18), than to the judges themselves.

3. the city which is nearest: the Code of Hammurabi, paras. 23, 24 (cf. *ANET*, 167) stipulates that the city nearest to the scene of a crime for which nobody has been apprehended is responsible for compensating the victim or the community to which he belonged. For parallels in other texts, cf. Gordon, *Revue d'Assyriologie et d'Archéologie orientale* 33, 1936, 1ff. **worked:** the form of the verb is very rare, appearing otherwise only in Isa. 14:3. But this hardly justifies the *NEB* 'mated', following Driver's proposal (*VT* 2, 1952, 356f.) to emend *'ubbad* to *'ubbar*. The latter is a form of the verb *'br* which never otherwise occurs, and a sense of it which appears otherwise only in Job 21:10. The closest parallel to this description in Num. 19:2 uses neither form.

4. a valley with running water: better is the *NEB* 'a ravine where there is a stream that never runs dry'. The meaning of the word *'ēṭān* was early forgotten, and was unknown to the ancient versions where it is variously rendered depending on the context. Here LXX and Vulg conjecture 'rough' or 'rocky' (cf. *AV*). The cognate Arabic *watana*, 'be perpetual', is used especially of water. **neither ploughed nor sown:** the ground is a waste area, not cultivated land used in the normal way by the settled Israelites. **break the heifer's neck:** the breaking of the neck of an animal is referred to otherwise only in Exod. 13:13; 34:20 (cf. also Isa.

66:3) in connection with the ritually unclean firstling of an ass which is not redeemed by a lamb. Zevit, *JBL* 95, 1976, 384, suggests that the original law in the present context demanded that the heifer should be sacrificed; the deuteronomic legislator then changed this into the demand that its neck be broken, since for this legislator sacrifice could be carried out only at the central sanctuary. However, if the washing of the hands over the animal is an original part of the ritual it is more likely that what is prescribed here is simply a means of ensuring that the animal, bearing the bloodguilt which the washing has transferred to it (see comment on v. 6), remains outside the community and cannot return with the contagion which it has removed.

5. The verse is a late addition which has come in by two stages. V. 5*a* (**And the priests ... the name of the Lord**) was introduced because of the cultic nature of the event which, it was understood, must have taken place in the presence of the priests. Secondly, the judicial nature of the proceedings led to the introduction of v. 5*b*, for it was known from 17:8ff. that the Levitical priests played a role in judicial decision making. However, it is only in this verse that the priests appear; they otherwise play no part in the proceedings, and, like the judges in v. 2, they have been brought in to make the law conform with what the deuteronomic law has already prescribed elsewhere. **the priests the sons of Levi:** the deuteronomic law does not otherwise use this expression (cf. 17:9, 18; 18:1; 24:8, which refer to 'the Levitical priests'), but it does appear in the late 31:9. **to minister to him and to bless in the name of the Lord:** see comment on 10:8.

6. wash their hands: this action, combined with the declaration which follows, is not simply a symbolic act of cleansing (cf. Pss. 26:6; 73:13), but the means whereby the bloodguilt for the murdered man is transferred from the elders representing the community to the animal over which they perform the ceremony. In particular at this point a comparison may be made with the priestly ritual of the scapegoat (cf. Lev. 16:20ff.), in which the goat, bearing the sins of the community, was driven out into the wilderness in order to remove the contagion from the people.

7. they shall testify: the Hebrew uses two verbs: 'they shall declare and say'. These form a fixed pair, as 25:9; 26:5; 27:14, 15 indicate, and are used of solemn declarations and affirmations either in a legal or in a cultic context. On the first of the verbs, *ʿānāh*, see also comment on 5:20. In this declaration the elders deny both having played a part in the murder and having seen it done; the latter would have obliged them to report it. **shed:** the *keṭîḇ* is third person feminine singular form: *šāpᵉḵāh*, while the *qᵉrê* is third person plural *šāpᵉḵû*. That the former is in fact an old third person feminine plural form, as in Accadian and Old Aramaic (cf. Gordon, *Ugaritic Textbook*, 70 n.3) is very doubtful. Driver argues that the subject here (**our hands**) is understood as a collective singular (see also the analogous case with the imperfect of the verb in Ps. 37:31), so making the *qᵉrê* an unnecessary correction; see also GK § 44m.

8. Forgive: the basic meaning of the verb *kpr* is uncertain. The sense of 'cover' is perhaps chiefly supported by the late technical term *kappōreṭ*, used for the cover of the ark (cf. e.g. Driver, Wijngaards; however, for a proposed Egyptian origin of this word, not from the root *kpr*, cf. Görg, *ZAW* 89, 1977, 115ff.); but the meaning 'cover' for the root is clearly attested only in Arabic. Alternatively, the sense may be 'to wipe off' or 'cleanse'; in this sense biblical usage exactly parallels that of Accadian. So the word *kōper*, translated 'ransom' or 'expiation', would mean the payment made in order to 'wipe off' or 'cleanse' guilt. Here the translation would be 'wipe away (the guilt of) thy people'. See the discussion in Levine, *Presence*, 56ff. **redeemed:** see comment on 7:8. **the guilt of innocent blood:** see comment on 19:10.

9. As in 19:13 this verse is the deuteronomic conclusion to the law using material from 13:5. The two halves of the verse fit together very abruptly, however, and it is possible that LXX preserves an original reading in having 'and it shall be well with you' after **from your midst.** The final clause, **when you do what is right in the sight of the Lord,** may be a late deuteronomistic supplement; cf. 6:18; 19:13.

(E) LAWS ON RESPECT FOR LIFE, ESPECIALLY IN FAMILY RELATION-
SHIPS: **21:10–22:30**

The laws of this section fall into three major groups: 21:10–23, consisting of three laws on family relationships with a supplement in the last two verses; 22:1–12, laws of different origins brought together to illustrate a concern that different forms of life should be respected; and 22:13–30, laws on marriage and sexual relationships. The first and third sections are closely related in subject, and also in their casuistic form. Deuteronomic editing, introducing the use of the direct form of address, is to be found mainly in the first and last laws of each of the two sections. Otherwise, the pre-deuteronomic casuistic laws are fairly faithfully preserved. The middle section is at first sight foreign to its context, but several links connect it not only with its immediate context but also with earlier sections. So, for example, it is connected with the third section in that both are closely concerned with respect for life. This appears in the last section in so far as contravention of the laws there most often brings the death penalty, and on one occasion (22:26) a direct connection is explicitly made with the case of murder: these laws are presented as dealing with cases of attacks on the lives of individuals. Moreover, this same concern with life constitutes a link between the second and third sections on the one hand and the laws of chs. 19f. on the other hand, a connection which is strengthened by the fact that the first section of the present division has a war situation in view. It is, therefore, respect for life which informs the whole of 21:10–22:30 along with the laws of the previous major division.

(i) Laws on family relationships and the treatment of a criminal **21:10–23**
This section contains three laws regulating family relationships, with a supplement in vv. 22–23. The first, in vv. 10–14, on a man's treatment of a captive woman whom he wishes to marry, has its place here because of the war laws in the immediately preceding section. The law betrays signs of old material having been brought into a new context. This is particularly so in that while the section is clearly chiefly concerned with establishing the rights of the female captive, it also has subsidiary, and in the present context quite superfluous, provisions dealing with the actions to be performed by the captive when taken into her master's house. The deuteronomic law in vv. 10–12a, 13b–14 is formulated in the second person singular, and deals with the master's duties towards the captive female whom he wishes to marry. Vv. 12b–13aα, which prescribe that the captive should shave her head, pare her nails, and change her clothing, are distinct not only in their content, but in the change from direct address to third person singular subject. This does not indicate, however, as Merendino, *op. cit.*, 243f., proposes, that this section is a secondary insertion in the deuteronomic law. Rather, these are ancient provisions which belong in the context of rules of war. The deuteronomic legislator in taking them up provided the additional clause in v. 13aβ, 'and

shall remain . . . a full month', in order to connect the laws with his own formulated law, which was concerned with regulating the relationship of the husband to his captive wife in the context of family law.

The second law, in vv. 15–17, on the rights of the firstborn son, has a clear casuistic structure, with no later additions. There is nothing deuteronomic in its formulation nor does it express any specifically Israelite view. The right of the firstborn was widely acknowledged in the ancient Near East (see comment on v. 17). However, it was also apparently widespread custom for the father to select his 'firstborn', not only at Nuzi, Ugarit, and Alalakh, but also in Israel (cf. Gen. 48:13–20; 49:3–4; 1 Chr. 5:1–2, and Mendelsohn, *BASOR* 156, 1959, 38ff.; Weinfeld, *JAOS* 90, 1970, 193), and it is this practice that the law is concerned to counteract.

The third law, in vv. 18–21, on the treatment due to the disobedient son, also is a clear pre-deuteronomic casuistic law in impersonal formulation. On this occasion, however, there is some deuteronomic editing (see comment on v. 21). The older law is preserved intact in vv. 18–21aα. Merendino, *op. cit.*, 245f., is undoubtedly too critical in wishing to excise the reference to the actions of the parents in vv. 19f. as an interpretative addition. They play an analogous role in the next pure casuistic law, in 22:13ff., and in both places the reference to them should be taken as original.

Seitz, *op. cit.*, 117, thinks that the order of subjects treated in vv. 15–21 is a traditional one, paralleled in the Code of Hammurabi, paras. 165–168. It is true that there is a common theme of inheritance and bringing a son to justice; however, the Code of Hammurabi has both subjects within the context of inheritance, the second being the case of a father who wishes to disinherit his son. That is not the case in the present connection. Yet the law of vv. 18–21 has a clear affinity with the previous one, both belonging in the context of family law; so it is not necessarily as a result of deuteronomic editing that the two are first found together.

The supplement to these laws in vv. 22–23 is a casuistic form of law using the direct form of address, as frequently in deuteronomic laws (see the introduction to 12:29–13:18). The deuteronomic legislator is here expressing and modifying an ancient customary method of dealing with condemned criminals. Their bodies may be exposed, but not indefinitely. In content there is a natural connection with the conclusion of the immediately preceding law.

10. For the deuteronomic structure here, see comment on 17:14.

12, 13. shave her head and pare her nails . . . put off her captive's garb: the shaving of the head and putting off of the clothes is referred to in the Mari texts where it has the purpose of getting rid of everything that would remind the captive of home (cf. du Buit, *RB* 66, 1959, 576f.). In the present context these are neither mourning rites (on the cutting of the hair as a mourning rite cf. 14:1) nor rites marking the conclusion of a period of mourning. They symbolize a change of life and home, following which comes the period of mourning. **captive's garb:** i.e. the clothes she was wearing when taken captive, which belong, therefore, with her old life. **a full month:** this is the mourning period also in 34:8; Num. 20:29. Other references (Gen. 50:10; 1 Sam. 31:13; 1 Chr. 10:12) give seven days as the mourning period. **she shall be your wife:** there is some conflict between this provision and the deuteronomic parenetic introduction in 7:3, a conflict similar to that between 7:1ff. and 20:10ff. (see introduction to 20:10–20). As in 20:10ff. so here the traditional context is that of war in general; the deuteronomic legislator, however, has modified this (in 20:10ff. explicitly; here by implication, by describing the case as one in which Israel shall 'go forth to war') in order to restrict the traditional context to that of war against enemies outside her land. In this way the conflict with ch. 7 is resolved.

14. you shall let her go: as well as being used of the freeing of slaves (e.g. 15:12), the verb is also used for divorce (22:19, 29). That is probably the sense of it here too. The following word, *lᵉnapšāh* (translated here **where she will**), serves to reinforce the point that the former captive, having become her master's wife, must now be treated as a wife: if the husband wishes to divorce her he may do so, but his action leaves her free (cf. *lᵉnapšām* in Jer. 34:16); she is not any longer a captive who may be sold to another master. **treat . . . as a slave:** the verb *hiṯʿammēr*, which is thus translated by the *RSV* (*NEB* 'treat harshly'; *AV* 'make merchandise'), is found only here and in 24:7. Its origin and precise meaning are uncertain. Alt, *VT* 2, 1952, 153ff., points to the existence of a cognate term, in the form of a masculine plural noun, in the Ugaritic texts, where it designates a group of people liable for military service. It is thus taken basically to designate the action of one who claims unlimited power of disposal over others. At Ugarit it is a question of the power of the state over its subjects, while here it is an assumed legal claim in the relations of individuals. **humiliated her:** for the sense of the verb ʿānāh here see particularly its use in Gen. 34:2; Jg. 19:24; 20:5; 2 Sam. 13:12, 14, 22, and Dt. 22:24, 29 (translated 'violated'). A better translation perhaps is 'had (your) will with her'. The use of the verb in 22:24 of the women who did not cry for help indicates that it is not a case of the woman having been humiliated through rape or ill-treatment.

16. in preference to: see comment on 5:7.

17. he shall acknowledge: the verb is a technical legal term signifying formal legal acknowledgement (cf. also 33:9, and Daube, *Studies*, 5ff.). **a double portion:** the phrase occurs also in 2 Kg. 2:9 and Zech. 13:8. The latter passage, however, indicates that the sense is rather 'two thirds' (cf. Noth, *Ursprünge*, 19f.). The accordance of a privileged status to the firstborn son is an ancient custom in the ancient Near East, widely represented in extra-biblical texts. The Hammurabi Code, however, betrays a definite weakening in the custom (para. 165, cf. *ANET*, 173). This is explained by Mendelsohn, *BASOR* 156, 1959, 40, as the result of changes in the economic structure of society which tended to reduce the role of the eldest brother in the family. **for he is the first issue of his strength:** it is unusual to find such clauses coming at this stage of a casuistic law. However, the lack of any theological motive in the clause, and the parallel in Gen. 49:3, indicate that it is an old idea. For the translation 'procreative power' instead of **strength,** cf. Fohrer, in *Words and Meanings*, 99.

18. stubborn and rebellious: this combination is found also in v. 20; Jer. 5:23; Ps. 78:8.

19. the elders of the city: the appearence of the elders in their traditional judging capacity is at variance with the law of 16:18ff., and indicates the pre-deuteronomic origin of the law (cf. the introduction to 16:18–17:7). **at the gate:** the gate of the city is often mentioned as the place for the administration of justice; cf. e.g. Am. 5:10, 12, 15; Isa. 29:21; Ps. 127:5; Ru. 4.

20. he is a glutton and a drunkard: the Hebrew lacks 'he (is)'; the phrase is an addition based on Prov. 23:21, introduced here in order to give precision to what was seen as a too general accusation.

21. The punishment prescribed in v. 21aα completes the case.

The two clauses of v. 21aβb, which revert to the direct form of
address, use the purging formula found on several earlier occasions
(13:5; 17:7; 19:19) and other material which has also been used
before (cf. 13:11; 17:13; 19:20). The clauses are clearly deuteronomic editorial additions to the law (see comment on 13:5, 11).
stone him: the verb here, *rāgam*, does not otherwise occur in
Deuteronomy (which in 13:10 uses *sāqal*), but is found otherwise
in the Holiness Code and P.

22. hang him on a tree: it is clear from Jos. 8:29; 10:26;
1 Sam. 31:10; 2 Sam. 4:12 that hanging was in fact the exposure
of the corpse of a condemned man already executed by other
means. The purpose of such exposure is not certain. Phillips
points to 2 Sam. 21:1–14 as indicating that it may have originally
been designed to appease the deity who, because of the actions
of the condemned man, brought punishment on the land. There
may also be present the idea of an unburied body as additional
punishment for the executed criminal. In any case, the deuteronomic legislator has strictly limited this aspect of the judicial
process.

23. all night: not in the Hebrew, but clearly implied. **accursed
by God:** the Hebrew phrase is 'a curse of God' which may be
taken as *RSV* or, following some Jewish interpretations, 'a curse'
or 'a reproach to God' (cf. Phillips, *Law*, 25 'repudiation of God';
and *NEB* 'offence in the sight of God'). However, the latter is
not supported by the traditional understanding of the text,
represented by LXX and Vulg (cf. also Gal. 3:13). It is better to
translate the phrase as *RSV*: a condemned man has brought the
curse of God on himself, and as the bearer of this curse his visible
presence threatens the land with impurity; see the discussion in
Plöger, *Untersuchungen*, 98ff. **which the Lord your God gives
you:** a deuteronomic phrase, found also in the first verse of this
chapter.

(ii) Laws on respect for different forms of life **22:1–12**
With the exception of v. 5, all the laws in this collection have a
common apodictic form, in contrast to the casuistic form of the
surrounding laws. In content it is a heterogeneous collection of
laws which, however, has been brought together under a single
point of view. With the exception of the final law in v. 12, which
was probably attracted to its present place because of a coincidence
of subject matter with the immediately preceding law, all the

laws are concerned with respect for different forms of life. This
may not indeed have been the original intention of the individual
laws. So, for example, the first law was probably originally
intended to protect the property of a fellow-Israelite. But in its
present context it is also concerned with the prevention of unnecessary suffering.

The deuteronomic legislator is ultimately responsible for this
collection, though it is difficult to say to what extent the laws may
already at an earlier stage have been connected. Of the individual
laws only vv. 9–11 have an inner coherence together with a common form, indicating the existence of an original unit.

The first law in the collection, in vv. 1–4, on an Israelite's duty
towards his brother's property, is composed of two parallel demands in vv. 1 and 4, which have been supplemented by interpretative material in vv. 2f. Vv. 1 and 4 have the same formulation
and structure. Their source is the casuistic law of Exod. 23:4f.,
which the deuteronomic legislator has modified through giving
it an apodictic expression and substituting 'brother' for 'enemy'.
The deuteronomic legislator in vv. 2f. has brought in supplementary material, expanding this law, based partly on the law itself
and partly on Exod. 22:9, which is apparently the source of the
list in v. 3 of the present law.

The law of vv. 6f., which is basically concerned to safeguard
food supplies for the future, also necessarily expresses a respect
for life and an unwillingness to sanction the destruction of any
particular species.

The law of v. 8 has an analogy in the Code of Hammurabi,
paras. 229f. (cf. *ANET*, 176), and so takes up an old custom; here,
however, there is nothing of compensation or punishment (as in
the Code, and also in the analogous law in Exod. 21:33f.).
Rather, it is solely with honouring and preserving life that this
law, like the previous one, is concerned.

Vv. 5, 9–11 all prohibit unnatural mixtures of one kind or
another. The reasons, which are not now clear, may well be very
different in each case; however, the prohibitions are brought
together out of a concern for the integrity of all forms of life and
the preservation of the distinctions of the created order.

1. your brother: the corresponding law in Exod. 23:4f.,
which is the source of the present law, speaks of 'your enemy' and
'one who hates you'. The change does not represent a limitation
in the application of the law, but the opposite. The Exodus law

undoubtedly also has in view the Israelite (von Rad interprets it as an enemy at law); the deuteronomic legislator generalizes it to apply to every fellow-Israelite. **(you shall not) withhold your help:** this is a reflexive form of the verb 'to conceal' (cf. *AV*), which is perhaps better rendered in this context, as JB, 'there must be no evasion'.

2. seeks it: the same verb in 23:21 is translated 'require'. The sense of the verb in this context is of claiming by right.

3. you may not: on the sense of duty implied in this verb see comment on 12:17.

4. The structure of the verse, a prohibition followed by a command, is the exact counterpart of v. 1.

5. anything that pertains to: the term *keli* has a very general sense, and can denote weapons (1:41), utensils (23:24), as well as clothes. The background of the prohibition of transvestism is not certain. The reason given for it, that it is **an abomination to the Lord,** suggests that the practice prohibited is a cultic one associated with non-Israelite cults (see comment on 7:25). Even if this reason is a later addition to the prohibition this is probably still the background. Römer, in *Travels*, 219ff., has collected examples in Mesopotamian sources from the old Akkadian period onwards, of transvestism or mixing of the sexes in general or emasculation, in connection with the cult of the goddess Ishtar. For references to sources from the Graeco-Roman period, cf. Driver.

6, 7. The law protecting the mother bird and allowing the young to be taken is often held to have a humanitarian motive. However, this was never the main emphasis. It is basically concerned with the continuity of life in general and with the source of food in particular; when only the young are taken the continuance of the life of the species is assured. See also Carmichael, *Laws*, 153ff., who compares the law with 20:19f. prohibiting the destruction of fruit trees. **that it may go well with you, and that you may live long:** these two motive clauses are found together in 4:40; 5:16, and separately in 4:26; 5:33; 6:2; 11:9; 17:20; 25:15; they may be late deuteronomistic additions here.

8. On the use of the flat top of the house for sleeping, recreation, etc.; cf. Jos. 2:6; Jg. 16:27; 1 Sam. 9:25f., etc. **the guilt of blood:** see comment on 19:10.

9. The basis of the prohibition is not clear; it may have originated in a desire to avoid foreign practices which had some magical or cultic associations; it may have a utilitarian reason in the inappropriate and wasteful use of crops and land. The motive supplied here, **lest the whole yield be forfeited,** which does not appear in the Leviticus law (Lev. 19:19) on the subject, does not clarify the matter, though if it is an original motivation for the prohibition it would associate it with the cultic sphere (see below). **vineyard:** the parallel law in Lev. 19:19 reads 'field'. The latter is undoubtedly original, as being more suitable to the verb **sow.** The verb expected with 'vineyard' is 'plant' (cf. Isa. 5:2). The change probably came about as the result of the incorporation of the law in its present place immediately following the law on the new house, for 'house and vineyard' is a frequent pair (cf. Am. 5:11; Dt. 20:5–7; 28:30). **be forfeited to the sanctuary:** König is not correct in objecting that this translation does not suit the word *zeraᶜ*, for the latter is not just the seed which is sown but also the **crop** which results. The translation is a paraphrase of the Hebrew, which is simply 'become holy'; this implies that it is not available for common use.

10. Lev. 19:19 has no parallel to the law of this verse; however, as the first of its three prohibitions Lev. 19:19 mentions the mating of different breeds of animals, and Carmichael, *op. cit.*, 159f., proposes that this is in fact the true sense also of the deuteronomic law in this verse. On this view the verb **plough** must be understood as meaning to have sexual relations, a sense which, while not found otherwise in the Old Testament, does appear in Rabbinic literature. This interpretation suits better the context of unnatural mixtures than does the apparent meaning of the text; for the latter seems to have the humanitarian motive of ensuring that a weak and a strong animal are not yoked up together.

11. mingled stuff: the word *šaᶜaṭnēz* is not of Hebrew origin, and its precise significance is known only from the present passage. It appears only here and in Lev. 19:19; the present passage defines it as a combination of wool and linen. The background of this prohibition is unknown; but for some references to sources documenting the use in magical practices of garments made of different cloths, cf. Goldziher, *ZAW* 20, 1900, 36f.

12. The reason for this demand is unknown. The priestly legislator in Num. 15:38f. demands it as a method of reminding Israelites of their obligations to the divine commandments; the lack of any such explanation in Deuteronomy would suggest,

however, that the priestly explanation is not original. The place
of the law here is perhaps to be explained from the fact that it
deals with clothing, as does the immediately preceding law. It
has no other apparent connection with its context. On the later
application of the law in Judaism, cf. Driver.

(iii) Laws on marriage and sexual relationships **22:13-30**
The six laws of this section are all concerned with the area of
marriage and sexual relations. With the exception of the final
law in v. 30, which acts as a transition to the prohibitions in the
following section, all the laws have a casuistic form. This, along
with the parallels in other codes, the only slight contact in the
laws with anything specifically Israelite or Yahwistic, and the
reference in vv. 15f. to the elders acting in a judicial capacity,
shows the antiquity of the laws.

The work of the deuteronomic editor is here not very obtrusive:
it comes to expression mainly in the use of the purging formula in
vv. 21, 22 and 24. Two other peculiarities of these laws also
deserve notice, although it is not certain that they are the responsibility of the deuteronomic legislator. Firstly, the law of
vv. 13-19 has been secondarily supplemented by vv. 20f. This is
suggested not only by v. 14 (see comment), but also by the fact
that it is difficult to see what the basic concern of this law could be
unless it is with the case of a husband attempting fraudulently to
recover the bride price paid to his father-in-law on marriage. It is
this which gives unity to vv. 13-19. Through the addition of vv.
20f., on the other hand, the law now revolves around the question
of the truth or falsehood of the charge. That this change is to be
ascribed to the deuteronomic editor is, however, unlikely. It is
only the purging formula at the end of the addition which,
through its direct form of address, shows its deuteronomic origin.
Secondly, the emphasis of the law on the seduction of an unbe-
trothed girl in vv. 28f. is considerably modified over against its
counterpart in Ex. 22:16f. While there it is the father's financial
compensation which stands at the forefront, here it is the security
of the seduced girl.

13. spurns her: in 2 Sam. 13:15 the same verb is translated
'hated'.

14. shameful conduct: the Hebrew expression has been given
a variety of translations. The difficulty concerns the word ʿ*alîlōt*.
LXX, Vulg, Ibn Ezra, and also the *AV* ('occasions') connect it

with the Aramaic *'illāh*, 'affair', 'occasion'. However, this sense is
not found otherwise for the root *'ll* in biblical Hebrew. The root
comes to expression in the Hithpael with the sense of 'act wantonly'
or 'act ruthlessly' (cf. Num. 22:29; Jg. 19:25; 1 Sam. 6:6; 31:4),
and in the plural noun *taᶜᵃlûlîm*, 'wantonness', 'caprice' (cf. Isa.
3:4; 66:4). The *RSV* thus translates 'wantonness of deeds' (**shameful conduct**), with reference to the actions of the woman charged,
which suits the whole situation described in vv. 13–21. Better,
however, is 'wantonness of words' or 'caprice of words', i.e.
baseless accusations, with reference to the charges brought by
the husband (cf. *NEB* and also v. 17). This suits vv. 13–19, but
not vv. 20–21. The latter, however, as noted in the introduction
above, are a later addition to the law. **the tokens of virginity:** the
term *beṯûlîm* is usually taken to refer to the bloodstains resulting
from the first sexual union (on the widespread importance of
such signs among eastern peoples, cf. e.g. Knobel). For a different
interpretation, arguing that the reference is to proofs of menstru-
ation immediately before marriage, as a sign that the bride is not
already pregnant at the time of her marriage, cf. Wenham, *VT*
22, 1972, 331ff. This interpretation suits the context well, and is
a necessary one if Wenham's view of the related word translated
'virgin' is correct; see comment on v. 23.

15. That the case is brought before **the elders of the city in
the gate** is a pointer to the antiquity of the law. As noted in the
introduction to 16:18–17:7, it appears that under Jehoshaphat
the judicial functions of the elders were taken over by professional
judges.

17. shameful charges: the same phrase as that translated
'shameful conduct' in v. 14.

18. whip him: although this is how the versions also understood
the verb here, it is not in fact certain that the intention is to prescribe corporal punishment. Apart from this doubtful passage
this is not otherwise specifically prescribed as a punishment.
Although the verb may imply this in 21:18, it is elsewhere used
with the general sense of 'admonish' or 'discipline'. Moreover,
where a case of corporal punishment being administered is
referred to, a different verb is used (25:1–3). Thus, here the
translation should perhaps be 'punish him', with the following verse
prescribing a fine, not being an additional punishment, but
standing in apposition giving the particular form of punishment
(cf. *NEB*).

19. Although the evil name is brought on the girl, it is her father's reputation which is particularly at stake. He has been implicitly accused of not looking after his daughter, or alternatively of trying to pass her off deceitfully as a virgin (on the word translated **virgin** see, however, the comment on v. 23). So the fine is paid to him by way of compensation. It would seem from v. 29 that the bride price was fifty shekels of silver; here the husband compensates his father-in-law by paying him twice what he tried to get from him (see the introduction to this section).

20, 21. These verses are apparently a subsequent addition to the law; the latter is concerned not with proving or disproving the charge brought but rather with punishing the man who brings a false charge. On the purging formula included in the verses see comment on 13:5. **folly in Israel:** an expression found also in Gen. 34:7; Jos. 7:15; Jg. 20:6, 10; Jer. 29:23; cf. also Jg. 19:23f.; 2 Sam. 13:12; Job 42:8. Noth, *System*, 106, understands an amphictyonic background for the formula: it deals not specifically with sexual crimes, but with the violation of the unwritten customary law which governed the life of the amphictyony. However, such a specific context is not demanded by the formula; the recent study by Phillips, *VT* 25, 1975, 237ff., explains *nᵉbālāh* ('folly') as a general expression for serious disorderly conduct resulting in the breakup of an existing relationship, whether between tribes, within the family, in marriage or with God; it indicates the end of an existing order.

22. Adultery was forbidden not just in order to protect the husband's property, but perhaps primarily to assure the husband of the paternity of his children. Phillips suggests that originally only the man would have been liable to execution, and that Hos. 2:2; Jer. 3:8 indicate that the penalty as far as the woman was concerned was that she should be divorced by her husband; it is the deuteronomic reform which is then understood to have changed this, by making the woman equally responsible before the law. However, see the comment on 5:18.

23. betrothed: it is clear from the punishment prescribed in the law, which refers to the betrothed virgin as 'wife' (v. 24) that betrothal meant considerably more than merely engagement. It implied the completion of all the legal arrangements preceding the marriage, especially the payment of the bride price, leaving no further obstacles in the way of the marriage taking place (cf.

also Gen. 29: 21). **virgin:** Wenham, *VT* 22, 1972, 326ff., points out that several occurrences of the Hebrew word *beṯûlāh* do not suggest this translation (cf. Jer. 2:32; 31:13; 51:22; Job 31:1; Est. 2:17, 19), and it is absolutely precluded in a number of occurrences of cognate terms in other Semitic languages. In particular the description in the Ugaritic texts of Anat as *btlt* is quite inconsistent with her activities if this term is understood to mean 'virgin'. The term designates rather a 'girl of marriageable age'. **in the city:** an unwilling victim would cry out; in the city her cries would be heard. That no such cries were heard suggests her consent. The distinction between the case of the consenting woman and one forced is formulated in rather different terms in extra-biblical law; cf. *ANET*, 162 para. 26; 171 para. 130; 181f. paras. 12, 23; 196 para. 197.

24. The impersonal formulation of casuistic law breaks down in this verse; moreover, the use of the second person plural form of address is remarkable. It is further noteworthy that the elders make no appearance here, in contrast to the law of vv. 13ff. It may be that the second person represents a secondary change from an original third person plural: 'they shall bring . . .', 'they shall stone . . .' On the purging formula see comment on 13:5. It is a deuteronomic addition to the casuistic law here.

26, 27. The original law probably concluded with v. 25. Vv. 26f. add nothing new to the law and are probably a deuteronomic addition. V. 26*b* is apparently modelled on 19:11, and has the purpose of emphasizing the connection between these marriage laws and the earlier complex by showing that in these marriage laws it is also a question of life and death.

28. who is not betrothed: the verbal form used here is a passive of the perfect, whereas vv. 23, 25, 27 use a passive participle. As Weiss, *JBL* 81, 1962, 67ff., notes, the more accurate translation here (reflecting the difference in grammatical form) must be 'who has never been betrothed'. The fine which is imposed in this law is compensation to the father for the loss of, or diminution to, the bride price which he might normally expect. Had his daughter ever been betrothed the bride price would have already been paid to the father.

The law of vv. 28f. is probably concerned with seduction rather than rape. This is made explicit in Exod. 22:16f. Here it is implied in the use of the phrase **they are found.** Moreover, the verb translated **seizes** is not the same verb as that found in v. 25.

Here it is the verb *tāpaś*, which has the general sense of 'hold' or 'handle'; see comment on 20:19, and Weinfeld, *Deuteronomy*, 286f. On 'violated' in the next verse see the use of the term in connection with the consenting woman in v. 24, and comment on 21:14.

29. The law of Exod. 22:16f. allows for the possibility that the father of the girl might not wish to give his daughter to the man as his wife; but that in any case the man must pay the father the bride price. The deuteronomic law gives the father no option in the matter; it protects the girl by ensuring that she is not left unmarried, and it also prevents the possibility of the father receiving a second bride price. On the other hand, the deuteronomic law also guards against the possibility (present under the Exodus law) that having married his victim the seducer might divorce her. **fifty shekels:** this was probably considered to be an average bride price.

30. This law is a connecting link between what precedes and what follows. As a prohibition it is connected in form with the following laws, while in content it is closely related to the preceding marriage laws. The parallel laws in the Holiness Code (Lev. 18:8; 20:11) are set in the context of other degrees of relationship within which sexual relations are forbidden. The reason for the specific reference to the father's wife here is not immediately clear, but two points are relevant. Firstly, the father's wife is probably to be understood as step-mother rather than mother; secondly, it was an ancient and widespread custom that the son and heir should inherit his father's wives and concubines (cf. Gen. 35:22; 49:4; 2 Sam. 3:7; 16:22; 1 Kg. 2:22). It is this custom that the law is concerned to prohibit rather than simply sexual relations with a near relative. So the law connects the marriage laws with the earlier inheritance laws in this section (21:15ff.).

uncover her who is his father's: the Hebrew is 'uncover his father's skirt'. Ru. 3:9 and Ezek. 16:8 show that the phrase 'to cover with the skirt' means 'to marry'. 'To uncover the skirt' must then mean to invade the privacy of the father's marriage relationship.

(F) LAWS ON PURITY AND HUMANITARIAN BEHAVIOUR IN THE PEOPLE OF YAHWEH: **23:1–25:19**
Within this section two concerns predominate: (a) the purity of the people of Yahweh: and (b) the humanitarian behaviour which is required of the people of Yahweh. The first of these

subjects dominates the beginning of the section: 23:1–8 lays down
the limits of membership in the people; 23:9–14 sees Israel as a
military camp, the purity of which in both place and person is
to be respected and preserved; 23:15–18 introduces the first of the
humanitarian laws, on the treatment of the fugitive slave, as
a binding link with later parts of the section, and continues with
the theme of the sexual purity of the community; 23:19–25
stands rather apart from its context; the presence here of the
laws which it contains probably results from contact between
these verses and the context in the Book of the Covenant which
is the source of many of the laws in the section, and from catchword connections or simple association of subject matter; 24:1–4
brings the first part of the section to a close, again on the subject of
the community and its (sexual) purity.

The humanitarian laws, already prepared for by 23:15f.,
continue in 24:5–25:4, a collection of laws of diverse origins
brought together under the humanitarian principle which is
to be extended to a variety of particularly deserving sections of
the people. The theme of the purity of the people, however, is
also continued in so far as 24:8 alludes to Moses' command to
exclude from the camp one suffering from leprosy. Both purity and
humanitarian concerns are also apparent in the two laws of
25:5–12, while 25:13–16, in having an anti-Canaanite theme, is
closely connected with the laws on the assembly at the beginning
of the section. The whole section is then completed by a related,
though secondary, law on the Amalekites.

The theme of war which appears at the end, and also in 23:9–
14; 24:5, links the section as a whole with 19:1–21:9, while the
theme of marriage and other laws on sexual matters in 23:17f.;
24:1–4, 5; 25:5–12 link the section with 21:10–22:30. The taking
up of similar subjects in different contexts is thus characteristic
of the whole collection.

(i) Membership in the assembly of Yahweh 23:1–8

The rules governing membership of the 'assembly of the Lord'
probably have a varied background. Vv. 2b, 3b, 8 are later
additions, vv. 4b–6 derive from the deuteronomic legislator,
and v. 4a is probably later than Dt. 2 (see comment on the individual verses). The form of the basic laws which remain is not,
however, uniform. So the double law of v. 7 is a direct address,
unlike the earlier laws of the section. In content too there is lack

of uniformity: the specific reference to Ammonites, Moabites, Edomites, and Egyptians, does not fit well with the general exclusions in the first two laws.

Galling, in *Festschrift*, 176ff., has shown that the present collection of laws goes back to two, or more probably three, separate passages: vv. 1–2a, v. 3a, v. 7. They now form a series of laws, but did not originate as such a series. Vv. 3a, 7 are concerned with the attitude of Israel to peoples who (with the exception of Egypt) bordered her territory. The most likely setting for the laws is border sanctuaries where the acceptance or rejection of these non-Israelites in Israel's cultic life would have been an issue. The laws excluding Moabites and Ammonites may have been applied at the sanctuary of Mizpah, where at one time Israel gathered to oppose Ammon (Jg. 10:17), while that concerning Egypt and Edom might be set at the southern sanctuary of Beersheba. On the other hand, the general laws on membership of the Israelite community would have belonged to a west Jordan sanctuary.

As a collection, according to Galling, the laws may have been preserved at Gilgal, Israel's most significant west Jordan border sanctuary, where they would have been used in the ritual by which foreigners would be accepted into the Israelite community. (Bächli, *Wort*, 21ff., sees Jos. 2:9–11; 9:9–10 as two confessions which would have belonged in the context of such a ceremony.) The date of the collection, and indeed also of the individual laws, is uncertain. Galling thinks in terms of the pre-monarchic period.

1. The background and reason for this prohibition are not certain. It could be (a) cultic, in the sense that castration featured in certain non-Israelite cultic practices abhorrent to Israel (cf. e.g. Bertholet, Buis); (b) an affirmation of the inadmissibility of physical mutilation as contrary to the design of God's creation (cf. e.g. Driver); or (c) a specific rejection of any action which destroys the procreative power of Israelites (cf. e.g. Galling, *op. cit.*, 178). One or more of these explanations may have been considered basic to the prohibition at different times. The Israel from which such people are excluded is called **the assembly of the Lord,** a phrase whose pre-deuteronomic origin is indicated by Mic. 2:5. It is clearly a cultic term; as a designation for all those eligible for membership it denotes the fully enfranchised male citizens not only in cultic gatherings in the narrow sense, but also in the military levy.

2. bastard: the designation not of one born out of wedlock, but rather of the issue of a prohibited union. This is not to say that it refers exclusively to the issue of the union prohibited in 22:30, or any other incestuous marriage; the reference may be much more general and include the offspring of intermarriage between Israelites and non-Israelites. The latter is perhaps suggested particularly by the use of the word in Zech. 9:6. The former interpretation, on the other hand, is suggested by the Mishnah (Mishnah Jebamoth IV 13) and is frequently supported through the connection of the law with the following one on Ammon and Moab understood to have had incestuous origins (though see comment on v. 4). The second half of the verse **(even to the tenth generation...)** is repeated in v. 3 (with one slight change due to the different context). In both places it is undoubtedly an addition to the basic law.

3. If **the tenth generation** is taken literally rather than in general terms as a reference to even very distant descendants (cf. Knobel with reference to Gen. 31:7; Num. 14:22), there is some inconsistency with the last two words, **for ever.** The latter, however, should probably be seen as the original end of the prohibition of the reception of Ammonites and Moabites, while the intervening reference to the tenth generation is an addition here as in the previous verse.

4. This verse is a late expansion of the prohibition. It came in by two stages. In the first place, v. 4*b* was added to explain the exclusion of the Moabites (the Hebrew is 'He [viz. the king of Moab] hired...'), with reference to the story of Num. 22:4ff. No comparable explanation for the exclusion of the Ammonites could be found; however, this lack was in time made up through the addition of v. 4*a*. This, in contrast to the second part of the verse, is in the second person plural form of address. It has reference only to the Ammonites and is related to, and presupposes, the silence of Dt. 2 on the Ammonites having given Israel food and drink in the course of their wanderings. Dt. 2:29 does, on the other hand, relate that the Moabites did do this. Both parts of the verse, then, are later additions, attempting to account for the basic law. The first of them (in chronological terms) in v. 4*b* is in singular address form and may be from the hand of the deuteronomic legislator taking up the older law. It is very remarkable that the verse makes no reference whatever to the account of the incestuous beginnings of Ammon and Moab in Gen. 19:30ff.

The author cannot have known that story; had he known it, reference to it here would have been inevitable. (For this reason it is advisable not to refer uncritically to the exclusion of the Ammonites and Moabites, interpreted against the background of Gen. 19:30ff., in discussing the meaning of 'bastard' in v. 2.) The precise historical reason for this prohibition is not now discernible; the adverse relations between Israel on the one hand and the Ammonites and Moabites on the other, which the prohibition probably presupposes, featured over a long period of Israel's early history (cf. Num. 25:1ff.; Jg. 3:12ff.; 10:6ff.; 2 Sam. 8:2; 10:1ff.). **Mesopotamia:** in Hebrew *'aram nah*a*rayim*, 'Aram of the two rivers', i.e. strictly speaking the land between the Tigris and the Euphrates. On the variations in the actual territory covered by the term, see Gordon, in *IDB* vol. 3, 359.

5, 6. These verses continue v. 4*b*, and, like it, may be from the hand of the deuteronomic legislator. **their peace and their prosperity:** this is treaty terminology with parallels in the Sefire treaties. Hillers, *BASOR* 176, 1964, 46f. (cf. also Moran, *JNES* 22, 1963, 173ff.), proposes the translation '(a treaty of) friendship and peace with them'.

7. A treaty background for the reference to the Edomites as **your brother** has been proposed by Fishbane, *JBL* 89, 1970, 313ff., who points out that the word for 'brother' in Akkadian is also used as a technical term for 'treaty partner', even in the context of vassal treaties; and so the subjugation of Edom to vassaldom by David (2 Sam. 8:13f.) might explain the use of the term here. This may indeed have contributed to the use of 'brother' for the Edomites, but there is no indication of its having been understood in this way in the present passage and certainly not in 2:1–8. In the latter passage Edom is identified with Esau, the brother of Jacob/Israel, an identification which resulted from Edom's occupation of Seir, inhabited by the sons of Esau. This background of ethnic movements is probably also presupposed in the present law, even though the identification of Edomites and sons of Esau is not here explicit; see also comment on 2:4. Bartlett, in *Peoples*, 244ff., emphasizes the similarities between the religions of Edom and Israel, similarities known to, and appreciated by, Israel; this point is especially relevant here since, as von Rad notes, the terms in which the prohibition here is expressed suggest cultic reasons for the prohibition. The verb **abhor** (*tā'ab*) may mean 'to treat as unclean from a cultic point of view', particularly in view of the use of the related noun *tōʿēḇāh*; see comment on 7:25.

The reason given for accepting an Egyptian takes no account of the period spent in Egypt as a time of hardship and slavery. The thought here may be of individual Egyptian 'sojourners' (*gērîm*; see comment on 1:16) in Israel, rather than of Egypt as a nation.

8. The expression here is reminiscent of vv. 2*b*, 3*b*, and the verse may very well derive from the same hand.

(ii) The cleanliness of the camp **23:9-14**
The law on the cleanliness of the camp has a deuteronomic framework in vv. 9, 14, which brings together two laws, the one a casuistic law in vv. 10f., on the purity of the person, and the other a pair of direct commands in vv. 12f. on the purity of the place. These are laws of the holy war, and their connection with that context is emphasized through the framework which has clear contacts with 20:1; 21:10. However, the place of the laws here is perfectly intelligible: while the earlier holy war laws dealt with the conduct of war, here the subject is the ritual cleanliness of the participants and their camp. The purity of the assembly of Yahweh, as the subject of the immediately preceding section, clearly links up closely with the present verses.

9. every evil thing: the same expression occurs in a different context in 17:1, where it is translated 'any defect whatever'. So there is no essential moral content in the phrase; it denotes rather what is unfitting. **and are in camp:** the Hebrew has only *maḥᵃneh*; Gen. 32:2 justifies the translation 'army' for this word rather than 'camp', so giving the sense: 'when you go forth as an army'.

10. This law on the cleanliness of the person has general application in Lev. 15:16f. It is a casuistic law which is probably of ancient origin. Only in the word *bᵉḵā,* **among you,** is there any direct address, and this word probably came in secondarily as a result of the direct address in the framework.

11. The evening is the beginning of the new day.

12. a place: so LXX. The Hebrew is *yāḏ,* usually translated 'hand' or 'side'. The more general sense of 'place' is supported by Num. 2:17 and Jer. 6:3. The translation 'sign' (*NEB*) finds support in 1 Sam. 15:12; 2 Sam. 18:18. Translated in this way it could be taken as metonymy, standing for the place indicated by the sign (König).

13. stick: only here does the word *yāṯēḏ* occur in the sense of

a tool for digging. Otherwise, it means a pin or tentpeg. De Vaux,
VT 9, 1959, 399ff., points to the application of this law in the
community at Qumran, and suggests the identification of an
implement found there with the tool required for the fulfilling of
the law. **your weapons:** the word occurs only here in biblical
Hebrew, but is known from Aramaic. De veux, *op. cot.*, 405,
recommends a change in one of the consonants (to read 'ᵉzōreḵā
instead of 'ᵃzēneḵā) with the LXX, to give the meaning '(in) your
waistband'.

14. walks: the Hithpael of the verb is used here, as also in
Gen. 3:8 (cf. also e.g. 2 Sam. 7:6). **anything indecent:** see
comment on 24:1.

(iii) Laws on the fugitive slave and cultic prostitution **23:15–18**
Both of the laws in this section concern the community of the
people of Yahweh, and so are closely related to what precedes.
The fugitive slave who escapes to the land of Israel now belongs
to the community, which then assumes responsibility for him.
Cultic prostitution brought sexual impurity into the community,
and the latter is a concern of many earlier laws (cf. 22:13ff.;
23:1ff., 10ff.).

The hand of the deuteronomic legislator is not very obtrusive
in the two laws. In the first he has introduced the centralization
formula into a quite new context; in the second his contribution
is perhaps more extensive. The basis of this law is to be found
in v. 18*a*, prohibiting a particular practice in relation to cultic
prostitution. This has been later generalized into a complete prohibition in v. 17, along with which v. 18*b* was added. The reference to 'Israel' and the apposition 'your God' indicate that this
extension may well be deuteronomic.

15, 16. The pre-deuteronomic basis of this law seems to be the
law of Exod. 22:21: 'You shall not wrong a stranger or oppress
him, for you were strangers in the land of Egypt'. The motivation
to this prohibition describes Israel's period of *slavery* in Egypt as a
time when they were 'strangers' (*gērîm*) there. This motivation
provided the basis for the application of that prohibition of
oppression to the slave in the present law, so that in effect the
slave is here treated as a *gēr* who may live where he wishes within
Israel. That the deuteronomic legislator is responsible for this
form of the law is not certain. The phrase, **in the place which
he shall choose within one of your towns,** which, with its

affinity to the centralization formula (cf. 12:5, 11, 14, etc), is clearly deuteronomic, may be a deuteronomic addition to the existing law.

The law here goes against general custom in the ancient Near East, according to which fugitive slaves should be returned. The Code of Hammurabi, paras. 15–20 (cf. *ANET*, 166f.), also decrees the death penalty for harbouring runaway slaves.

17. On cultic prostitution on the part of both sexes, cf. Gen. 38:21f.; 1 Kg. 14:24; 15:12; 22:46; 2 Kg. 23:7; Hos. 4:14; Job 36:14. They appeared in Israel's cultic life at different stages of her history.

18. The price paid for the services of a temple prostitute was paid into the temple treasury (cf. Mic. 1:7). **the wages of a dog:** for a study of the term 'dog' with reference to both biblical and other texts, cf. Winton Thomas, *VT* 10, 1960, 410ff. It is used in two ways: firstly, as a term of self-abasement or generally in a pejorative sense; and, secondly, as a term descriptive of a faithful servant and follower. In this latter sense it is used both within the secular and within the religious sphere. So although the context of its use demands that it should be understood as the designation of a male prostitute, it does not necessarily have a pejorative connotation. It means 'a devoted follower' of a god. The last phrase of the verse, **for both of these . . .,** follows badly on the first half (which has a single action as its subject, so that the continuation should be 'for that is . . .'), and clearly refers back to v. 17. For the phrase **an abomination to the Lord** see comment on 7:25.

(iv) Laws on interest, vows, and the property of one's neighbour **23:19–25**
This collection of three different laws has no immediate connection with its context, and the laws themselves are apparently quite unrelated. There are some contacts, however, and these may be strong enough to suggest that it was on the basis of simple associations that the laws were brought together here. First of all, the Exodus law on the treatment of strangers and the law on lending at interest are found together in Exod. 22:21–27, which may account for vv. 19f. being placed immediately after the previous collection where the law on the treatment of strangers is taken up and applied to slaves (vv. 15f.). Secondly, the vow mentioned in v. 18 perhaps suggested the deuteronomic teaching on vows formulated in vv. 21ff. These verses have, moreover,

evidently been constructed on the pattern of the law of vv. 19f.
Finally, the law of vv. 24f. is concerned with honouring the neighbour's property, and so has an association in theme with vv. 19f.
All three laws have a deuteronomic formulation, though at least
the first and the third are in substance of ancient origin.

19, 20. The law here is of ancient origin, and the social evils
to which lending at interest often led were widely appreciated
both in Israel (cf. Prov. 22:7) and elsewhere (cf. the Egyptian
Book of the Dead, B14, in *ANET*, 35). Over against the form of
the law in Exod. 22:25 two chief changes are made here: firstly,
the very general clause at the end of v. 19 has no counterpart in
Exodus; and, secondly, it is only in the Deuteronomic law that
permission to lend on interest to a **foreigner** is made explicit.
The use of the word **brother** in the Deuteronomic law, the
phrase **in all that you undertake** (see 12:18, and the comment
on 12:7), and the concluding phrase of the law indicate deuteronomic formulation and so also responsibility for these changes.
On the distinction between the Israelite and the foreigner in the
application of the law see also 15:2f.

21. The content of vv. 21-23 is not so much law as instruction. It
has no source in the Book of the Covenant in Exodus, but has a
close parallel in Ec. 5:4f. It is a wisdom saying (on wisdom
influence on Deuteronomy, see Introduction, pp. 104f.), the introduction of which at this point was prompted by the reference to a
vow in v. 18. It is probably of deuteronomic formulation; it
follows the pattern of the immediately preceding law, viz. a
central phrase (v. 22) which is antithetical to the two parallel first
and third elements (vv. 21, 23).

23. voluntarily: the word $n^e\underline{d}\bar{a}\underline{b}\bar{a}h$ is here used adverbially;
see 12:6 (and comment) for the same word in the sense of 'free-
will offerings'. The last phrase in the verse, **what you have
promised with your mouth,** is a gloss on **what has passed
your lips.** It disrupts the chiastic structure which is otherwise
clear in these verses: v. 22aα being parallel to v. 24b; v. 22aβ to v.
24a; v. 22bβ to v. 23b; cf. Seitz, *op. cit.*, 177f. The translation of
the second half of v. 23 then is: 'as you have voluntarily. . .'.

24, 25. The two laws here, providing for the sustenance of travel-
lers but also protecting the farmer from robbery, have the same
form of casuistic law using the direct form of address. This is a
deuteronomic formulation of an old and established custom.
The laws are peculiar to Deuteronomy.

(v) *Divorce and remarriage* 24:1-4

This is an old divorce law, which in its present context is concerned solely with the abomination of the remarriage of a divorced woman to her first husband, having already been the wife of a second man. In its structure it is a casuistic law with the protasis in vv. 1-3 and the apodosis in v. 4. The *AV* translation, which finds both a protasis and apodosis in v. 1, makes it a law stipulating the procedure to be followed by the husband who wishes to divorce his wife. However, if this were the intention of the law, it would undoubtedly have included further matter, regarding especially the husband's obligation to repay the bride price in certain circumstances and to make provision for his former wife (for this in the Hammurabi Code, paras. 138ff. cf. *ANET*, 172).

That the pre-deuteronomic law also was concerned to prohibit the marriage of a divorced woman to her first husband after already having remarried, is indicated by the parallel to this law in Jer. 3:1-5. Both passages have the same concern, but the differences between them suggest that they are developments of an earlier law; there is nothing to show, however, that this earlier law was substantially different in intent. See the study by Hobbs, *ZAW* 86, 1974, 23ff. The contribution of the deuteronomic legislator to the law is apparent only in the addition of the abomination formula.

1. Three formal actions are mentioned in both vv. 1 and 3 as required of the husband who divorces his wife: (a) he must write a document attesting his wish to divorce her (cf. also Jer. 3:8; Isa. 50:1); (b) it must be given to her in person by her husband; (c) the husband must formally expel his wife from the home. Provided these formalities are carried out the husband seems to have been completely free in the matter of divorcing his wife. The clause giving the reason for his action, **if then she finds no favour in his eyes because he has found some indecency in her,** is probably a later addition (it has a new beginning with the word *wᵉhāyāh*; see comment on 18:19). That no substantial reason for the divorce was in fact required is clearly enough indicated by v. 3. **some indecency:** it is not clear what this means. It cannot be adultery since this is the subject of other laws and brings with it not divorce but the death penalty (cf. 22:22). The phrase occurs in 23:14, with reference to that which violates the purity and holiness of the camp. So probably it signifies some state of impurity in general, rather than any particular act of indecency.

2. **and becomes . . . wife:** on the meaning of the phrase *weḥāyetāh le*, which properly signifies 'come to belong to', 'become the property of', cf. e.g. Jg. 14:20; 15:2.

4. **she has been defiled:** since the remarriage of a divorced woman was permitted it is unlikely that the defilement was a general state brought about simply by that remarriage. Rather, the woman is defiled by her remarriage only in relation to her first husband (cf. *NEB* 'she has become for him unclean'). **that is an abomination:** the reference could be either to the act of remarriage to her first husband having been divorced by her second (cf. König), or (the word **that** is in fact pointed as a third person singular feminine pronoun) to the wife who commits the act. The abomination formula (for which see comment on 7:25) is referred to the person rather than to the deed in 18:12; 22:5; 25:16. As L'Hour, *Bib* 44, 1963, 24 n. 2, notes, this is the only case where the abomination formula occurs in a casuistic law. It is to be ascribed to deuteronomic editing of the older law. The final clause of the verse is an even later addition, caused mainly by Jer. 3:1 where the consequence of breaking this law is the pollution of the land. The deuteronomic law is concerned with the action of the woman as an abomination to Yahweh rather than with the effect of the action on the land.

(vi) Humanitarian behaviour, especially to the needy **24:5–25:4**
The laws in this collection are very diverse, but have in common a humanitarian attitude extending to fellow Israelites in general, and in particular to the newly married, the borrower, the servant, the socially weak, the guilty at law, and even the animal. In some cases it is possible to understand the basis for the order in which the laws come (for example, there is a coincidence of subject between 24:1–4 and 24:5, and within vv. 19–21; there is a catchword connection between 24:15 and 16); otherwise, however, the order of the laws cannot easily be explained. Some of them are clearly predeuteronomic both in form and content; but those in which direct address appears in a casuistic context (e.g. 24:19ff.) probably have a deuteronomic formulation (see introduction to 12:29–13:18), even though this expresses a pre-deuteronomic custom.

5. The law here is in an impersonal casuistic form, as the preceding law with which it also has a clear connection in subject. It is closely connected too with the war laws in 20:5–7. Here, however, the newly married man (in the war laws he need only be 'betrothed') is exempt from all forms of public service. The basis of the law is undoubtedly the concern that a man should not die childless, but this fundamental aim is now almost lost in the new emphasis on the individual himself and his right to enjoy Yahweh's blessing. This new emphasis is particularly clear in the last part of the verse (**to be happy . . .**), which is probably a deuteronomic addition to the law.

6. a mill or an upper millstone: i.e. both millstones, as together constituting the mill, or even the upper one alone. The millstones were not taken for any monetary value they might have, but (like the cloak in vv. 12f.) as a means of putting pressure on the debtor through depriving him of something essential to his everyday life. It is a law against oppression.

7. The subject of this law appears frequently in extra-biblical law codes (e.g. Hammurabi, para. 14; cf. *ANET*, 166). The parallel law in Exod. 21:16 is in a different form. For the deuteronomic form of the present casuistic law using direct address see the introduction to 12:29–13:18. It is only in the deuteronomic form that it is made explicit that the law refers to the kidnapping of an Israelite. In the context of Deuteronomy this is significant, since occasionally it is made clear that the laws do not apply to relations between Israelites and non-Israelites (cf. 14:21; 15:3; 23:20). **his brethren:** on this deuteronomic usage see comment on 1:16. The following phrase, **the people of Israel,** is an expression which occurs in later parts of Deuteronomy (cf. 1:3; 3:18; 4:44ff.) and is an addition here. **treats him as a slave:** see comment on 21:14.

8, 9. The law on leprosy has been considerably edited by a post-deuteronomic editor. The sudden appearance of the second person plural form of address is one indication of this. In addition, the reference to an already given direction of Moses to the Levitical priests (analogous to 17:18, and note that in the present passage LXX and *Sam* read 'according to all the *tôrāh* that the Levitical priests . . .'), which is probably intended as a general reference to the existing deuteronomic law (see comment on 17:18), points to late deuteronomistic editing here. The original deuteronomic law, in singular address form, may have been (cf. Merendino, *op. cit.*, 301): 'Take heed in an attack of leprosy; remember what the Lord your God did to Miriam'. The reference of the law would have been to Num. 12:14f., where, at the divine direction, Miriam when suffering from leprosy was excluded from the camp for seven days. This was edited through the introduction of the Levitical priests understood as successors of Moses, whose directions are to be followed. It was for rebellion against Moses that Miriam was stricken with leprosy, and it was at the divine command mediated through Moses that she was excluded from the camp. The law in its original form is then closely linked with earlier laws in the complex 23:1ff.

leprosy: according to Hulse, *PEQ* 107, 1975, 87ff., the disease now known as leprosy cannot be shown to have been present in the Near East in Old Testament times. It is not possible to give a precise medical term to translate the word *ṣāraʿaṭ*, but the *NEB* translation 'malignant skin disease' implying skin cancer, is not justified. Rather it would have been some form of 'repulsive scaly skin disease', most likely the modern psoriasis or favus.

10. The form of this law is deuteronomic (**when you …;** cf. also 23:21ff.). It takes up an older law, however, to be found in Exod. 22:26f. It is from this law that the word **neighbour,** in place of the expected 'brother', comes. The Deuteronomic law is distinct from its Exodus counterpart, however, in not allowing the creditor to enter the borrower's home. **pledge:** there is a clear connection with the law of v. 6, but the verbs used are different.

12. The main case of vv. 10f. deals with pledges in general. The subsidiary case in vv. 12f. deals specifically with the taking of a cloak or mantle in pledge. This only becomes clear in the next verse, however. The law of Exod. 22:26f., which deals primarily with this, is presupposed.

13. It is clear from Am. 2:8; Prov. 20:16; 27:13 and Job 22:6, that garments taken in pledge were frequently retained. The last clause, **it shall be righteousness …,** is the counterpart to the declaratory formula 15:9; 24:15 (cf. 6:25; 23:22).

14, 15. The original prohibition would have been simply **you shall not oppress a hired servant** (the *NEB* 'you shall not keep back the wages…' is based on the reading *śekar* for *śākîr*, following a Qumran text. However, this reading probably came in secondarily under the influence of the appearance of the word *śekārô*, 'his wages', in v. 15, after the phrase 'poor and needy' was secondarily added appositionally to v. 14. So the *MT* reading should be retained). The rest of v. 14 has typical deuteronomic vocabulary: **brethren** (cf. v. 7), **sojourners** (see on 1:16), **your towns** (e.g. 12:15). V. 15, which in fact restricts the original law by confining the notion of oppression to the withholding of wages, was added by the deuteronomic legislator to bind the law to the immediately preceding one by reference to the sun going down (which properly belongs to the pledge law) and by the use of the antithetical expressions: **cry against you** instead of 'bless you'; **sin in you** instead of 'righteousness to you'.

16. This law, quoted by the compiler of Kings in 2 Kg. 14:6, concerns the human administration of justice, and not divine justice, and so it is not directly comparable with the decalogue in Dt. 5:9. It is not in the form expected of a deuteronomic law (viz. expressed in the second person singular form of address) and gives no sign of being a late addition; it must, therefore, be an older law quoted by the deuteronomic legislator. It affirms a principle which is by no means a late phenomenon in Israelite history. Jos. 7:24 and 2 Sam. 21:1–9 are exceptional cases which find no reflection in pre-deuteronomic Old Testament law. The inclusion of the law at this point has the purpose of emphasizing individual responsibility in the laws of the context (which is particularly relevant here since the laws of the Book of the Covenant which the deuteronomic legislator is partially reproducing, Exod. 22:21ff., mention the effect of punishment on wives and children). There is also a catchword connection with the previous verse **(sin)**, which is probably sufficient to explain the presence of the law at precisely this point.

17. The protection of the rights of the socially weak is a classic ancient Near Eastern theme, especially in the wisdom literature (e.g. the second chapter of the Instruction of Amen-em-opet, cf. *ANET*, 422; cf. also Prov. 22:22; Job 24:3, etc.). Moreover, this particular group of those deserving charity is mentioned three further times in the immediately following verses. However, it is unlikely that all three members of the group were originally mentioned in this verse; **fatherless** is awkwardly added, without any conjunction, on the basis of its occurrences later. On the subject of the verse, cf. also Exod. 23:6; Dt. 27:19.

18. This formula is found in slightly different forms in 15:15; 24:22. Since it is the context of 15:15 that has slavery as its subject it was probably there that the formula originally belonged. Then it became a fixed saying which could be applied to other laws of a humanitarian nature in a somewhat looser way.

19–22. These verses have a parallel in Lev. 19:19f., though the differences between them preclude any direct literary dependence. Apart from other differences, it is only Deuteronomy which refers to olives. Both go back to the ancient custom of leaving behind a portion of the produce of the field as an offering for the gods or spirits of fertility. It now appears, however, as a humanitarian obligation only. The final formula in v. 19, **in all the work of your hands,** is usually a concluding formula (see 14:29, 16:15), and its appearance here in the middle of the law is surprising. Merendino, *op. cit.*, 307f., suggests that v. 19 is to some extent independent of vv. 20–22, but the common structure of vv. 19, 20 and 21 holds all three together.

25:1–3. Here the deuteronomic legislator has taken up what were originally separate casuistic laws and has appended his own comment in v. 3. V. 1, referring to 'judges' is an independent law prescribing that disputes should be brought before the courts. V. 2, referring to 'the judge', prescribed that punishment should be administered in the presence of the judge, in order to ensure that the guilty did not get more (or less) punishment than he deserved. V. 3 takes no notice of v. 2, but simply sets a general limit on the number of stripes which may be given in punishment. This verse passes over into second person singular form of address; its use of the word 'brother' also indicates deuteronomic authorship.

1. dispute: the word *rîb* is a legal term, designating a 'case at law'; cf. Exod. 23:2, 3, 6; Dt. 21:5; 2 Sam. 15:2, 4; Mic. 7:9; Jer. 50:34, etc. **innocent ... guilty:** these forensic terms are also frequently translated 'righteous ... wicked'; see comment on 16:18.

2. The verse has a new beginning (*wᵉhāyāh*; see comment on 18:19), indicating that in the present complex arrangement the apodosis begins at this point. The overall concern of the present law is, therefore, to ensure that the guilty is not punished excessively. **deserves to be beaten:** for a parallel to the Hebrew 'a son of beating', cf. e.g. 1 Sam. 20:31 'a son of death', for 'deserves to die'. For the form of punishment here, cf. Exod. 21:20; Prov. 10:13; 19:25; 26:3; Isa. 50:6.

3. Forty stripes ... but not more: the number forty also appears in prescribed punishments in extra-biblical law (e.g. Middle Assyrian Law A 18; cf. *ANET*, 181). In order to avoid accidental excess punishment, and so a breach of this law, the number was later fixed at thirty-nine (cf. Josephus, *Antiquities*, IV. viii, 21, 23; 2 Cor. 11:24).

4. An isolated law on showing kindness to animals; it has no connection with its immediate context, but does have some contact with 24:19ff. The law is given an allegorical interpretation by Paul in 1 Cor. 9:9, though Rabbinic exegesis generally understood it literally; see the study by Lisowsky, in *Das ferne und nahe Wort*, 144ff.

(vii) The preservation of the family 25:5-12

The two laws in this section are associated in that both are concerned with the possibility of a family becoming extinct. This is obvious in the case of the first of the laws; with the second law, it is a probable interpretation, for the crime here is not immodesty on the part of the woman so much as the possibility of her damaging male sexual organs thus destroying procreative ability. The deuteronomic legislator has in fact strengthened the link between the laws through an addition in v. 11 which makes it a case of brothers fighting (see comment).

The reason for the laws having been brought in just here is not clear; there is general affinity of subject in that laws on marriage have already appeared in the section (24:1ff.), and the present laws can also be seen in the humanitarian context of the whole, in that they warn against maltreatment both of the one who has the right of Levirate marriage and of a man involved in a fight.

5. The purpose of Levirate (from the Latin *levir*, 'husband's brother') marriage, so far as this law is concerned, is clear from the reference to the possibility of the widow marrying a stranger: it is to avoid the loss of property to the family. It is not so much a question of the family name being extinguished (which is referred to only in v. 6) as of division of the ancestral property. The unity of the family on its land is emphasized by the opening clause: **If brothers dwell together.** The word translated **son** was understood by LXX (cf. also Mt. 22:24; Mk. 12:19; Lk. 20:28 and *AV*) to mean 'child'. Since the issue is one of inheritance, this translation presupposes the possibility that daughters could inherit; this possibility is provided for in Num. 27:8, though the time of origin of the latter is uncertain. **husband's brother:** Hebrew has a special term, *yāḇām*, for this particular relation, so indicating that the custom presupposed by the law was a fixed institution in Israel. It was in fact a widely diffused custom (cf. de Vaux, *Ancient Israel*, 37f.), which varied somewhat in different cultures and times. Within Israel too there was modification over the course of time. Gen. 38 apparently understands that all the

children of a Levirate marriage are reckoned as the family of the
deceased brother; here it is only the firstborn son. Moreover, a
certain weakening in the institution is discernible in the law
here in that failure to fulfil the duty is seen as a disgrace but not as
a crime deserving of punishment. In the later Holiness Code
(Lev. 18:16; 20:21) such marriages are forbidden.

7. The reference to the elders and the gate indicates the pre-
deuteronomic origin of this law; see introduction to 16:18-17:7.
A brother might refuse to perform the duty required of him
simply because (as with Onan) the child would not be his.
It is sometimes suggested, however, that there may be a further
motive here. The property of the deceased brother, if his widow
did not marry again (see comment on v. 5), would pass back to
his family. On the assumption that the father is dead (only the
brothers are mentioned in v. 5), it is the surviving brother who
will then inherit the property. So the prospect of personal gain
may play a significant role in the brother's refusal to fulfil what is
seen as his duty. However, procedure in inheritance rights is very
uncertain, and this particular view makes for difficulties in the
interpretation of v. 9. If through marriage to a foreigner the
deceased husband's land would go to the foreigner (cf. v. 5), presumably also the widow could sell her deceased husband's land for
the sake of her own sustenance (cf. Ru. 4:3), or indeed retain it
for herself (cf. 2 Kg. 8:3).

9. pull his sandal off his foot: this action is undoubtedly to
be seen in the light of the fact that ownership of land was legally
effected through the walking over it by the owner (cf. Gen. 13:17).
The plain significance of taking off the shoe is the renunciation of
any claim to ownership, and by passing the shoe to another a
legal transfer of claim is indicated (cf. Ru. 4:7). If it is understood,
however, that the refusal of the brother-in-law to perform his duty
is motivated by personal gain (see comment on v. 7), then the
action here must be interpreted as deliberately ironical (cf.
Phillips); but there is no sign of this. In fact, the brother has
renounced (prospective) ownership of the land. The legal indication of this is the removal of his shoe; that the widow should
do this for him, and at the same time spit in his face, is a sign that
the brother's renunciation is a disgrace. By it he has not only
given up ownership of the land but also has left the widow in a
situation of insecurity. For a study of the action, cf. Rengstorf,
Re-Investitur, 46ff. **shall answer and say:** see comment on 21:7.

11. with one another: the Hebrew includes the phrase 'a man and his brother', which, if taken literally, constitutes a clear point of contact with the previous law. The phrase is, however, most probably a deuteronomic addition made precisely in order to provide such a link.

12. you shall cut off her hand: this is the only place in the Old Testament where physical mutilation is prescribed by law as a punishment, apart from the *lex talionis* (19:21). Such punishment is, however, quite characteristic of extra-biblical law; cf. the Middle Assyrian Laws, A 4ff., *ANET*, 180f., etc., and the study by Gordon *JPOS* 15, 1935, 29ff, **your eye shall have no pity:** significantly, in 19:21 this phrase introduces the *lex talionis*.

(viii) Laws on trade and on Amalek **25:13–19**
The abomination law in vv. 13–16 has been edited by the deuteronomic legislator in vv. 15f. (see comment). The pre-deuteronomic law consisted of the two prohibitions of vv. 13f. followed by the abomination clause. The latter otherwise characterizes laws which are anti-Canaanite in tone (see comment on 7:25), and this law too is seen by L'Hour, *RB* 71, 1964, 499 (cf. also Buis), as anti-Canaanite. It was from the Canaanites that Israel learned the art and ways of commerce. This is supported especially by Hos. 12:7f. (where 'trader' is the translation of the Hebrew $k^e na^c an$). However, while the anti-Canaanite element may be found in the law, it is certainly no essential part of it; the morality which the law advocates is a traditional wisdom concern appearing in both biblical and extra-biblical wisdom literature (cf. Prov. 11:1; 16:11; 20:23; the Instruction of Amen-em-opet, chapter 16, *ANET*, 423, etc.).

The law on Amalek in vv. 17–19 is a late addition. Not only does it change in one place to second person plural form of address, but it has no connection in content with any other part of the deuteronomic law. The verses are a redactional addition intended to round off the section 23:1–25:19, taking up ideas from the beginning of the section. Just as certain categories of people and certain peoples are utterly excluded from membership in the people of Yahweh, so also Amalek is to be utterly destroyed. This is supported by the clear connection between the verses and the late 23:4a. The verses may also be intended to round off the whole corpus of law, for with the motif of 'rest' they form a counterpart to 12:9f. at the beginning of the law corpus. The authorship of the verses is not quite certain; but connection with other passages in Deuteronomy, and the style, using both singular and plural forms of address, would indicate the late deuteronomistic editor.

13. two kinds of weights: literally 'a stone and a stone'; for this idiom, cf. Prov. 20:23; Ps. 12:2; and on the fraudulent use of weights and measures cf. Am. 8:5. Standard weights were used for measuring: through using a heavier weight for buying than for selling, the merchant could easily defraud his customers to his own profit.

14. two kinds of measures: the Hebrew refers here to the ephah, a measure of quantity used for grain, flour, etc.; for a detailed treatment, cf. de Vaux, *Ancient Israel*, 199ff.

15. A positive command is out of place in this law, particularly as an immediate prelude to the abomination clause in v. 16. The latter is made logically ambiguous by the presence here of v. 15. Since, moreover, the motivation clause in v. 15*b* is probably deuteronomistic (see comment on 22:6f.), it is best to see the whole verse as an addition to the original pair of prohibitions.

16. On the abomination clause, which is otherwise attached directly to negative laws, see comment on 7:25. **all who act dishonestly:** this is an addition, made necessary by the addition of v. 15. Apart from 32:4, the word *ʿāwel* (translated here **dishonestly**) does not otherwise occur in Deuteronomy, but only in Jeremiah (2:5) and later.

17. as you came out of Egypt: the use of the second person plural form of address here in an otherwise singular context is remarkable. The phrase is in the plural also in 23:4; 24:9.

18. There is no basis for the information contained in this verse in the tradition in Exod. 17:8-17 to which reference is presumably being made (compare v. 19 and Exod. 17:14). According to Weinfeld, *Deuteronomy*, 275, the deuteronomic author could not see justification for the command to destroy Amalek simply in the fact that Amalek had attacked Israel, and so supplied the idea that Amalek carried out a particularly cruel and inhuman form of attack.

19. has given you rest: see comment on 3:20; 12:9.

(G) TWO LITURGICAL CONFESSIONS: **26:1-15**
The two sections brought together here, in vv. 1-11 and 12-15, are from the hand of the second deuteronomist, as their language indicates. Their presence here is puzzling, for the subject with

which they deal has already appeared in the deuteronomic law, in 14:22–29. In relation to this law, however, 26:1–15 performs a specific function: the verses provide a historical-theological foundation to the ancient custom of offering first-fruits and tithes, Thereby, this agricultural custom is firmly assimilated into Israelite faith. The reference to the exodus from Egypt, and to the gift of the land, perform this function.

(i) Ceremony for the offering of first-fruits 26:1–11

There are two difficulties in particular in this text, which indicate that it is not a uniform composition. Firstly, it contains two confessions, one in v. 3 and the other in vv. 5ff., which are simply set side by side. Secondly, whereas v. 4 states that the priest lays the basket before the altar, in v 10. it is the worshipper himself who does this. Vv. 3f. belong together and they should probably be taken as a late addition to their present context. Their concern to emphasize the role of the priest points to the work of a post-exilic priestly redactor (cf. Seitz, *op. cit.*, 248, and comment on vv. 3f.), and also perhaps to a desire to effect some agreement with 18:4, according to which the first-fruits are given to the priest. V. 5 is, therefore, the original continuation of v. 2.

Main interest in this section has centered on vv. 5–9 since von Rad first proposed that in these verses there is an early summary of salvation history in the form of a creed (see comment on 6:21–25). Though presently cast in the familiar terminology of Deuteronomy, the verses were held by von Rad to have the form of an early creed, such as appears in several other Old Testament passages. This creed was understood to be basic to the whole form of the Hexateuch which in fact is then an expansive elaboration of the creed.

Although von Rad found wide following for his conclusions, more recent study (for which see especially Hyatt, in *Translating*, 152ff.) has cast considerable doubt both on the possibility of assigning an ancient date to these verses and on the view that they have the form of a creed. Von Rad admitted the presence of deuteronomic language in vv. 5–9, but this he regarded as the result of editorial work which could be removed in order to recover the original ancient form. However, such literary-critical work on the verses is not possible. Rost in particular (*Credo*, 11ff.) has shown that the last part of v. 5 together with vv. 6–9 form a unit of which the language has its closest parallels in the framework passages of Deuteronomy (see comment on vv. 8, 9). Furthermore, it is also clear that the verses cannot be abstracted from their context and presented as an independent form. The parallel passage in 6:21ff. has already been seen to be an integral part of its context, and here too it is not possible to establish the existence of an independent form simply adopted for the present context. The verses rather constitute a historical summary composed for the present context with the purpose of giving a historical foundation to the custom of offering first-fruits (cf. Carmichael, *VT* 19, 1969, 273ff.). Just as the deuteronomic legislator in 16:12 referred to Israel in Egypt to give an Israelite historical foundation to the originally Canaanite Feast of Weeks, so here Israelite history once again is referred to in order to give a particularly Israelite foundation to an agricultural rite adopted by Israel.

The author of vv. 5–9 uses expressions which appear in older sources (see comment on vv. 5, 6), but the whole is nevertheless a deuteronomistic composition which in its form has no older prototype. This does not mean that the verses should then be taken as a summary of the Hexateuchal tradition, a simple reversal of von Rad's theory, for it is doubtful that any such direct relationship between the two exists. Childs, *VTS* 16, 1967, 30ff., has pointed out that quite apart from problems associated with the place of the Sinai tradition, the verses do not refer to the Reed Sea episode, which is so central to the presentation in the book of Exodus. This excludes direct derivation or dependence of the one on the other. The verses cannot, therefore, be taken as an ancient form nor as an independent creed. They are a historical summary composed for the offering of first-fruits.

The offering of first-fruits is itself, of course, older than the deuteronomic law, and it is on a formula associated with this rite that the historical summary has been built. This formula is now to be found in vv. 5 and 10: 'A wandering Aramean was my father, but now I bring the first of the fruit of the ground which thou, O Lord, hast given me' (see comment on vv. 5, 10), a formula in which the offerer contrasted the status of his ancestors with his own situation in the context of giving thanks for the gift of the land on which his prosperity was based. The elaboration of this through the prefixing of vv. 1f. and the insertion of the rest of v. 5 and vv. 6–9 is the work not of the deuteronomic legislator but, as the language indicates, of a later deuteronomistic editor. From this same editor came also the rest of v. 10 and v. 11.

2. first: on the translation of *rē'šîṭ* see comment on 18:4. The end of the verse clearly presupposes the deuteronomic legislation on the central sanctuary. That this alone is a later addition to the text is unlikely; all of vv. 1–2 is from the one hand, and the structure (see comment on 17:14) and vocabulary (**inheritance; which the Lord your God gives you; the place which the Lord your God will choose, to make his name to dwell there**) are typical of Deuteronomy.

3, 4. The two verses belong together and are clearly a later supplement to the text. They introduce the priest who otherwise plays no part in the proceedings (cf. also 21:5), and act as a corrective to v. 10 where it is the worshipper who himself lays the first-fruits before Yahweh. The verses should therefore be assigned to a late priestly redactor. **who is in office at that time:** an expression which properly belongs to the office of judge in 17:9; 19:17; it is here secondarily understood also of the priest.

5. you shall make response: a translation of a fixed pair of Hebrew verbs: 'you shall declare and say'; see comment on 21:7. **wandering:** alternatively 'ready to perish' (*AV, RV*). However, the context, which contrasts the situation of the landless ancestor with that of the present worshipper, favours the *RSV* translation (cf. also *NEB* 'homeless'). **Aramean:** it is often simply understood that Jacob is intended here; but this is in fact not stated and can be justified only on the basis of a direct reference to the Genesis tradition of Jacob's descent into Egypt. However, the reference to the descent into Egypt and the events there in the remainder of v. 5 and in vv. 6–9 belongs to a secondary deuteronomistic elaboration of an old text which referred only to the **wandering Aramean**. This makes the identification with Jacob quite uncertain, even though this identification was probably understood by the deuteronomistic interpolator. Whoever may be intended, however, the father of Israel is here connected with a people with whom Israel in the monarchic period was frequently at war. There is no indication that the intention is to make a disparaging comment on the ancestor's origin; rather, the designation refers factually to his origin from the east as tradition related it. So the designation must be an ancient one. In the words **a wandering Aramean was my father** we have the old beginning of a text here brought into a deuteronomistic setting. For a study of the phrase, cf. Beek, *OTS* 8, 1950, 193ff. The remainder of the verse belongs, however, with vv. 6–9, forming a unit secondarily interpolated into the old text. This unit is a late deuteronomistic composition using some words and phrases derived from older tradition. The connection with Exod. 1 is particularly clear. In the present verse this chapter (Exod. 1:9) is the source of the phrase **mighty, and populous** (cf. also 7:1; 9:14). **sojourned:** i.e. lived as an 'alien'; see comment on 1:16.

6. In this deuteronomistic continuation there is again contact with Exod. 1 in the words **afflicted** (Exod. 1:11f.) and **hard bondage** (Exod. 1:14, a verse usually assigned to P). The phrase **treated us harshly,** and in the next verse the reference to Israel crying to Yahweh, have parallels in Num. 20:15f.

8. a mighty hand . . . signs and wonders: see comment on 4:34.

9. a land flowing with milk and honey: see comment on 6:3.

10. The first half of the verse continues the old text at the beginning of v. 5. The second half **(And you shall set it down . . .)** is a deuteronomistic supplement bringing the text into its new context of centralized worship. On the phrase **the Lord your God:** see comment on 1:6.

11. This verse continues the deuteronomistic v. 10*b*. By it the deuteronomistic editor has strengthened the connection of first-fruits and tithes, mentioned in the following verses: the command **you shall rejoice** points to a meal, to be enjoyed by the worshipper with his household and **the Levite and the sojourner,** at the sanctuary (see comment on 12:18; 14:23), and it is to this that the following verses, dealing with the tithes, refer. See the discussion of the topic in the introduction to 14:22–29; the precise relationship between first-fruits and tithes remains a problem.

(ii) Ceremony for the offering of the triennial tithe **26:12–15**
This section deals with the triennial tithe to be given to the needy. From v. 14 in particular (see comment) it is clear that in this section older material has been adapted to a new context. The precise place and time of origin and use of this older material are obscure, but in the present context it is a deuteronomistic editor (see comment on vv. 13, 14, 15) who has brought an ancient confession of cultic purity into the context of a confession of obedience to the commandments in general.

12. the year of tithing: it is clear from 14:22 that the produce was tithed annually. The later editor of these verses emphasizes

that the tithe is given every three years. The annual levy is that
of the first-fruits. **the sojourner, the fatherless and the widow:**
see comment on 1:16; 14:29.

13. before the Lord your God: the section nowhere refers to
the central sanctuary, though it is probably implied in this
phrase; cf. 14:23; 15:20; 16:11, 16. Centralization is here presupposed as well known in so far as the section depends on the
law of 14:22-29—a further indication that it is a post-deuteronomic compiler at work here. **I have removed:** the same verb is
used here as that translated 'purge' in the formula found in 13:5;
17:7, 12, etc. The need for such a strong expression is indicated
by the description of the tithe as **the sacred portion,** i.e. something in which secular participation and to which any secular
claim is totally prohibited.

14. The first half of the verse contains three negative statements
which have been classified by Galling, *ZAW* 47, 1929, 125ff., as a
confession of innocence through which the worshipper would
declare to the priest his ritual fitness to participate in cultic
festivals. The confession, however, stands in some tension with
its present context. According to the latter (cf. v. 12) the
whole tithe was given to the Levite, the sojourner, the fatherless,
and the widow. It is then, at least superfluous to detail these three
particular ways in which this requirement might not have been
fulfilled. Secondly, if the confession is concerned with the ritual
purity of the one giving the tithe or with the ritual purity of the
tithe itself, it indicates that the tithe is being offered to Yahweh
rather than to the poor. Ritual purity would scarcely have been
a consideration in the latter case.

Both of these points suggest that this confession now stands in
a secondary context. The closer definition of the original context
is difficult. It concerned an offering to Yahweh which was
accompanied by a denial that any part of the offering or part of
the crop from which the offering was taken, had been eaten in a
context made unclean through contact with the dead. Cazelles,
RB 55, 1948, 54ff., has attempted to be more specific, through
connecting the words translated **mourning** and **unclean** (which
he takes as direct objects of the verbs rather than adverbially:
'(the bread of) mourning' (as Hos. 9:4) and 'the unclean thing')
with a formal meal held as part of a ritual lamentation over the
death of the Canaanite vegetation god Baal who is taken to be
referred to in the words **the dead.** The suggestion is uncertain

though it fits the general context well. The confession has some
such original reference as this; it has been taken up by the
deuteronomist whose contribution continues in the second half of
the verse. For the phrase **obeyed the voice of,** cf. 27:10; 28:1,
2, 15, 45, 62; 30:2, 8, 10, etc.

15. The idea of God dwelling in heaven and looking down on
the earth appears in the deuteronomistic 1 Kg. 8:30 and other
late passages, cf. 2. Chr. 30:27; Jer. 25:30; Zech. 2:13. **a land
flowing with milk and honey:** see comment on 6:3.

D. THE SEALING OF THE COVENANT: 26:16-27:26
This section is composed of five fragments, all of which (with
the possible exception of 26:16-19 and 27:9-10) are apparently
unrelated. They are all late, the last being perhaps the latest of
all. Although none of the passages can clearly be claimed as
pre-deuteronomistic, there is some indication that in some places
they do ultimately depend on an older covenant tradition (see
comment on 27:2, 12, 13; and the introduction to 27:11-13). It
is difficult to account for the emphasis which is put on the fact that
the covenant-making, explicitly associated with Shechem, is to
be carried out as soon as the land is entered, otherwise than by
assuming that a covenant tradition, historically located at
Shechem, is here consciously divorced from its setting, and made
to serve the purpose of indicating that Israel's entry into the
land brings with it automatically and immediately her entry
into the covenant relationship (see also comment on 11:30; 27:2).

The section as a whole occurs in a transitional stage between
the proclamation of the law and the blessings and curses which
follow on obedience and disobedience. In it the covenant is
sealed, Israel's status as the people of Yahweh is affirmed, and
she is pointed in summary fashion on a number of occasions
(including 27:15-26 which belongs in this context) to the whole
law which must now govern her existence.

(A) THE COVENANT FORMULA: 26:16-19
V. 16 both concludes the previous section (through connection
with 12:1), and provides a transition to the following 'covenant
formula' in vv. 17-19. Although the word 'covenant' is not used
in the verses this designation is not altogether a misnomer, for vv. 17
and 18f. clearly contain the two parts of a formal declaration

whereby an agreement was sealed. Indeed, it has even been proposed (cf. Smend, *Bundesformel*, 9) that this formula goes back to the covenant concluded between Josiah and the people in the course of Josiah's reform, as mentioned in 2 Kg. 23:1–3. It may indeed be the case that vv. 17–19 ultimately depend on some cultic ceremony of covenant conclusion (on the reform of Josiah see above Introduction, pp. 85ff.); but certainly in their present form the verses are late deuteronomistic. The closest parallels to the threefold combination 'statutes . . . commandments . . . ordinances' are to be found only in late passages (5:31; 6:1; 7:11; 8:11; 11:1), and other expressions both in v. 16 ('statutes and ordinances', 'be careful to do', 'with all your heart and all your soul') and in the covenant formula ('obey his voice', 'a people for his own possession', 'a people holy to the Lord your God') are all to be set within the literature of the deuteronomic-deuteronomistic writers.

That the covenant formula has a history before the deuteronomic writings is an uncertain point. Smend not only linked this particular example of it with Josiah's reform, but also took that as the time and place of the formula's origin. Similarly, Perlitt, *Bundestheologie*, 106f. sees pre-deuteronomistic history for the formula only in Hos. 2:23, which, however, is argued to be an isolated theological forerunner of the covenant formula which grew out of Hosea's own message and has no background in Israelite tradition in any covenant festival or any covenant theology. Even if 2 Sam. 7:24 and 2 Kg. 11:17 are to be included with Hos. 2:23 as pointers to a pre-deuteronomic history of the covenant formula (cf. Lohfink, *ZKTh* 91, 1969, 525f.), it certainly remains true that it is in deuteronomic and later literature that the language and thought of the covenant are prominent (see also above, Introduction, pp. 64ff.). In its present context the formula plays a significant role: it marks the conclusion of the law, establishes the formal status of the covenant partners in relation to that law, and leads over to the blessings and curses to be proclaimed in the next part of the book.

16. Through the words **statutes and ordinances** a connection is established with 12:1 and the collection of law is brought formally to a close. The connection of other phrases in the verse with late passages (**commands to do** as in 4:5; **this day** as in 4:8; 5:1; 6:6, etc.; **be careful to do** as in 4:6; 7:12, etc.) shows that it is the late deuteronomistic editor rather than the deuteronomic compiler at work here.

17. You have declared this day concerning the Lord: the verb in this clause (and in the corresponding clause in v. 18) is the Hiphil of the verb 'āmar, 'to say', which in this form occurs only in these two places in the Old Testament. As an alternative to the *RSV* (cf. also *NEB* 'recognized the Lord') it may be taken in the usual Hiphil causative sense 'you have caused the Lord to declare'. This would have the effect of making the content of v. 17 a declaration on the part of Yahweh and of vv. 18f. a declaration by Israel. Lohfink, *ZKTh* 91, 1969, 529ff., proposes the causative translation, pointing out that this may mean not simply 'to cause someone to say' but 'to let someone say' or 'to accept what someone says'. So here the translation would be 'You have agreed this day to the declaration of the Lord that . . .', and in v. 18 'the Lord has agreed this day to your declaration that . . .' The translation is somewhat awkward, however, and apart from following the normal significance of the Hiphil it has in its favour only the point that the phrases in vv. 18f. 'as he has promised you' and 'as he has spoken' are perhaps more suitable in a declaration of Israel rather than in one of Yahweh. Whatever translation is adopted, each declaration refers to the obligations undertaken by both parties to the covenant, and the reference is to a solemn legal act whereby the covenant is agreed.

18. a people for his own possession: see comment on 7:6. Each declaration refers to the obligations incumbent on both parties. So v. 17 refers to one obligation undertaken by Yahweh (that he will be Israel's God) and three obligations undertaken by Israel (that they will walk in his ways, that they will keep his statutes and his commandments and his ordinances, and that they will obey his voice). On the other hand, vv. 18f. refer to three obligations undertaken by Yahweh (that Israel will be his special possession, that he will set Israel above all nations, and that Israel will be a people holy to the Lord) and only one obligation undertaken by Israel (that they will keep all the commandments).

19. in praise and in fame and in honour: the context seems to indicate that praise, fame and honour will be conferred on Israel through the action of Yahweh. However, the same phrase in Jer. 13:11 (cf. also Jer. 33:9) justifies the sense expressed in the *NEB* translation here: 'to bring him praise and fame and glory'. **a people holy:** Exod. 19:6, which undoubtedly stands behind vv. 18f., has 'a holy nation'. For Deuteronomy, however, the nations (as in this verse) are the non-Israelite peoples. Other

distinctive characteristics of Deuteronomy over against Exod.
19:3–8 are noted by Wildberger, *Jahwes Eigentumsvolk*, 18f., 92ff.;
however, the differences between the two are not sufficiently
great to justify Wildberger's view that Exod. 19:3–8 represents an
old pre-deuteronomic election tradition. See also comment on 7:6.

(B) THE WRITING OF THE LAW: **27:1–8**

This is the first section of a very fragmentary chapter in which
there is little relationship between the sections within the chapter
or between the chapter as a whole and its context. Within this
section too there is disunity. The repetition of vv. 2f. in vv. 4*b*,
8 (which probably originally stood together) seems to have
arisen because of a misunderstanding of the relationship between
v. 2 and v. 4 (see comment on v. 4), and vv. 5–7 are a later addition
in deuteronomic-deuteronomistic-style, which stand nevertheless
in some conflict with deuteronomic-deuteronomistic thought on
the central sanctuary. The language of the basis of the section, vv. 1–
4*a*, is deuteronomistic and probably comes from the second deuteronomistic editor, though the idea that it expresses, that of the writing of the law, is an old and essential aspect of treaty and covenant
making.

1. Moses is spoken of in the third person otherwise in 1:1–5;
4:41ff.; 5:1; 29:1f., all of which are late passages. A further
indication of the late deuteronomistic origin of the present
verse is the comprehensive use of the word **commandment;**
see comment on 5:31. The verse probably contains an even
later addition in the words **and the elders of Israel.** These
otherwise never appear in Deuteronomy alongside Moses in
this way, and their unsuitability here is indicated by the words
which I command you. Alternatively (cf. Smith), there may
be a fusion of two introductions here: 'Moses commanded the
elders . . .' and 'Moses commanded the people . . .'

2. on the day you pass over the Jordan: this definite
statement cannot be taken vaguely as 'when you pass over the
Jordan' in order to accommodate the verse with v 4. The latter,
prescribing that the inscribed stones are to be set up on Ebal,
near Shechem (and so probably at a place which Israel would
not reach on the day of crossing the Jordan), is inconsistent with
this verse; the latter points to an action to be undertaken as soon
as the Jordan has been crossed. As in 11:30 (see comment) so here
it must be supposed that there is an intentional conflation of

traditions, those of Shechem where Israel's covenant tradition was particularly preserved, and those of Gilgal, the sanctuary on the border of west Jordan where memories of Israel's first entry into the land were preserved. This conflation would have had the purpose of strengthening the connection of covenant and land, law and life in the promised land; the law is designed for the regulation of Israel's life in the land, and from the moment she sets foot there the provisions of the law become operative.

3. Vv. 2 and 3 belong together as the continuation of v. 1. They are all late deuteronomistic. This is supported in the present verse by the use of the word **law** (*tôrāh*), which presupposes the law of Deuteronomy as an existing entity (see comment on 1:5). The writing on plastered stone was evidently an Egyptian practice, distinct from engraving on stone (cf. Job 19:23f). Elsewhere (Jos. 24:27; cf. also Gen. 31:48, 52; Isa. 19:19f.) the stone is witness to the covenant rather than bearer of the written record. McCarthy, *Treaty*, 126, explains this as an application of the treaty tradition of writing to the old Israelite concept of the stone as witness. On treaty influence on Deuteronomy see above, Introduction, pp. 31ff. **a land flowing with milk and honey:** see comment on 6:3.

4. Ebal: the stones are to be erected on the mountain traditionally associated with the curse rather than on Gerizim which was associated with the blessing; see comment on 11:29. *Sam* reads 'Gerizim' here for the *MT* Ebal, a difference which is usually explained as an arbitrary change on the part of *Sam*, since Gerizim became the sacred mountain of the Samaritan community. However, in support of the *BHS* proposal that the *Sam* text preserves a better reading than *MT*, it is certainly possible that after the Samaritan schism Gerizim was changed to Ebal in *MT* as a result of anti-Samaritan polemic (cf. also Bülow, *ZDPV* 73, 1957, 104 n. 14). The second half of the verse (**and you shall plaster them with plaster**) repeats the command already given in v. 2. The words should be taken, along with v. 8, as a late addition from the hand of a late editor conscious of the discrepancy between vv. 2 and 4 in the matter of when and where the stones were to be erected (see comment on v. 2). For this editor, apparently, the stones to be set up on Ebal are a second set, for which the same procedure is adopted as for those to be erected as soon as the Jordan is crossed; cf. also Mittmann, *Deuteronomium 1:1–6:3*, 14.

5–7. The absence of any reference to 'the place which the Lord your God shall choose' puts these verses outside the deuteronomic and deuteronomistic context, and in so far as this description of the central sanctuary characterizes deuteronomic-deuteronomistic literature, these verses clearly conflict with that context. Yet in a number of respects there are links with that context: first, in the familiar deuteronomic-deuteronomistic phrase **the Lord your God;** secondly, in the reference to eating at the sanctuary (cf. e.g. 12:7, 18); and, thirdly, in the clause at the end of v. 7 **and you shall rejoice before the Lord your God** (cf. 12:7, 12, 18; 14:26; 16:11). It seems likely, therefore, that the verses are a secondary insertion into this context from the hand of someone familiar with deuteronomic and deuteronomistic terminology, who thought that the setting up of stones inscribed with the law implied the presence of a sanctuary and an altar. This, however, is outside the real concern of the deuteronomistic context, which is focused rather on the idea of Israel's subjection to the law on the point of entry into the land. The one responsible for the addition of the verses drew on the altar law of Exod. 20:24f., though he did not follow the latter in allowing for the possibility of an altar of earth. Jos. 8:30–35, where the fulfilment of this commandment is recorded, presupposes the presence of this addition and understands that the inscribed stones and the stones with which the altar was built were the same.

6. burnt offerings: see comment on 12:6.

7. peace offerings: Levine, *Presence*, 45ff., suggests that the sacrifice translated 'peace offerings' was an ancient one which in early time was largely reserved for royal and/or national celebrations of a dedicatory or commemorative character. It is only in later times, in Ezekiel and the priestly writing, that it becomes an element of regular public cultic worship, being prescribed for Pentecost (Lev. 23:15ff.). Levine also thinks that the worshipper participated in the consumption of the animal sacrificed as a 'peace offering' (cf. also de Vaux, *Studies*, 32f.). However, the latter point is not really certain; when a meal is mentioned after reference to the peace offering (cf. Exod. 32:6; 2 Sam. 6:17ff.; 1 Kg. 3:15 and the present passage) it is not necessarily implied that the latter formed part of the meal, for in all these passages 'burnt offerings' and 'peace offerings' belong together as a fixed pair, and what is implied of the former is probably also implied

of the latter. Furthermore, when peace offerings are mentioned in
the context of fasting and lamentation (Jg. 20:26; 21:4) any
meal on the part of the worshippers is unlikely.

8. For this verse as a late addition see comment on v. 4. **very
plainly:** the phrase incorporates a form of the verb translated
'explain' in 1:5 (see comment there).

(c) ISRAEL IS THE PEOPLE OF YAHWEH: **27:9-10**
These verses have a new beginning and have no particular
connection with the preceding section; they are, however, closely
related to 26:16-19 (see comment on v. 10) and are frequently
seen as the original continuation of that section. They are theologi-
cally significant in stating explicitly that Israel's obedience is a
necessary consequence and not the condition of its becoming the
people of Yahweh.

9. the Levitical priests: the use of the first person singular
in the next verse makes doubtful the originality of this reference
to the Levitical priests (cf. also v. 1). They may have been
added here in order to legitimate the later functions of the
Levitical priests as spokesmen of the law standing in the Mosaic
tradition.

10. The terminology of this verse (**obey the voice of the Lord
your God, commandments and statutes, this day**) has
clear links with 26:16ff.

(D) BLESSING AND CURSE ON GERIZIM AND EBAL: **27:11-13**
This section is distinct from what precedes (see comment on v. 11)
and what follows (see comment on vv. 12, 13). Like the other
sections, it is a fragment of covenant ceremonial. Although it
incorporates a traditional listing of the tribes, the peculiar
division of them into two groups is not found elsewhere. The
sudden transition to plural address in v. 12 argues against this
section having belonged to the original Deuteronomy and in
favour of assigning it along with other sections to a later deuteronomistic editor.

11. The verse is clearly the beginning of a new section, so that
there is here no direct continuation of v. 10.

12, 13. On the association of Gerizim and Ebal with blessing
and curse, see comment on 11:29. In the list of tribes comprising
Israel a traditional form has been used which appears in several
other passages and is dependent on the story of the birth of the

sons of Jacob in Gen. 29–30 (cf. my *Israel*, 22). Genealogical considerations also explain in large measure the particular form of division of the tribes into two groups of six, those which stand on Gerizim and those which stand on Ebal. The former group comprises the sons of Jacob's wives Leah and Rachel, while the latter comprises the sons of his concubines along with two sons of his wife Leah, Reuben (who according to Gen. 49:3f. forfeited his birthright) and Zebulun (the last of Jacob's sons by Leah). Geographical factors may also have influenced the division (cf. Nielsen, *Shechem*, 69ff.; Buis-Leclercq), for those tribes which are assigned to Ebal, the northern mountain of cursing, are the less important Galilean and Transjordanian tribes, while those assigned to Gerizim, the southern mountain of blessing, are the significant mid-Palestinian and Judean tribes.

The form of ceremony envisaged here is far from clear. If through the incorporation of a traditional list of twelve tribes it was intended simply to indicate a ceremony in which all Israel was involved, then the distinctive role assigned to the Levites in v. 14 is no reason for separating vv. 11–13 from what follows. However, vv. 11–13 refer to blessing and curse, while vv. 15ff., to which v. 14 is apparently the introduction, mention only curses (and these not real curses, see introduction to the next section). Vv. 11–13 are therefore scarcely the original prelude to vv. 14ff. Moreover, a division of the people into two groups has little bearing on a situation where all the people respond together, as in vv. 15ff. It seems likely, therefore, that vv. 11–13, in so far as they have a ceremony in view, envisage each group proclaiming in turn the blessings and the curses of the law, and not a situation (as understood in Jos. 8:30–35) where a third party proclaims blessings and curses before the two groups.

(E) PROHIBITED BEHAVIOUR IN THE PEOPLE OF YAHWEH: **27:14–26**
Vv. 15 and 26, the first and the last elements of the series, are probably secondary additions to an original series of ten curses (see comment on v. 15). The latter is frequently understood to be a very ancient series which a deuteronomistic editor brought into this context, and various proposals have been made on its possible place of origin. Alt, *Essays*, 114f., points to it as a series of apodictic laws concerned with crimes committed in secret, the punishment for which is 'exclusion from the common life shared by Yahweh and Israel'; Wallis, *HUCA* 45, 1974, 47ff., takes it

as an oath text which belongs in the context of a ceremony for
young men being inducted into full citizenship; Wagner, *Rechtssätze*, 32ff., proposes that it is a non-cultic, legal text, brought into
a secondary cultic context, which has as its background the administration of justice in the nomadic context when the one cursed
was expelled from the clan (for other proposals see also the
commentaries).

However, it must be emphasized that not only in content,
but probably also in form, this is a late series. On the latter point
see also the introduction to 5:1–6:3, where the same holds for the
decalogue. As a general form-critical rule it is probable that longer
series like the present one only developed in later time on the
basis of shorter series (apart from the introduction to 5:1–6:3;
cf. also Schulz, *Todesrecht*, 61ff.), and in the present case one may,
with Gese, *ZThK* 64, 1967, 129f., point to five pairs which make up
the form and on which it is based (omitting vv. 15, 26): the first
is concerned with the family, the second with social and humanitarian behaviour, the third and fourth with the sphere of sexual
behaviour and the last with legal custom.

The form-critical approach yields a result corresponding to
what is indicated by the content of the series, for in some cases
it may be shown that the particular action cursed (as marriage
with half-sister through father or mother, or marriage with
mother-in law) was the subject of prohibition in late time, while
in others the closest parallels to the curses are to be found in the
Holiness Code and not in earlier legislation (see comment on
individual verses).

It must be concluded, therefore, that this is a late composition,
and not an ancient collection secondarily adopted here. Its
authorship is not clear; if, however, the series originally existed
independently of its present context, and was not compiled for
that context, it seems at least clear, from the language of v. 14,
that its incorporation here took place later than (both stages of)
the deuteronomistic editing of Deuteronomy. The purpose of
the composition is difficult to discern. It is not in fact a series of
curses (since a curse describes the content of misfortune rather
than the cause of it; cf. Buis, *VT* 17, 1967, 478f.), but rather a
series of what are in effect strong prohibitions. It is not specifically
concerned with 'crimes committed in secret', but rather in its
allusions to various laws, either earlier in Deuteronomy or in
the Holiness Code, it may function in a representative way (see

comment on vv. 20, 21) to bring to mind the whole field of law and morality which must characterize the life of the people of Yahweh.

14. the Levites: a deuteronomic or deuteronomistic author would have said 'the Levitical priests' (as e.g. 18:1). **shall declare:** see comment on 21:7. **all the men of Israel:** the only other occurrence of this phrase in Deuteronomy is in 29:10, in the context of a list of members of the people; it is not a deuteronomic or deuteronomistic phrase; in the latter context 'all Israel' would be expected (as in v. 9).

15. This is the longest element in the series. It is distinct also in form from the others, being constructed with a relative clause rather than a participle, following the word **cursed.** For this reason, and also because in content it is the only element (apart from v. 16) having specific reference to the concerns of the deuteronomic law, it is generally held to be a later addition. Wagner, *Rechtssätze*, 33, suggests that it is a late addition caused by the addition of v. 26; the latter was brought in secondarily as a summary of the whole, but was later understood as one element of the series. The resulting total of eleven conflicted, however, with the number of tribes mentioned in verses 11ff. as participating in the ceremony, and thus brought about the addition of v. 15. As far as its content is concerned, the subject was probably chosen primarily in order to anchor the following series in the context of the deuteronomic law.

cursed: this word makes the theory of a cultic origin and context of use of the series especially attractive. However, as Schottroff, *Fluchspruch*, 199ff., and others have shown, the word does not have an essential or original cult-ritual, or magical, content. The word means to place under ban or expel from the community, the one cursed being the one formally excluded from the clan (if that is the place of origin of the form of speech using the expression). The word then has a legal rather than a cultic background. **graven or molten image:** see 4:16; 9:12, 16. **an abomination to the Lord:** see comment on 7:25.

16. dishonours: the parallels in Exod. 21:17; Lev. 20:9 use the verb *qll*, 'curse', which differs in only one letter from the verb used here. The latter, however, offers a more exact counterpart of the decalogue commandment to honour one's father and mother. The subject is also treated in Dt. 21:18ff.

17. On the subject of this clause see comment on 19:14.

18. This clause finds its closest parallel in the Holiness Code, in Lev. 19:14.

19. The list of needy is to be found in 14:29; 16:14; 24:17, 19, 20, 21; 26:12f. On the subject treated here, cf. 24:17.

20. uncovered her who is his father's: see comment on 22:30. For the subject see also Lev. 18:7f. Schulz, *Todesrecht*, 65, suggests that the present clause stands here as representative of that category of disallowed sexual unions mentioned in Lev. 20:11f., 17, 19, 20f.

21. Schulz proposes that this clause is representative of that category of sexual unions prohibited in Lev. 20:13-16, 18; cf. also Lev. 18:23. The Book of the Covenant mentions only this particular sexual offence (Exod. 22:19); as Phillips suggests, this may be because this practice was known in non-Israelite cults as a means of achieving physical union with the deity represented in a sacred animal, and so is mentioned in the Book of the Covenant alongside the condemnation of sacrificing to any god except Yahweh as a form of apostasy.

22. According to older family law, marriage with a half-sister was not prohibited (cf. Gen. 20:12; 2 Sam. 13:13). It is prohibited, however, in Lev. 18:9; 20:17, besides the present passage. There is nothing to show that there was an older form of this curse which did not include the specification **whether the daughter of his father or the daughter of his mother,** and had in view only marriage with a full sister.

23. This particular union would not have been prohibited in ancient times, according to Phillips, since the mother-in-law would not have lived in the family home, that being the criterion by which the limits of marriage unions were fixed. It is prohibited, however, in the Holiness Code, Lev. 18:17; 20:14.

24. slays: more accurately 'strikes' (as *NEB*). Often when the meaning 'kill' is intended an additional verb is used, as for example Exod. 21:12. However, in that the action here is put under the curse, the *RSV* translation (here and in the next verse) undoubtedly expresses the sense of the verb in this context.

25. The subject of bribery is common, cf. Exod. 23:8; Dt. 16:19; Isa. 1:23; Prov. 17:23. The particular case here, however, appears only in Ezek. 22:12. **an innocent person:** the expression appears also in the Hebrew of 19:10; 21:8. The *NEB* translation here, 'a man with whom he has no feud', implies the possible existence of a situation, that of the practice of blood revenge, in which killing would not come under the curse. This is not, however, the ordinary interpretation of the phrase **an innocent person,** which designates rather a person the slaying of whom would amount to murder; cf. Jer. 26:15.

26. Both in structure (as v. 15) and content this clause is separate from the preceding series. It has a summary character and does not refer to a specific action. It was undoubtedly added in the first stage of the incorporation of the series into its present context. For the comprehensive use of the term **this law** see comment on 1:5.

E. DECLARATION OF THE BLESSINGS AND THE CURSES: 28:1–68

For the history of research into these chapters, cf. Plöger, *Untersuchungen*, 130ff. and Seitz, *op. cit.*, 254ff.

The form of ch. 26 as speech of Moses, which broke down in ch. 27, is continued now in ch. 28 (except for two clauses in vv. 20, 68). This, however, does not completely clarify the relationship of the chapter to the book as a whole. In the first place, all of ch. 26 has already been seen to be of post-deuteronomic origin, along with the final part of ch. 25. Is ch. 28 to be treated as related in any way to the original deuteronomic law, or is it wholly of later origin? The answer usually given is that ch. 28 contains at least a nucleus which accompanied the original Deuteronomy. Not only does this explain Josiah's discomfiture at the contents of the lawbook (understood as the original Deuteronomy; cf. 2 Kg. 22:11), but it suits best the analogy with the extra-biblical treaty forms and lawcodes where sections of blessing and curse are frequently found.

However, caution is necessary on both these points. In the first place, the isolation of pre-deuteronomistic elements of the story of Josiah's reform in 2 Kg. 22f. from their present deuteronomistic context is a difficult undertaking. We have already seen (Introduction, pp. 89ff.) that a pre-deuteronomistic basis may be traced only in the oracle of Huldah and in the account of the actual reform measures of Josiah in 2 Kg. 23. The present story of 2 Kg. 22f. is a theological construction which indeed points to Deuteronomy, and probably to Deuteronomy in much its present form. To that extent the story presupposes the presence of ch.

28, or part of that chapter, with Deuteronomy; but that in fact says nothing about the relationship of ch. 28 to the original Deuteronomy. The second point is more difficult. The extra-biblical texts have been invoked not only as a reason for seeing ch. 28 as a necessary part of the original Deuteronomy, but also in favour of the unity of the chapter as a single whole (see especially Hillers, *Treaty Curses*, 30ff., Weinfeld, *Deuteronomy*, 128f.). The first part of this argument cannot be accepted. Law collections existed without blessings and curses attached to them, and it may have been only as a result of the later addition of the blessings and curses of ch. 28 that the original deuteronomic lawbook came to bear a similarity to the law collections and treaties which do have such sections. On the second side of the argument, it is undoubtedly true that extra-biblical texts exhibit within the framework of a single text a variety of styles and a degree of repetition. However, one may not transpose this observation immediately to the biblical context. The situations are different: in the one case a treaty text dependent on a ceremony for which the text was composed; in the other a narrative framework incorporating passages which have at most an indirect relationship to any ceremony. Furthermore, given that an analogy between biblical and extra-biblical texts does exist, the means by which the latter affected the biblical writings must be clarified before the composition of the biblical texts may be explained by reference to the extra-biblical texts. Finally, the variety within ch. 28 (see particularly the difference between vv. 1–46 and 47ff.; see comment on vv. 45f.) requires the supposition of different authors behind the chapter.

The chapter must, therefore, be subjected to an internal study in order to determine its origin and development on the one hand, and its relationship to the rest of Deuteronomy on the other. It falls into three major paragraphs; vv. 1–46, 47–57, and 58–68. The first section contains conditional blessing and curse, the second a promise of curse, and the third a conditional curse. The first and third are, then, related in form; but the content indicates clearly that the third is in fact the latest of all three sections. Not only does it use expressions found in the latest parts of Deuteronomy and other literature (see comment on v. 58), but it clearly has the character of a concluding section. The first and second sections are connected by a transitional passage in vv. 45f., which was clearly composed by the author of vv. 47–57 on the model of v. 15 (see comment on vv. 45f.). The second section is, therefore, a later supplement to the first. The first section is full of language typical of other parts of Deuteronomy, apart from two passages which stand out for their lack of any such contact. These are vv. 3–6 and 16–19. They contain parallel series of blessings and curses which are closely related in subject, style and rhythm. They make no explicit reference to Yahweh and none to the law. It is only through prose introductions in vv. 1f., 15 that they are given this context.

The basis of the chapter is, therefore, to be found in vv. 3–6, 16–19. The content and form of the verses indicate an original setting in a liturgical ceremony, but there is nothing to show that this ceremony had any relation to the law or the covenant (in which connection it is apposite to note that the forms 'blessed shall you be . . .' and 'cursed shall you be . . .' are not forms of treaty curses; see also the introduction to 27:14–26). The lack of any allusion to law and covenant in the verses should be taken to show that they did not in fact originate in that context. A more likely origin has been suggested by Seitz, *op. cit.*, 271ff. If one thinks in terms, in the first place, of an origin for just one of the series of blessings and curses in these verses, reference may be made to 1 Sam. 2:20; Ps. 118:26 to show that it was customary for blessings to be imparted to worshippers by the priest at the sanctuary. Since the blessings are concerned with agriculture, it may be suggested that the occasion of their use was when the worshipper left the first fruits at the sanctuary. From this context the blessings have been taken, provided with an introduction to relate them to the law, and on their model a similar series of curses has been formed and also provided with an introduction relating them to the law.

From this point, expansion took place in a number of stages. First of all, the curses were expanded through the addition of the basis of vv. 20–46. In the course of this, various existing series of curses were used, such as a series of 'smiting' curses in vv. 22, 27, 28, 35 (cf. Plöger, *op. cit.*, 189f.) and another series in vv. 38–40 (see comment). On the basis of the expanded curses the blessings were also extended, through the addition of vv. 7–14. So, vv. 7–8a are secondary in relation to vv. 20, 25 and vv. 12b, 13a in relation to v. 44. The author of the second section in vv. 47–57 attached his composition to the first section through the transitional vv. 45f. The connection was strengthened through the editing of the

first section by the addition of further curses. This brought in
vv. 23-26, 29-34, 36f., 41f. (cf. Seitz, *op. cit.*, 296), which caused
the break up of the older series of 'smiting' curses. The origin of
all this material cannot be fixed in detail, but undoubtedly it
mostly goes back to traditional curses which make their appearance in various treaties (cf. especially Hillers, *Treaty Curses*, 30ff.,
McCarthy, *Treaty*, 121f., and Weinfeld, *Bib* 41, 1960, 417ff.).
Weinfeld in particular has argued for the extensive use of existing
treaty texts in this respect by the scribal authors of ch. 28 (see
comment on v. 29).

In this way there originated a text which was composed very
largely of curses. The preponderance of the latter and the relatively insignificant place assigned to blessings undoubtedly
reflects the Mesopotamian treaty tradition in which the curses
play this remarkable role (cf. McCarthy, *Treaty*, 68ff.). The
blessings give the impression of being no more than what Noth,
Laws, 126, called 'a purely formal counterpart to the curse'.
However, this is not because the nature of blessing as such is
foreign to law—the latter demands obedience which is then a
duty and can claim no reward. Blessings and curses are closely
associated with law from ancient times; their relative weighting
in ch. 28 reflects a peculiar tradition which in Mesopotamia
attached particular importance to the curses.

It is difficult to relate this process of growth with any certainty
to the rest of Deuteronomy. Outside the basic blessing and curse
series with their introductions, the rest of the chapter has closest
contacts with deuteronomistic and later literature (see comment
on vv. 7, 20, 25, 26, 47). It seems also that it is to a deuteronomistic editor that we owe the introductions to the blessings and
curses in vv. 1f., 15 (see comment on v. 1). If this is the case,
then it must have been first within the deuteronomistic stage
of editing the original deuteronomic lawbook that the series of
blessings and curses came into its present place.

1. obey the voice of: a phrase mostly found in deuteronomistic and later passages, cf. 8:20; 13:18; 15:5, etc. and comment on 26:14. **careful to do:** again a typically deuteronomistic phrase, cf. 4:6; 5:32; 6:3, etc. **the commandments
which I command you this day:** cf. 4:2; 11:13, 22, 27, 28,
etc. The second half of the verse (**the Lord your God will set
you...**) has no counterpart in the corresponding v. 15; since,
moreover, it contains a special blessing, it is unlikely that it is an

original part of the introduction to the blessings which follow in vv. 3ff. It is an addition based on 26:19.

2. The conditional clause in the second half of the verse presupposes the blessing given in v. 1*b*, and like the latter is a late addition.

3. Although the form 'blessed be you' (and 'cursed be you') is very likely of ancient origin, cf. 1 Sam. 15:13; 26:25 (Gen. 3:14; 4:11), it is only here in vv. 3–6 (16–19) that the form is extended by additional clauses (**in the city,** etc.) and found gathered in a series. **in the city... the field:** a combination known also from Gen. 34:28; 1 Kg. 14:11; 16:4; 21:24; Jer. 14:18; Ezek. 7:15; 33:27, but only here in a blessing (and v. 16 in a curse). The combination expresses totality: everywhere that you go. See also comment on 6:7.

4. For the objects of blessing mentioned here cf. 7:13. **and the fruit of your beasts:** this is not mentioned in 7:13 nor in the corresponding 28:18. It is also lacking in the chief MSS of LXX, and so may not be an original part of the verse. **the increase of your cattle, and the young of your flock:** see comment on 7:13.

5. basket ... kneading trough: a combination which appears only here and in v. 17. Once again, the combination expresses totality; Israel's sustenance both at the stage of harvest (**basket,** cf. 26:4) and at the stage of preparation for eating (**kneading trough,** cf. Exod. 12:34) will be blessed.

6. come in ... go out: this phrase is found in texts of cultic, judicial and military-political content (cf. Exod. 28:35; Num. 27:17; 1 Sam. 18:13, 16, etc. and Plöger, *op. cit.*, 174ff.). By analogy with the interpretation of the combinations in vv. 3 and 5, so here the reference should be taken to be to the totality of life, all the daily activities in which one may be engaged. For this general use, cf. also 2 Kg. 11:8 (=2 Chr. 23:7); 19:27; Jer. 37:4; Ps. 121:8.

7. seven ways: the number seven is used in a wide variety of both biblical and extra-biblical contexts; cf. Num. 23:1, 14, 29; Jos. 6:4, 15; 1 Kg. 18:43f., 2 Kg. 5:10, 14; and, for the Ugaritic texts, cf. Gray, *Legacy*, 298; Kraus, *Worship*, 85ff. The number is clearly used to carry a notion of completeness and fullness; but along with this it has particular associations with evil, destruction and death, as in the seven plagues mentioned in v. 22. See also Gaster, *Myth*, 305, 321.

Vv. 7ff. use late forms ('establish' v. 9, only otherwise in 29:13

in this particular context; 'all the peoples of the earth', v. 10, cf. the deuteronomistic Jos. 4:24; 1 Kg. 8:43, 53, 60; also Ezek. 31:12; 'called by the name of the Lord' v. 10, cf. Jer. 14:9; Isa. 63:19), and seem to represent a late secondary compilation, based in part on material already existing in ch. 28. The blessings of vv. 7–8a have their counterpart in vv. 25, 20 where, however, they occur in a better order (general blessing/curse 'all that you undertake', followed by the particular); cf. Seitz, *op. cit.*, 275f.

8. in all that you undertake: see comment on 12:7. The peculiar language of Deuteronomy is particularly clear from the second half of the verse on to the end of the section of blessings (v.14); compare especially 7:6ff.

9. as he has sworn to you: throughout Deuteronomy the use of the verb 'swear' with Yahweh as subject is with reference to the promise to the patriarchs (cf. e.g. 1:8; 4:31; 6:10; 7:12 etc.; though cf. 2:14). This is a remarkable use of the phrase with reference to the Sinai covenant.

10. you are called by the name of the Lord: as 2 Sam. 12:28 shows, this phrase expresses the idea of ownership; proclaiming the name over something was a legal act by which ownership was claimed and established, cf. Galling, *ThLZ* 81, 1956, 65ff. (see also comment on 12:5).

12. The idea of heaven as a reservoir for rain was well known (cf. Gen. 1:7; 7:11; 8:2; Ps. 33:7; Job 38:37). For the phrase **all the work of your hands** in agricultural contexts, see comment on 2:7. The blessings of vv. 12b, 13a have their counterpart in the curses of v. 44. However, while the latter has a rhythmical form, vv. 12b, 13a are prose. They give the impression of having been formed in dependence on v. 44 (see also comment on v. 7).

13. For the figurative use of **head** and **tail** cf. Isa. 9:14f.; 19:15.

15. The introduction to the curses in this verse is almost the exact counterpart to the introduction to the blessings in vv. 1f. (omitting the two secondary clauses from the latter). **and his statutes:** this is missing in LXX. Although there is a chiastic correspondence with v. 45 where the word appears, the relationship to vv. 1f., where the word does not appear, is closer, since both are introductory sentences. It is, therefore, probably best to omit the word here, with LXX, and understand it as a secondary insertion in *MT* on the basis of its appearance in v. 45. On vv. 16–19 see comments on vv. 3–6.

20. confusion: as in 7:23, the panic sent by God into the enemy in war. **frustration:** the form *migʿeret* occurs only here. Its root and other derivative noun are usually translated 'rebuke'. Macintosh, *VT* 19, 1969, 471ff., proposes, however, that its true sense is not that of moral reprimand but rather of angry protest or wrath. With God as subject it may also denote the effective working out of his anger, and so come close to the sense of 'curse'. **the evil of your doings:** not otherwise in Deuteronomy but frequent in Jeremiah (e.g. 4:4). The second half of the verse (from **and perish quickly . . .**) is frequently taken as an addition; cf. also the anomalous use (Moses is evidently the speaker) of first person at the end.

22. The first two terms **consumption** and **fever** occur only here and in Lev. 26:16; the next two are found only here. **drought:** this translation is based on a slightly changed Hebrew text (*ḥōreḇ* for *ḥereḇ*) following the Vulg. Both the Hebrew (emended) and Latin (*aestus*) may also mean a feverish illness (cf. Job 30:30), which would suit better with the preceding terms. The last two words are normally translated as referring to a blight on corn (caused by the drying east wind). However, Plöger, *op. cit.*, 151, refers to 1 Kg. 8:37; 2 Chr. 6:28 (for the first) and to the root *yrq*, 'be pallid' (for the second), to suggest that in both cases an illness is intended. In any case it is remarkable that seven plagues are mentioned altogether; see comment on v. 7.

23. When the heavens are **brass** the rain cannot get through, and with the earth as **iron** the plants cannot grow up. The verses thus form the counterpart to v. 12*a*. For a parallel to this curse in the Esarhaddon treaty, lines 528–531, cf. Wiseman, *Iraq* 20, 1958, 88.

25–37. A chiastic structure has been discerned in these verses (cf. Thompson), though it involves taking a whole series of particular curses as the focal point (vv. 30–32) as well as reversing the order of the last two elements in vv. 36 and 37 to achieve a correspondence with the first two in vv. 25*a* and 25*b*, 26.

25. On Israel as a **horror** cf. Jer. 15:4; 24:9; 29:18; 34:17.

26. For this verse cf. also Jer. 7:33; 34:20.

27. The precise identification of the diseases mentioned here (which are all, apparently, diseases of the skin) is uncertain. The **boils of Egypt** may be elephantiasis, a peculiarly Egyptian disease; another possibility is a skin infection common in the Near East known as the 'Baghdad Button' or 'Jericho Rose', an ulcerous boil which leaves a scar. The term occurs in Job where (if Job's symptoms may all be ascribed to it) its symptoms are inflammation, itching, disfigurement, etc. (cf. Job 2:7f., 12; 7:5, 14; 16:16; 19:17, 20; 30:17, 30). For a discussion of the second, which apparently means hemorrhoids, cf. Driver, *Samuel*, 51f. The word translated **scurvy** (*gārāḇ*) is suggested by Weinfeld, *Bib* 41, 1960, 418 n.3, to have been a form of leprosy.

28. All three of the afflictions mentioned here are found also in Zech. 12:4. They there occur in the context of panic and confusion in war; here, however, the continuation in the next verse would indicate that general physical afflictions are intended.

29. Weinfeld, *Bib* 41, 1960, 420ff., has pointed out that the association of skin diseases on the one hand with the curse of darkness and lawlessness on the other, in vv. 27ff., is impossible to explain except in the context of Mesopotamian religion. The plague of leprosy is always associated with the god Sin, while darkness, symbolizing the absence of law and justice, is associated with the god Shamash. Sin and Shamash are, however, invariably paired at the head of Assyrian catalogues of gods, which explains also how the afflictions associated with them are also found together.

only: the *NEB* ('also') apparently follows the *Sam* reading *raq* (for '*aq*; cf. also v. 33).

30. The background of the three curses mentioned here lies in the catalogue which comes to expression, in slightly changed form, in 20:5–7, where the man who has just built a house, planted a vineyard or married is exempt from military service for a year. Not even these, which are reckoned as fundamental blessings, will hold good. **lie with her:** the verb is stronger; cf. *NEB* 'ravish her'. **use the fruit of it:** translated 'enjoyed its fruit' in 20:6; see comment there.

35. On this curse, cf. also v. 27.

36. Cf. also 4:28; 13:6. The service of other gods by exiled Israel would not be simply a matter of choice; land and religion were closely connected, to the extent that separation from the land involved separation from the faith proper to that land (cf. 1 Sam. 26:19).

38–40. The three staple products of Palestine: corn, wine, and oil, are referred to in this fixed combination on several occasions in the Old Testament and also in the Ugaritic texts; see comment on 7:13. The particular form in which they are referred to in these verses may be compared with Mic. 6:15; Hag. 1:6. There is no question of literary dependence.

39. nor gather the grapes: perhaps an addition here; it comes rather late after reference has already been made to drinking the wine.

40. On the rite of anointing, cf. 2 Sam. 12:20; 14:2; Ru. 3:3; 2 Chr. 28:15.

43. sojourner: see comment on 1:16. The structure of society is turned completely upside down.

44. See comment on v. 12.

45, 46. The summary character of these two verses, which take up the beginning of the section in v. 15, clearly indicates a conclusion. However, there are certain differences between vv. 45f. and what precedes, which indicate that the verses are not from the same author. V. 45 refers to disobedience as something of which Israel is already guilty, whereas v. 15 refers to it simply as a future possibility. V. 45 also refers to the proclamation of the law as something which occurred in the past (**he commanded you**), whereas v. 15 refers to it as something happening in the present ('I command you this day'). The first of these differences connects vv. 45f. with the following section, indicating that the two verses perform a bridging role to the new section. Vv. 45f. are, therefore, probably from the hand of the author of the next section, who composed them on the model of v. 15 in order to link up his own material; cf. Seitz, *op. cit.*, 263ff.

46. a sign and a wonder: see comment on 4:34.

47. The new section, extending to v. 57, proclaims a curse which is to come for the acts of disobedience already committed, not a conditional curse. It has several contacts with Jeremiah; cf. Jer. 4:13; 5:15, 17; 19:9; 28:14; 48:40; 49:22. **by reason of the abundance of all things:** the danger of abundance leading to forgetfulness is frequently alluded to in Deuteronomy; see comment on 6:12.

49, 50. The expressions used to describe the enemy in these verses are in many cases stereotyped; they could be used of any conqueror. It is the existence of a common tradition and not direct literary dependence which explains the contacts between the two verses and Isa. 5:26–29; Jer. 5:15–19; 6:22–24; Hab. 1:5–11. Seitz, *op. cit.*, 295ff., suggests that descriptions of the enemy as coming from a distant land, speaking an unintelligible language, being of stern appearance, causing fear, powerful and

merciless, destructive and rapacious etc., have their origin in
the king's praise of himself and his power as found in Sumerian
and Accadian royal inscriptions. In the prophets a democra-
tization of terminology has taken place in that these statements
are now applied to the enemy as a whole and not just to the
king. This is reflected also in the present verses, and to that
extent there is dependence here on the prophets; but behind
both there is a common tradition.

51. The verse is apparently inspired by 7:13 and 28:4.

53. On the horrors of siege, cf. Lev. 26:29; 2 Kg. 6:28f.; Jer. 19:9;
Lam. 2:20; 4:10; Ezek. 5:10. They are common in the lists of
curses, as in the Esarhaddon treaty, lines 448, 549f., 568ff. **in the
siege and in the distress:** a refrain taken up again in vv. 55,
57, and also in Jer. 19:9.

54. will grudge food to: the phrase is literally 'his eye will
be evil against'; the following verse, however, supports the *RSV*
interpretation of the phrase. See also comment on 15:9.

58. The final section, in vv. 58–68, returns to the form of the
conditional curse. It is a very late section in which Deuteronomy
is understood as an existing book (vv. 58, 61). **this law:** see
comment on 1:5. On the **fear** of Yahweh see comment on 4:10.
The use of **name** points to a late period; it is paralleled in Lev.
24:11; Mic. 6:9 (which is probably late); Isa. 59:19; Mal. 4:2.

59. lasting: the word *ne'emānîm* usually has a moral content,
'faithful'. For the sense here, cf. also 1 Sam. 25:28 (translated 'sure').

60. all the diseases of Egypt: see comment on 7:15, where
Israel is promised freedom from these in the event of her obedience.

61. the book of this law: several of the versions follow the
normal expression 'this book of the law' (as 29:21; 30:10; 31:26).

62. Two late passages are combined in this verse; cf. 1:10;
4:27. Seitz, *op. cit.*, 264ff., points out that vv. 62f. perform a
bridging function holding together the two parts of the section.
The words **because you did not obey the voice of the Lord
your God** refer back to the written law mentioned in vv. 58, 61,
while the threat that they **shall be left few in number** points
forward to the following verses threatening Israel's dispersion
among the nations.

64. See comment on v. 36.

65. soul: see comment on 4:9. For Deuteronomy **rest** is a
condition frequently alluded to; it consists of security in the
land. See comment on 3:20; 12:9.

67. For the thought cf. Job. 7:4.

68. The verse may be an addition. Vv. 65–67 are held together in thought and style, but here there is a change in both.

The verse represents the culmination of all the curses, for in returning to Egypt Israel's whole history, the history of its relationship with Yahweh, is nullified. But whereas at the beginning Israel at least had the security of slavery, now even this will be denied her. **in ships:** the point of this is obscure. Driver thinks of the slave trade as practised by the Phoenicians (cf. Am. 1:9; Ezek. 27:13; Jl 3:6). Their contact with Egypt would have been by sea (cf. Isa. 23:2f.). However, the second half of the present verse seems rather to indicate a voluntary return to Egypt on the part of Israelites, where they will not even be able to sell themselves as slaves. The *NEB* translation, 'sorrowing', presupposes a slight change in the pointing of the *MT* (*baʾaniyyôt* for *boʾoniyyôt*). **which I promised:** this divine word is alluded to also in 17:16, but is not itself preserved.

III. The Third Address of Moses to Israel: 29:1–30:20

The question of the limits of the section introduced by 29:1 has been discussed especially by Lohfink, *BZ* 6, 1962, 32ff. He thinks that it extends as far as 32:47, so including the installation of Joshua as Moses' successor, together with the Song of Moses and its introduction. The installation of a new leader is a subject with close covenant associations, while the Song of Moses was included as a threat of divine punishment for apostasy. Thus the covenant content of the heading in 29:1 is suitable as a superscription for all the material extending to 32:47. However, the proposal is doubtful. Chs. 29–30 possess a certain unity which is destroyed if the unit is extended into the following chapters, and, moreover, 31:1 contains what was probably originally a concluding formula (see comment). Apart from that, the last section in 30:15–20 has the summarizing purpose of a conclusion which suits well as a counterpart to 29:1. There is little to suggest that the latter was composed with anything further in view.

This is not, however, a conclusion to be drawn on the basis of the supposed covenant or treaty structure of chs. 29–30. This structure has been suggested particularly by Baltzer, *Covenant Formulary*, 34ff. (cf. also Wright), who points to the 'antecedent history' or historical prologue in 29:2–8, the basic stipulation in

29:9, the blessing and cursing in 30:16–18 and the witness in 30:19. Yet, it is clear that however much the treaty form, thought and vocabulary may have influenced what lies in these chapters, there is no treaty or covenant conclusion ceremony standing directly behind them. The one really essential element of such a ceremony (and so also of the form), the stipulations, is missing; furthermore, the chapters in fact fall into almost self-contained units. They indeed follow one another in logical order, but the impression they give is of artistically formed literary creations rather than formally organized documents.

The units constitute a series of speeches or sermons which aim to inculcate a spirit of faithful obedience to a law already promulgated and known. The speeches follow a logical order: the first in 29:1–9 introduces the covenant law, advocating obedience to it on the basis of the history which led up to its promulgation; the second in 29:10-15 centres on the covenant formula, proclaiming its binding nature on Israel of the present and Israel of the future; the third in 29:16–21 addresses the individual and warns him not to be over-confident because of his membership of the covenant community; the fourth in 29:22–28 proclaims the consequences of the covenant for the nation as a whole in the event of disobedience; the fifth in 29:29–30:14 proclaims blessing and restoration after the destruction of the covenant curse, centering once more on the law and the need for obedience; and the final section in 30:15–20 sets the law once more before the people, with its blessing and curse, and concludes with an urgent appeal for obedience. These are exhortations, addressed to a people in exile, with the purpose of explaining the causes of the present plight and the means of avoiding its recurrence.

Since the whole section clearly presupposes the existence of the law as an existing independent entity, obedience to which may be inculcated through sermons and speeches, it is clear that we are in the deuteronomistic rather than the deuteronomic world. Moreover, this concern with the law connects the section with ch. 4, rather than with chs. 1–3, so it is to the second deuteronomistic editor that the section should be ascribed.

A. EXHORTATION TO OBEDIENCE TO THE COVENANT LAW: 29:1–9

The first unit within this larger complex formed by chs. 29f. is, apart from the general heading to the whole in v. 1, a self-contained and complete unit. In its allusion to history as the basis for the demand for obedience to the law, there is here clear contact with the historical prologues of the extra-biblical treaties. However, such a use of history should not be confined within the rigid limits of treaty or covenant ceremonies. The present passage does not necessarily go back to any ceremony. It is a literary unit in itself (cf. 8:2–6), a short sermon encouraging obedience to the existing law.

 1. In the *MT* this verse appears as the last verse of ch. 28, and is the conclusion of the preceding chapters. From a grammatical point of view it may be either a conclusion or a superscription to the next section. The *MT* view is followed by several scholars (e.g. Driver; cf. also Kutsch, *Verheissung*, 140f.) on the grounds that the **words of the covenant** or the terms and conditions of the relationship to which the verse refers are nowhere specified in what follows, but are to be found only in the earlier chapters. On the other hand, it is significant that the verse is taken up by v. 9, and that the word 'covenant' appears five times in the chapter apart from this first verse (vv. 9, 12, 14, 21, 25), while it is used only once in the whole law corpus (17:2) in what is probably a deuteronomistic addition. Moreover, if in addition chs. 29f. are taken as texts which depend on and preach the law as an existing entity, understood as covenant law, then it is preferable to understand that this verse introduces these following texts rather than concludes the preceding. The verse also depends on the preceding chapters, and never existed without these chapters; but that is the case with all the material contained in chs. 29f.

A more difficult problem concerns the purpose of the author here in distinguishing sharply between the original covenant at Sinai and what is now understood to be a second covenant in the land of Moab on the border of the land. It is clear from the original introduction to the deuteronomic law (cf. 4:45; 7:1–3, etc.) that the original deuteronomic law was understood to have been imparted to Israel by Moses on the border of the land, just before his death and the beginning of the conquest of the land by Israel. The later addition of the decalogue, understood as spoken directly to the people by Yahweh at Sinai, at the beginning of the law raised the question of the relationship between this law given directly by Yahweh at Sinai and that given by Moses in Moab. This was resolved through the idea of the Mosaic law as Moses' mediation to the people of all the law which Yahweh had imparted to him alone at Sinai: decalogue and Mosaic law were thus given equal standing as will of Yahweh. It is this equal authority which is proclaimed in this verse. The decalogue was already covenant law belonging in the context of the Sinai covenant. The law of Moses is now seen to be no less binding just because it was not given on that occasion. It too is covenant law, proclaimed to Israel not at Sinai but indirectly through Moses (5:31ff.) in Moab. This is too a divine covenant, equally binding on Israel (see also above, introduction to 5:1–6:3). **Horeb:** see comment on 1:2.

2. The historical prologue (vv. 2–9) begins, using plural form of address, with a reference to Egypt. It falls into three shorter sections, vv. 2–4, 5–7a and 7b–9. The first two correspond in structure, beginning with a reference to the past and ending with a reference to the present, and in style suddenly using singular form of address briefly in the middle; also in both theological interpretation (vv. 4, 6b) is attached to the statements they contain. Cf. Lohfink, *BZ* 6, 1962, 37. For the form of the whole section as that of argument from history, see comment on 8:2–6.

3. trials ... signs ... wonders: see comment on 4:34.

4. mind: the word is *lēḇ*, the longer form of which, *lēḇāḇ*, is translated 'heart' in, for example, 4:29; for the sense see comment there. For the thought of the verse, compare Isa. 6:10; Jer. 5:21.

5. I have led you: the speaker is apparently Moses; but in the next verse it is clear that a transition has been made to divine speech. In the form of preaching which these texts represent such an unconscious transition, or identification of human and divine 'I', is not altogether unexpected; cf. also Am. 2:10. On the thought and expression of the verse see also the deuteronomistic 8:4.

6. that you may know that I am the Lord your God: this theological conclusion uses a form of the first person pronoun (*'anî*) which is very unusual in Deuteronomy (apart from the Song of Moses, only 12:30); this supports the suggestion that the whole phrase is in fact a fixed form used in different contexts (cf. e.g. Exod. 6:7; 7:17; 8:22; 10:2, etc.), and here quoted by the writer. This then may have influenced the use of the first person in the previous verse. On the verb **know** in the sense of 'legally recognize', 'acknowledge', see comment on 9:24. In thought the verse is closest to 8:3.

7, 8. V. 7*a* (which is strictly a main clause: 'and you came to this place') completes the section beginning in v. 5. Vv. 7*b*, 8 stand in stark contrast to the preceding in their quite untheological language and thought. There is no reference to Yahweh's having given Sihon and Og into the hand of Israel (cf. 2:31ff.; 3:1ff.; 31:4); it is an action carried out from beginning to end by Israel herself. Lohfink, *BZ* 6, 1962, 38, suggests that the passage may have been added in order to localize this covenant clearly in the land of Moab, or it may reflect the lack of theological importance which the deuteronomist attached to east Jordan. However, the theological form of the record of this event in other deuteronomistic passages favours the former alternative. (On the subject of the passage see commentary on 2:26ff.; 3:1ff.) **we ... gave it:** the LXX use of the first person singular here is in conformity with 3:12ff. (Moses speaking).

9. In the literary form of the argument from history (see comment on 8:2–6) the third and final element is an exhortation to keep the commandments as a practical application of the theological understanding derived from reflection on what Yahweh has done in history. This verse is thus the conclusion of the unit which begins in v. 2.

B. PRESENT AND FUTURE GENERATIONS ENTER INTO THE COVENANT RELATIONSHIP: 29:10–15

The second section is concerned with the entry of all Israel, present and future, into the covenant relationship. In a formal way the theme of the section is brought to prominence through its chiastic structure: vv. 10f. and 15 correspond in referring to those who 'stand ... before the Lord your (our) God', the first part listing all the members of present Israel, the second emphasizing that future generations also are included; vv. 12 and 14 correspond in referring to this relationship as a 'sworn covenant'; and v.13, with the covenant formula, is the focal point of the whole.

10. the heads of your tribes, your elders: the *MT* is 'your heads, your tribes, your elders'; but 'your tribes' can scarcely be original in that context, between the other two. The *RSV* trans-

lation follows the Syr in reading *rāʾšê šiḇṭêkem* instead of *MT*
rāʾšêkem šiḇṭêkem. Better perhaps is to read *šōpṭêkem* for the second
of the two terms in *MT* (so involving only one consonantal
change in *MT*) to give the translation 'your heads, your judges,
your elders'. Note the appearance of the 'judges' in the lists in
Jos. 23:2; 24:1, even though the order in those lists is different.
LXX clearly felt the omission here, for it added a reference to
'judges' after 'elders'; see also 31:28. **heads:** see comment on 1:13;
elders: see introduction to 16:18–17:7; **officers:** see comment on
1:15.

11. sojourner: see comment on 1:16. **he who hews your**
wood and he who draws your water: a traditional fixed
expression to describe the socially inferior responsible for the
most menial tasks; cf. also Jos. 9:27. In the Ugaritic texts (KRT
A (iii) 110ff.; cf. *ANET*, 144) these are referred to as women's
tasks.

12. enter into: only here does this verb (*ʿāḇar*) appear in this
context; it has a parallel in Exod. 30:13f., where it is used of
those who pass over into the numbered body of the people.
sworn covenant: the phrase, which appears again in v. 14,
combines two Hebrew words: *bᵉrît*, 'covenant' (for which see
comment on 4:13) and *ʾālāh*. The latter word means both 'oath'
and 'curse' (for the second see especially v. 20), but is here
treated as parallel if not synonymous with 'covenant' (the
translation being: 'the covenant of the Lord your God and his
oath'). The 'oath' by which allegiance to the covenant would have
been sworn would have involved a self-cursing formula to guard
against disobedience. The word, therefore, in both its senses
suits with 'covenant', and is perhaps particularly suggested for
the present context by the subject of the immediately preceding
chapter. For a similar parallel use of the terms cf. Gen. 26:28;
Ezek. 17:18f.

13. The focal point of the section in this verse is the covenant
formula giving formal expression to the relationship established
between Yahweh and Israel; see the introduction to 26:16–19.
as he swore to your fathers: the oath to the patriarchs is
usually with explicit reference to the bestowal of the land (as 1:8);
in 4:31 it too is described as a 'covenant'.

14, 15. Besides wishing to establish the equal authority of the
law of Moses with the decalogue, through referring to the former
as covenant law (see comment on v. 1), the deuteronomist also

wished by the same means to indicate that the covenant obligation
was not limited solely to that generation which had direct and
immediate experience of the covenant established at Sinai. This
view is made explicit in the present verses. The covenant concluded by Moses (for a parallel to the role of Moses here, cf.
Jos. 24:25) involves not only those present at the time, but those
not present, the future generations; cf. also 5:3.

C. WARNING AGAINST IDOLATROUS WORSHIP:
29:16–21

The third section begins with a reference to Egypt, not on this
occasion in the context of illustrating the power of Yahweh and
his election of Israel, but in order to draw the attention of the
individual to the idolatrous worship of the nations which he, as a
committed member of the covenant people, must avoid.

16. we dwelt in the land of Egypt: in fact the generation
which came out of Egypt died in the wilderness according to
the earlier deuteronomistic account (cf. 2:14ff.), and those now
being addressed are the next generation. On the contradiction
see comment on 5:3.

17. detestable things . . . idols: the two Hebrew words only
occur here in Deuteronomy, and only the second occurs again
(Lev. 26:30) in the Pentateuch. They are both frequent, however,
in Jeremiah and Ezekiel.

18. This is the only allusion in this chapter to a specific demand,
that of the sole worship of Yahweh; yet it is an allusion to a
demand rather than a demand itself. The latter is presupposed as
already given and accepted. The previous section proclaimed
Israel's entry into the covenant; now Israel is warned against
the danger of temptation to defection in spite of its commitment
already given. **poisonous and bitter fruit:** the terms are frequent in prophetic contexts condemning the perversion of justice
in Israel; cf. Hos. 10:4; Am. 5:7; 6:12.

19. sworn covenant: see comment on v. 12. Only the second
of the two terms used in the earlier passage (*'ālāh*) appears here
(cf. *NEB* translation: 'the terms of this oath'); the *RSV*, however,
is undoubtedly correct in understanding that the reference here
is the same as in vv. 12, 14. **stubbornness of . . . heart:** apart
from this passage and Ps. 81:12, this expression is confined to

Jeremiah where it appears on eight occasions (3:17; 7:24; 9:13; 11:8; 13:10; 16:12; 18:12; 23:17). **This would lead to the sweeping away of moist and dry alike:** the translation and meaning of this phrase are very uncertain. The LXX understands 'moist and dry' to refer to sinners and sinless. *JB*, 'much water drives away thirst', takes the words as a continuation of the speech of the apostate who declares in effect that the way to deal with temptation is to yield to it. Probably the phrase 'moist and dry' is an expression of totality (cf. also 28:3–6, 16–19). Yet it is unlikely that reference is being made to the whole people who will suffer because of the sins of the individual (as Driver and others), for the transition back to the individual in the next verse would then be too abrupt, and the sense would be incompatible with v. 21. Perhaps the reference is to the totality of that individual's life. Continuing the metaphor of v. 18, the 'moist' or 'watered' is the man's life in covenant with Yahweh (compare Jer. 31:12), while the 'dry' or 'thirsty' is his life away from Yahweh in service of the gods of the nations (compare Isa. 44:3; 55:1). The fact that he is, or has been, a member of Yahweh's covenant people will not save him.

20. Weinfeld, *Deuteronomy*, 107ff., points out that the motifs of this verse—the divine anger, the curse settling on the malefactor, the reference to the book/document, and the obliteration of the name—are also met with in extra-biblical treaties and legal documents. There, as here, they come in the concluding part of the document. **jealousy:** see comment on 4:24. **curses:** the same word (*'ālāh*) as that which is used in the expression 'sworn covenant' in vv. 12, 14 (cf. also v. 19). **blot out his name:** see comment on 9:14.

D. PUNISHMENT FOR DISOBEDIENCE: 29:22–28

This section stands apart from the preceding in referring to destruction not as a threat for the future but as a characteristic of the present (see especially v. 28). Furthermore, while the previous section was focused on the behaviour of the individual member of the covenant people, here it is the people as a whole whose punishment and destruction is presupposed. The section is a unit with a question and answer literary form, which has a close parallel in an extra-biblical text; it apparently belongs to the

treaty or covenant context (see comment on v. 24). In this
passage the form is extended by the addition of a traditional
reference to cities which exemplified utter destruction brought by
Yahweh as punishment for sin.

22. foreigner: see comment on 15:3.

23. According to Weinfeld, *Deuteronomy*, 109ff., the razing and
burning of a city and its being sown with salt and brimstone was
the conventional punishment for breach of treaty, and had the purpose of preventing resettlement of the site. The four cities mentioned here appear together also in Gen. 10:19; 14:2, 8. An
account of their overthrow exists only with reference to Sodom
and Gomorrah, however (Gen. 19); and these two cities are
referred to on other occasions in this context (Am. 4:11; Isa. 1:9;
13:19). Admah and Zeboiim are similarly referred to in Hos. 11:8.
Probably all four are intended in 'Sodom and Gomorrah and
their neighbour cities' in Jer. 49:18; 50:40. It may be that the
present verse and the passages from Jeremiah represent a conflation of two traditions: a northern tradition coming to expression
in Hos. 11:8 told only of the complete destruction of Admah and
Zeboiim, while a southern tradition appearing in Amos and
Isaiah knew only of Sodom and Gomorrah as examples of such
complete destruction.

24. In the annals of Asshurbanipal, part of the record of his
campaign against the Arabs reads (cf. *ANET*, 300): 'Whenever
the inhabitants of Arabia asked each other: *On account of what
have these calamities befallen Arabia?* (they answered themselves:)
Because we did not keep the solemn oaths (sworn by) *Ashur, because we
offended the friendliness of Ashurbanipal, the king, beloved by Ellil'*. The
similarity of form with the present verses is unmistakable, and
its presentation in this extra-biblical text in the context of breach
of treaty suggests that it is a literary form associated with that
setting whence it was adopted by the deuteronomist. It appears
also, with little change, in 1 Kg. 9:8f.; Jer. 16:10f.; 22:8f.

25. The continuation in the next verse, explaining what **forsook
the covenant** means, suggests that **covenant** here means specifically the decalogue; see comment on 4:13.

26. gods whom they had not known: see comment on 11:28;
allotted to them: cf. 4:19.

27. curses: here the word used is not *'ālāh* as in v. 21, but
rather *qᵉlālāh*, as in 28:15.

28. uprooted them: the verb does not otherwise appear in

Deuteronomy or the rest of the Pentateuch. It is found chiefly in
Jeremiah (cf. e.g. 1:10; 12:14f.; 18:7). On the synonymous
words for 'anger' cf. also Jer. 21:5; 32:37; and, for **another land**
cf. Jer. 22:26. **and cast them into another land, as at this
day:** clearly the exile is presupposed as the background of the
late deuteronomistc editor at work here.

E. REPENTANCE AND RESTORATION: 29:29–30:14

29:29 stands somewhat isolated in its context, but its connections
with 30:11–14 suggest that it acts as a framework to 30:1–10
(see comment on 29:29). However, this framework, if such it is,
remains almost independent of what it contains in both form
and thought. Whereas 30:1–10 has a chiastic structure and is
concerned with the restoration of Israel, its purification through
the action of God, and Israel's obedience to the law, the framework is concerned with the ready access to the law which Israel
enjoys as the source of her guidance for life. Furthermore, while
the framework still projects the situation of Moses addressing
Israel, this fiction is completely abandoned in 30:1–10.

However, despite the disparity both framework and content
have a common link with ch. 4, and otherwise show evidence of
late deuteronomistic authorship (see comment on 30:1, 2, 9, 10,
11, 14). Moreover, when the structure of 30:1–10 is appreciated
it is clear that its major concern is by no means incompatible with
the framework. The structure is that of the chiasm (cf. Lohfink,
BZ 6, 1962, 41; however, the detailed form suggested here differs
slightly from Lohfink's proposal), which is largely determined
by the use of the verb *šûḇ* (see comment on 30:2: vv. 1f. correspond
with v. 10 ('return'/'turn'); vv. 3f. with v. 9*b* ('restore', 'again'/
'again'); v. 5 with v. 9*a*. The focal point is formed by vv. 6 and 8
(v. 7 is probably an addition; see comment) in which the double
aspect of Israel's restoration is brought to prominence: on the
one hand there is the inward renewal brought about by Yahweh;
and, on the other, its result in Israel's renewed ('again', v. 8)
obedience to the law. It is the ready availability of this law which
is the subject of the framework.

The late deuteronomistic authorship of this passage is shown
not only by its affinities with other such deuteronomistic passages
(see above), but also by its clear connection with the book of

Jeremiah (see comment on 30:3, 6), and by its content in which the exilic situation is presupposed (see comment on 30:1). The theme of 'return' which is so prominent here is a deuteronomistic theme (see comment on v. 2), and, in the presentation of curse and blessing, not as alternate possibilities dependent on disobedience or obedience, but as successive periods of Israel's history, there is a clear connection with the deuteronomistic ch. 4 (see comment on 4:29; Lohfink, *Höre Israel*, 119f. and above, Introduction, p. 70).

29. The **secret things** are usually understood as a reference to the future which only God can know (cf. Driver, Wright, Buis, etc.), and the passage may then be interpreted in the sense that what lies in the future, whether a continuation of the present conditions or a happy restoration, should not be the object of speculation. It lies in God's hands. But for the present God has revealed his law, and that is all that Israel needs to know. Weinfeld, *Deuteronomy* 63f. n.5, suggests that the verse should be seen in the light of the treaty practice of drawing up duplicate copies of the treaty text, each of which would be kept by one party to the treaty. Since God dwells in secret abode, so his copy of the covenant would be hidden and concealed; the copy possessed by Israel, on the other hand, is revealed and belongs **to us and to our children for ever.** However, this does not explain the contrast between the secret things of God and the things revealed to Israel (since on that view the contents of that which is concealed and that which is revealed would be identical), which seems to be the main point of the verse. It seems rather to be a wisdom maxim, which affirms the limits of any human wisdom apart from the law which God has revealed (cf. also 4:6ff.). This associates the verse with 30:11–14 rather than with what precedes (cf. also Rennes, Buis), for there too it is a matter of the ready accessibility of the law for the direction of Israel's life. The verse thus acts with 30:11–14 as a framework to 30:1–10.

1. has driven you: the exile is clearly presupposed here. The verb is not otherwise used in this sense in Deuteronomy, but does appear frequently in Jeremiah (e.g. 8:3; 16:15; 24:9).

2. See comment on 4:29f., with which the verse has clear contacts. For a study of the root *šûḇ* in the covenant context, cf. Holladay, *Root ŠÛBH*. The verb is determinative for vv. 1–10, being used six times: 'return', v. 2; 'restore', v. 3; 'again', vv. 3, 8, 9; 'turn', v. 10. It expresses both the returning of Israel to Yahweh and the returning of Yahweh to Israel. The theme of 'return' is, as Wolff,

Studien, 371f., has shown, a significant one in the deuteronomistic work; cf. also 1 Kg. 8:46ff. In these passages it is the work of a late (exilic) deuteronomistic editor, not that of the (pre-exilic) deuteronomist responsible for an earlier stage of the deuteronomistic historical work. See above, Introduction, pp. 41ff.

3. restore your fortunes: the phrase was formerly translated as if it had a direct reference to return from exile, cf. *AV* 'turn thy captivity'. However, the word translated 'captivity', *šᵉḇûṯ*, is probably better derived from the root *šûḇ*, 'return', than *šāḇāh*, 'take captive', and the phrase then translated 'turn a turning', i.e. effect a decisive change. This more general sense for the phrase, which is now most widely accepted, is reflected in the *RSV* translation. See the discussion in Driver, and also Holladay, *op. cit.*, 110ff. The phrase is a common one in the Old Testament, but particularly frequent in Jeremiah (e.g. 29:14; 30:3, 18; 31:23). Although the phrase then does not of itself necessarily refer to the exile, that is clearly its reference in the present context.

4. the uttermost parts of heaven: the same phrase as 'end of heaven' in 4:32.

5. make you more prosperous and numerous: the same two verbs appear together in 28:63. The comparative *min* may here apply to both (as *RSV*) or only to the second (*AV*, *NEB*).

6. circumcise your heart: on the metaphor see comment on 10:16. While in the latter passage Israel is herself commanded to do this, here it is Yahweh who will effect the conversion in Israel which the expression signifies. The figure is found with Jeremiah (cf. 4:4), and the idea that inward renewal in Israel will be accomplished by Yahweh himself is also prominent there (cf. Jer. 31:31ff.; 32:39ff.; cf. also Ezek. 11:19; 36:26f.).

7. The thought of the verse is paralleled in 7:15. The whole verse interrupts the clear continuity of vv. 6 and 8 (cf. also on v. 8); moreover, it uses *'ālôṯ* for **curses** (as 29:20f.) rather than *qᵉlālāh*, as in 30:1. It may be an addition here, intended to link this passage closely with the earlier section.

8. The focal point of the construction in vv. 6 and 8 emphasizes the double aspect of Israel's restoration: Yahweh makes possible Israel's ability to return, and Israel responds in obedience. V. 8 begins with an emphatic **you;** this can only be intended to contrast with the action of Yahweh in v. 6, not with his action in v. 7.

9. V. 9*a* (**... your ground;**) repeats 28:11 with very slight change. The main difference consists in the addition of the phrase **all the work of your hand** (which appears, however, in 28:12, though *RSV* there translates the plural 'hands'), for which see comment on 2:7.

10. commandments ... statutes: the combination appears in the deuteronomistic 27:10; 28:15, 45.

11. this commandment: for the comprehensive use of 'commandment' in later passages, see comment on 5:31. **too hard:** the word may be used of the acts of God, cf. Ps. 118:23; Job 37:14, or generally of those things which are beyond human comprehension, cf. Ps. 131:1; Prov. 30:18. The verse, then, affirms what has already been indicated in 29:29—the law by which Israel is to live has been revealed to her by God, and so is readily available to her.

12. not in heaven: it is not among the 'secret things' (29:29) which God has not revealed to his people. **that we may hear it:** the verb is a third person singular imperfect of the Hiphil, and so a more accurate translation is: 'and tell it to us', as *NEB* (so also v. 13).

14. As in 4:7 God himself is near to Israel (see comment), so here his word is **very near.** Earlier passages have also spoken of it in terms similar to **in your mouth and in your heart,** cf. 6:6f.; 11:18f.

F. CHOICE BETWEEN LIFE AND DEATH: 30:15–20

The final section is sometimes seen as the original conclusion of the original Deuteronomy (Buis). However, its connections of language and thought are with the deuteronomistic rather than the deuteronomic sections of the book. Yet the verses do clearly function as a conclusion. They bring together the covenant themes of the whole book: commandments, blessing and curse, witnesses, and end with an appeal for obedience so that the ancient promises to the patriarchs might be fulfilled.

15. The alternatives set before Israel in 11:26ff. are formulated as 'blessing and curse'. The implications in both passages are the same. **Good** and **evil** here do not have a moral sense; they refer to 'prosperity' (cf. e.g. 26:11, and the cognate verb 'go well with' in 4:40; 5:29, etc.) and 'misfortune' (cf. e.g. Jer. 7:6; 25:7).

16. The Hebrew text lacks the introductory conditional clause: **If you obey the commandments of the Lord your God,** which should be restored with LXX. The rest of the verse uses expressions well known from earlier chapters: **by loving the Lord your God, by walking in his ways** (see comment on 10:12); **his commandments and his statutes and his ordinances** (cf. 5:31; 6:1; 7:11; 8:11, etc.); **you shall live and multiply** (cf. 8:1, plural); **the land which you are entering to take possession of it** (cf. 7:1).

17. drawn away: for this verb in the sense of temptation to idolatry, cf. 4:19, where too it is followed by the verbs **worship** and **serve.**

18. you shall perish: cf. 4:26, and comment on 8:19, where, as here, this phrase occurs in the plural form of address in a singular context.

19. I call heaven and earth to witness: see comment on 4:26; 32:1. **choose life:** the contrast between life and death seems to be especially a wisdom theme; it is found in Prov. 11:19; 14:27; 18:21; and also Jer. 8:3; 21:8. For a parallel to the present use of the idea of choosing life, i.e. the service of Yahweh in obedience to the commandments, cf. Jos. 24:15.

20. loving the Lord your God: see comment on 6:5. **cleaving to him:** see comment on 10:20.

IV. Appendix: 31:1–34:12

This appendix breaks down into three major sections: 31:1–13; 31:14–32:44 and 32:45–34:12. In the first, two topics are treated: the institution of Joshua and provision for the reading of the law. In both cases Moses is providing for the future life of the people. The second section deals with three topics; the institution of Joshua by Yahweh, as confirmation of what has already been done by Moses; the provision for the preservation of the law; and the Song of Moses, the last mentioned being anchored to the previous topics through the incorporation there of an introduction to the Song (31:16–22). The third section has four topics: a parenetic conclusion to the law; the announcement of Moses' death; Moses' farewell blessing on the tribes; and, finally, the account of his death.

In no case can pre-deuteronomistic material be seen here. Most of it is deuteronomistic, taking up the deuteronomistic chapters at the beginning of the book and providing a transition to the story of Joshua in the next book of the deuteronomistic history (31:1-8, 14f., 23; 34:1-6), or is from the second deuteronomist concentrating on the law (31:9-13, 24-29; 32:45-47). The Song of Moses and the Blessing of Moses with their introductions are post-deuteronomistic additions, however, since the deuteronomistic context clearly does not presuppose their presence. The Song is probably as late in composition as the time of its insertion here, but the Blessing shows signs of being considerably older. Priestly material is also present, particularly in the announcement of Moses' death in 32:48-52, and also in some verses of the story of his death (34:7-9). The final three verses of the book are also the latest, reflecting on the picture of Moses through the whole Pentateuchal tradition.

A. MOSES' PROVISION FOR THE FUTURE: 31:1-13

(A) THE INSTITUTION OF JOSHUA BY MOSES: 31:1-8

The first part of this section uses language familiar from chs. 1-3 and is clearly the deuteronomistic continuation of 3:27f. The passage uses what Lohfink has described as a formula for institution to an office (see comment on vv. 7, 8), as part of the description of the transfer of leadership from Moses to Joshua. For the account of this transfer comparison may be made with other deuteronomistic passages in Jos. 23:2ff.; 1 Sam. 12:2ff. There is nothing to show, however, that the whole passage is anything other than a literary creation of the deuteronomist. Its occurrence in other deuteronomistic passages does not indicate the existence of a particular legal model which is being followed (cf. Baltzer *Covenant Formulary*, 69ff.; Buis); the passage as a whole (apart from the formulaic language of vv. 7f.) is a discursive text, a sermon, composed by the deuteronomist.

1. So Moses continued to speak: the LXX and Dead Sea Scrolls text read 'and Moses finished speaking'. The textual difference between the two is fairly slight (*wayᵉkal mōšeh lᵉdabbēr* for *MT wayyēlek mōšeh wayᵉdabbēr*), but it is difficult nevertheless to assume an accidental change from either reading to the other. The fact that a deliberate change from the *MT* to the text presupposed by LXX and offered by the Dead Sea Scrolls is less credible than a deliberate change in the other direction (in view of the fact that the following chapters do contain further words of

Moses), suggests that LXX and Dead Sea Scrolls do preserve the
better reading of the two. If this is so then v. 1 was originally the
concluding formula which brought to an end the section begun in
29:1. The change to the present *MT* would have been made after
the inclusion of additional words of Moses, particularly the Song
of Moses in ch. 32.

2. a hundred and twenty years old: the deuteronomist
usually makes a general reference to old age, as in Jos. 23:2;
1 Sam. 12:2. This precise figure may derive from the priestly
writer who comes to expression in 34:7. **go out and come in:** in
view of the context the reference here may be specifically to
ability to exercise leadership in war. However, see comment on
28:6 in justification of the *NEB* 'move about as I please'. **the
Lord has said:** cf. 3:27f. (of which this is the continuation); also
1:37; 4:21f.

3. and Joshua will go over at your head: the Hebrew text
lacks the conjunction and for the rest it is an exact repetition
(substituting **Joshua** for **the Lord your God**) of the beginning
of the verse. However, if any part of the verse is secondary, it must
be the first part, for v. 2 requires a reference here to Joshua as
Moses' successor and not simply a general reference to the leadership of Yahweh. The latter may be an intrusion modelled on
9:3.

4. Compare the form which this record takes in 29:7f. **when he
destroyed them:** the *NEB* translation 'he will destroy them',
which understands here a reference to the conquest and dispossession of the nations in west Jordan, is unlikely, particularly as the
immediate prelude to the beginning of the next verse.

5. all the commandment: i.e. that given in 7:2ff.

6. On the expressions used see 1:21, 29; 3:28; 4:31, and vv. 7f.
of the present chapter. The use of identical expressions here and
in the actual commissioning of Joshua in the next verses serves to
emphasize the equality of the people with Joshua and the sole
leadership of Yahweh.

7, 8. Lohfink, *Schol* 37, 1962, 38f., has pointed out that these
two verses follow a form which appears again in v. 23 and also in
Jos. 1:6, 9b. It is a formula of institution to an office, which is
composed of the following elements: (a) a formula of encouragement **(be strong and of good courage):** (b) a description of the
task which the office involves (introduced by **for you . . .**); and
(c) a formula of support **(he will be with you).** These two verses

are a rather expanded form of the shorter, and probably basic, form found in v. 23. The latter may have served as prototype for the form here and in Jos. 1. Lohfink believes that this is a fixed form, which is not just a literary creation; rather, it is a formula deriving from a real life situation dealing with institution to an office and adopted here by the deuteronomist.

(B) THE FUTURE READING OF THE LAW: 31:9–13

The second part of this section is a deuteronomistic passage in which Moses is first clearly stated to have written the law. The connection of the passage with its context is not very close; it may, in view of its interest in the law, be ascribed to the second deuteronomistic editor. So it is from a later time than 31:1–8.

The reference to the writing of the law and the command to read it every seven years is often seen in the context of the treaty requirement for the regular public recitation of the written treaty documents. However, even before the application of the treaty analogy to Deuteronomy, it was suggested by Alt (now in *Essays*, 127ff.) that there is here the record of an ancient custom in Israel. The connection between the law and the feast of Booths was thought by Alt to be understandable when that feast was seen as the New Year festival, a time of renewal in nature; for that would form a suitable context for the proclamation of the law and the people's assent to the law, which would constitute a corresponding renewal in man. The festival, therefore, came to be seen as one of covenant renewal, at least on the occurrence of its celebration every seven years.

However, it should be noted that it is only here that this festival is connected with the reading of the law, and since it is certainly a deuteronomistic passage it is doubtful that it can easily be interpreted as reflecting an ancient custom. Moreover, it is not particularly likely that ancient custom would have connected an agricultural festival with the notion of covenant renewal, for the latter was related to the historical events of Israel's past rather than to the cycles of nature (cf. Perlitt, *Bundestheologie*, 123f.). This passage cannot really indicate the existence of a covenant renewal festival in ancient Israel. The deuteronomist here prescribes the reading of the law; that he prescribes it for the feast of Booths may be explained simply on the basis of his wish to locate the reading in a context of Israel's life which would guarantee the presence of a large number of worshippers. The feast of Booths was the chief festival in the Israelite cultic calendar (see introduction to 16:1-17).

9. The view and the explicit assertion that **Moses wrote** the laws is an inevitable development of his role of proclaimer of the law which is otherwise dominant. His role as writer is understood also in the addition in 1:5 (see comment). **this law:** see comment on 1:5. **the priests the sons of Levi:** see comment on 18:1. **who carried the ark of the covenant:** see comment on 10:8. **the elders of Israel:** the intention in referring to the elders here seems to be to indicate that the law is for application in the life of the community and not just for preservation. Where preservation only is in mind, as in vv. 25f., only the Levites are mentioned.

10. at the end of every seven years ... year of release: see comment on 15:1. **the feast of booths:** see introduction to 16:1-17 and comment on 16:13ff.

11. to appear before the Lord: see comment on 16:16.

12. sojourner: see comment on 1:16.

13. On the concern of Deuteronomy with the transmission of the faith to the future generations, see comment on 4:9. **who have not known it:** i.e. who have no personal and direct experience of the great saving actions of Yahweh on Israel's behalf; see comment on 11:2. For the last phrase cf. 4:14; 6:1.

B. YAHWEH'S PROVISION FOR THE FUTURE, AND THE SONG OF MOSES: 31:14-32:44

(A) YAHWEH'S INSTITUTION OF JOSHUA AND COMMAND TO MOSES TO WRITE THE SONG: 31:14-23

These verses fall into two sections: vv. 14-15, 23 and vv. 16-22. The former is concerned with the institution of Joshua and the latter with the Song of Moses. They are quite distinct sections; they clearly do not form an original unit, but represent a secondary combination. Vv. 16-22 have been secondarily placed in their present position, breaking the essential connection of vv. 14f. and 23.

Vv. 14f., 23 are usually seen as a duplication of vv. 7f., since both concern the institution of Joshua and use similar expressions. However, there are some essential differences which show that the case is not quite so simple (see comment on v. 23). In fact, vv. 14f., 23 function as divine confirmation of what Moses has already done, according to vv. 7f. It is a deliberate deuteronomistic construction in which use is made of old formulaic material (see comment on vv. 7f.). Vv. 14f., 23 are thus a continuation of that deuteronomistic account.

Vv. 16–22, on the other hand, introduce the new and quite separate subject of the Song of Moses, which then follows in ch. 32. The verses have the purpose of giving an interpretation to the Song making it suitable to its present context in Deuteronomy. The Song is interpreted in the section in wholly negative terms as testifying to Yahweh's destructive anger, an interpretation not adequate to the whole of the Song (cf. especially 32:36ff.), but deliberately intended as a means of adapting the Song to its context. The terms in which this interpretation is expressed indicate that the deuteronomistic vv. 24ff. are presupposed (see comment on v. 19); so the section is post-deuteronomistic. This is supported by the strong determinism which characterizes the verses: Israel's forsaking of Yahweh is inevitable, not something that only may happen. This characteristic also points to a late time (cf. von Rad, *Gottesvolk*, 70f.). The language is not in contradiction of this, for it is mostly untypical of Deuteronomy generally, though showing acquaintance with it at least in v. 20 (see comment).

This means either that vv. 16–22 derive from the hand of the one who introduced the Song of Moses into its present place, or they derive from a later hand with the purpose of strengthening the connection of the Song to Deuteronomy, the Song having at first been added simply by means of v. 30 alone (see comment on v. 30). It is difficult to decide which is the correct view, but in either case there is no indication that the deuteronomistic editor at work in this chapter was aware of the Song. The latter, with its heading in 31:30 and its introduction in 31:16–22, are post-deuteronomistic additions.

14. the tent of meeting: only in this and the following verse does Deuteronomy refer to the tent of meeting. The significance of the tent and its connection (if any) with the ark have been problems extensively discussed in recent years. For an elaborate discussion which strictly separates the two, associating each with a quite distinct theology of God's presence with his people, cf. Newman, *People*, especially pp. 55ff. A distinction between the two, on both literary and theological grounds, has been widely accepted; cf. Maier, *Ladeheiligtum*, 1ff.; von Rad, *Problem*, 103ff. The ancient

Pentateuchal traditions do not explicitly associate them, and the sparse information with which we are provided seems to suggest that while the tent was the place where Yahweh appeared from time to time in the cloud to answer specific questions (so Cazelles suggests the translation 'oracular tent'; cf. Exod. 33:7ff.; Num. 11:24ff.; 12:4ff.), the ark was the throne of Yahweh, the place of his permanent presence, cf. 1 Sam. 4-6; 2 Sam. 6. However, the differences can be exaggerated. David pitched a tent for the ark in Jerusalem (2 Sam. 6:17), and an ambiguous phrase in Exod. 33:7 suggests that his action was justified by ancient custom in that it was precisely in the tent of meeting that the ark was kept in the pre-settlement period; if so, the tent may have been the place where (occasional) meetings with Yahweh took place simply because it was there that the ark, his throne, was to be found. For a recent discussion of the problem, cf. de Vaux, in *Bible*, 136ff. See also comment on 10:1.

15. Weinfeld, *Deuteronomy*, 201f., describes the **cloud** as a kind of divine chariot by which God descends (LXX reads *wayyēreḏ*, 'came down', for MT *wayyērā'*, 'appeared', though this should probably be taken as a change to make the image conform with Exod. 33:9) to earth, cf. Exod. 34:5; Num. 11:25; 12:5. Reference may be made to the use of similar imagery in the Ugaritic texts where Baal is described as 'rider of the clouds', an epithet which has influenced Old Testament imagery, cf. Ps. 68:4.

16. play the harlot after: a frequent term (e.g. Exod. 34: 15f.; Hos. 2:5; 4:15; Jer. 3:1) for forsaking Yahweh to follow other gods. Its background is the practice of cultic prostitution among Israel's neighbours. **strange gods:** apart from 32:12, the Song of Moses, of which this verse begins the introduction, the phrase does not otherwise occur in Deuteronomy. **the land where they go to be among them:** the phrase is very awkward in its context, and in fact the Hebrew should be translated 'in its (i.e. the people's) midst' rather than 'among them' (i.e. the gods of the land). The best solution is to omit **the land where they go (to be)** as an addition intended to indicate that the original 'the strange gods in its (the people's) midst' referred in fact not to the present but to the future when the land would be occupied.

17. This verse clearly points forward to the Song of Moses in the next chapter, and introduces particularly 32:19ff.

19. this song: the *NEB* has emended the text and translates 'this rule of life'. The emendation, which has no support in the versions, arises from the difficulty attaching to the idea of a song standing as **witness** for Yahweh against Israel. More appropriate to this role is the law (or 'rule of life') which, as given to Israel by Yahweh, may function as witness in the sense that through its existence throughout Israel's history it stands as a constant indictment of her sins and as proof that Yahweh had warned Israel against disobedience and provided the means of avoiding the destruction which was to come in the future. This is the function ascribed to the law in the deuteronomistic v. 26, and in so far as **witness** is a legal term that is certainly its more appropriate context. It is probably on the basis of what is said there of the law that a later editor, perhaps the one who introduced the Song of Moses and attached it to Deuteronomy (see the introduction to this section), formulated this verse to strengthen the connection between Deuteronomy and the Song. **write:** the verb is plural, which seems to conflict with v. 22; however, cf. 32:44, according to which both Moses and Joshua recited the Song.

20. The verse points forward to and introduces 32:15ff., but also uses phrases appearing elsewhere in Deuteronomy; cf. 6:10, 11; 8:12. **flowing with milk and honey:** see comment on 6:3.

21. the purposes: the word is *yēṣer*, used in Gen. 6:5; 8:21 for the tendency (*RSV* 'imagination') to do evil which is characteristic of man (see further Pss. 10:2; 140:2; Prov. 6:18; Lam. 3:60f.). Later Judaism saw this evil tendency, which is the source of man's sinfulness, as an impulse implanted in man by God at birth. The law is the means given by God to conquer the tendency; cf. my article in *ITQ* 40, 1973, 262f.

23. See comment on vv. 7, 8. **And the Lord commissioned:** in the Hebrew the subject is not made explicit (LXX understood it to be Moses speaking as in the previous verse, and consequently at the end of the verse read: 'which the Lord swore to give them; he will be with you'), but it is clear from the rest of the verse that Yahweh is speaking. In its original position immediately following v. 15, the verse would not have needed to mention Yahweh by name. This verse, and vv. 14f. which belong with it, are not a simple repetition of vv. 7f. Whereas there Moses is the actor here it is Yahweh who confirms the action of Moses. In vv. 7f. Moses commissioned Joshua to the dual task of taking the land and dividing it among the tribes ('put them in possession of it'). Here in vv. 14f., 23, only the first of these tasks is mentioned. The second

appears in the deuteronomistic Jos. 1:6. This is a deliberate construction in which the deuteronomistic presentation of events
proceeds step by step; cf. Lohfink, *Schol* 37, 1962, especially
pp. 40f.

(B) PROVISION FOR THE PRESERVATION OF THE LAW: **31:24–29**
The deuteronomistic authorship of vv. 24–29 is clear. The verses
constitute the continuation of vv. 9–13 and so come from the
second deuteronomistic editor (see also comment on vv. 27, 28, 29
for contacts with other passages from this editor). While vv. 9–13
are concerned to ensure the regular public recital of the law, here
Moses is concerned with its preservation as a witness against
Israel. Its existence means that Israel cannot plead ignorance of
the ways of behaviour demanded by Yahweh.

The deuteronomistic continuation of the present passage is now
to be found in 32:45ff. That connection is broken through the
insertion of the Song of Moses in ch. 32 with its heading in 31:30.
Both the Song and its heading are post-deuteronomistic insertions,
neither known nor alluded to in the deuteronomistic context.

24. this law: the view (cf. Steuernagel, Bertholet) that the text
originally read 'this song' arises from the desire to give a unity to
the whole paragraph in vv. 24–30 (cf. v. 30), but it is in fact quite
improbable. V. 30 is no original part of the section (see comment
there); and otherwise the paragraph is the continuation (not a
parallel, as Smith thinks) of vv. 9–13 which are concerned with the
writing and proclamation of the law.

25. the Levites who carried the ark of the covenant: see
comment on 10:8.

26. by the side of the ark: the tablets of the covenant containing the decalogue were put *in* the ark (cf. 10:2, 5; also Exod.
40:20; 1 Kg. 8:9). The **book of the law,** the laws of chs. 5–26,
are set beside it. On the equal authority ascribed to the decalogue
and the Mosaic law see comment on 29:1. Lohfink, *Bib* 44, 1963,
468 n.1, suggests that the verse may indicate that in the late
monarchic period the ark was no longer opened but that it was
known to contain the oldest covenant document, while the
covenant document actually used was only deposited beside the
ark. **a witness:** see comment on v. 19.

27. On the expressions used in this verse cf. 1:26; 9:6f., 13, 23f.;
10:16.

28. the elders of your tribes: the expression does not otherwise occur. LXX reads 'heads of your tribes and your elders', cf. 1:15; 5:23; 29:10. As in 29:10 so here LXX also adds a reference at this point to 'your judges'. **officers:** see comment on 1:15. **these words:** it is most unlikely that this should be a reference to the Song in ch. 32 (as understood by Driver, Smith, Wright, etc.). That would make the transition from law (v. 26) to Song (v. 28) intolerably abrupt. The reference is to the preceding law, as in 'the words of this law' in v. 24. When the continuation of vv. 24–29 is seen to lie in 32:45ff., the interpretation of **these words** here as a reference to the law causes no difficulty. **call heaven and earth to witness:** there is no allusion here to the beginning of the Song in 32:1. Rather, the allusion is to 4:26; 30:19. On the meaning of the phrase see comment on 4:26; 32:1.

29. act corruptly: cf. 4:16, 25. **turn aside:** cf. 9:12, 16; 11:28. **in the days to come:** see comment on 4:30. **provoking him to anger:** a deuteronomistic phrase; see comment on 4:25.

(c) THE SONG OF MOSES: **31:30–32:44**

This section comprises the Song of Moses with its introduction and conclusion. Apart from the longer introduction in 31:16–22, there is otherwise no reference to the Song, and it is clearly not presupposed in its present position by the deuteronomistic context. It is, therefore, a post-deuteronomistic insertion (see also introduction to 31:14–23), though this, of course, of itself gives no sure indication of the time of its composition.

The form of the Song is an expanded version of the *Rib*, or lawsuit, form (cf. especially Harvey, *Bib* 43, 1962, 172ff.; Wright, in *Heritage*, 26ff. Labuschagne, in *De Fructu*, 85ff., argues, though unconvincingly, against this). This is a form which appears elsewhere in the Old Testament (cf. especially Isa. 1; Jer. 2; Mic. 6; Ps. 50); it comprises the following elements: 1. an introduction in which witnesses are summoned (vv. 1–3); 2. an introductory statement of the case at issue (vv. 4–6); 3. a speech of prosecution, recalling the good actions of Yahweh (vv. 7–14); 4. the indictment in which Israel is accused of apostasy (vv. 15–18); 5. declaration of guilt and threat of total destruction (vv. 19–25).

The form may have its origin in international law, as the standard means by which a suzerain declared war on a rebellious vassal (Harvey, *op. cit.*, 180ff., points to extra-biblical examples of the form; cf. also Delcor, *VT* 16, 1966, 19ff.); but the use of the form in the present chapter stands far from that context. Here the form has been adapted and expanded to serve a purpose quite different from that for which it was first created. Even within the verses comprising the form there is expansion, particularly in vv. 2f., where wisdom elements foreign to the first section of the *Rîb* pattern have been introduced. However, the chief expansion of the form lies in what follows, in vv. 26ff. Through the use of the idea of the preservation of Yahweh's honour, vv. 26–27 mark a turning point in the Song. Complete destruction of Israel would be misinterpreted by the enemies whom Yahweh would use to carry out his punishment. So Israel will not be destroyed; rather, those enemies, unable to discern the meaning of these events in history, and themselves corrupt, are soon to meet their doom. So Yahweh will manifest himself also to the nations as the only God. The declaration of punishment and destruction has become a promise of vindication and salvation.

The context within which this adaptation of the form took place is not certain. Both von Rad and Boston, *JBL* 87, 1968, 198ff., have pointed to the wisdom influences which the Song betrays (see comment on vv. 1, 2, 20, 24, 28f.). However, contact between the Song and later prophecy (see comment on vv. 2, 12, 13, 15–18, 21f., 26f., 31, 39, 41) is sufficiently clear and consistent to indicate that it is to late prophetic circles that we should chiefly look for its background. Linguistic arguments do not contradict this and arguments based on possible historical allusions may be taken to support it.

As far as language is concerned, it is not possible to follow Albright, *VT* 9, 1959, 344, in his declaration that the style is intermediate between archaic repetitive parallelism such as we find in the Song of Miriam (Exod. 15) and the Song of Deborah (Jg. 5), and the tenth century style of the lament of David (2 Sam. 1). The poem has its own style which cannot be used to date it precisely in such a scheme of development (cf. Wright, *op. cit.*, 41 n.29), and the most thorough study of its morphology and vocabulary (cf. Robertson, *Linguistic Evidence*, 154f.) must conclude that such archaic elements as the Song does exhibit may well be the result of conscious archaizing rather than an actual early date.

For possible historical allusions reference has been made particularly to v. 21, where the 'no people' has been identified with a variety of Israel's enemies (see comment). However, this has led to no clear conclusion. It is more profitable to consider the whole Song in general terms, to seek the background which is presupposed by this use of the lawsuit form and the complete inversion of the intention of that form. The best background is undoubtedly an exilic or post-exilic one, in which the adoption of the lawsuit form was suggested by the need to explain the disasters which had in fact overtaken Israel (this was punishment for sin in forsaking Yahweh who had created them), and its drastic modification was motivated by the knowledge that punishment had come and by the desire to offer encouragement for the future (cf. also Fohrer, *Introduction*, 190, who dates the Song to around, or shortly after, the middle of the sixth century). All the indications (historical, contact with late prophecy and wisdom, lack of knowledge of the Song in the deuteronomist's work) are, therefore, that the Song is a late composition, composed probably at, or not long before, the post-deuteronomistic time in which it was inserted in its present position.

30. The deuteronomistic continuation in 32:45ff. is interrupted by the Song of Moses and this heading (which is neutral compared with the interpretation given to the Song in 31:16–22), by which the Song may originally simply have been introduced. Both the heading and the Song are post-deuteronomistic additions to the present context.

32:1. The appeal to heaven and earth should be interpreted in the light of their regular appearance as witnesses in extra-biblical treaty texts (cf. Huffmon, *JBL* 78, 1959, 291f.; Moran, *Bib* 43, 1962, 317ff.). They are invoked, not as witnesses of the punishment which God is bringing on Israel, but rather as witnesses to the earlier covenant between Yahweh and Israel which Israel has broken. Delcor, *VT* 16, 1966, 16f., has suggested a possible connection between these two witnesses and the Israelite law which requires two witnesses to a capital charge (Num. 35:30; Dt. 17:6); however, it is probably better to see heaven and earth as a natural pair, which are named together as a totality, so that in effect the whole of the created order is thus summoned (see also comment on 28:3ff.). See further comment on 4:26. There is also clear wisdom influence in the verse, in the double invocation **Give ear … hear,** cf. e.g. Prov. 7:24 and, outside the Old Testament, the first chapter of the Instruction of Amen-em-opet, *ANET* 421, lines 9–10; cf. Boston, *JBL* 87, 1968, 199f. These are the words by which the teacher introduces his instruction to his pupil.

2. The wisdom influence continues in this verse in the word **teaching** (which otherwise appears only in wisdom literature, cf.

e.g. Prov. 1:5, 4:2; 7:21) and in the general thought: the effective-
ness and fruitfulness of the words of the master on his pupil. On
the general thought, cf. also, however, Isa. 55:10f.; Ps. 72:6.
gentle rain: the context makes it clear that the word *šeʿîrim*
refers to something which waters the ground. If the root is *šāʿar* it
must be 'storm rain' (cf. Snaith, *VT* 25, 1975, 116). The context,
however, would rather indicate something less violent and more
quietly effective in its fructifying work. Moran, *Bib* 43, 1962,
321f., suggests that metathesis has taken place and that the word
should be identified with the Ugaritic *šrʿ* which is found in a
context which includes reference to dew and rain: 'no dew, no
rain, no welling-up (*šrʿ*) of the deep . . .'.

3. The verse has a clear hymnic quality; compare Pss. 22:22;
29:1f.; 96:7f. To **proclaim the name of the Lord** is to make
open declaration of his character as shown in his actions with his
people and with individuals.

4. Rock: this word appears again as a title in vv. 15, 18, 30, 31,
37, and is fairly frequent elsewhere in the Old Testament. Its
plural form stands parallel with 'hills' in Num. 23:9, where it is
correctly translated 'mountains' in *RSV*. The word corresponds to
the Ugaritic *ġr*, 'mountain' (cf. Albright, *VT* 9, 1959, 345), and
should be translated as such. 'Mountain' is one of Baal's appellations at Ugarit and it is as a divine appellative that the word is
used here. Although an archaic usage, it is also found in later Old
Testament literature, e.g. Isa. 44:8. The *NEB* 'creator' (as also in
v. 18; though cf. vv. 15, 30, 31, 37) presupposes repointing *haṣṣûr*
to read *haṣṣawwār*. The parallelism in v. 18 perhaps supports this,
but apart from that it seems unnecessary.

5. The first half of this verse is quite uncertain. It is clearly
overloaded and perhaps also corrupt. Literally: 'he has dealt corruptly with him not his sons their blemish'. The versions offer a
variety of readings and various proposals for emendation of the
text have been made (see especially Driver's review). The last
word, *mûmām*, **their blemish,** should probably be omitted as an
original marginal comment on the disqualification of Israel as sons
of Yahweh, which has been awkwardly introduced into the text.
The subject of the singular verb at the beginning may be taken as
the **perverse and crooked generation** of the second half of the
verse. **perverse:** the word occurs most frequently in Proverbs
(e.g. 10:9; 11:20; 19:1) as the opposite of that which is 'blameless'
and 'perfect'.

6. foolish: i.e. such that commit 'folly', *nᵉbālāh*; see comment on 22:21. **created:** the meaning 'create' (rather than 'get' or 'buy' as *AV*) for the verb *qānāh* is well established in Ugaritic. Its use in Exod. 15:16 (translated 'purchased' in *RSV*) indicates that in its use in this context particular reference is being made to the exodus from Egypt. In that deliverance God **created** his people. **established:** the cognate verb in Ugaritic means 'to be', and it is found also in a causative form 'create' (cf. Gordon, *Ugaritic Textbook*, 418; and Fisher, *Ras Shamra Parallels* 1, 96, who points to the use of the word in parallelism with 'father'). Probably here too, then, the translation 'begot you' or 'brought you into being' (as a synonym of the previous two verbs) is a better translation.

7. the days of old: the reference is particularly to the period of Israel's formation, from Egypt onwards, as vv. 8ff. show. **many generations:** rather 'every generation'; cf. the same phrase in Ps. 90:1. On the responsibility of parents for the transmission of the faith to the children, see comment on 4:9.

8. the Most High: the Hebrew is *'elyôn*, which appears in extra-biblical texts as a divine title. Johnson, *Sacral Kingship*, 48ff., connects the worship of Elyon particularly with Jerusalem in pre-Israelite times, in the light of Gen. 14:18ff. As he also notes (*ibid.*, 74ff.), it is an honorific title of Yahweh in the Old Testament, see for example Ps. 47:2; cf. also Rendtorff, in *Jewish Studies* 1, 167ff. **sons of God:** the *MT* reads 'sons of Israel'. This is difficult, and it is doubtful that Driver's view, that God determined the boundaries of the nations in such a way as to reserve for Israel a place adequate to its numbers, is a correct interpretation. On the face of it, the interpretation of *MT* is that the number of boundaries established by God for the peoples corresponded to the number of Israelites; cf. the Targum which adds 'seventy' after **the number,** connecting the seventy nations of Gen. 10 with the seventy sons of Jacob in Gen. 46:27; Dt. 10:22. See also Zimmermann, *JQR* 29, 1938–39, 241. On this view, however, the verse is scarcely relevant to the context, which is clearly concerned with Yahweh's actions on behalf of Israel. It is, therefore, better to follow the reading of LXX and Qumran which is adopted by *RSV*. The meaning here is that the nations were divided up and given their land in such a way that to each was assigned its divine protector, one of **the sons of God.** The verse, taken with the following one, then follows very closely the thought 4:19f., and anticipates the later doctrine as expressed in Dan. 10:13, 20f.;

12:1. For the idea of subordinate divine beings generally, with whom God holds council, cf. Ps. 82, and the study of Wright, *Old Testament*, 30ff. Why the change was made to the present *MT* text is not clear. Skehan's view (*CBQ* 12, 1951, 154f.), that it was because of the religious susceptibilities of pious Jews living in a polytheistic context, is not very likely in view of the fact that such a passage as Ps. 82 did not cause embarrassment to a similar degree, and especially in view of the later Jewish doctrine of guardian angels watching over the nations, as expressed in the Daniel passages noted above.

9. It is unlikely that the intention is to say that just as the 'sons of God' received their nations from the Most High, so also did Yahweh, himself one of the divine beings subordinate to the Most High (so, for example, Eissfeldt, *JSS* 1, 1956, 25ff.). Although Elyon is not an original epithet of Yahweh (see comment on the previous verse), it did become so; so in these two verses 'Most High' and **the Lord** stand parallel; cf. Albright, *VT* 9, 1959, 343. For the thought of the verse, Yahweh's special relationship with Israel, cf. also 7:6; 10:15.

10. Following Hos. 9:10, so here Israel's origins are traced not to Egypt but rather to the wilderness period. The intention, however, is not to reproduce a special tradition of Israel's origins, but rather to emphasize the enormity of Israel's ungratefulness once she was settled in the rich land. **wilderness:** the word is *tōhû*, a part of the expression *tōhû wāḇōhû*, used in Gen. 1:2 to describe the empty waste (*RSV* 'without form and void') before creation, and in Jer. 4:23 (*RSV* 'waste and void') to describe the state to which the world will return. **the apple of his eye:** i.e. the pupil of his eye, symbolizing that which is precious and particularly worthy of protection; cf. also Ps. 17:8; Prov. 7:2.

11. eagle: see comment on 14:12. The image is that of the bird training its young to make their first flight, yet always ready to support them to safety (Driver). The *NEB* 'watches over', for **stirs up,** apparently follows LXX which may have read *yiṣṣōr* for the *MT yā'îr*; but no change is required.

12. For the thought of the verse cf. Isa. 43:12.

13. Having described Yahweh's choice of Israel (v. 9) and his leading of Israel through the desert (vv. 10–12), the poet here refers to Israel's entry into the promised land. **high places:** 'high place' in the Old Testament is a term primarily used in a cultic sense with reference to a sanctuary (e.g. 1 Kg. 3:4). With the exception of one occurrence in the Moabite Stone this is not the case with the term in other Semitic languages. There the word is used in a topographical ('open country', 'hillside') or anatomical ('flank', 'back') sense. The former sense suits the present passage and for the latter cf. 33:29. See the study by Vaughan, *Meaning of 'BĀMÂ'*. The phrase used here is not without connection with the fairly common 'tread upon the high places', used of Yahweh (cf. Am. 4:13; Mic. 1:3; Hab. 3:19; Job 9:8), which Vaughan suggests indicates ownership of land in the context of a divine theophany. The expression here may then indicate Israel's establishing ownership of the land. **he ate:** following *Sam*, LXX, a change in the pointing (from *wayyōʾkal* to *wayyaʾᵃkēl*) yields the perhaps preferable 'he fed (him)', as a better continuation of the first part of the verse. Isa. 58:14, which is certainly related to the present text, though not a quotation of it, presupposes the emended text. **honey out of the rock:** not necessarily a picture of miraculous richness of barren land; rather, an accurate description of the land where wild honey may be found among rocks, and oil from the olives growing in stony soil.

14. curds: for curdled milk as a beverage, cf. also Gen. 18:8; Jg. 5:25, etc. **herds of Bashan:** see comment on 3:1. **the finest of the wheat:** literally 'the kidney-fat of wheat'. The phrase 'the fat of wheat' to denote the best wheat is known from Pss. 81:16; 147:14, which may be sufficient to justify the fuller phrase which is found only here: the fat about the kidneys being the richest (Lev. 3:4; Isa. 34:6). However, *NEB* ('the fat of lamb's kidneys') is perhaps better in understanding that the word *kilyōṯ*, **kidneys,** has been accidentally displaced from its original position after the first occurrence of the word *ḥēleḇ*, **fat,** to its present place after the second occurrence. **you drank:** *NEB* follows LXX in reading third person. However, a similar sudden change from third to second person appears in vv. 15, 18. At the end of the verse LXX and *Sam* add 'and Jacob ate and was full' (added by *NEB* to the beginning of v. 15), but it is not at all certain that this was an original part of the text.

15. The connection between prosperity and apostasy has already featured on several occasions in Deuteronomy, cf. 6:10ff.; 8:10ff. **Jeshurun:** a rare title for Israel, found again in 33:5, 26; Isa. 44:2. It is of uncertain origin, but probably related to the word *yāšār*, 'upright'. As an honourable title its application at this point is particularly ironic. Cazelles suggests an allusion to the word

šôr, 'ox', referring to the use of the verb **kicked**. However, the
latter, occurring only here and 1 Sam. 2:29, is of uncertain meaning; cf. Rabin, *VTS* 16, 1967, 228ff., who points to a rare Arabic
cognate root which suggests the meaning 'despise'. This suits well
in both passages. **you waxed fat:** the three verbs in second person
are harmonized with the context to third person by LXX (cf. also
NEB). See also comment on previous verse. **became sleek:** this
is the only occurrence of the word in the Old Testament; it is
probably correctly explained from an Arabic root meaning 'be
gorged with food'. The *AV* 'covered', connects the verb with
kāsāh, 'cover', with particular reference to the use of the latter in
Job 15:27. The connection is made improbable through the
necessity of adding the phrase 'with fatness' in order to accommodate it to the present passage. **scoffed at:** the root is that
from which 'foolish' and 'folly' are derived: 'treat as foolish' or
'behave as a foolish person'; see comment on 22:21. **Rock:** see
comment on v. 4.

    16. jealousy: see comment on 4:24. **strange gods:** the Hebrew
is simply 'strangers'. On the use of the term with reference to
strange gods, cf. Jer. 2:25, 3:13. **abominable practices:** the
word is rather 'abominations', meaning concretely the idols
worshipped (cf. also 2 Kg. 23:13; Isa. 44:19) rather than the rites
by which they were worshipped. See also comment on 7:25.
provoke him to anger: see comment on 4:25.

    17. demons: an Accadian loan word occurring only here and
in Ps. 106:37 (cf. Dahood, *Psalms* III, 74). From the latter passage
it appears that they were the object of human sacrifice. **no gods:**
the denial of the reality of the objects of idolatrous worship is
reminiscent particularly of second Isaiah(cf. Isa. 44:6ff.; 45:14ff.);
see also Jer. 5:7. **they had never known:** i.e. with whom they
had no contact in history, with whom they stood in no (covenant)
relationship; see also comment on 9:24. **new gods:** as distinct
from Yahweh who has been Israel's God from the beginning of
her history. **dreaded:** the verb is found in Jer. 2:12; Ezek. 27:35;
32:10, but only here in the context of the service of a god. Clearly
a parallel for the previous **known** is required; this is probably to
be found in the cognate Ugaritic *tʿr*, 'serve', cf. Gray, *Legacy*,
30 n.8, 195.

    18. You were unmindful: this translation presupposes an
emendation of the *MT* *teši* (in form from *šāyāh*, a root not otherwise known) to *tiššeh*, from the root *nāšāh*, 'forget'. The parallelism

supports the emendation; cf. also Dahood, *Bib* 54, 1973, 356, who
refers to Jer. 18:14f. where a slight change in the *MT* would yield
a further instance of the parallel use of the roots *nāšāh* and *šākah*,
'forget', as in this (emended) verse. **Rock:** see comment on v. 4.
begot: the verb in this form occasionally clearly means 'begot'
(e.g. Gen. 4:18), but most often means 'bore', and so is used with
the mother rather than the father as subject. Only here and
Num. 11:12 is it found with Yahweh as subject and Israel as
object. If the translation **begot** is adopted here, the verse may be
understood to combine images of both fatherhood and mother-
hood in order to express how Israel owes its origin completely to
Yahweh (cf. Bertholet). Otherwise, the imagery is that of mother-
hood only. For comparable expressions, cf. Num. 11:12; Isa.
49:15; 66:13.

20. I will hide: cf. 31:17f. Dahood, *Bib* 54, 1973, 405, proposes
to read the verb *'astîrāh* not as from the verb *sātar*, 'hide', but as an
infixed *-t-* conjugation of the verb *sûr*, 'turn away', so giving a
better parallel to the root *hāpak*, 'turn', from which the word
perverse is derived. The chief problem concerns the existence of
this conjugation in biblical Hebrew, on which there is some doubt.
Furthermore, unless all the frequent instances of the use of this
form of the verb in this context are to be claimed as belonging to
this conjugation, there is nothing to recommend the present case
in particular. **perverse:** the word is found otherwise only in
Proverbs (2:12, 14, etc.)

21. idols: this is a figurative use of the word meaning 'vapour'
or 'breath', i.e. what is insubstantial; it is used particularly by
Jeremiah in the sense found here (e.g. Jer. 8:19; 10:15; 16:19;
51:18). **no people:** this has been taken as a positive historical
allusion, and so through attempted identifications a particular
historical context has been sought for the Song as a whole. So the
no people has been identified as Canaanite (cf. Cassuto, *Studies* 1,
43), the Philistines (especially Eissfeldt, *Lied Moses*), and most
other non-Israelite peoples who threatened Israel's existence. However, there is no real basis to any of these proposals. The terms
used are not intended as a concrete description of the enemy
through whom Yahweh will punish his people. They are used
rather by analogy with **no god.** Just as Israel has rejected Yahweh's
exclusive claim on them so stirring him to **jealousy** (see comment
on 4:24), so Yahweh will provoke their **jealousy** by turning to a
non-Israelite nation, a **no people** (for it is to Israel that the term

people belongs), to carry out his purposes. **foolish:** see comment on v. 6.

22. For the first clause cf. also Jer. 15:14; 17:4. **Sheol:** a term for the abode of the dead which is of frequent occurrence in the Old Testament. Its etymology is quite uncertain and also its precise meaning. The idea that one 'returns' to Sheol in the same way as one 'returns' to the ground (Gen. 3:19) is found in Ps. 9:17, Sheol here being understood perhaps as 'the depths of the earth' where man is formed (Ps. 139:15).

23. I will heap: this presupposes a repointing of the Hebrew to read *'ōsipāh* (the verb *yāsap*, 'add'; cf. Ezek. 5:16; Lev. 26:21) instead of *MT 'aspeh*, 'I will sweep up' (the verb *sāpāh*; only here in this form). Alternatively, with a different change in the pointing (to *'ōs^epāh*), one may translate 'I will gather' (the verb *'āsap*; cf. Mic. 4:6). For the figurative use of **arrows** for divine punishment (as detailed in the following verses), cf. also v. 42: Ezek. 5:16; Pss. 7:13; 38:2; Job 6:4.

24. devoured: apart from the present passage and Ps. 141:4, the verb is used only in Proverbs (e.g. 4:17; 9:5; 23:6). **burning heat:** the Hebrew is *rešep*, which appears in Ugaritic texts as the name of the god of plague or pestilence (cf. Gray, *Legacy*, 276); here, then, better 'devoured by plague' (cf. *NEB*).

25. virgin: the term properly refers to a girl of marriageable age (see comment on 22:23), and in the present context is better translated 'young girl'.

26, 27. These two verses represent the turning point in the whole Song, from a threat of destruction to a promise of vindication. For the thought, compare the prayer of Moses in 9:25ff.; also Isa. 48:9-11; Ezek. 20:9, 14, 22, 44; 36:21, etc. Israel is saved from destruction because her enemies would see it as the result of their own power and not as the punishment of Yahweh. **I will scatter them:** this translation is apparently based on an emendation of the text (following LXX) to read *'ap̄îṣēm* for the *MT 'ap̄'êhem*. The latter is from an unknown root *pā'āh*; but it has an Arabic cognate with the sense of 'cleave' (cf. *NEB* 'strike them down'), which is not unsuitable to this context.

28. Terms are used in this and the following verse which are reminiscent of earlier statements relating to Israel (cf. vv. 6, 20), so that it is difficult to decide if the **nation** here is Israel or the enemy used by Yahweh to punish Israel. On the former interpretation, which would involve a sudden reversion to the thought

of the earlier part of the poem, the unit cannot extend beyond
v. 29 (30), for in what follows 'they' clearly means the enemy. On
the latter interpretation vv. 28-33 may be taken together and the
section as a whole follows well on the turning point of vv. 26f.
The latter is, then, the better approach. The poet here, in distinction to the previous verses, is clearly thinking of a particular
nation standing as Israel's enemy.

29. understand: the verb appears again, Ps. 106:7 (*RSV*
'consider'), with reference to the understanding of the meaning
of Yahweh's activities in Israel's history. Wisdom vocabulary is
prominent in vv. 28f.: **counsel, understanding, wise,
discern.**

30. Whereas the holy war tradition tells of a few routing the
many with the help of Yahweh (especially Jg. 7:2ff.), here the
many Israelites are routed by the few enemy; Yahweh has left
them. On this inversion of holy war ideas and vocabulary, cf. also
1:28f. (see comment). **Rock:** see comment on v. 4.

31. The thought that Israel's enemies, **judges** themselves of
the evidence put before them, should acknowledge the superiority
of Yahweh, has a clear echo in Isa. 41:1-4. Instead of *pelilîm*,
judges, the *NEB* follows LXX in reading *:ewilîm*, 'fools'.

32. Sodom ... Gomorrah: see comment on 29:23. Here,
however, the cities are referred to not as examples of utter destruction wrought by God, but as places of corruption and perversion.
Israel's enemies are so corrupt that their victory over Israel cannot
be ascribed to Yahweh's having helped them; it is, rather, the
result of Yahweh's desertion of Israel. **fields:** used in parallelism
with *gepen*, **vine,** as here, also in Isa. 16:8; Hab. 3:17. However,
the specific translation 'terraces' or 'vineyards' (cf. Craigie),
rather than the general **fields,** is unlikely in view of the use of the
word also in 2 Kg. 23:4; Jer. 31:40 (Qr). For an elaborate discussion of the word, which sees in it a technical term associated with
a cult of the god Mot, cf. Lehmann, *VT* 3, 1953, 361ff.

33. serpents ... asps: a parallel pair also found at Ugarit;
cf. Fisher, *Ras Shamra Parallels* I, 374f. The precise meaning of the
second term is not certain.

34. this: i.e. the 'latter end' of Israel's enemies (v. 29), or
perhaps the corruption of the enemies (vv. 32f.) which Yahweh
keeps in mind for the day of punishment. For a similar idea,
though using different verbs, cf. Hos. 13:12. **laid up in store:** the
meaning of the otherwise unknown *kāmus* is indicated by the

parallelism. Possibly the reading is an error for *kānûs* (as found in *Sam*), 'gathered up' or 'collected'.

35. Vengeance: for a study of the root *nqm*, from which the word comes, in its biblical and extra-biblical usages, cf. Mendenhall, *Tenth Generation*, 69ff. The usual translation, as given in *RSV*, is inadequate. The word does not belong in the context of 'private self-help'. Rather, it signifies 'the executive exercise of power by the highest legitimate political authority for the protection of his own subjects'. A more appropriate translation, then, is 'vindication'. Depending on the context this can take the form of either punishment or deliverance, these being the two aspects of this one meaning. For the latter, 1 Sam. 24:12 and Isa. 61:2 provide examples, while in the present case it is clear that 'punishment' is the intended sense. **is mine:** for *MT li*, *Sam* and LXX read *lᵉyôm*, 'for the day of'. This is probably a better reading, providing a good parallel for the following clause; the verse should then be directly connected with the previous one and translated: 'for the day of punishment and recompense . . .' (cf. *NEB*). **their foot shall slip:** a frequent expression for misfortune, cf. Pss. 38:16; 94:18, etc. **their doom:** literally 'the things prepared for them'; this, with the possible exception of Isa. 10:13, is a generally late expression.

36. vindicate: the verb is *dîn*, usually meaning 'judge'. As with its synonym *šāpaṭ*, however, there is overlap with the meaning of the root *nqm*, used in the previous verse; cf. Mendenhall, *op. cit.*, 77, 84. For the meaning 'give justice to' or **vindicate** for the word here, cf. also Gen. 30:6; Ps. 54:1, etc. **bond or free:** a pair of words (found also in 1 Kg. 14:10; 21:21; 2 Kg. 9:8; 14:26), whose precise reference is not clear. The words may refer to social (slave or free, imprisoned or free) or cultic (impure or clean) status. They may thus be used in a comprehensive way to include everybody (see comment on 28:3). Alternatively, they may be taken as synonymous, rather than antithetic, terms, with the sense '(even) helpless and destitute', so signifying the absence of even the most wretched survivors of a catastrophe; see the discussion in Gray, *I & II Kings*, 337f.

37. It is unclear if vv. 37ff. refer to Israel or to the nations. If it is Israel, the verses constitute a reversion to the indictment of Israel in vv. 15ff., as a prelude to the conclusion in vv. 39ff. which draws the consequence of what history has shown: Yahweh alone is God. (Buis suggests that the verses are in fact misplaced, that they originally belonged between the accusation of Israel in vv. 15–18 and the sentence in vv. 19–25, and that they were brought to their present place in order to apply them to the nations rather than to Israel.) It is more probable, however, that the verses continue the thought of Yahweh's destruction of the enemies, with the ironical questioning after the power of their gods in whom they have trusted.

38. who ate the fat of . . .: the LXX reads second person 'the fat of whose sacrifices you ate, the wine of whose drink offering you drank'. However, the reference is undoubtedly to the gods' eating of the fat and drinking of the wine.

39. The verse has a slight formal parallel in Hos. 5:14, but there is no doubt that its closest parallels and its thought world are to be sought in second Isaiah; cf. Isa. 41:4; 43:10, 13; 44:6; 45:6f., 22; 48:12. See also comment on 4:35, 39. **I kill and I make alive:** cf. 1 Sam. 2:6; 2 Kg. 5:7. This is hymnic language, probably derived from cultic use. The reference is to a reviving not from physical death but from threat of death which even sickness brings; see particularly Johnson, *Vitality*, 108f.: 'to be in sickness of body or weakness of circumstances is to experience the disintegrating power of death, and to be brought by Yahweh to the gates of Sheol; but to enjoy good health and material prosperity is to be allowed to walk with Him in fullness of life'. **I heal:** de Moor (see comment on 2:11) sees here the polemical appropriation for Yahweh of an epithet used in the Ugaritic texts of Baal: the Healer; cf. also Hos. 11:3.

41. For Yahweh as a warrior cf. Isa. 34:5f.; 63:1ff.; Jer. 46:10, where the language of vv. 41f. is particularly echoed. **vengeance:** see comment on v. 35.

42. long-haired: of the four passages where the noun *pera‘* occurs in various forms, two (Num. 6:5; Ezek. 44:20) clearly refer to locks of hair. The other two (the present passage and Jg. 5:2) are less certain. *RSV* in Jg. 5:2 translates 'leaders' (cf. also *NEB* in the present passage: 'princes'), a translation based on a possible Arabic cognate 'be lofty'. If this is adopted the verse refers comprehensively to the destruction of the enemy, both ordinary soldiers and chiefs. In fact, however, both Jg. 5:2 and the present passage offer suitable contexts for the translation 'long locks of hair'. Num. 6:5; Ezek. 44:20 refer to hair permitted to grow long as the fulfilment of a vow of consecration. Warriors too, in ancient times were consecrated for war, and it is to these

consecrated warriors with their unshorn locks that Jg. 5:2 and
the present passage may be taken to refer.

43. LXX and Qumran offer considerably longer texts than *MT*.
Material has probably been lost from *MT*: in the present structure
there is considerable lack of balance between the first part
summoning the nations to praise and the second part in which the
reason for praise being due is given (cf. also Skehan, *CBQ* 12, 1951,
156; *idem*, *BASOR* 136, 1954, 12ff.). Moreover, the summons to
praise the people and the reason given for it do not fit well. The
MT has probably also suffered corruption of the text which it has
preserved. **Praise his people, O you nations:** that the nations
should be summoned to praise Israel is sudden and unjustified in
this context. LXX and Qumran read 'heavens' for **nations,** and
LXX reads 'with him' (*'immô*) for **his people** (*'ammô*). Furthermore, the present *MT* offers the only passage where the verb
rānan is used in the Hiphil with a direct object and the sense of
praise. The verb otherwise means 'give a cry of joy', 'rejoice'.
This usual meaning may be followed if the LXX and Qumran
readings as noted above are adopted. Immediately following, LXX
and Qumran add (cf. also Heb. 1:6): 'bow down to him (all)
gods (or: sons of God)', a clause adopted by Albright, *VT* 9,
1959, 340f., in his attempted reconstruction (cf. also *NEB*). The
originality of this is more probable than the further LXX addition,
also adopted by Albright: 'Rejoice with his people, O nations, and
work hard (?) for it, O angels of God'. This is more like a variant
reading to the earlier summons to rejoice than an original element
of the verse. **his servants:** *NEB* follows LXX and Qumran in
reading 'his sons'. **vengeance:** see comment on v. 35. The last
line of the verse hangs awkwardly, and possibly should be preceded
by the addition (offered by LXX and Qumran) of: 'those who hate
him he requites' (cf. *NEB*). **make expiation:** see comment (on
'Forgive') on 21:8. **the land of his people:** the *MT* is 'his land
his people', the *RSV* being based on the reading of Qumran, *Sam*,
LXX and Vulg. The restored verse would read: 'Rejoice with him,
O heavens; bow down to him (all) gods (or: sons of God); for he
avenges the blood of his servants (or: his sons), and takes vengeance on his adversaries; those who hate him he requites, and
makes expiation for the land of his people'.

44. The final clause of the verse, **he and Joshua the son of
Nun,** is probably a late addition to this conclusion, intended to
remind the reader that Joshua, having been commissioned by

Moses and Yahweh (31:7f., 23), now stands with Moses as leader of the people. Joshua is not referred to otherwise in the introduction and conclusion to the Song, and the form his name takes, Hoshea, is otherwise found only in the priestly writing (cf. Num. 13:8, 16).

C. CONCLUSION: 32:45–34:12

(A) CONCLUSION TO THE LAW: **32:45–47**
This closing section of the deuteronomistic edition of Deuteronomy continues 31:29 after the interruption caused by the late insertion of the Song of Moses, and so should be ascribed to the second deuteronomistic editor (see also comment on vv. 46, 47 for contacts with this editor).

45. This is the deuteronomistic continuation of 31:29 (see introduction to 31:24–29), in which **all these words,** now apparently referring to the immediately preceding Song of Moses, originally referred to the law corpus of Deuteronomy before the post-deuteronomistic insertion of the Song.

46. enjoin: the verb is that used in 31:28 and translated 'call to witness'; cf. also 4:26. It is to this solemn act of calling heaven and earth to witness the covenant that the present verse alludes. On the teaching of children see comment on 4:9.

47. trifle: literally 'empty word'; cf. Isa. 55:11. On the thought of the verse cf. 4:26, 40.

(B) ANNOUNCEMENT OF MOSES' DEATH: **32:48–52**
The agreement between this passage and the priestly Num. 27:12–14 is so close that it cannot be taken (as von Rad) as an independent variant of the latter. This is rather a secondary repetition of Num. 27:12–14, as Noth, *Studien,* 190f., has shown. Its purpose is to recover the connection between the announcement of Moses' death (Num. 27:12–14) and the actual account of his death (the priestly portions of Dt. 34), after those two elements of the priestly writing were secondarily separated through the insertion of Deuteronomy between them. The section thus belongs to the time of the formation of the Pentateuch.

48. that very day: i.e. the day specified in the priestly 1:3. This is a familiar priestly expression (cf. e.g. Gen. 7:13; 17:23).

49. cf. Num. 27:12. **Abarim:** apparently the range of mountains in Moab, east of the Dead Sea, of which **Nebo** formed a single mountain; cf. also Num. 33:47f. The deuteronomist refers earlier (3:27) to Mount Pisgah as the mountain which Moses was commanded to ascend. See also comment on 34:1. **a possession:** the Hebrew is *'aḥuzzāh*, not the usual deuteronomistic word, *naḥalāh* (see comment on 4:20f.).

50. people: in each of its occurrences in this verse the word is the plural of *'am* with a suffix. The word seems originally to have meant 'father's kin', a sense preserved in this context (cf. *NEB*), while it is usually used generally to mean **people.** The expression 'be gathered to your father's kin' is a frequent one in P (e.g. Num. 20:24; 27:13; 31:2). **Mount Hor:** so P as the site of Aaron's death in Num. 20:22-29; 33:37-39. The late addition in 10:6 gives Moserah as the mountain where Aaron died. The location of neither mountain is known. See also comment on 10:6.

51. you broke faith: a verb found mostly in the priestly writer or later (e.g. Num. 31:16). The deuteronomistic historian in the early chapters of Deuteronomy emphasizes the innocence of Moses. It is the priestly writer who introduced the thought of Moses himself having sinned; see comment on 3:26. The precise nature of Moses' offence is nowhere specified, a lack which has given rise to various suggestions, especially concerning the interpretation of Num. 20:1-13 where the priestly account of events at **Meribath-kadesh** is given. The latter story is now apparently supplemented with material taken from Exod. 17, but the original priestly account seems to have reported Moses' question to the people (Num. 20:10) as an expression of doubt on the part of Moses that Yahweh would or could produce water from the rock. **Meribath-kadesh:** or 'Meribah of Kadesh'; a priestly expression, Num. 27:14; cf. also Num. 20:13, 24. The name is apparently simply an alternative to 'Kadesh' (on which see comment on 1:2); it arose because it was at Kadesh that the 'strife' or 'argument' (*merîḇāh*) between the people and Moses and Aaron, or between Moses and Aaron and Yahweh, took place. **the wilderness of Zin:** another geographical expression of the priestly writer. From the various references to it (e.g. Num. 33:36; Jos. 15:1, 3), it is presupposed as adjoining the southern border of Judah towards the Dead Sea. **revere me as holy:** cf. Num. 20:12; 27:14, though there the Hiphil (*RSV* 'sanctify') rather than the Piel of the verb *qāḏaš* is used. There may be an intended connection with the name Kadesh, *qāḏēš*, where the offence was committed.

52. before you: better 'from a distance' (cf. *NEB*); see the same expression in 2 Kg. 2:15 (*RSV* 'over against them').

(C) MOSES' FAREWELL BLESSING: 33:1-29

The Blessing of Moses is a second long interpolation in Deuteronomy. Its place, however, is in no way incongruous for the custom of a father imparting his blessing shortly before death is well known from the Old Testament (cf. Gen. 27:27ff.; 48:15f.; 49:1-28). Moses, therefore, is here understood as the father of Israel now about to die. From a second point of view, too, the place of the chapter is suitable. The Song of Moses in the previous chapter concludes (32:26ff.) with the assurance of Israel's vindication. The present chapter, which is composed solely of blessings on each tribe, functions then as a detailed illustration of the way in which the vindication promised earlier will take concrete form.

The chapter comprises a series of sayings about the individual tribes embedded in a framework consisting of vv. 2-5, 26-29. The framework (omitting v. 4 as a secondary addition; see comment) has its primary focus on Yahweh who became king in Israel and gives his people victory; it holds together as a single unit, a psalm of praise, celebrating kingship, victory and prosperity, and may well have existed independently of the tribal sayings now incorporated in it. Just at the point where the psalm refers to 'all the tribes of Israel' it has been broken in order to act as a framework for the sayings.

The sayings relate to twelve tribes in all: however, one of the familiar tribes, Simeon, is missing. The traditional total of twelve is maintained through dividing Joseph into Ephraim and Manasseh, while keeping Levi, the tribe normally omitted from the tribal lists when Joseph is considered as two tribes (see my study of the subject in *Israel*, 16ff.). Simeon is omitted, not simply because it was absorbed into Judah and had no independent existence, but because no tribal saying on Simeon was available. This in turn, of course, may well have been a result of Simeon's loss of effective tribal status. The peculiarity of the list of tribes in this respect over against the other tribal lists (which are mostly to be derived from Gen. 49 and Num. 1:5-15), is emphasized by the order in which the tribes are mentioned. This does not follow the order to be found in either of the other basic tribal lists; it seems rather to have a geographical basis: beginning with Reuben in east Jordan it then mentions Judah and Levi in the west, then

moves northwards to Benjamin and Joseph, and then takes the
rest of the tribes in a roughly anti-clockwise order of the place of
settlement.

The sayings are a collection which was probably not composed
as an original unit but represents the bringing together of formerly
independently existing sayings. The diversity in form and presentation of these sayings suggests this. They are of very diverse
length and literary form. Sometimes the tribe is personified in its
eponymous ancestor (cf. vv. 8, 12, 22, 24); sometimes it is the
tribe itself which stands in the foreground (vv. 6, 7, 13, 18, 20, 23).
Sometimes the blessings are strongly Yahwistic (vv. 7, 8, 12, 13,
19, 21, 23); occasionally they are sayings with no religious content
(vv. 22, 24).

The problem of the time of origin of the sayings is complicated
by this diversity. In most cases, moreover, it is quite impossible to
determine precisely the historical situation which they presuppose,
and consequently a reconstruction of the history of the tribes based
on the sayings and the relationship between them and the sayings
in Gen. 49 and Jg. 5, as attempted especially by Zobel, *Stammesspruch*, can be only very tentative. Occasionally (see comment on
vv. 6, 7, 8) it is possible to say with some confidence that they
reflect the period of the judges, but this can determine at best the
time of origin of those particular sayings, but not the time of
origin of the others nor of the collection as a whole. Linguistic
arguments, too, are ambiguous. Cross and Freedman, *JBL* 67,
1948, 192, argued for an eleventh century date (see also Wright),
but Robertson, *Linguistic Evidence*, 49ff., 54f., inclines to about the
eighth century. It is certainly true that at least some sayings (see
comment on vv. 8–11) use language which points to the later
rather than the earlier date. This means that for the collection as a
whole it is this later date which should be preferred.

However, the collection was probably in existence some considerable time before its incorporation in its present place in
Deuteronomy. If it has a relationship with ch. 32 as described
above, then it was perhaps incorporated at the same time or later
than ch. 32, that is in post-deuteronomistic time.

1. the man of God: a title of Moses found in the heading to
Ps. 90 and in Jos. 14:6. It is frequently used of prophets (e.g. 1 Kg.
17:18; 2 Kg. 4:7, 9, etc.), and more generally of a messenger of
God in Jg. 13:6, 8.

2. Sinai: see comment on 'Horeb' in 1:2. This is the only

occurrence of **Sinai** in Deuteronomy. **Seir:** see comment on 1:2.
us: the Hebrew is 'them'. However, several of the ancient versions
read as *RSV* (*lānû* rather than *lāmô*); an emendation to *lᵉʿammô*,
'his people', is sometimes suggested (cf. *BHS*; Seeligmann, *VT* 14,
1964, 76), though without any convincing argument. **he shone
forth:** as Miller, *Divine Warrior*, 77f., has noted, the verb is found
in the Ugaritic texts in battle contexts: it denotes the appearance
of the gods in battle. This sense is found also used of Yahweh in
Ps. 80:1ff., and suits well the present context. Labuschagne, *OTS*
19, 1974, 99f., disputes the usual description of this and the
following verses as theophany, suggesting rather that terms and
motifs adopted from that context are given a new function, that of
describing God's acts of salvation. However, there is more here
than just a narrative description. The psalm to which the verse
belongs (see introduction above) is a victory psalm, proclaiming
the kingship of Yahweh over his people and the destruction of his
enemies as he manifests himself in terrifying majesty. Elements of
that theophany description are taken up in other passages, cf. Jg.
5:4; Ps. 68:7f.; Hab. 3:3f. **Mount Paran:** of unknown location.
The 'wilderness of Paran' is referred to on several occasions as
lying south of Palestine, but attempts to locate it precisely have
not been successful. It is referred to here along with Sinai, Seir and
perhaps also Kadesh (cf. below) as the region beyond the frontiers
of the land where Yahweh showed himself in power. **he came
from the ten thousands of holy ones:** a clause apparently as
puzzling to the ancient translators as it is today. The verb is an
Aramaic word, sometimes found in Hebrew poetry (cf. e.g. v. 21;
Isa. 21:12, etc.), while the significance of the **holy ones** is
unclear. That it should refer to the heavenly council of Yahweh
(cf. especially Ps. 89:7) is possible but unexpected at this stage of
the verse after Sinai, Seir and Mount Paran have already been
mentioned; furthermore, Yahweh in Ps. 68:17 manifests himself
in the midst of his holy ones rather than away from them. Con-
jectures from this point onwards are very diverse. Some, claiming
some support from the LXX which reads 'with myriads of Kadesh',
propose to emend *mēribᵉbōṯ qōḏeš*, 'from the ten thousands of holy
ones', to *mimᵉribaṯ qāḏēš*, 'from Meribath-kadesh' (cf. e.g. Smith;
Margulis, *VT* 19, 1969, 205f.; and *BHS*). However, it is unlikely
that the poet intended to name Meribath-kadesh (on which see
comment on 32:51) alongside Sinai, Seir and Mount Paran, as the
source of God's theophany. Kadesh was a too familiar site in

Israelite history for this significance to be attached to it. Possibly
one should read simply *meribat qādēš* '(to) Meribath-kadesh', in
view of the fact that the poem goes on to deal with Israel's
receiving law and it is with Kadesh that lawgiving to Israel is
associated in Exod. 15:25. However, the simplest treatment of the
text is that followed by *NEB* (cf. also Miller, *op. cit.*, 78): to emend
we°āṭāh, 'and he came', to *wē°ittô*, 'and with him', and translate:
'and with him ten thousands of holy ones'. This agrees with the
theophany description in Ps. 68 and also with the use of *qdš* as a
designation of divine beings in both biblical and non-biblical
texts, cf. Cross and Freedman, *JBL* 67, 1948, 199. **flaming fire:**
one word in the Hebrew, *°ēšdāṭ*, which is, however, pointed by the
Massoretes as two words, understood by the Vulg (*ignea lex*) and,
following that, by the *AV*, as 'fiery law'. The second of the two
words, *dāṭ*, is, however, a late Persian loan word in Hebrew, and
unlikely in this context; and the fact that the consonants of the
alleged two words are written together as a single word suggests
that the Massoretic treatment of the word is not correct. *RSV*
seems to understand *°ēš lappiḍōt*, 'fire of flames', but this involves
considerable interference in the text, and does not really result in
anything credible. Driver, *VTS* 16, 1967, 50f. (followed by *NEB*),
proposes to understand a Hebrew verb *°šd*, 'to pour out', cognate
to the Syriac, and to repoint the consonants here: *°ašuḍôṭ*, 'poured
out', and in this context: 'streaming along at his right hand'.

3. he loved: the verb is found only here in biblical Hebrew,
though it is common in Aramaic. It is either an active participle
or (cf. Cassuto, *Studies*, 51) a Polel form; in either case it is perhaps
better translated 'he loves'. **his people:** the Hebrew is 'peoples'.
In view of Gen. 28:3; 48:4, and especially v. 19 of this chapter,
the form could be taken as it stands to refer to Israel. LXX, however, reads 'his people'. **all those consecrated to him:** this is
either a reference to the 'holy ones' of the previous verse, or,
standing parallel to 'his people' here, a reference to Israel (cf.
7:6; 14:2, 21; 26:19; 28:9; Lev. 19:2; Num. 16:3, etc.). **in his
hand:** the Hebrew *beyāḍekā*, 'in your hand', is emended by *NEB*
following the Syriac to *yebārēk*, 'he blesses'. It is simpler to follow
some MSS of the LXX in reading (as *RSV*) a third person suffix
beyāḍô; for this in the sense 'at his side', cf. Zech. 4:12. **they
followed:** the Hebrew is *wehēm tukkû*; the verb is quite unknown.
It is best to combine the two words to read *wehimtakkû*, the
Hithpael of the verb *mākak*, known from Ps. 106:43; Ec. 10:18 and

Job 24:24 in the sense 'be low', 'be humiliated'. So here: 'and they prostrate themselves' (cf. also Cross and Freedman, *JBL* 67, 1948, 200). **receiving direction from thee:** this is not an acceptable rendering of the Hebrew *yiśśā' middabbᵉrōṭekā*, where the verb is third person singular, rather than plural as the translation presupposes. A possible approach (cf. *BHS*) is to redivide the words and repoint the first: *yiśśᵉ'úm dabbᵉrōṭekā*, 'your direction lifts them up', which provides a good contrasting parallel to the first half of the line as emended.

4. The verse on the face of it presents no problems, but its relationship to its context is problematical. **law** (*tôrāh*; see comment on 1:5) is the first word in the sentence, indicating that the verse begins something quite new. There is certainly no likelihood of an identity of this **law** and the 'direction' of the previous verse (as *NEB* takes it); in the one case it is Yahweh speaking directly to his people, in the other it is a question of the law delivered by Moses. The whole idea of Moses as lawgiver is otherwise foreign to the poem (cf. also Seebass, *VT* 27, 1977, 159). Possibly at least the first half of the verse is a late addition, a gloss on the end of the previous verse, intended to explain what this 'direction' was in terms of the existing deuteronomic law. If the second half of the verse is retained, *môrāśāh*, 'a possession', may be repointed *môrāśōh*, 'his possession'; the half verse would suit either as an introduction to v. 5 or following 'Jeshurun' in v. 5a. On Israel as Yahweh's possession cf. e.g. 4:20 (though there with a different word).

5. the Lord became king: the Hebrew is 'he became king' or 'there was a king'. The impersonal translation is unlikely since such an isolated reference to the assembly electing its king makes little sense in the context. To take the subject as Moses (for which cf. e.g. Porter, *Moses*, 14 and n. 35) is suggested by the fact that Moses is the subject of v. 4; however, as already noted, this is probably an addition. The subject is, therefore, most likely Yahweh and the reference is to the acclamation of Yahweh as king on the basis of the victory which he gives to his people (cf. Exod. 15:18; Num. 23:21; Jg. 8:22f.; Isa. 33:22). **Jeshurun:** see comment on 32:15.

6. An introduction to the Reuben blessing is lacking. An original 'of Reuben he said' (cf. *NEB*) may have been lost in the course of transmission of the text. **nor let his men be few:** this is an incorrect translation. There is no negative particle and the negative particle in the subordinate clause of the first part of the line cannot govern the second part (cf. Driver). A possible alternative is to translate 'so that his men be few', leading on the thought of the previous words (cf. e.g. Buis); however, that translation does not in fact provide a sensible continuation of **and not die.** The only acceptable translation is 'and (but) let his men be few', which means that this must be understood as a qualified blessing: let Reuben survive, but not in any great number. This should be seen against the background of the fact that Reuben was the firstborn son of Jacob and consequently the leader of the tribes (cf. Gen. 29:32; 49:3); historically, however, Reuben is known only as an insignificant tribe in danger of extinction. In Gen. 49:4 this is explained as a consequence of an incident in Reuben's past, here simply as corresponding to the blessing of his father.

7. bring him in to his people: the historical background is not certain, but clearly Judah's effective isolation from the other tribes is presupposed, and the blessing here includes a prayer for Judah's union with its fellow-tribes. The most probable background is the period of the judges when Judah was separated from the other tribes by the continued existence of foreign enclaves in the land (cf. my *Israel*, 100f.; see further, below); others suggest the early part of David's monarchy when he was king over Judah only while Israel was ruled by Ishbaal (cf. Labuschagne, *op. cit.*, 108ff.); or generally the period of the divided monarchy. **with thy hands contend for him:** some such sense as this is demanded by the continuation; the Hebrew, however, is '(with) his hands he contended for him (or: it)', and the *RSV* translation presupposes two emendations of the text: *yāḏekā*, 'thy hands', for *yāḏāw*, 'his hands', and *rîḇ*, 'contend', for *rāḇ*, 'he contended'. Dahood (in Fisher, *Ras Shamra Parallels* II, 26) has made the very plausible suggestion of emending *rāḇ*, 'he contended', to *rabbeh*, 'increase' (cf. Jg. 9:29): 'increase his hands (i.e. his forces) for him'. This suits the context admirably and demands only very slight change in the Hebrew text. **his adversaries:** the historical background of the saying will to a large extent determine the identity of the enemy: if it is the period of the judges it could be the Canaanites or Philistines; in any later period it is difficult to see who could be described as preventing Judah's joining with the other tribes, unless one is to think of internal political opponents of any scheme for union.

8–11. The verses containing the blessing on Levi raise considerable difficulties. In general terms, the blessing is unusually long. Secondly, vv. 8–9a speak of Levi the tribe in the singular, while vv. 9b–10 speak of Levites in the plural. Thirdly, v. 11 (see comment) associates Levi with characteristics which are otherwise not familiar, and it provides a most unexpected conclusion to what has gone before. Finally, there are language differences between vv. 8–10 on the one hand and v. 11 on the other (use of definite article, sign of definite object and relative pronoun in vv. 8–10, but not in v. 11 or elsewhere in the poem; cf. Cross and Freedman, *JBL* 67, 1948, 203f.) which preclude their belonging together as an original unit. These linguistic peculiarities of vv. 8–10 suggest, moreover, that these verses are later than their context.

Rather than that v. 11 should be seen as the original blessing on Levi, to which vv. 8–10 were subsequently added, it seems in fact better to divorce v. 11 from Levi altogether and regard it as the original conclusion of the Judah blessing of v. 7 (see comment on v. 11, and Cassuto, *op. cit.*, 55f.; Labuschagne, *op. cit.*, 111f.). Vv. 8–10 comprise the blessing on Levi which was later formulated in two stages: the singular section in vv. 8–9a makes more archaic claims for Levi than does the remainder (see comment on Urim and Thummim in v. 8, and Cody, *History*, 114ff.), and is probably the original blessing, to which vv. 9b–10 were subsequently added. The giving of Torah ('law') by priests, in the sense suggested by v. 10 (see comment there), belongs particularly to the end of the ninth and the eighth centuries (cf. Hos. 4:6; Mic. 3:11). Why the Levi blessing should have been inserted at this point is difficult to say; but it reflects close association of the Levites with Judah which would have come into existence particularly after the fall of the northern kingdom in 721 BC. So the insertion of the blessing on Levi at this point is probably not earlier than this. In its basis, however, the blessing may be considerably older in formulation.

8. Give to Levi: not in the *MT*, but present in LXX; its adoption here leads to a better balanced line. The reason for its omission is difficult to say; it may be connected with the lack of clarity in the rest of the verse. The reference to **Massah** and **Meribah** apparently connects the verse with Exod. 17:1–7, but there is nothing there of Yahweh's having tested Levi. Exod. 17 is a story of how the people found fault with Moses and put Yahweh to the test. It may be the absence of reference to Levi and the prominence of Moses in that story which led to the deliberate omission here of **Give to Levi,** the object of the testing and striving being here understood as Moses, cf. Zobel, *Stammesspruch*, 30 n.10. However, as Zobel, *op. cit.*, 32ff., has also shown, there seem to have existed different forms of the Massah-Meribah testing tradition: so, for example, Dt. 32:51 and Ps. 106:32 point to a story of Moses and Aaron having opposed Yahweh, while Ps. 81:7 apparently tells of how Yahweh tested Israel at Meribah. The background to the present verse may be found in Exod. 15:25 where those whom Yahweh 'proved' were probably the Levites, since they in particular are associated with the statute and ordinance (cf. v. 10 here). The **Thummim** and **Urim** (which otherwise are referred to in reverse order, cf. Exod. 28:30; Lev. 8:8, etc.) were oracular media by which divine responses to particular questions could be ascertained. Apparently, only a yes or no answer could be given through the use of this method; furthermore, both the meanings of the words and the forms of objects which they designated are quite uncertain. Examples of their use are probably recorded in 1 Sam. 14:18f., 41f.; 23:9ff. They seem, however, to have dropped out of use in the monarchic period.

9. The verse refers to the tradition of Levi's having shown itself as a tribe pairtcularly zealous for Yahwism, which in Exod. 32:25ff. is attached to the story of the golden calf. As Daube, in *Von Ugarit*, 34, has shown (cf. also comment on 21:17), it is formal legal language which is used here by which family relationships are formally and legally severed. **ignored:** the verb is *yāḏaʿ*, 'know', with a negative particle; for the legal use of this verb see comment on 9:24. The reference to the **mother** is possibly an addition. It breaks the rhythm and is not presupposed in the object suffix 'him' (not **them** as in *RSV*) of the following verb. The **covenant** which Levi kept is not necessarily that special covenant by which priesthood was granted exclusively to Levi (Num. 25:12f.; Jer. 33:21; Mal. 2:4ff.; Neh. 13:29), which as a covenant granted to Levi would scarcely be referred to in these terms. More likely the reference is to the covenant between Yahweh and Israel.

10. they shall teach: the reference is rather to present practice; so 'they teach' (see also comment on 17:10), and similarly 'they put' rather than **they shall put. law:** see comment on 1:5. The parallel with **ordinances** here suggests that the particular Levitical function being described is not simply the giving of detailed direction on individual queries concerning ritual and worship (which may be seen as an original priestly function), but rather the more comprehensive teaching for which they were responsible in later times, as presupposed in Hos. 4:6; Mic. 3:11. **incense:** the word means generally the smoke of sacrifices; cf. 1 Sam. 2:16; Hos. 4:13; 11:2; Isa. 1:13. **before thee:** literally 'in thy nostril'; cf. Gen. 8:21 for the suitability of this. **whole burnt offering:** see comment on 13:16.

11. The view that this is an unexpected conclusion to the blessing on Levi and that Levi is not usually associated with the characteristics which the verse suggests, is well founded. It is not satisfactory to avoid the difficulty by saying simply that the early history is not known (cf. Bertholet), for the preservation of a blessing so completely out of keeping with the known history and character of the object of that blessing then demands explanation. **substance:** neither this nor **the work of his hands** can easily be applied to the Levitical priestly occupation. In both cases the reference is to material prosperity and possessions. The **adversaries** and **those that hate him,** interpreted as opponents of Levitical claims to exclusiveness in priestly functions (cf. Zobel, *op. cit.*, 31f.), seems not only a use of unnecessarily strong language but also gives expression to a theme which does not appear elsewhere. On the other hand, the idea has already appeared in the blessing on Judah in v. 7. It is probable, therefore, that this verse should be regarded as the original conclusion to the blessing on Judah, now separated from it through the insertion of vv. 8–10 (see also above, introduction to vv. 8–11).

12. It is only in the introduction to the saying that the subject is explicitly identified as Benjamin. The saying is itself anonymous. There is no real reason, however, for seeing it as having originally been part of another saying only secondarily ascribed to Benjamin, as sometimes suggested. The saying is complete in itself and internally is perhaps better understood of Benjamin than of any other tribe. **The beloved:** there is here probably an allusion to the status of Benjamin as the youngest son, particularly loved by his father, cf. Gen. 44:20. **by him:** not only is this redundant in the context (the clause coming more naturally to a conclusion without the word *'ālāw*), but it represents a peculiar use of the preposition *'al*, which is never otherwise found in the sense 'beside' with this verb **dwells.** The LXX reading, *ho theos*, suggests the possibility that *'ālāw* is a corruption of an original *'elyôn*, the Most High (for which see comment on 32:8), which could then be the subject of the following verb: 'the Most High encompasses him . . .' (cf. *NEB* and Zobel, *op. cit.*, 35, following earlier commentators, such as Smith). **and makes his dwelling:** the *NEB* understands the subject to be Benjamin dwelling 'between the shoulders' (i.e. under the protection) of God. Better, however, is the *RSV* understanding, which takes the subject to be Yahweh dwelling 'between the shoulders' (i.e. among the hills; for 'shoulders' in this sense cf. Num. 34:11; Jos. 15:8, 10f.) of Benjamin. The verb translated 'dwell' is the usual verb used not only for Yahweh making his name dwell at a sanctuary (e.g. 12:11), but also elsewhere for Yahweh dwelling among his people (e.g. Isa. 8:18). The allusion here is then to a sanctuary in Benjamin: possibly Bethel, but more likely Jerusalem which, according to Jos. 15:8; 18:28, was a city of Benjamin.

13. choicest gifts: the word *meged* is used always of the gifts of nature. It appears on four further occasions in this saying on Joseph, variously translated 'choicest fruits' and 'rich yield' (v. 14, in each case connected with another word meaning 'produce'), 'abundance' (v. 15), 'best gifts' (v. 16). The saying as a whole is full of natural fertility imagery, as also the closely related blessing on Joseph in Gen. 49:25f. The two passages have a common background in traditional formulaic blessings on the tribe. **above:** this presupposes an emendation of the Hebrew *miṭṭāl*, 'from the dew', to *mēʿal* (cf. also Gen. 49:25). A reference to the dew would form a good parallel to the following reference to **the deep,** and it may be this which led to the introduction of the word here. **the deep:** see comment on 8:7. It is here personified, as in Gen. 49:25; Exod. 15:5, 8; Hab. 3:10, and frequently also in Ugaritic. The Deep is thought of as a monster which **couches** below the earth.

15. For the parallelism of **ancient mountains** and **everlasting hills** see also Gen. 49:26; Hab. 3:6. This is a traditional expression, the source of which, like that of the fertility thought and expression throughout the saying, is Canaanite.

16. him that dwelt in the bush: this, if correct, is the only other reference in the Old Testament to the incident recorded in Exod. 3:1ff. The problem of the relevance of the reference has prompted the suggestion to emend *sᵉneh*, 'bush', to *sinay*, 'Sinai' (cf. e.g. Steuernagel), but this has no textual support; for a history of discussion of the passage from Rabbinic times cf. Beek, *OTS* 14, 1965, 155ff.; Beek points to other passages associating a bush (though not a *sᵉneh*; the latter is usually identified as a thorn bush, but no further precision is possible) in the wilderness with

divine revelation: Gen. 21:14ff.; 1 Kg. 19. There may be here a
deliberate contrast between the fruits of the fertile land and the
desert dwelling of the donor of those fruits, and so an implicit
claim that the favour of fertility comes from Yahweh and not
from the nature gods of the Canaanites. **let these come:** the
verbal form (*tāḇôʾṭāh*) is quite impossible. It seems to have arisen
as a result of the combination of an original *teʾeṭeh* (from the
Aramaic verb '*th*, 'come'; see comment on v. 2) with its explanatory *tāḇôʾ* (from the usual verb *bāʾ*, 'come'), which was erroneously
brought into the line immediately before the word which it was
intended to explain. **prince:** the Hebrew *nāzîr* is used of a person
set apart and consecrated; so, generally, **prince** (cf. also Lam.
4:7), but also specifically a 'Nazirite', one dedicated to Yahweh
(as Samson, Jg. 13:5, 7; cf. also Num. 6:2; Am. 2:11f.). Cazelles
finds here an intended play on the word *rōʾš*, which may mean
either **head** or 'summit of a hill', and the word *nāzîr*, which
means not only **prince** but also 'Nazirite' and (in the form *nēzer*)
the long hair characteristic of consecration, and sees a reference
to the lush growth on the hills of Joseph's land.

17. His firstling bull: the meaning of this is not certain,
primarily because the reference of the pronominal suffix in *šôrô*,
'his bull', is obscure. Bertholet, understanding the suffix to refer
to Joseph, thinks that the **firstling bull** is the king (Jeroboam II),
though such a specific reference at this stage would be at the least
surprising. Motzki, *VT* 25, 1975, 484, finds here a reference to the
bull cult practised at Bethel, a sanctuary of the tribe of Joseph; but
this does not suit the continuation which refers to tribal expansion.
Driver and Smith see a reference to Ephraim, given the blessing
of the firstborn son of Joseph (Gen. 48:13ff.). This last view is the
most probable. Alternatively, one may omit the suffix, with support from Qumran, *Sam*, LXX, Syr and Vulg, and translate: 'a
firstling bull, he has majesty' (cf. *NEB*), so that it is Joseph himself
who is addressed as **firstling bull,** the most powerful of the
powerful. The expression clearly belongs with the stock of
Canaanite imagery already used in the saying; and in fact 'bull' is
well known as an epithet of El in the Ugaritic texts, where the
word *reʾēm*, **wild ox,** also occurs. **all of them:** the word used is
yaḥdāw, 'together', which may well be a corruption of *yiddaḥ*, or
yidḥeh, 'he shall thrust', which would form a much better parallel
to **he shall push** in the first half of the line.

The last part of the verse, making reference to Ephraim and

Manasseh, is an addition to the saying, most probably from the hand of the compiler of the collection of sayings. It may have arisen from the wish to ensure that the saying as a whole was understood of both Ephraim and Manasseh, and not Ephraim only to which the first part of the verse pointed (see above). There may also have been the purpose of ensuring that the total number of tribes mentioned in the chapter was twelve: cf. Seebass, *VT* 27, 1977, 158.

18. The heading to the saying mentions Zebulun only, but the saying concerns both Zebulun and Issachar. These two tribes are elsewhere associated, cf. Gen. 30:17ff.; 49:13ff.; Jg. 5:14f. **going out ... in your tents:** this may be interpreted to refer to the whole life of the tribes (being a variation of the usual expression 'go out ... come in'; see comment on 28:6); but since the phrase is divided so that one activity is predicated of one tribe and the other of the other, a contrast may be intended rather than a comprehensive statement. If so, **going out** may be taken to mean the sea voyages in which Zebulun engaged (for the use of the verb in that context, cf. Ezek. 27:33; and for Zebulun's connection with the sea cf. Gen. 49:13), while **in your tents** may mean by contrast the sedentary life at home on the part of Issachar. This contrast is brought up again in the next verse.

19. Although the text is not very clear, the *RSV* translation at the beginning of the verse is not misleading. **their mountain:** the Hebrew is 'a mountain' though the context demands that this be taken to refer to a specific mountain and the site of a sanctuary. Mount Tabor is a likely identification, for not only was it the site of a Yahwistic sanctuary (cf. Jg. 4:6, 12: Hos. 5:1), but it also lay at the point of meeting of the borders of the two tribes mentioned in the verse (together with Naphtali, cf. Jos. 19:12, 22, 34). For a study of the cult of Tabor and the significance of the sanctuary, cf. Eissfeldt, *Kleine Schriften* II, 29ff.; Zobel, *op. cit.*, 38f., 82f. The **peoples** (see comment on v. 3, 'his people') who are summoned by the tribes must in this context be Israelites; the **right sacrifices** are sacrifices offered to Yahweh; cf. Pss. 4:5; 51:19. **the hidden treasures:** the text is an awkward construction, combining two passive participles. A good parallel to **they suck** is achieved by the emendation of the first of them, *ûś*ᵉ*pûnê*, to *w*ᵉ*yispûn*, 'and they draw out (the treasures of the sand)'; cf. *NEB* and Buis-Leclercq. The reference in any case may be to caravan trade as a source of wealth.

20. he who enlarges Gad: this is a strange and obscure allusion. If correct, it may refer to Yahweh, but it is improbable that a tribal saying should begin in such a way. *NEB* (apparently through repointing *marḥib,* **he who enlarges,** to *merḥāḇ,* 'a broad place') offers the very suitable: 'Blessed be Gad in his wide domain'. Gad's martial character is also referred to in Gen. 49:19; 1 Chr. 12:8. It was the strongest east Jordanian tribe, cf. Num. 32:34ff.; Jos. 13:24ff.

21. the best of the land: the word is *rē'šît,* 'first', which is used in Gen. 49:3 of Reuben, the firstborn son of Jacob. The history of the tribe of Gad and its relations with Reuben suggest that what is hinted at here is Gad's absorption of the tribe of Reuben and its land, and so also its assumption of, or claim to, leadership. Jg. 5:15 presupposes the independence of Reuben, but thereafter the picture seems to have changed. A comparison of Jos. 13:15ff. with Num. 32:34ff. shows Reubenite towns having become Gadite, and the Moabite Stone, line 10, at a point where reference to Reuben is expected, mentions rather Gad (for the historical reconstruction, see especially Zobel, *op. cit.,* 64f.). **for there a commander's portion was reserved:** the verb, which usually means 'to cover, panel', hardly bears the meaning here assigned to it. A good suggestion (cf. *BHS* and Driver) is that *yiššōm,* 'he pants after', should be read for *šām,* **there,** involving the supposition of the omission through haplography of one consonant only; and that for *sāpûn wayyēṯē',* **was reserved; and he came,** one should read (understanding an accidental transposition of the consonants of the two words) *wayyiṯ'assᵉpûn,* 'and they gathered together', the subject being **the heads of the people.** This clause might then be understood to be a gloss, perhaps intended to direct the reader's attention to v. 5 where the phrase occurs and to suggest that the latter verse should be interpreted as Gad's assumption of kingship/leadership over the tribes. The first part of the verse would then read: 'He chose the first for himself, for he pants after the commander's portion'. **the commands:** the Hebrew is 'the righteousness', i.e. what Yahweh considers right (cf. *NEB*). What this and the following **just decrees** (or, better, 'ordinances', as elsewhere for this word; e.g. 4:45) refer to is not clear; perhaps the ruler's function of executing justice.

22. from Bashan: if a correct translation the saying apparently alludes to Dan as launching attacks from Bashan in east Jordan, perhaps on Laish in the course of its movement towards settlement

(Jg. 18). However, Bashan is never otherwise presented as the base of Danite military activity in the form the translation presupposes. Bertholet proposes that the words **that leaps forth from Bashan** refer to the **lion's whelp** only and not to Dan. Better is the suggestion of Cross and Freedman, *JBL* 67, 1948, 208, that the word *bāšān* should be taken not as the proper name Bashan, but as the Ugaritic *bṯn*, 'viper', so giving the translation: 'that leaps forth (i.e. shies away) from a viper'. This would have to be understood as a traditional saying on Dan of uncertain provenance and significance, but it gains credibility from the association of Dan with a viper (though a different Hebrew word) in Gen. 49:17.

23. the lake: perhaps the Sea of Galilee is intended here, though Naphtali settled to the north and west of that lake. Alternatively, *yām*, 'sea', may be translated 'west', which is perhaps more in keeping with the other geographical term used.

24. Blessed above sons: better, 'most blessed of sons', since, as the verse goes on to say, Asher is to be **the favourite of his brothers,** the sons of Jacob. **dip his foot in oil:** i.e. oil will be so abundant that Asher will not only anoint his feet, but will dip them in the oil. For a similar image of extravagant prosperity, cf. Gen. 49:11. Asher was established on rich land along the coastline.

25. The verse probably alludes to the military power Asher requires to maintain its settlement area. The word translated **strength** is otherwise unknown in Hebrew. The *RSV* translation suits the context, and this meaning is also suggested by the context in which the word appears in the Ugaritic texts, cf. Cross, *VT* 2, 1952, 162ff. Asher's strength will be sufficient for the whole of its life.

26. like God, O Jeshurun: a slight change in pointing (from *kā'ēl* to *kᵉ'ēl*) gives the better sense 'like the God of Jeshurun' (cf. LXX). As Driver notes, the point of the passage is not the uniqueness of God as such, but rather the uniqueness of Israel's God. On **Jeshurun,** see comment on 32:15. **who rides:** the idea of God riding on a chariot through the heavens occurs a number of times (cf. Pss. 18:10; 68:33; Isa. 19:1; Ezek. 1); it has a Canaanite background in which it is found associated with Baal. **to your help:** this is unobjectionable and fits well in the context; but (cf. Cross and Freedman, *BASOR* 108, 1947, 6f.) a division of the letters of the word *bᵉʿezrekā*, and the assumption that a *b* has been omitted by haplography or corrupted into the conjunction which follows, yields the two words *be'uzzô rōkēḇ*, 'in his strength, who rides', to give the excellent couplet: 'who rides the heavens in his strength, who rides the clouds in his glory' (cf. *NEB*). Not only does this provide a good form with parallels in Ugaritic literature, but it gets rid of the sudden and awkward change from second to third person suffixes in the text as it stands.

27. The lack of parallelism in the first part of the verse has prompted several suggestions for alternative renderings. Dahood, *Proverbs*, 45f., repoints *me'ōnāh*, **dwelling place**, to *me'annēh*, and *ûmittaḥaṯ*, **and underneath**, to *ûmuttaḥēṯ* (infixed -*t*- conjugation of the root *nḥt*, 'descend'), and takes *'ōlām*, **everlasting**, as a divine name, 'the Eternal' (following a widespread usage of the term), getting the translation: 'the God of Old is a conqueror, one who lowers his arms, the Eternal', the lowering of the arms being in the context of waging war (cf. Isa. 30:30). The *NEB* translation: 'who humbled the gods of old and subdued the ancient powers', presupposes a similar change in pointing to that of Dahood for the word *me'ōnāh*, taking *me'anneh*, however, in its participial sense 'one who humbles'; and changes *ûmittaḥaṯ* to *ûmeḥattēṯ*, a parallel participial form, 'one who subdues'. The *NEB*, though involving some change in the text, seems to be the better approach from the point of view of context. The verse goes on to praise the actions of God in the past, as a prelude to which the *RSV* translation is clearly unsuitable. It interrupts, moreover, the progress of thought from v. 26 (God's theophany in power) to v. 27 (the purpose of that theophany: to help his people). **thrust out:** the verb used here (*grš*) is not the term otherwise found in Deuteronomy in this context (*yrš*; cf. 4:38; 9:5), but is elsewhere used almost as a technical term for Yahweh's activity in the conquest; cf. Exod. 23:28ff.; 33:2; 34:11; Jos. 24:12, 18; Jg. 2:3; 6:9.

28. fountain: perhaps a reference to posterity (cf. Ps. 68:26, where, however, a different Hebrew word is used); but by a small change (*'ên* to *'ān*) the translation 'Jacob dwells' is possible, so providing a better parallel. **alone:** i.e. having expelled the Canaanite inhabitants of the land. References to **grain and wine** (see comment on 7:13) and the **dew** of heaven are traditional in blessings and descriptions of prosperity; cf. the blessing of Isaac in Gen. 27:28.

29. shield: Dahood, *Psalms* I, 16f., distinguishes between *māgēn*, 'shield', and *māgēn*, 'suzerain', the latter deriving from a root *māgan*, frequent in Ugaritic in the meaning 'bestow', and appearing in such passages as Gen. 15:1; Ps. 84:11, etc. The *RSV* translation in the present context remains the more suitable of the two meanings of the word. **and the sword:** the Hebrew text includes the relative pronoun *ʾašer*, which is difficult here. This should be either omitted or perhaps emended to *šadday*, the divine name translated 'the Almighty' (e.g. Pss. 68:14; 91:1): 'the Almighty is the sword . . .'. **high places:** see comment on 32:13; the better translation here is 'backs'.

(D) THE DEATH OF MOSES: **34:1–12**

The basis of these closing verses is formed by the deuteronomistic vv. 1–6 in which the fulfilment of 3:27 is described in Moses' ascent of the mountain and his death; the deuteronomist at work in 34:1–6 is, therefore, the deuteronomistic historian already encountered in chs. 1–3. As Noth, *Studien*, 212f., has shown, there is no pre-deuteronomistic material in this chapter: there is nothing to connect the verses with any early Pentateuchal sources.

The priestly writer has made an addition in v. 1, 'from the plains of Moab to Mount Nebo', in accordance with his own tradition of the name of the mountain from which Moses viewed the land; in vv. 7–9 he has given information on Moses corresponding to that already given on Aaron, and has finally taken up the theme of Joshua as Moses' successor. The concluding three verses of the chapter are a post-deuteronomistic addition, deriving from the time of the formation of the Pentateuch and based on reflection on the role and significance of Moses in tradition.

1. from the plains of Moab: a geographical term of the priestly writing (cf. Num. 22:1; 26:3, 63; 31:12, etc.). The reference to **Mount Nebo** is likewise priestly, as 32:49. The deuteronomist, in fulfilment of the command in 3:27, related simply that **Moses went up ... to the top of Pisgah.** Pisgah is the mountain of Moses' ascent to see the land according to the deuteronomist; for the priestly writer it is Nebo. **And the Lord showed him all the land:** Daube, *Studies*, 25ff., suggests that basic to the account there is an original version according to which Moses was granted actual possession of the land. Transfer of ownership of property in Roman law and also in biblical law (Gen. 13:14f.; Mt. 4:8f.) was effected through showing the object to be transferred to the new owner. It is only a later theological view of the original story which introduced the idea of sin in order to explain why Moses did not enter the land (cf. also 3:27). It is indeed possible that the idea of transfer of ownership is present in some contexts mentioned by Daube, but the deuteronomistic passages in Deuteronomy are doubtful instances. There is nothing to indicate an earlier version of what is told here; there is nothing said of Moses' taking 'possession' of the land, and indeed the deuteronomist reserves the word 'possession' for the context of the actual entry of the tribes into the land and their expulsion of the Canaanites (e.g. 3:28; 4:22). It seems generally best to take the deuteronomistic passages at face value: Yahweh gives Moses a view of the land which he is giving Israel in fulfilment of his promise. See also Schwertner, *ZAW* 84, 1972, 44. The land of which Moses is given a view is detailed at the end of the verse and in vv. 2f. in a description going from the southern limit of east Jordan (**Gilead**) to the northern (**Dan**), and then in the next verse from the northern limit of west Jordan through the centre to the south, then in v. 3 to the southern limit of west Jordan and finally back to the point of departure in the Jordan valley. The whole detailed description is only one way of describing the land; other descriptions were perhaps more usual. *Sam*, instead of **Gilead as far as Dan** here, the next verse as far as 'Judah', and all of v. 3, reads the traditional 'from the river of Egypt to the great river, the river Euphrates' (cf. Gen. 15:18; Dt. 1:7; 11:24, etc.).

2. the Western Sea: see comment on 11:24.

3. the Negeb: see comment on 1:7. **the Plain:** the word *kikkār* is frequently used as a geographical term; it refers to the circular plain (the word means a round district, a round loaf, or a round weight) of the Jordan rift valley at both northern and southern ends of the Dead Sea; cf. also Gen. 13:12; 19:17, 25, 28, 29. **the city of palm trees:** cf. also 2 Chr. 28:15; the description is used without explicit reference to **Jericho** in Jg. 1:16; 3:13, though Jericho is undoubtedly there too the place intended. **Zoar:** of unknown location, but probably at the southern end of the Dead Sea, cf. Gen. 14:2.

4. The deuteronomistic authorship of the verse is confirmed by a comparison of its first half, dealing with the oath to the patriarchs, with 6:10; 9:5; 29:12f.; 30:20, and of its second half with 3:27.

5. the servant of the Lord: cf. also Jos. 1:1, 7, 13, etc. **in the**

land of Moab: the phrase is superfluous in view of the use of **there** earlier in the sentence. It may be an addition by someone expressly noting that Moses did not die in Canaan. **according to the word of:** literally, 'at the mouth of', a frequent idiom for 'at the command of'; cf. e.g. Num. 33:38.

6. he buried him: it is doubtless intended that the subject of the verb is Yahweh. It is hardly correct to say (as Noth, *Pentateuchal Traditions*, 196ff.) that **in the valley in the land of Moab opposite Beth-peor** gives the impression that Moses' grave was still well known in earlier days, while the rest of the verse indicates that in the course of time the knowledge of it was lost and in the opinion of the narrator the site ought never to be known to men. In so far as any precise location for the grave is given, it is sufficient (and intended to be sufficient) only to show that Moses died and was buried before the tribes entered the land. There is no indication here of the existence of any grave tradition of Moses attaching to a specific place in Moab. Yahweh buried him, so the place is unknown. **Beth-peor:** see comment on 3:29.

7. a hundred and twenty years old: so also 31:2. However, the rest of the verse stands in some conflict with 31:2, for in the latter (a deuteronomistic passage) Moses describes himself as weakened physically. The present passage is from the priestly writer, giving for Moses the information already given for Aaron in Num. 33:39. **natural force:** the only occurrence of the noun in Hebrew, though the related adjective does occur with the meaning 'moist, fresh'. The noun is found in two passages in the Ugaritic texts. Albright, *BASOR* 94, 1944, 32ff., thinks that its precise connotation is 'sexual power'. **abated:** the word *nās* is pointed as if from the verb *nûs*, 'flee'; with the slight change in pointing to *nas* it may be derived from *nāsas*, 'be sick, fail', to give a more appropriate sense (cf. *NEB*).

8. The verse is again from the priestly writer, and corresponds to the information already given in relation to Aaron in Num. 20:29.

9. The final verse of the priestly contribution to the chapter refers to the priestly account of Moses' instituting Joshua as his successor in Num. 27:18–23.

10. The presentation of Moses here stands in some conflict with 18:18, and can scarcely derive from the same hand. The final verses of the book are in fact to be seen as very late, deriving from the time of the combination of the deuteronomistic work with the

Tetrateuch (see Introduction, p. 47), and so are post-deuterono-mistic. They are a reflection on Moses based on tradition con-cerning him in the Tetrateuch. For the present verse cf. Exod. 33:11; Num. 12:6ff. The phrase **knew face to face** expresses the two ideas of God's 'choice' of Moses (cf. Hos. 13:5; Am. 3:2; and on the verb 'know' see also comment on 9:24) and his 'speaking' with Moses (Exod. 33:11). Moses is both prophet and lawgiver.

11. The late reflection on Moses in Israel's tradition is con-tinued here in a reference to the part he played in the plagues brought on Egypt. For **signs and wonders** in this context, see comment on 4:34.

12. mighty power ... great and terrible deeds: the same phrase is used in 4:34 ('mighty hand', 'great terrors', cf. also 26:8) in describing the power and actions of God at the exodus. The power and activities of Moses are here exalted to the level of those of Yahweh himself.

INDEX